# Assurance

# Assurance

## Overcoming the difficulty of knowing forgiveness

*John Owen*

CHRISTIAN
HERITAGE

Introduction © Sinclair B. Ferguson 2013
Copyright © Christian Focus Publications 2013

paperback ISBN 978-1-84550-974-3

This edition first published in 2013
in the
Christian Heritage Imprint
of
Christian Focus Publications Ltd.,
Geanies House, Fearn, Ross-shire,
IV20 1TW, Scotland

www.christianfocus.com

Cover design by Daniel Van Straaten

Printed by Bell & Bain, Glasgow

# CONTENTS

THIS EDITION   13

INTRODUCTION   15

TO THE READER   23

PSALM 130—A PARAPHRASE AND INTRODUCTION   27
   General Scope of the Whole Psalm   30

1   OUT OF THE DEPTHS   33

   Sin Brings Saints into the Depths   36
      Experiencing the Depths   37
   When Believers Fall into the Depths   43
      The Provisions of the Covenant of Grace   43
      Why Believers Fall into the Depths   49
   The Sins that Cast Believers into the Depths   51
      Great Sins Bring Great Distress   51
      Aggravating Circumstances   52
      Guilt Intensified   56

The Behaviour of a Believer Under Distress   58
   He Comes to God Alone   60
   He Cries to God with Great Earnestness   63

2   LORD, WHO SHALL STAND?   73
   Apprehensions of a Sin-Perplexed Soul   76
      Dread as God Marks Sin According to the Law   78
      Weighing up Grounds for Hope?   81
   The Attitude of an Awakened Soul   85
      A Sincere Sense of Sin   85
      Acknowledgment of Sin   91
      Self-condemnation   93
   Self-condemnation Is not the Goal   95
      Sinful Despondency Provokes the Lord   96
      Conviction Is not Conversion   98

3   BUT THERE IS FORGIVENESS WITH YOU   101
   No Approach to God without Forgiveness   107
   Forgiveness—A Rare Attainment   109
      Conscience Opposes Forgiveness   111
      The Law Opposes Forgiveness   113
      Human Thinking Rejects Forgiveness   116
   False Notions of Forgiveness   118
      'God Is Like Ourselves'   119
      'God Will Forgive Me; That's His Job'   120
      How to Identify False Notions of Forgiveness   120
   True Gospel Forgiveness   125
      Its Relation to the Gracious Heart of the Father   126
      Its Relation to the Blood of Christ   133
      Its Relation to the Promise of the Gospel   137
      Only Faith Discovers Forgiveness   141
   The Benefit of Discovering Forgiveness in God   144
      Assurance of Forgiveness Is Possible   144
      Forgiveness without Assurance Is Possible   147
      Forgiveness without Assurance not to be Despised   149
      Discovering Forgiveness in God Nurtures Assurance   153
      Supports to Spiritual Life   155

The True Concept of Believing   161
    Many Pretend to Believe   161
    Many Have not Laid the Foundation   162

4   'THERE IS FORGIVENESS'—THE EVIDENCE   165
The Wrong Place to Look for Proof   165
    The Light of Nature   165
    Inbred Notions of the Acts of God   166
    God's Dealing with Sinning Angels   169
    The Law God Gave to Adam   170
Preliminary Considerations   170
    Forgiveness Is a Rare Discovery   170
    The Foundation of Our Communion with God   171
    A Matter for Serious and Diligent Enquiry   171
How God Dealt with Our First Parents   173
    The First Sin—the Greatest Sin   173
    Man Knew What He Deserved   174
    God Had Declared How He Would Deal with Sin   174
    Nothing Without God Could Halt His Wrath   174
The Institution of Sacrifices   175
    Appointed by God   176
    After Sin Came into the World   176
    The Greatest Part of Old Testament Worship   178
The Prescription of Repentance   179
    True Repentance Lays Hold of Forgiveness   180
    The Call to Repent is Founded on Forgiveness   181
    Why So Many Arguments?   185
God's Pleasure with His Saints   187
    The Saints Above Were All Sinners   189
    Some Were Great Sinners   190
God's Patience Towards the World   193
    After Adam's Fall   193
    Throughout History   194
    Constantly Abused   194
    More than Sufferance   194
    Reaches All for the Sake of Some   195
    Points to God's Willingness to Forgive   196

## Saints' Faith and Experience in this World    199

Profession without Power    201

Profession with Power    204

## The Institution of Religious Worship    211

To Glorify God    211

God Chooses What He Will Receive as Worship    212

Fallen Angels Are not Called to Worship    213

God's Call to Worship Declares Forgiveness    214

Ordinances That Specifically Confirm Forgiveness    216

Commands to Pray for Pardon    220

## The New Covenant    223

Any Covenant Between God and Man Is a Marvel    224

Covenant Abrogation Requires Momentous Cause    225

Why 'a New Covenant'?    228

## The Oath of God    230

The Nature of the Oath    231

The End of His Oath    231

Unspeakable Condescension    232

'As I Live'    233

## The Name of God    234

God Reveals Himself by His Name    234

God Reveals Himself by an Appropriate Name    235

Every Name Confirmed in Jesus Christ    237

'The God of Forgiveness'    238

## The Nature of God    239

Eternally Glorious    239

He Made All Things for Himself    240

He Can Add Nothing to Himself    240

We Know Only What He Is Pleased to Reveal    243

He Reveals His Properties in Fitting Acts    243

Properties Revealed in Their Effects After Creation    244

Mercy, Grace, and Patience    245

## God's Sending of His Son    246

The Source of the Sending—the Counsel of Peace    246

The Only Begotten of the Father    248

In the Likeness of Sinful Flesh    250

The Purpose   251
He Lives Again   253
God's Greatest Work   253

## God Requires Us to Forgive One Another   257

Many Testimonies   257
The Characteristic of a Good Man   260
The Mark of a True Christian   261

5   Forgiveness and Unbelievers   263

## Forgiveness Becomes God   263

His Thoughts Are not Our Thoughts   264
Have You not Known?   266

## Forgiveness Glorifies God   269

## Most Men Do not Believe Forgiveness   271

Gospel Truth   273
Believe Forgiveness in God—Obtain Forgiveness   274
Easy Believers   275
How Did You Come to Believe?   276
Have You More than a General Belief?   277
Have You Been Convicted of Your Sin?   279
Do You Live in Sin?   281
All of Grace?   283

## An Exhortation to Unbelievers   284

There Are Terms of Peace   286
No Room for Delay or Excuses   290
Pleasing Terms   294
Where Does Your Hope Rest?   312

6   Rules for Finding Gospel Peace   321

I   Let Christ Be Your Judge   322

His Judgments often Contradict Men's Judgments   323
How Christ Pronounces His Sentence   326

II   Expect to Carry Hell in One Hand
and Heaven in the Other   328

Attendants to Assurance   330
The Effects of Evangelical Assurance   334

III   Wait   337

IV   Search Out Sin   339
    Consider What Areas of Sin Disturb Your Peace   341
    Consider Sin at Various Stages of Life   341

V   Distinguish Between Unbelief and Jealousy   343
    Unbelief Weakens   345
    Unbelief Is Selfish   346

VI   Distinguish Between Faith and Feeling   347
    Peace and Joy Are not Essential to Faith   348
    Grace May Work Unrecognised   350

VII   Do Not Mix Foundation and Building Work   351

VIII   'Get Up!'   353
    Spiritual Wisdom Is Essential   356
    Beware Unbalanced Spiritual Counsel   356

IX   Guard Your Thoughts of God   358

X   Lay Hold of Every Appearance of Grace   361

XI   Pinpoint the Cause of Your Restlessness   363

7   CAUSES OF SPIRITUAL DISQUIET   365

Afflictions   365
    What Aggravates Afflictions   366
    How to Avoid Spiritual Trouble Under Affliction   371

Inner Turmoil About the State of the Soul   377
    Uncertainty About Regeneration   377

A Digression on Judging Others   384
    Many Christian Duties Require us to Judge Others   384
    One Spirit—One Body   385
    Some Duties Require Certainty of Regeneration   388
    Rules for Dealing with Doubts of Regeneration   389

Inner Turmoil over a Sense of Spiritual Poverty   398
    Add One Grace to Another   399
    More Spiritual Men See Their Unspiritualness More   401
    Hypocrisy   401
    God Does not Despise Small Things   402
    Christ Makes Our Little a Great Deal   403
    Believe Now to Obey Now   403

The Power of Indwelling Sin    404

Unexpected    404
Universal    405
Endless    405
Not Inconsistent with Grace    406
Your Opposition to Sin Is the Measure    406

8    MY SOUL WAITS    409

'I Wait...'    415
How We Wait    416
Why We Wait    421
'...for the Lord'    426
Himself    426
A Great and Sovereign Ruler    428
'In His Word I Hope'    450
God's Promises Reveal Him to Believers    450

9    HE SHALL REDEEM ISRAEL    455

Israel, 'Hope in the Lord'    458
'With Him Is Plenteous Redemption'    459
'...from All His Iniquities'    460
'Consider How it Was with Me'    462
Final Words    463

# THIS EDITION

The contents of this book were first published as an exposition of Psalm 130. The text here is unchanged apart from the following features, designed to make the book more user-friendly:

1. The text has been divided into nine chapters.
2. Subheadings, sometimes extending to four levels and mainly based on the original numeric structure, have been inserted. The contents pages include primary and secondary subheadings to aid navigation.
3. Sentences enumerating more than five or six items, lists of more than one sentence, selected notes, and some 'digressions' are broken off from the main text and displayed.
4. The style and placement of biblical references has been made consistent with modern practice and Roman numerals have been changed to Arabic.
5. Words such as 'unto' become 'to' or 'doth consist' becomes 'consists'.

# INTRODUCTION

---

'I have been accustomed,' wrote John Calvin on the Psalms, 'to call this book, I think not inappropriately, "An Anatomy of all the Parts of the Soul."'[1] Perhaps even more appropriately, as a former colleague once commented to me, 'An Anatomy and Physiology' of the soul. It is for this reason that the people of God in every age have found them a treasure trove buried deep in the heart of sacred Scripture. They speak *to us*, as all God's Word does; but they also speak *for us*. Here are words for the voiceless. It has always been the experience of afflicted saints that they discover that even although they knew the words of the Psalms, now they understand what the psalmist meant when he penned them.

All this is wonderfully evident in John Owen's exposition of Psalm 130. Remarkable in the length to which it extends (it is somewhere north of four hundred pages long in this edition), it is even more remarkable in the breadth of his discussions of Christian experience, in the depth to which it penetrates, and in the heights which it ultimately reaches in leading the reader into the high privilege of the assurance of forgiveness.

---

1  John Calvin, *Commentary on the Book of Psalms*, trs., James Anderson (Calvin's Commentaries, Calvin Translation Society, Edinburgh, 1843-1855), xxxvi-xxxvii.

In addition, *A Practical Exposition upon Psalm CXXX* is obviously in large measure an anatomy of the author's soul and in places a transcript of the spiritual experience which contributed in a major way to John Owen becoming perhaps the greatest English theologian of all time, and certainly her greatest exponent of spiritual theology. His colleague David Clarkson perhaps best expressed this in his funeral sermon:

> I need not tell you of this who knew him, that it was his great design to promote Holiness in the life and Exercise of it among you...He was a burning and a shining light, and you for a while rejoiced in his light. Alas! It was but for a while

And then, almost as an afterthought, Clarkson added, 'and we may Rejoyce in it still.'[2] And one obvious way in which that is true — probably far beyond Clarkson's expectation — is to be found in the pages of this volume which Dr Philip Ross has, with his usual expertise, edited for the modern reader.

Owen rarely spoke of himself. The general outline of his life is well known. Born 1616; son of a minister; educated at Oxford; parish minister in Fordham and later in Coggeshall; chaplain to Oliver Cromwell; Vice Chancellor (read 'President') of the University of Oxford; scholar and prodigious author (his collected writings amount to 24 volumes each of around 600 pages in length); and, towards the end of his life, pastor of an independent congregation in London. He died in 1683.[3]

Somewhere in his twenties, Owen appears to have gone through a prolonged period of deep personal struggle. He never fully removed the veil that hung over those years, nor does he provide us with any self analysis that would explain the period of spiritual melancholy through which he passed. What we do know is that he

---

2  David Clarkson, *A Funeral Sermon on the Most Lamented Death of the late reverend and learned divine John Owen, D.D.*, preached on 9th September 1683. Clarkson (1622–86) was appointed pastoral colleague to Owen in 1682 and succeeded him.

3  See A. Thomson, *The Life of John Owen*, in Owen's *Works*, ed. W.H. Goold, Edinburgh: Johnstone & Hunter, 1850-53, volume 1 pp. XIX-CXII. Separately published as *John Owen, Prince of Puritans*, Tain: Christian Focus, 1996.

was already a preacher of Christ's gospel who through dark hours came to a fresh sense of light and joy in Christ.

The depth of Owen's experience may well explain why he would become weary of all superficial religion. It certainly helps to explain why he devotes around seventy-five percent of his work on Psalm 130 to the fourth verse: 'There is forgiveness with thee, that thou mayest be feared.' Once fully recovered and strengthened, Owen determined to preach on the truth that had set him free and raised him up, and, as with a number of his works, the public exposition of the text became the impetus for and foundation of the subsequent book, first published in 1668.[4]

In the standard edition of Owen's *Works*, edited by William Goold, the exposition of Psalm 130 was bound together with three other massively penetrating works, *Of the Mortification of Sin in Believers,* his work *Of Temptation: The Nature and Power of It*, and its twin volume *The Nature, Power, Deceit, and Prevalency of the Remainders of Indwelling Sin in Believers.* Taken together they represent a massive theological, spiritual, and psychological analysis of the power of sin. If you would read Owen, noted Professor John ('Rabbi') Duncan, 'prepare yourself for the knife.' But Owen's deep penetrating unmasking of the human heart is matched by his exposition of the sheer wonder of the grace of God in the gospel. For Owen these were ever the twin *sine qua non* for any authentic exposition of the Christian gospel.

There is much here that is striking. One is Owen's emphasis on the fact that real believers may find themselves in considerable soul distress because of their sin. They need to learn from the psalmist how to respond to this reality, and then how to recover from it. The great key is the discovery of forgiveness.

Owen takes us patiently by the hand and leads us on in our understanding and grasp of grace. All this is predicated on his

4 The subject of the assurance of grace and salvation was a major theme in the writings of the seventeenth century Puritans following in the tradition of the Reformation. For an extended discussion see Joel R. Beeke, *The Quest for Full Assurance*, Edinburgh: Banner of Truth Trust, 1999. Dr Beeke's work contains an extended treatment of Owen's view, pp. 165-213.

conviction that a deep sense of forgiveness is not as common a reality among believers as we might like to think. He himself had once lacked it. In another context he shrewdly observed that in fact many Christians view the Father 'with anxious, doubtful thoughts.' Sadly, he noted, 'What fears, what questionings are there, of his good-will and kindness.'[5] All of this, of course, was in keeping with the statements of the *Westminster Confession of Faith* (in which Owen had no hand) and its daughter confession *The Savoy Declaration* (in which he played a major role) that genuine Christians might have to pass through long struggles and deep waters before they experienced the full assurance of their salvation. Owen had done so himself. The key for the Westminster and Savoy Divines, however, as for Owen, was that such assurance could be experienced through the right use of the ordinary 'means of grace', that is the instruments God uses to help us experience the fulfillment of his promises.

Within this context, Owen both challenges our generation of surface thinking and models for us what a ministry of these 'means' might be. This is what we discover in his detailed exposition of Psalm 130 verse 4 ('There is forgiveness with thee, that thou mayest be feared'). While our inclination may be to point the soul struggling for assurance to read a few texts that describe assurance, Owen does more. He does not merely cite biblical texts; he uses his detailed knowledge of the whole of Scripture as an instrument by which he actually transitions us from doubts and fears to a settled assurance of grace and salvation. In this sense he preaches us out of lack of assurance into the joy of assurance.

This explains the detailed character of Owen's work. While we moderns do not find detail unusual in an academic text book in our own discipline, or on the financial or sporting statistics of the newspaper, when it comes to spiritual experience we tend to prefer 'instant' to 'freshly ground, slowly percolated.' We are impatient with the laws or principles that govern the spiritual life. It is here that Owen teaches us to slow down, think, understand, and apply.

5   *The Works of John Owen*, ed. W. H. Goold (1850-53), reprinted Edinburgh: Banner of Truth Trust, II.32.

Owen thus provides us with an extended exposition of the wonder of forgiveness, where and how we can discover it, and how it is revealed to us in Christ. He then takes us through a series of eleven 'rules' which serve to guide us safely in this area of experience.

We live in an antinomian age which honours the rules of the sports more than the rules of God's word. Perhaps it is as well, therefore, to point out that these are not an expression of a legalism that will lead us into bondage, but an exposition of the basic principles of God's word and gospel grace which will deliver us from bondage into spiritual liberty.

Here, then, we have spiritual anatomy and physiology at its best. Owen excels in diagnosis—no stone is left unturned in his examination of the soul. By comparison, few books today will give us the principles by which we may 'search out sin' in our hearts; and equally few will clarify the importance of distinguishing between faith and spiritual sense (rule vi), and avoiding the error of mixing the foundation and the 'building' work (rule vii). But these, along with their companions, are vital to our spiritual health and stability.

In this vein Owen continues his exposition until he quietly reflects in the closing sentences that he has probably written enough, and draws his work to a close.

Like many of Owen's other works, *A Practical Exposition upon Psalm CXXX* was written to be read as a single book. But it would be unwise to read it in isolation from Owen's other works, or at least without knowing that all of Owen's emphasis on experimental Christianity and subjective experience is securely rooted in his understanding and exposition of the glory of Christ's Person and Work, the character of God as Trinity and our fellowship with him, and the ministry of the Holy Spirit.[6] Anyone for whom this volume constitutes a first encounter with Owen would certainly be both wise and well-served by turning to one or other of these works next. It will then become clear that the enjoyment of assurance takes place within the context of fellowship of the Spirit, centered

---

6   Owen treats these subjects in *Works* vols 1–3 respectively. See also the companion volumes in this series edited by Philip Ross.

on Jesus Christ, and bringing us to the knowledge of God as our Heavenly Father.

Perhaps the most fitting way to bring these words of introduction to a close is by adding two personal testimonies.

The first is now three hundred and forty years old, and comes from the sermon preached at Owen's funeral by his colleague and successor David Clarkson:

> A great light is fallen; one of eminency for holiness, learning, parts, and abilities; a pastor, a scholar, a divine of the first magnitude; holiness gave a Divine lustre to his other accomplishments, it shined in his whole course, and was diffused through his whole conversation.
>
> I need not tell you of this that knew him, and observed that it was his great design to promote holiness in the power, life, and exercise of it among you. It was his great complaint that the power of it declined among professors. It was his care and endeavour to prevent or cure spiritual decays in his own flock. He was a burning and a shining light, and you for a while rejoiced in his light: alas! that it was but for a while, and that we cannot rejoice in it still!
>
> He had extraordinary intellectuals [i.e. intellectual gifts] a vast memory, a quick apprehension, a clear and piercing judgment; he was a passionate lover of light and truth, of Divine truth especially; he pursued it unweariedly, through painful and wasting studies, such as impaired his health and strength, such as exposed him to those distempers with which he conflicted many years: and some may blame him for this as a sort of intemperance, but it is the most excusable of any, and looks like a voluntary martyrdom. However it showed he was ready to spend, and be spent, for Christ: he did not bury his talent, with which he was richly furnished, but still laid it out for the Lord who had intrusted him. He preached while his strength and liberty would serve, then by discourse and writing.
>
> That he was an excellent preacher none will deny who knew him, and knew what preaching was, and think it not the worse because it is spiritual and evangelical. He had an admirable facility in discoursing on any subject, pertinently and decently,

and could better express himself extempore, than others with premeditation. He was never at a loss for want of expression; a happiness few can pretend to; and this he could show upon all occasions, in the presence of the highest persons in the nation, and from the greatest to the meanest. He hereby showed he had the command of his learning. His vast reading and experience was hereby made useful, in resolving doubts, clearing what was obscure, advising in perplexed and intricate cases and breaches, or healing them which sometimes seemed incurable. Not only we, but all his brethren will have reason to bewail the loss of him. His conversation was not only advantageous in respect to his pleasantness and obligingness; but there was that in it which made it desirable to great persons, natives and foreigners, and that by so many, that few could have what they desired.

I need speak nothing of his writings, though that is another head that I intimated; they commend themselves to the world. If holiness, learning, and a masculine unaffected style can commend anything, his practical discourses cannot but find much acceptation [acceptance] with those who are sensible of their soul concerns, and can relish that which is Divine, and value that which is not common or trivial. His excellent Comment [commentary] upon the Hebrews gained him a name and esteem, not only at home, but in foreign countries. When he had finished it (and it was a merciful providence that he lived to finish it) he said, Now his work was done, it was time for him to die.[7]

The second testimony is more recent and indeed more personal.

Mountain climbers are reputed to respond to the question 'Why climb mountains?' by saying 'Because they're there.' If asked why I began to read Owen, the answer would probably be the same. I was seventeen or eighteen, and Owen was 'there' (his *Works* were in the process of their first major reprinting in over one hundred years). Clearly he was a theological and pastoral mountain worth climbing. As I began to read him I felt as if someone had come into a wood paneled room, and led me by the hand to the wall to show me that one panel had a handle and was in fact a door into a larger

7  Clarkson, *loc. cit.*

room. Therein treasures in abundance awaited my exploration. Owen seemed to go down deeper, stay up longer, come up with more treasure, lead to greater heights of understanding grace than anything I had read before.

Now, decades later, I still find myself turning to the old master and thinking, 'Why do I spend time reading other books when such riches are available to me here?' Of course, the world is full of valuable Christian books and we should read as many as we can. But Owen belongs to a special category of well-tried and fully proved authors whom to read is to invest for a lifetime.

As a schoolboy, still a few years short of encountering Owen I was required to read a number of the *Essays* of Sir Francis Bacon (1561–1626). Although lacking the experience fully to appreciate that knight's wisdom, one of his comments has lingered in my memory over the years:

> Some books are to be tasted, others to be swallowed, and some few to be chewed and digested: that is, some books are to be read only in parts, others to be read, but not curiously, and some few to be read wholly and with diligence and attention.[8]

*A Practical Exposition upon Psalm CXXX* undoubtedly fits into this last category—'to be read wholly and with diligence and attention'. Dr Ross has again placed us in his debt by preparing this attractive edition to enable us to do just that. All that remains therefore is that I encourage you to set aside the time, slow down part of your life, and begin to chew on Owen. For this book may be one of the most nutritious meals you ever digest!

*Sinclair B Ferguson*
*First Presbyterian Church*
*Columbia, South Carolina*

---

8   Francis Bacon, 'Of Studies' in *Essays*, ed. with intro and notes, F.G. Selby, London: MacMillan & Co., 1889, p.129.

# TO THE READER

Christian Reader, The ensuing exposition and discourses are intended for the benefit of those whose spiritual state and condition is represented in the psalm here explained. That these are not a few, that they are many, yea, that to some part or parts of it they are all who believe, both the Scriptures and their own experience will bear testimony. Some of them, it may be, will inquire into and after their own concerns, as they are here declared. To be serviceable to their faith, peace, and spiritual consolation has been the whole of my design. If they meet with any discovery of truth, any due application of it to their consciences, any declaration of the sense and mind of the Holy Ghost in the Scriptures, suitable to their condition and useful to their edification, much of my end and purpose is obtained.

I know some there are that dislike all discourses of this nature, and look upon them with contempt and scorn; but why they should so do I know not, unless the gospel itself, and all the mysteries of it, be folly to them. Sin and grace in their original causes, various respects, consequents, and ends, are the principal subjects of the whole Scripture, of the whole revelation of the will of God to mankind. In these do our present and eternal concerns lie, and from and by them has God designed the great and everlasting exaltation of his own glory. Upon these do turn all the transactions that are between God and the souls of men. That it should be an endeavour needless or superfluous, to inquire into the will of God about, and our own interest in, these things, who can imagine? Two ways there are whereby this may be done. First, speculatively, by a due investigation of the nature of these things, according as their doctrine is declared in the Scripture. An endeavour according to the mind of God herein is just and commendable, and comprehensive of most of the chief heads of divinity. But this is not to be engaged in for its own sake. The knowledge of God and spiritual things has this proportion to practical sciences, that the end of all its notions and doctrines consists in practice. Wherefore, secondly, these things are to be considered practically; that is, as the souls and consciences of men are actually concerned in them and conversant about them. How men contract the guilt of sin, what sense they have and ought to have thereof, what danger they are liable to thereon, what perplexities and distresses their souls and consciences are reduced to thereby, what courses they fix upon for their relief; as also, what is that grace of God whereby alone they may be delivered, wherein it consists, how it was prepared, how purchased, how it is proposed, and how it may be attained; what effects and consequents a participation of it produces; how in these things faith and obedience to God, dependence on him, submission to him, waiting for him, are to be exercised, is the principal work that those who are called to the dispensation of the gospel ought to inquire into themselves, and to acquaint others withal. In the right and due management of these things, whether by writing or oral instruction, with prudence, diligence, and zeal, consists their principal usefulness in reference to the glory of God and the everlasting welfare of the souls of men. And they are under a great mistake who suppose it an easy and a common matter to treat of these practical things usefully, to the edification of them that do believe; because both the nature of the things themselves, with the concerns of the souls and consciences of all sorts of persons in them, require that they be handled plainly, and without those intermixtures of secular learning and additions of ornaments of speech which discourses of other natures may or ought to be composed and set off withal. Some, judging by mere outward appearances—especially if they be of them from whom the true nature of the things themselves treated of are hid—are ready to despise and scorn the plain management of them, as that which has nothing of wisdom or learning accompanying of it, no effects of any commendable ability of mind for which it should be esteemed. But it is not expressible how great a mistake such persons, through their own darkness and ignorance, do labour under. In a right spiritual understanding, in a due perception and comprehension of these things—the things of the sins of men and grace of God—consists the greatest part of that wisdom, of that soundness of mind, of that knowledge rightly so called, which the gospel commands, exhibits, and puts a valuation upon. To reveal and declare them to others in words of truth and soberness fit and meet; to express them to the understandings of men opened and enlightened by the same Spirit by whom the things themselves are originally revealed; to derive such sacred spiritual truths from the word, and by a due preparation to communicate and apply them to the souls and consciences of men— contains a principal part of that ministerial skill and ability which are required in the dispensers of the gospel, and wherein a severe exercise of sound learning, judgment, and care, is necessary to be found, and may be fully expressed.

Into this treasury, towards the service of the house of God, it is that I have cast my mite in the ensuing exposition and discourses on Psalm 130. The design of the Holy Ghost was therein to express and represent, in the person and condition of the psalmist, the case of a soul entangled and ready to be overwhelmed with the guilt of sin, relieved by a discovery of grace and forgiveness in God, with its deportment upon a participation of that relief. After the exposition of the words of the text, my design and endeavour has been only to enlarge the portraiture here given us in the psalm of a believing soul in and under the condition mentioned; to render the lines of it more visible, and to make the character given in its description more legible; and withal, to give to others in the like condition with the psalmist a light to understand and discern themselves in that image and representation which is here made of them in the person of another. To this end have I been forced to enlarge on the two great heads of sin and grace—especially on the latter, here called the 'forgiveness that is with God.' An interest herein, a participation hereof, being our principal concern in this world, and the sole foundation of all our expectations of a blessed portion in that which is to come, it certainly requires the best and utmost of our endeavours, as to look into the nature, causes, and effects of it, so especially into the ways and means whereby we may be made partakers of it, and how that participation may be secured to us to our peace and consolation; as also into that love, that holiness, that obedience, that fruitfulness in good works, which, on the account of this grace, God expects from us and requires at our hands. An explication of these things is that which I have designed to ensue and follow after in these discourses, and that with a constant eye, as on the one hand to the sole rule and standard of truth, the sacred Scriptures, especially that part of it which is under peculiar consideration; so, on the other, to the experience and service to the edification of them that do believe, whose spiritual benefit and advantage, without any other consideration in the world, is aimed at in the publishing of them.

# PSALM 130

## A PARAPHRASE AND INTRODUCTION

1 Out of the depths have I cried to you, O LORD.
2 Lord, hear my voice;
let your ears be attentive
to the voice of my supplications.

O Lord, through my manifold sins and provocations, I have brought myself into great distresses. Mine iniquities are always before me, and I am ready to be overwhelmed with them, as with a flood of waters; for they have brought me into depths, wherein I am ready to be swallowed up. But yet, although my distress be great and perplexing, I do not, I dare not, utterly despond and cast away all hopes of relief or recovery. Nor do I seek to any other remedy, way, or means of relief; but I apply myself to you, Jehovah, to you alone. And in this my application to you, the greatness and urgency of my troubles makes my soul urgent, earnest, and pressing in my supplications. Whilst I have no rest, I can give you no rest. Oh, therefore, attend and hearken to the voice of my crying and supplications!

> 3 If you, LORD, should mark iniquities,
> O Lord, who shall stand?

It is true, O Lord, God great and terrible, that if you should deal with me in this condition, with any man living, with the best of your saints, according to the strict and exact tenor of the law, which first represents itself to my guilty conscience and troubled soul; if you should take notice of, observe, and keep in remembrance, mine, or their, or the iniquity of any one, to the end that you might deal with them, and recompense to them according to the sentence thereof, there would be, neither for me nor them, any the least expectation of deliverance. All flesh must fail before you, and the spirits which you have made, and that to eternity; for who could stand before you when you should so execute your displeasure?

> 4 But there is forgiveness with you,
> that you may be feared.

But, O Lord, this is not absolutely and universally the state of things between your Majesty and poor sinners; you are in your nature infinitely good and gracious, ready and free in the purposes of your will to receive them. And there is such a blessed way made for the exercise of the holy inclinations and purposes of your heart towards them, in the mediation and blood of your dear Son, that they have assured foundations of concluding and believing that there is pardon and forgiveness with you for them, and which, in the way of your appointments, they may be partakers of. This way, therefore, will I, with all that fear you, persist in. I will not give over, leave you, or turn from you, through my fears, discouragements, and despondencies; but will abide constantly in the observation of the worship which you have prescribed, and the performance of the obedience which you require, having great encouragements so to do.

> 5 I wait for the LORD,
> my soul waits,
> and in his word do I hope.

And herein, upon the account of the forgiveness that is with you, O Lord, do I wait with all patience, quietness, and perseverance. In this work is my whole soul engaged, even in an earnest expectation of your approach to me in a way of grace and mercy. And for my encouragement therein have you given out to me a blessed word of grace, a faithful word of promise, whereon my hope is fixed.

> 6 My soul waits for the Lord
> more than they that watch for the morning:
> I say, more than they
> that watch for the morning.

Yea, in the performance and discharge of this duty, my soul is intent upon you, and in its whole frame turned towards you, and that with such diligence and watchfulness in looking out after every way and means of your appearance, of the manifestation of yourself, and coming to me, that I excel therein those who, with longing desire, heedfulness, and earnest expectation, do wait and watch for the appearance of the morning; and that either that they may rest from their night watches, or have light for the duties of your worship in the temple, which they are most delighted in.

> 7 Let Israel hope in the Lord:
> for with the LORD there is mercy,
> and with him is plenteous redemption.
> 8 And he shall redeem Israel
> from all his iniquities.

Herein have I found that rest, peace, and satisfaction to my own soul, that I cannot but invite and encourage others in the like condition to take the same course with me. Let, then, all the Israel of God, all that fear him, learn this of me, and from my experience. Be not hasty in your distresses, despond not, despair not, turn not aside to other remedies; but hope in the Lord: for I can now, in an especial manner, give testimony to this, that there is mercy with him suited to your relief. Yea, whatever your distress be, the redemption that is with him is so bounteous, plenteous, and unsearchable, that the undoubted issue of your performance of this duty will be, that you shall be delivered from the guilt of all your sins and the perplexities of all your troubles.

## General Scope of the Whole Psalm

The design of the Holy Ghost in this psalm is to express, in the experience of the psalmist and the working of his faith, the state and condition of a soul greatly in itself perplexed, relieved on the account of grace, and acting itself towards God and his saints suitably to the discovery of that grace to him—a great design, and full of great instruction.

And this general prospect gives us the parts and scope of the whole psalm; for we have:

1. The state and condition of the soul therein represented, with his deportment in and under that state and condition: 'Out of the depths have I cried to you, O LORD. Lord, hear my voice; let your ears be attentive to the voice of my supplications' (v. 1–2).

2. His inquiry after relief. And therein are two things that present themselves to him; the one whereof, which first offers the consideration of itself to him in his distress, he deprecates: 'If you, LORD, should mark iniquities, O Lord, who shall stand?' (v. 3). The other he closes withal, and finds relief in it and support by it: 'But there is forgiveness with you, that you may be feared' (v. 4). Upon this, his discovery and fixing on relief, there is the acting of his faith and the deportment of his whole person:

   a. Towards God: 'I wait for the LORD, my soul waits, and in his word do I hope. My soul waits for the Lord more than they that watch for the morning: I say, more than they that watch for the morning' (v. 5–6).

b. Towards the saints: 'Let Israel hope in the LORD: for with the LORD there is mercy, and with him is plenteous redemption. And he shall redeem Israel from all his iniquities' (v. 7–8).

All which parts, and the various concerns of them, must be opened severally.

And this also gives an account of what is my design from and upon the words of this psalm, namely, to declare the perplexed entanglements which may befall a gracious soul, such a one as this psalmist was, with the nature and proper workings of faith in such a condition; principally aiming at what it is that gives a soul relief and support in, and afterward deliverance from, such a perplexed estate.

The Lord in mercy dispose of these meditations in such a way and manner as that both he that writes and they that read may be made partakers of the benefit, relief, and consolation intended for his saints in this psalm by the Holy Ghost!

1

## OUT OF THE DEPTHS

---

[1] Out of the depths have I cried to you, O LORD.
[2] Lord, hear my voice;
let your ears be attentive
to the voice of my supplications.

The state and condition of the soul here represented as the basis on which the process of the psalm is built, with its deportment, or the general acting of its faith in that state, is expressed in the two first verses: 'Out of the depths have I cried to you, O LORD. Lord, hear my voice: let your ears be attentive to the voice of my supplications.'

The present state of the soul under consideration is included in that expression, 'Out of the depths.'

Some of the ancients, as Chrysostom, suppose this expression to relate to the depths of the heart of the psalmist: Τί ἐστιν ἐκ βαθέων·, not from the mouth or tongue only, ἀλλ' ἀπὸ καρδίας βαθυτάτης—'but from the depth and bottom of the heart;' ἐξ αυτῶν τῆς διανοίας τῶν βάθρων—'from the deepest recesses of the mind.'

And, indeed, the word is used to express the depths of the hearts of men, but utterly in another sense: 'The heart is deep' (Ps. 64:6).

But the obvious sense of the place, and the constant use of the word, will not admit of this interpretation: 'E profundis' from עָמַק, 'profundus fuit' is מַעֲמַקִּים in the plural number, 'profunditates,' or 'depths.' It is commonly used for valleys, or any deep places whatever, but especially of waters. Valleys and deep places, because of their darkness and solitariness, are accounted places of horror, helplessness, and trouble: 'Though I walk through the valley of the shadow of death' (Ps. 23:4); that is, in the extremity of danger and trouble.

The moral use of the word, as expressing the state and condition of the souls of men, is metaphorical. These depths, then, are difficulties or pressures, attended with fear, horror, danger, and trouble. And they are of two sorts:

1. Providential, in respect of outward distresses, calamities, and afflictions: 'Save me, O God; for the waters are come in to my soul. I stick in the mire of the deep, and there is no standing. I am come, בְּמַעֲמַקֵּי־מַיִם, into the depths of waters, and the flood overflows me' (Ps. 69:1–2). It is trouble, and the extremity of it, that the psalmist complains of, and which he thus expresses. He was brought by it into a condition like to a man ready to be drowned, being cast into the bottom of deep and miry waters, where he had no firm foundation to stand upon, nor ability to come out; as he farther explains himself (v. 15).

2. There are internal depths—depths of conscience upon the account of sin: 'You have laid me in the lowest pit, in darkness, in the deeps' (Ps. 88:6). What he intends by this expression, the psalmist declares in the next words, 'Your wrath lies hard upon me' (v. 7). Sense of God's wrath upon his conscience upon the account of sin, was the deep he was cast into. So, speaking of the same matter, says he, 'I suffer your terrors' (v. 15); and, 'Your fierce wrath goes over me' (v. 16); which

he calls water, waves, and deeps, according to the metaphor before opened.

And these are the deeps that are here principally intended. '*Clamat sub molibus et fiuctibus iniquitatem suaxum,*' says Augustine on the place; 'He cries out under the weight and waves of his sins.'

This the ensuing psalm makes evident. Desiring to be delivered from these depths out of which he cried, he deals with God wholly about mercy and forgiveness; and it is sin done from which forgiveness is a deliverance. The doctrine, also, that he preaches upon his delivery is that of mercy, grace, and redemption, as is manifest from the close of the psalm; and what we have deliverance by is most upon our hearts when we are delivered.

It is true, indeed, that these deeps do oftentimes concur; as David speaks, 'Deep calls to deep' (Ps. 42:7). The deeps of affliction awaken the conscience to a deep sense of sin. But sin is the disease, affliction only a symptom of it: and in attending a cure, the disease itself is principally to be heeded; the symptom will follow or depart of itself.

Many interpreters think that this was now David's condition. By great trouble and distress he was greatly minded of sin; and we must not, therefore, wholly pass over that intendment of the word, though we are chiefly to respect that which he himself, in this address to God, did principally regard.

This, in general, is the state and condition of the soul managed in this psalm, and is as the key to the ensuing discourse, or the hinge on which it turns. As to my intendment from the psalm, that which arises from hence may be comprised in these two propositions:

1. Gracious souls, after much communion with God, may be brought into inextricable depths and entanglements on the account of sin; for such the psalmist here expresses his own condition to have been, and such he was.
2. The inward root of outward distresses is principally to be attended in all pressing trials—sin, in afflictions.

## SIN BRINGS SAINTS INTO THE DEPTHS

Before I proceed at all in the farther opening of the words, they having all of them respect to the proposition first laid down, I shall explain and confirm the truth contained in it; that so it may be understood what we say, and whereof we do affirm, in the whole process of our discourse.

It is a sad truth that we have proposed to consideration. He that hears it ought to tremble in himself, that he may rest in the day of trouble. It speaks out the apostle's advice, 'Be not high-minded, but fear' (Rom. 11:20); and that also, 'Let him that thinks he stands take heed lest he fall' (1 Cor. 10:12). When Peter had learned this truth by woeful experience, after all his boldness and frowardness, he gives this counsel to all saints, 'That they would pass the time of their sojourning here in fear' (1 Pet. 1:17); knowing how near, in our greatest peace and serenity, evil and danger may lie at the door.

Some few instances of the many that are left on record, wherein this truth is exemplified, may be mentioned: 'Noah was a just man, perfect in his generations, and Noah walked with God' (Gen. 6:9). He did so a long season, and that in an evil time, amidst all sorts of temptations, 'when all flesh had corrupted his way upon the earth' (v. 12). This put an eminency upon his obedience, and doubtless rendered the communion which he had with God, in walking before him, most sweet and precious to him. He was a gracious soul, upon the redoubled testimony of God himself. But we know what befell this holy person. He that shall read the story that is recorded of him (Gen. 9:20–27) will easily grant that he was brought into inextricable distress on the account of sin. His own drunkenness (v. 21), with the consequent of it, gives scandal to and provokes the unnatural lust of his son (v. 22); and this leads him to the devoting of that son and his posterity to destruction (v. 24–5): all which, joined with the sense of God's just indignation, from whom he had newly received that tremendously miraculous deliverance, must needs overwhelm him with sorrow and anxiety of spirit.

The matter is more clear in David. Under the Old Testament none loved God more than he; none was loved of God more than he. The paths of faith and love wherein he walked are to the most of us like the way of an eagle in the air—too high and hard for us. Yet to this very day, the cries of this man after God's own heart sound in our ears. Sometimes he complains of broken bones, sometimes of drowning depths, sometimes of waves and water-spouts, sometimes of wounds and diseases, sometimes of wrath and the sorrows of hell; everywhere of his sins, the burden and trouble of them. Some of the occasions of his depths, darkness, entanglements, and distresses, we all know. As no man had more grace than he, so none is a greater instance of the power of sin, and the effects of its guilt upon the conscience, than he. But instances of this kind are obvious, and occur to the thoughts of all, so that they need not be repeated. I shall then show, *first*, what in particular is intended by the depths and entanglements on the account of sin, into which gracious souls, after much communion with God, may be cast. *Secondly*, whence it comes to pass that so they may be, and that oftentimes so they are.

### EXPERIENCING THE DEPTHS

For the first, some or all of these things following do concur to the depths complained of.

### *A Loss of the Sense of God's Love*

Loss of the wonted sense of the love of God, which the soul did formerly enjoy. There is a twofold sense of the love of God, whereof believers in this world may be made partakers. There is the transient acting of the heart by the Holy Ghost with ravishing, unspeakable joys, in apprehension of God's love, and our relation to him in Christ. This, or the immediate effect of it, is called 'Joy unspeakable and full of glory' (1 Pet. 1:8). The Holy Ghost shining into the heart, with a clear evidence of the soul's interest in all gospel mercies, causes it to leap for joy, to exult and triumph in the Lord, as being for a season carried above all sense and thought of sin, self-temptation, or trouble. But as God gives the bread of his house to all his children, so these dainties and high cordials he reserves only for the seasons and persons wherein and to whom he knows them to be needful and useful. Believers may be without this sense of love, and yet be in no depths. a man may be strong and healthy who has wholesome food, though he never drinks spirits and cordials.

Again; there is an abiding, dwelling sense of God's love upon the hearts of the most of those of whom we speak, who have had long communion with God, consisting in a prevailing gospel persuasion that they are accepted with God in Christ: 'Being justified by faith, we have peace with God' (Rom. 5:1). I call it a prevailing persuasion, denoting both the opposition that is made to it by Satan and unbelief, and its efficacy in the conquest thereof. This is the root from whence all that peace and ordinary consolation, which believers in this world are made partakers of, do spring and grow. This is that which quickens and enlivens them to duty (Ps. 116:12–13), and is the salt that renders their sacrifices and performances savoury to God and refreshing to themselves. This supports them under their trials, gives them peace, hope, and comfort in life and death: 'Though I walk in the valley of the shadow of death, I will fear no evil, for you are with me' (Ps 23:4). a sense of God's presence in love is sufficient to rebuke all anxiety and fears in the worst and most dreadful condition; and not only so, but to give in the midst of them solid consolation and joy. So the prophet expresses it (Hab. 3:17–18):

> Although the fig tree shall not blossom, neither shall fruit be in the vines; the labour of the olive shall fail, and the fields shall yield no meat; the flocks shall be cut off from the fold, and there shall be no herd in the stalls: yet I will rejoice in the LORD, I will joy in the God of my salvation.

And this is that sense of love which the choicest believers may lose on the account of sin. This is one step into their depths. They shall not retain any such gospel apprehension of it as that it should give them rest, peace, or consolation, that it should influence their souls with delight in duty or support in trial; and the nature hereof will be afterward more fully explained.

### Conscious of One's Ungratefulness

Perplexed thoughtfulness about their great and wretched unkindness towards God is another part of the depths of sin-entangled souls. So David complains, 'I remembered God,' says he, 'and was troubled' (Ps. 77:3). How comes the remembrance of God to be to him a matter of trouble? In other places he professes that it was all his relief and support. How comes it to be an occasion of his trouble? All had not been well between God and him; and whereas formerly, in his remembrance of God, his thoughts were chiefly exercised about his love and kindness, now they were wholly possessed with his own sin and unkindness. This causes his trouble. Herein lies a share of the entanglements occasioned by sin. Says such a soul in itself, 'Foolish creature, have you thus requited the Lord? Is this the return that you have made to him for all his love, his kindness, his consolations, mercies? Is this your kindness for him, your love to him? Is this your kindness to your friend? Is this your boasting of him, that you had found so much goodness and excellency in him and his love, that though all men should forsake him, you never would do so? Are all your promises, all your engagements which you made to God, in times of distress, upon prevailing obligations, and mighty impressions of his good Spirit upon your soul, now come to this, that you should so foolishly forget, neglect, despise, cast him off? Well! now he is gone; he is withdrawn from you; and what will you do? Are you not even ashamed to desire him to return?' They were thoughts of this nature that cut Peter to the heart upon his fall. The soul finds them cruel as death, and strong as the grave. It is bound in the chains of them, and cannot be comforted (Ps. 38:3–6). And herein consists a great part of the depths inquired after: for this consideration excites and puts an edge upon all grieving, straitening, perplexing affections, which are the only means whereby the soul of a man may be inwardly troubled, or trouble itself; such are sorrow and

shame, with that self-displicency and revenge   self-displicency:
wherewith they are attended. And as their reason   self-aversion
and object in this case do transcend all other occasions of them,
so on no other account do they cause such severe and perplexing
reflections on the soul as on this.

### Old Wounds Reopened

A revived sense of justly deserved wrath belongs also to these
depths. This is as the opening of old wounds. When men have
passed through a sense of wrath, and have obtained deliverance
and rest through the blood of Christ, to come to their old thoughts
again, to be trading afresh with hell, curse, law, and wrath, it is
a depth indeed. And this often befalls gracious souls on the account
of sin: 'Your wrath lies hard upon me,' says Heman (Ps. 88:7). It
pressed and crushed him sorely. There is a self-judging as to the
desert of wrath, which is consistent with a comforting persuasion
of an interest in Christ. This the soul finds sweetness in, as it lies in
a subserviency to the exaltation of grace. But in this case, the soul
is left under it without that relief. It plunges itself into the curse
of the law and flames of hell, without any cheering support from
the blood of Christ. This is walking in 'the valley of the shadow
of death.' The soul converses with death and what seems to lie in
a tendency thereunto. The Lord, also, to increase his perplexities,
puts new life and spirit into the law—gives it a fresh commission,
as it were, to take such a one into its custody; and the law will never
in this world be wanting to its duty.

### Overwhelmed by Affliction and Sin

Oppressing apprehensions of temporal judgments concur herein
also; for God will judge his people. And judgment often begins
at the house of God. 'Though God,' says such a one, 'should not
cast me off for ever, though he should pardon my iniquities; yet
he may so take vengeance of my inventions as to make me feed on
gall and wormwood all my days.' Says David, 'My flesh trembles
for fear of you, and I am afraid of your judgments?' (Ps. 119:120).

He knows not what the great God may bring upon him; and being full of a sense of the guilt of sin, which is the bottom of this whole condition, every judgment of God is full of terror to him. Sometimes he thinks God may lay open the filth of his heart, and make him a scandal and a reproach in the world. 'O,' says he, 'make me not a reproach of the foolish' (Ps. 39:8). Sometimes he trembles lest God should strike him suddenly with some signal judgment, and take him out of the world in darkness and sorrow: so says David, 'Take me not away in your wrath.' Sometimes he fears lest he shall be like Jonah, and raise a storm in his family, in the church whereof he is a member, or in the whole nation: 'Let them not be ashamed for my sake.' These things make his heart soft, as Job speaks, and to melt within him. When any affliction or public judgment of God is fastened to a quick, living sense of sin in the conscience, it overwhelms the soul, whether it be only justly feared or be actually inflicted; as was the case of Joseph's brethren in Egypt. The soul is then rolled from one deep to another. Sense of sin casts it on the consideration of its affliction, and affliction turns it back on a sense of sin. So deep calls to deep, and all God's billows go over the soul. And they do each of them make the soul tender, and sharpen its sense to the other. Affliction softens the soul, so that the sense of sin cuts the deeper, and makes the larger wounds; and the sense of sin weakens the soul, and makes affliction sit the heavier, and so increases its burden. In this case, that affliction which a man in his usual state of spiritual peace could have embraced as a sweet pledge of love, is as goads and thorns in his side, depriving him of all rest and quietness; God makes it as thorns and briers, wherewith he will teach stubborn souls their duty, as Gideon did the men of Succoth.

### Fear of Being a Reprobate at the Last Day

There maybe added hereunto prevailing fears for a season of being utterly rejected by God, of being found a reprobate at the last day. Jonah seems to conclude so, 'Then I said, I am cast out of your sight' (Jonah 2:4) — 'I am lost for ever, God will own me no more.' And Heman, 'I am counted with them that go down into the pit:

free among the dead, like the slain that lie in the grave, whom you remember no more: and they are cut off from your hand' (Ps. 88:4–5). This may reach the soul, until the sorrows of hell encompass it and lay hold upon it; until it be deprived of comfort, peace, rest; until it be a terror to itself, and be ready to choose strangling rather than life. This may befall a gracious soul on the account of sin. But yet because this fights directly against the life of faith, God does not, unless it be in extraordinary cases, suffer any of his to lie long in this horrible pit, where there is no water, no refreshment. But this often falls out, that even the saints themselves are left for a season to a fearful expectation of judgment and fiery indignation, as to the prevailing apprehension of their minds.

### Disconsolate Under God's Rebuke

God secretly sends his arrows into the soul, that wound and gall it, adding pain, trouble, and disquietness to its disconsolation: 'Your arrows stick fast in me, and your hand presses me sore' (Ps. 38:2). Ever and anon in his walking, God shot a sharp piercing arrow, fixing it on his soul, that galled, wounded, and perplexed him, filling him with pain and grievous vexation. These arrows are God's rebukes: 'When with rebukes you correct man for iniquity' (Ps. 39:11). God speaks in his word, and by his Spirit in the conscience, things sharp and bitter to the soul, fastening them so as it cannot shake them out. These Job so mournfully complains of (Job 6:4). The Lord speaks words with that efficacy, that they pierce the heart quite through; and what the issue then is David declares, 'There is no soundness,' says he, 'in my flesh because of your anger; nor is there any rest in my bones because of my sin' (Ps. 38:3). The whole person is brought under the power of them, and all health and rest is taken away.

### Lack of Zeal

Unspiritedness and disability to duty, in doing or suffering, attend such a condition: 'Mine iniquities have taken hold upon me, so that I am not able to look up' (Ps. 40:12). His spiritual strength was worn away by sin, so that he was not able to address himself to any communion with God. The soul now cannot pray with life and power, cannot hear with joy and profit, cannot do good and communicate with cheerfulness and freedom, cannot meditate with delight and heavenly-mindedness, cannot act for God with zeal and liberty, cannot think of suffering with boldness and resolution; but is sick, weak, feeble, and bowed down.

Now, I say, a gracious soul, after much communion with God, may, on the account of sin, by a sense of the guilt of it, be brought into a state and condition wherein some, more, or all of these, with other the like perplexities, may be its portion; and these make up the depths whereof the psalmist here complains. What are the sins, or of what sorts, that ordinarily cast the souls of believers into these depths, shall be afterwards declared.

## When Believers Fall into the Depths

Secondly, I shall now show both whence it is that believers may fall into such a condition, as also whence it is that oftentimes they actually do so.

### The Provisions of the Covenant of Grace

First, the nature of the covenant wherein all believers now walk with God, and wherein all their whole provision for obedience is inwrapped, leaves it possible for them to fall into these depths that have been mentioned. Under the first covenant there was no mercy or forgiveness provided for any sin. It was necessary, then, that it should exhibit a sufficiency of grace to preserve them from every sin, or it could have been of no use at all. This the righteousness of God required, and so it was. To have made a covenant wherein there was no provision at all of pardon, and not a sufficiency of grace to keep the covenanters from need of pardon, was not answerable to the goodness and righteousness of God. But he made man upright, who, of his own accord, sought out many inventions.

It is not so in the covenant of grace; there is in it pardon provided in the blood of Christ: it is not, therefore, of indispensable necessity that there should be administered in it grace effectually preserving from every sin. Yet it is on all accounts to be preferred before the other; for, besides the relief by pardon, which the other knew nothing of, there is in it also much provision against sin, which was not in the other.

### No Sin Can Void the Covenant

There is provision made in it against all and every sin that would disannul the covenant, and make a final separation between God and a soul that has been once taken into the bond thereof. This provision is absolute. God has taken upon himself the making of this good, and the establishing this law of the covenant, that it shall not by any sin be disannulled: 'I will,' says God, 'make an everlasting covenant with them, that I will not turn away from them, to do them good; but I will put my fear in their hearts, that they shall not depart from me' (Jer. 32:40). The security hereof depends not on any thing in ourselves. All that is in us is to be used as a means of the accomplishment of this promise; but the event or issue depends absolutely on the faithfulness of God. And the whole certainty and stability of the covenant depends on the efficacy of the grace administered in it to preserve men from all such sins as would disannul it.

### Constant Peace and Consolation

There is in this covenant provision made for constant peace and consolation, notwithstanding and against the guilt of such sins as, through their infirmities and temptations, believers are daily exposed to. Though they fall into sins every day, yet they do not fall into depths every day. In the tenor of this covenant there is a consistency between a sense of sin to humiliation and peace, with strong consolation. After the apostle had described the whole conflict that believers have with sin, and the frequent wounds which they receive thereby, which makes them cry out for deliverance (Rom. 7:24), he yet concludes that 'there is no condemnation to them' (Rom. 8:1); which is a sufficient and stable foundation of peace. So, 'These things I write to you, that you sin not. And if any man sin, we have an advocate with the Father, Jesus Christ the righteous' (1 John 2:1). Our great business and care ought to be, that we sin not; but yet, when we have done our utmost, 'If we say we have no sin, we deceive ourselves' (1 John 1:8). What, then, shall poor, sinful, guilty creatures do? Why, let them go to the Father by their advocate, and they shall not fail of pardon and peace. And, says Paul, 'God is abundantly willing that we might have strong consolation, who fly for refuge to lay hold on the hope set before us' (Heb. 6:17–18). What was his condition who fled of old to the city of refuge for safety, from whence this expression is taken? He was guilty of blood, though shed at unawares; and so as that he was to die for it, if he escaped not to the city of refuge. Though we may have the guilt of sins upon us that the law pronounces death to, yet, flying to Christ for refuge, God has provided not only safety, but 'strong consolation' for us also. Forgiveness in the blood of Christ does not only take guilt from the soul, but trouble also from the conscience; and in this respect does the apostle at large set forth the excellency of his sacrifice (Heb. 10). The sacrifices of the old law, he tells us, could not make perfect the worshippers (Heb. 10:1): which he proves (Heb. 10:2), because they did never take away, thoroughly and really, conscience of sin; that is, depths or distresses of conscience about sin. 'But now,' says he, 'Jesus Christ, in the covenant of grace, "has perfected for ever them that are sanctified" (Heb. 10:14); providing for them such stable peace and consolation, as that they shall not need the renewing of sacrifices every day' (Heb. 10:18). This is the great mystery of the gospel in the blood of Christ, that those who sin every day should have peace with God all their days, provided their sins fall within the compass of those infirmities against which this consolation is provided.

### Preservation from Ruinous Sins

There is provision made of grace to prevent and preserve the soul from great and enormous sins, such as in their own nature are apt to wound conscience, and cast the person into such depths and entanglements as wherein he shall have neither rest nor peace. Of what sort these sins are shall be afterward declared. There is in this covenant 'grace for grace' (John 1:16), and abundance of grace administered from the all-fulness of Christ. Grace reigns in it (Rom. 6:6), destroying and crucifying 'the body of sin.'

But this provision in the covenant of grace against peace-ruining, soul-perplexing sins, is not, as to the administration of it, absolute. There are covenant commands and exhortations, on the attendance whereunto the administration of much covenant grace depends. To watch, pray, improve faith, to stand on our guard continually, to mortify sin, to fight against temptations, with steadfastness, diligence, constancy, are everywhere prescribed to us; and that in order to the insurance of the grace mentioned. These things are on our part the condition of the administration of that abundant grace which is to preserve us from soul-entangling sins. So Peter informs us, 'The divine power of God has given to us all things that pertain to life and godliness' (2 Pet. 1:3). We have from it an habitual furnishment and provision for obedience at all times. Also, says he, 'He has given to us exceeding great and precious promises, that by these we might be partakers of the divine nature' (v. 4). What, then, is in this blessed estate and condition required of us, that we may make a due improvement of the provision made for us, and enjoy the comforting influence of those promises that he prescribes to us? 'Giving all diligence, add to your faith virtue, and to virtue knowledge, and to knowledge temperance, and to temperance patience, and to patience godliness, and to godliness brotherly-kindness, and to brotherly-kindness charity' (v. 5–7); that is, carefully and diligently attend to the exercise of all the graces of the Spirit, and to a conversation in all things becoming the gospel. What, then, shall be the issue if these things are attended to? 'If these things be in you, and abound, they make you that you shall neither be barren nor unfruitful in the knowledge of our Lord Jesus Christ' (v. 8). It is not enough that these things be in you, that you have the seed and root of them from and by the Holy Ghost; but you are to take care that they flourish and abound: without which, though the root of the matter may be in you, and so you be not wholly devoid of spiritual life, yet you will be poor, barren, sapless, withering creatures all your days. But now, suppose that these things do abound, and we be made fruitful thereby? Why then, says he, 'If you do these things, you shall never fall' (v. 10). What! Never fall into sin? Nay, that is not in the promise; and he that says, when he has done all, 'that he has no sin, he is a liar.' Or is it never fall totally from God? No; the preservation of the elect, of whom he speaks, from total apostasy, is not suspended on such conditions, especially not on any degree of them, such as their abounding imports. But it is that they shall not fall into their old sins, from which they were purged (v. 9)—such conscience-wasting and defiling sins as they lived in, in the time and state of their unregeneracy. Thus, though there be, in the covenant of grace through Jesus Christ, provision made of abundant supplies for the soul's preservation from entangling sins, yet their administration has respect to our diligent attendance to the means of receiving them appointed for us to walk in.

And here lies the latitude of the new covenant, here lies the exercise of renewed free-will. This is the field of free, voluntary obedience, under the administration of gospel grace. There are extremes which, in respect of the event, it is not concerned in. To be wholly perfect, to be free from every sin, all failings, all infirmities, that is not provided for, not promised in this covenant. It is a covenant of mercy and pardon, which supposes a continuance of sin. To fall utterly and finally from God, that is absolutely provided against. Between these two extremes of absolute perfection and total apostasy lies the large field of believers' obedience and walking with God. Many a sweet, heavenly passage there is, and many a dangerous depth, in this field. Some walk near to the one side, some to the other; yea, the same person may sometimes press hard after perfection, sometimes be cast to the very border of destruction. Now, between these two lie many a soul-plunging sin, against

*Between these two extremes of absolute perfection and total apostasy lies the large field of believers' obedience and walking with God. Many a sweet, heavenly passage there is, and many a dangerous depth, in this field.*

which no absolute provision is made, and which, for want of giving all diligence to put the means of preservation in practice, believers are oftentimes overtaken withal.

### Consolation for Sinning Believers

There is not in the covenant of grace provision made of ordinary and abiding consolation for any under the guilt of great sins, or sins greatly aggravated, which they fall into by a neglect of using and abiding in the fore-mentioned conditions of abounding actual grace. Sins there are which, either because in their own nature they wound and waste conscience, or in their effects break forth into scandal, causing the name of God and the gospel to be evil spoken of, or in some of their circumstances are full of unkindness against God, do deprive the soul of its wonted consolation. How, by what means, on what account, such sins come to terrify conscience, to break the bones, to darken the soul, and to cast it into inextricable depths, notwithstanding the relief that is provided of pardon in the blood of Christ, I shall not now declare; that they will do so, and that consolation is not of equal extent with safety, we know. Hence God assumes it to himself, as an act of mere sovereign grace, to speak peace and refreshment to the souls of his saints in their depths of sin-entanglements (Isa. 57:18–19). And, indeed, if the Lord had not thus provided that great provocation should stand in need of special reliefs, it might justly be feared that the negligence of believers might possibly bring forth much bitter fruit.

Only, this must be observed by the way, that what is spoken relates to the sense of sinners in their own souls, and not to the nature of the thing itself. There is in the gospel consolation provided against the greatest as well as the least sins. The difference arises from God's sovereign communication of it, according to the tenor of the covenant's administration, which we have laid down. Hence, because under Moses' law there was an exception made of some sins, for which there was no sacrifice appointed, so that those who were guilty of them could no way be justified from them—that is, carnally, as to their interest in the Judaical church and polity—

Paul tells the Jews that 'through Jesus Christ was preached to them the forgiveness of sins: and that by him all that believe are justified from all things, from which they could not be justified by the law of Moses' (Acts 13:38–9). There is now no exception of any particular sins as to pardon and peace; but what we have spoken relates to the manner and way wherein God is pleased to administer consolation to the souls of sinning believers.

### Why Believers Fall into the Depths

And this is the evidence which I shall offer to prove that the souls of believers, after much gracious communion with God, may yet fall into inextricable depths on the account of sin; whence it is that actually they oftentimes do so shall be farther declared.

The principles of this assertion are known, I shall therefore only touch upon them.

### *The Nature of Indwelling Sin*

First, the nature of indwelling sin, as it remains in the best of the saints in this life, being a little considered, will evidence to us from whence it is that they are sometimes surprised and plunged into the depths mentioned.

THE ROOT OF EVERY SIN REMAINS. Though the strength of every sin be weakened by grace, yet the root of no sin is in this life wholly taken away. Lust is like the stubborn Canaanites, who, after the general conquest of the land, would dwell in it still (Josh. 17:12). Indeed, when Israel grew strong they brought them under tribute, but they could not utterly expel them. The kingdom and rule belongs to grace; and when it grows strong it brings sin much under, but it will not wholly be driven out. The body of death is not utterly to be done away, but in and by the death of the body. In the flesh of the best saints there 'dwells no good thing' (Rom. 7:18); but the contrary is there—that is, the root of all evil: 'The flesh lusts against the Spirit,' as 'the Spirit lusts against the flesh' (Gal. 5:17).

As, then, there is a universality in the actings of the Spirit in its opposing all evil, so also there is a universality in the actings of the flesh for the furtherance of it.

SOME SINS ARE HARDER TO SUBDUE. Some lusts or branches of original corruption do obtain in some persons such advantages, either from nature, custom, employment, society, or the like circumstances, that they become like the Canaanites that had iron chariots; it is a very difficult thing to subdue them. Well it is if war be maintained constantly against them, for they will almost always be in actual rebellion.

INDWELLING SIN RETAINS ITS PROPERTIES. Indwelling sin though weakened retains all its properties. The properties of a thing follow its nature. Where the nature of any thing is, there are all its natural properties. What are these properties of indwelling sin I should here declare, but that I have handled the whole power and efficacy, the nature and properties of it, in a treatise to that only purpose. In brief, they are such as it is no wonder that some believers are by them cast into depths; but it is indeed that they do escape them. But thereof the reader may see at large my discourse on this particular subject.

### The Power of Temptation

Secondly, add hereunto the power and prevalency of temptation; which, because also I have already, in a special discourse to that purpose, insisted on, I shall not here farther lay open.

### God Deals with Sinning Saints in Various Ways

Thirdly, the sovereign pleasure of God in dealing with sinning saints must also be considered. Divine love and wisdom work not towards all in the same manner. God is pleased to continue peace to some with a 'non-obstante,' for great provocations. Love shall humble them, and rebukes of kindness shall recover them from their wanderings. Others he is pleased to bring into the depths we have been speaking of. But yet I may say generally, signal provocations meet with one of these two events from God. First, those in whom they are are left into some signal barrenness and fruitlessness in their generations; they shall wither, grow barren, worldly, sapless, and be much cast out of the hearts of the people of God. Or, secondly, they shall be exercised in these depths, from whence their way of deliverance is laid down in this psalm. Thus, I say, God deals with his saints in great variety; some shall have all their bones broken, when others shall have only the gentle strokes of the rod. We are in the hand of mercy, and he may deal with us as seems good to him; but for our parts, great sins ought to be attended with expectations of great depths and perplexities.

And this is the state of the soul proposed in this psalm, and by us, to consideration. These are the depths wherein it is entangled; these are the ways and means whereby it is brought into these depths. Its deportment in and under this state and condition lies next in our way.

### The Sins that Cast Believers into the Depths

But before I proceed thereunto, I shall annex some few things to what has been delivered, tending to the farther opening of the whole case before us. And they are:

1. What are, or of what sort those sins are, which usually cast the souls of believers into these depths.
2. Insist on some aggravations of them.

### Great Sins Bring Great Distress

First, sins in their own nature wasting conscience are of this sort; sins that rise in opposition to all of God that is in us; that is, the light of grace and nature also. Such are the sins that cast David into his depths; such are the sins enumerated. 'Be not deceived,' says the apostle: 'neither fornicators, nor idolaters, nor adulterers, nor effeminate, nor abusers of themselves with mankind, nor thieves, nor covetous, nor drunkards, nor revilers, nor extortioners, shall inherit the kingdom of God' (1 Cor. 6:9–10). Certain it is that believers may fall into some of the sins here mentioned. Some have done so, as is left on record. The apostle says not those who have committed any of these sins, but such sinners, shall not inherit the kingdom of God; that is, who live in these sins, or any like to them. There is no provision of mercy made for such sinners. These and the like are sins which in their own nature, without the consideration of aggravating circumstances (which yet, indeed, really in believers they can never be without), are able to plunge a soul into depths. These sins cut the locks of men's spiritual strength; and it is in vain for them to say, 'We will go, and do as at other times.' Bones are not broken without pain; nor great sins brought on the conscience without trouble. But I need not insist on these. Some say that they deprive even true believers of all their interest in the love of God, but unduly; all grant that they bereave them of all comforting evidence and well-grounded assurance of it. So they did David and Peter. And herein lies no small part of the depths we are searching into.

### Aggravating Circumstances

Secondly. There are sins which, though they do not rise up in the conscience with such a bloody guilt as those mentioned, yet, by reason of some circumstances and aggravations, God takes them so unkindly as to make them a root of disquietness and trouble to the soul all its days. He says of some sins of ungodly men, 'As I live, this iniquity shall not be purged from you until you die. If you are come to this height, you shall not escape. I will not spare you.' And there are provocations in his own people which may be so circumstantiated as that he will not let them pass before he has cast them into depths, and made them cry out for deliverance. Let us consider some of them.

### Under-valuations of God's Love

Miscarriages under signal enjoyments of love and kindness from God are of this sort. When God has given to any one expressive manifestations of his love, convinced him of it, made him say in the inmost parts of his heart, 'This is undeserved love and kindness;' then for him to be negligent in his walking with God, it carries an unkindness with it that shall not be forgotten. It is a remark upon the miscarriages of Solomon, that he fell into them after God had 'appeared to him twice.' And all sins under or after especial mercies will meet, at one time or other, especial rebukes. Nothing does more distress the conscience of a sinner than the remembrance, in darkness, of abused light; in desertions, of neglected love. This God will make them sensible of. 'Though I have redeemed them,' says God, 'yet they have spoken lies against me' (Hos. 7:13: so 13:4–7). When God has in his providence dealt graciously with a person—it may be delivered him from straits and troubles, set him in a large place, prevented him with many fruits and effects of his goodness, blessed him in his person, relations, and employments, dealt well with his soul, in giving him a gracious sense of his love in Christ— for such a one to fall under sinful miscarriages, it goes to the heart of God, and shall not be passed over. Under-valuations of love are great provocations. 'Has Nabal thus requited my kindness....' says David. 'I cannot bear it.' And the clearer the convictions of any in this kind were, the more severe will their reflections be upon themselves.

### Disregard for God's Discipline

Sins under or after great afflictions are of this importance also. God does not afflict willingly, or chasten us merely for his pleasure; he does it to make us partakers of his holiness. To take so little notice of his hand herein, as under it or after it not to watch against the workings and surprisals of sin, it has unkindness in it: 'I smote him,' says God, 'and he went on frowardly in the way of his own heart?' These provocations of his sons and daughters he cannot bear with. Has God brought you into the furnace, so that you have melted under his hand, and in pity and compassion has given you enlargement? If you have soon forgotten his dealings with you, is it any wonder if he mind you again by troubles in your soul?

## Resisting Convictions

Breaking off from under strong convictions and dawnings of love before conversion, are oftentimes remembered upon the conscience afterward. When the Lord by his Spirit shall mightily convince the heart of sin, and make withal some discoveries of his love and the excellencies of Christ to it, so that it begins to yield and be overpowered, being almost persuaded to be a Christian; if, then, through the strength of lust or unbelief, it goes back to the world or self-righteousness, its folly has unkindness with it that, sometimes shall not be passed by. God can, and often does, put forth the greatness of his power for the recovery of such a soul; but yet he will deal with him about this contempt of his love and the excellency of his Son, in the dawnings of them revealed to him.

## Forgetful of His Love

Sudden forgetfulness of endearing manifestations of special love. This God cautions his people against, as knowing their proneness thereunto: 'God the LORD will speak peace to his people, and to his saints; but let them not turn again to folly' (Ps. 85:8). Let them take heed of their aptness to forget endearing manifestations of special love. When God at any time draws nigh to a soul by his Spirit, in his word, with gracious words of peace and love, giving a sense of his kindness upon the heart by the Holy Ghost, so that it is filled with joy unspeakable and glorious thereon; for this soul, upon a temptation, a diversion, or by mere carelessness and neglect, which oftentimes falls out, to suffer this sense of love to be as it were obliterated, and so to lose that influencing efficacy to obedience which it is accompanied withal, this also is full of unkindness. An account hereof we have in Song of Solomon 5:1–6. In the first verse the Lord Jesus draws nigh, with full provision of gospel mercies for his beloved: 'I am come to you,' says he, 'O my sister. I have brought myrrh and spice, honey and wine, with me: whatever is spiritually sweet and delightful—mercy, grace, peace, consolation, joy, assurance—they are all here in readiness for you' (v. 2). The spouse, in her drowsy indisposition, takes little notice of this gracious visit; she is diverted by other matters, and knows not how to attend fully and wholly to the blessed communion offered to her, but excuses herself as otherwise engaged. But what is the issue? Christ withdraws, leaves her in the dark, in the midst of many disconsolations, and long it is before she obtain any recovery.

### Neglected Opportunities and Gifts

Great opportunities for service neglected and great gifts not improved are oftentimes the occasion of plunging the soul into great depths. Gifts are given to trade withal for God. Opportunities are the market-days for that trade. To napkin up the one and to let slip the other will end in trouble and disconsolation. Disquietments and perplexities of heart are worms that will certainly breed in the rust of unexercised gifts. God loses a revenue of glory and honour by such slothful souls; and he will make them sensible of it. I know some at this day whom omissions of opportunities for service are ready to sink into the grave.

### Warnings Ignored

Sins after especial warnings are usually thus issued. In all that variety of special warnings which God is pleased to use towards sinning saints, I shall single out one only: When a soul is wrestling with some lust or temptation, God by his providence causes some special word, in the preaching of the gospel, or the administration of some ordinance thereof, peculiarly suited to the state and condition of the soul, by the ways of rebuke or persuasion, to come nigh and enter the inmost parts of the heart. The soul cannot but take notice that God is nigh to him, that he is dealing with him, and calling on him to look to him for assistance. And he seldom gives such warnings to his saints but that he is nigh them in an eminent manner to give them relief and help, if, in answer to his call, they apply themselves to him; but if his care and kindness herein be neglected, his following reproofs are usually more severe.

### Scandal

Sins that bring scandal seldom suffer the soul to escape depths. Even in great sins, God in chastening takes more notice ofttimes of the scandal than the sin (as 2 Sam. 12:14). Many professors take little notice of their worldliness, their pride, their passion, their lavish tongues; but the world does, and the gospel is disadvantaged by it: and no wonder if themselves find from the hand of the Lord the bitter fruits of them in the issue.

And many other such aggravations of sins there are, which heighten provocations in their own nature not of so dreadful an aspect as some others, into a guilt plunging a soul into depths. Those which have been named may suffice in the way of instance; which is all that we have aimed at, and therefore forbear enlargements on the several heads of them.

### GUILT INTENSIFIED

The consideration of some aggravations of the guilt of these sins, which bring the soul usually into the condition before laid down, shall close this discourse.

### By a Principle of Grace

The soul is furnished with a principle of grace, which is continually operative and working for its preservation from such sins. The new creature is living and active for its own growth, increase, and security, according to the tenor of the covenant of grace: it 'lusts against the flesh' (Gal. 5:17). It is naturally active for its own preservation and increase, as newborn children have a natural inclination to the food that will keep them alive and cause them to grow (1 Pet. 2:2). The soul, then, cannot fall into these entangling sins, but it must be with a high neglect of that very principle which is bestowed upon it for quite contrary ends and purposes. The labourings, lustings, desires, crying of it are neglected. Now, it is from God, and is the renovation of his image in us—that which God owns and cares for. The wounding of its vitals, the stifling its operations, the neglect of its endeavours for the soul's preservation, do always attend sins of the importance spoken to.

### By the Full Provision Made in Jesus Christ

Whereas this new creature, this principle of life and obedience, is not able of itself to preserve the soul from such sins as will bring it into depths, there is full provision for continual supplies made for it and all its wants in Jesus Christ. There are treasures of relief in Christ, whereunto the soul may at any time repair and find succour against the incursions of sin. He says to the soul, as David to Abiathar, when he fled from Doeg, 'Abide with me, fear not: for he that seeks my life, seeks your life; but with me you shall be in safe-guard'—sin is my enemy no less than yours; it seeks the life of your soul, and it seeks my life. 'Abide with me, for with me you shall be in safety.' This the apostle exhorts us to, 'Let us come boldly to the throne of grace, that we may obtain mercy, and find grace to help in time of need' (Heb. 4:16). If ever it be a time of need with a soul, it is so when it is under the assaults of provoking sins. At such a time, there is suitable and seasonable help in Christ for succour and relief. The new creature begs, with sighs and groans, that the soul would apply itself to him. To neglect him with all his provision of grace, whilst he stands calling to us, 'Open to me, for my head is filled with dew, and my locks with the drops of the night;' to despise the sighing of the poor prisoner, the new creature, by sin appointed to die, cannot but be a high provocation. May not God complain and say, 'See these poor creatures. They were once intrusted with a stock of grace in themselves; this they cast away, and themselves into the utmost misery thereby. That they might not utterly perish a second time, their portion and stock is now laid up in another—a safe treasurer; in him are their lives and comforts secured. But see their wretched negligence; they venture all rather than they will attend to him for succour.' And what think we is the heart of Christ when he sees his children giving way to conscience-wasting sins, without that application to him which the life and peace of their own souls calls upon them for? These are not sins of daily infirmity, which cannot be avoided; but their guilt is always attended with a neglect more or less of the relief provided in Christ against them. The means of preservation from them is blessed, ready, nigh at hand; the concern of Christ in our preservation great, of our souls unspeakable. To neglect and despise means, Christ, souls, peace, and life, must needs render guilt very guilty.

Much to the same purpose may be spoken about that signal provision that is made against such sins as these in the covenant of grace, as has been already declared; but I shall not farther carry on this discourse.

And this may suffice as to the state and condition of the soul in this psalm represented. We have seen what the depths are wherein it is entangled, and by what ways and means any one may come to be cast into them. The next thing that offers itself to our consideration is the deportment of a gracious soul in that state or condition, or what course it steers towards a delivery.

### The Behaviour of a Believer Under Distress

The words of these two first verses declare also the deportment of the soul in the condition that we have described; that is, what it does, and what course it steers for relief. 'I have cried to you, O LORD. Lord, hear my voice: let your ears be attentive to the voice of my supplications.'

There is in the words a general application made in a tendency to relief; wherein is first to be considered to whom the application is made; and that is Jehovah: 'I have cried to you, Jehovah.' God gave out that name to his people to confirm their faith in the stability of his promises (Exod. 3): He who is Being himself will assuredly give being and subsistence to his promises. Being to deal with God about the promises of grace, he makes his application to him under this name: I call upon you, Jehovah.

In the application itself may be observed, first, the anthropopathy of the expression. He prays that God would cause his ears to be attentive; after the manner of men who seriously attend to what is spoken to them, when they turn aside from that which they regard not. Secondly, the earnestness of the soul in the work it has in hand; which is evident both from the reduplication of his request, 'Lord, hear my voice: let your ears be attentive to the voice of my supplications;' and the emphaticness of the words he makes use of: 'Let your ears,' says he, 'be קַשֻּׁבוֹת — diligently attentive.' The word signifies the most diligent heedfulness and close attention: 'Let your ears be very attentive.' And to what? לְקוֹל תַּחֲנוּנָי—'To the voice of my supplications.' *'Deprecationum mearum,'* generally say interpreters—'Of my deprecations,' or earnest prayers for the averting of evil or punishment. But the word is from חָנַן, *'Gratiosus fuit,'* to be gracious or merciful; so that it signifies properly supplication for grace. 'Be attentive,' says he, 'O Lord, to my supplications for grace and mercy, which, according to my extreme necessity, I now address myself to make to you.' And in these words does the psalmist set forth in general the frame and working of a gracious soul being cast into depths and darkness by sin.

The foundation of what I shall farther thence pursue lies in these two propositions:

1. The only attempt of a sinful, entangled soul for relief lies in an application to God alone: 'To you, Jehovah, have I cried; Lord, hear.'
2. Depths of sin-entanglements will put a gracious soul on intense and earnest applications to God: 'Lord, hear; Lord, attend.' Dying men do not use to cry out slothfully for relief.

What may be thought necessary in general for the direction of a soul in the state and condition described, shall briefly be spoken to from these two propositions.

Trouble, danger, disquiet, arguing not only things evil, but a sense in the mind and soul of them, will of themselves put those in whom they are upon seeking relief. Every thing would naturally be at rest. a drowning man needs no exhortation to endeavour his own deliverance and safety; and spiritual troubles will, in like manner, put men on attempts for relief. To seek for no remedy is to be senselessly obdurate, or wretchedly desperate, as Cain and Judas. We may suppose, then, that the principal business of every soul in depths is to endeavour deliverance. They cannot rest in that condition wherein they have no rest. In this endeavour, what course a gracious soul steers is laid down in the first proposition, negatively and positively. He applies himself not to any thing but God; he applies himself to God. An eminent instance we have of it in both parts, or both to the one side and the other, 'Asshur,' say those poor, distressed, returning sinners, 'shall not save us; we will not ride upon horses: neither will we say any more to the work of our hands, You are our gods: for in you the fatherless finds mercy' (Hos. 14:3). Their application to God is attended with a renunciation of every other way of relief.

Several things there are that sinners are apt to apply themselves to for relief in their perplexities, which prove to them as waters that fail. How many things have the Romanists invented to deceive souls withal! Saints and angels, the blessed Virgin, the wood of the cross, confessions, penances, masses, pilgrimages, dirges, purgatories, papal pardons, works of compensation, and the like, are made entrances for innumerable souls into everlasting ruin. Did they know the terror of the Lord, the nature of sin, and of the mediation of Christ, they would be ashamed and confounded in themselves for these abominations; they would not say to these their idols, 'You are our gods; come and save us.' How short do all their contrivances come of his that would fain be offering 'rivers of oil, yea, the fruit of his body, for the sin of his soul, his first-born for his transgression' (Mic. 6:7), who yet gains nothing but an aggravation of his sin and misery thereby! Yea, the heathens went beyond them in devotion and expense. It is no new inquiry, what course sin-perplexed souls should take for relief. From the foundation of the world, the minds of far the greatest part of mankind have been exercised in it. As was their light or darkness, such was the course they took. Among those who were ignorant of God, this inquiry brought forth all that diabolical superstition which spread itself over the face of the whole world. Gentilism being destroyed by the power and efficacy of the gospel, the same inquiry working in the minds of darkened men, in conjunction with other lusts, brought forth the Papacy. When men had lost a spiritual acquaintance with the covenant of grace and mystery of the gospel, the design of eternal love, and efficacy of the blood of Christ, they betook themselves, in part or in whole, for relief under their entanglements, to the broken cisterns mentioned. They are of two sorts—self, and other things. For those other things which belong to their false worship, being abominated by all the saints of God, I shall not need to make any farther mention of them. That which relates to self is not confined to Popery, but confines itself to the limits of human nature, and is predominate over all that are under the law; that is, to seek for relief in sin-distresses by self-endeavours, self-righteousness. Hence many poor souls in straits apply themselves to themselves. They expect their cure from the same hand that wounded them. This was the life of Judaism, as the apostle informs us (Rom. 10:3). And all men under the law are still animated by the same principle. They return, but not to the Lord. Finding themselves in depths, in distresses about sin, what course do they take? This they will do,

*...many poor souls in straits apply themselves to themselves. They expect their cure from the same hand that wounded them.*

that they will do no more; this shall be their ordinary course, and that they will do in an extraordinary manner; as they have offended, whence their trouble arises, so they will amend, and look that their peace should spring from thence, as if God and they stood on equal terms. In this way some spend all their days; sinning and amending, amending and sinning, without once coming to repentance and peace. This the souls of believers watch against. They look on themselves as fatherless: 'In you the fatherless finds mercy;' that is, helpless—without the least ground of hopes in themselves or expectation from themselves. They know their repentance, their amendment, their supplications, their humiliations, their fastings, their mortifications, will not relieve them. Repent they will, and amend they will, and pray, and fast, and humble their souls, for they know these things to be their duty; but they know that their goodness extends not to Him with whom they have to do, nor is He profited by their righteousness. They will be in the performance of all duties; but they expect not deliverance by any duty. 'It is God,' say they, 'with whom we have to do: our business is to hearken what he will say to us.'

There are also other ways whereby sinful souls destroy themselves by false reliefs. Diversions from their perplexing thoughtfulness please them. They will fix on something or other that cannot cure their disease, but shall only make them forget that they are sick; as Cain, under the terror of his guilt, departed from the presence of the Lord, and sought inward rest in outward labour and employment. He went and built a city (Gen. 4:17). Such courses Saul fixed on; first music, then a witch. Nothing more ordinary than for men thus to deal with their convictions. They see their sickness, feel their wound, and go to the Assyrian (Hos. 5:13). And this insensibly leads men into atheism. Frequent applications of creature-diversions to convictions of sin are a notable means of bringing on final impenitency. Some drunkards had, it may be, never been so, had they not been first convinced of other sins. They strive to stifle the guilt of one sin with another. They fly from themselves to themselves, from their consciences to their lusts, and seek for relief from sin by sinning. This is so far from believers, that they will not allow lawful things to be a diversion of their distress. Use lawful things they may and will, but not to divert their thoughts from their distresses. These they know must be issued between God and them. Wear off they will not, but must be taken away. These rocks, and the like, whereof there are innumerable, I say, a gracious soul takes care to avoid. He knows it is God alone who is the Lord of his conscience, where his depths lie; God alone against whom he has sinned; God alone who can pardon his sin. From dealing with him he will be neither enticed nor diverted. 'To you, O Lord,' says he, 'do I come; your word concerning me must stand; upon you will I wait. If you have no delight in me, I must perish. Other remedies I know are vain. I intend not to spend my strength for that which is not bread. To you do I cry.' Here a sin-entangled soul is to fix itself. Trouble excites it to look for relief. Many things without it present themselves as a diversion; many things within it offer themselves for a remedy. 'Forget your sorrow,' say the former; 'Ease yourself of it by us,' say the latter. The soul refuses both, as physicians of no value, and to God alone makes its application. He has wounded, and he alone can heal. And until any one that is sensible of the guilt of sin will come off from all reserves to deal immediately with God, it is in vain for him to expect relief.

## HE CRIES TO GOD WITH GREAT EARNESTNESS

Herein it is intense, earnest, and urgent; which was the second thing observed. It is no time now to be slothful. The soul's all, its greatest concerns are at the stake. Dull, cold, formal, customary applications to God will not serve the turn. Ordinary actings of faith, love, fervency; usual seasons, opportunities, duties, answer not this condition. To do no more than ordinary now is to do nothing at all. He that puts forth no more strength and activity for his deliverance when he is in depths, ready to perish, than he does, or has need to do, when he is at liberty in plain and smooth paths, is scarcely like to escape. Some in such conditions are careless and negligent; they think, in ordinary course, to wear off their distempers; and that, although at present they are sensible of their danger, they shall yet have peace at last: in which frame there is much contempt of God. Some despond and languish away under their pressures. Spiritual sloth influences both these sorts of persons. Let us see the frame under consideration exemplified in another. We have an instance in the spouse (S. of S. 3:1–3). She had lost the presence of Christ, and so was in the very state and condition before described (v. 1). It was night with her—a time of darkness and disconsolation; and she seeks for her beloved: 'By night on my bed I sought him whom my soul loves.' Christ was absent from her, and she was left to depths and darkness upon that account; wherefore she seeks for him. But, as the most are apt to do in the like state and condition, she mends not her pace, goes not out of or beyond her course of ordinary duties, nor the frame she was usually in at other times. But what is the issue? Says she, 'I found him not.' This is not a way to recover a sense of lost love, nor to get out of her entanglements. And this puts her on another course; she begins to think that if things continue in this estate she shall be undone. I go on, indeed, with the performance of duties still; but I have not the presence of my beloved—I meet not with Christ in them. My darkness and trouble abides still. If I take not some other course, I shall be lost.' Well, says she, 'I will rise now' (v. 2)—'I will shake off all that ease, and sloth, and customariness, that cleave to me.' Some more lively, vigorous course must be fixed on. Resolutions for new, extraordinary, vigorous, constant applications to God, are the first general step and degree of a sin-entangled soul acting towards a recovery. 'I will rise now.' And what does she do when she is thus resolved? 'I will,' says she, 'go about the streets, and in the broad ways; and seek him whom my soul loves'—'I will leave no ways or means unattempted whereby I may possibly come to a fresh enjoyment of him. If a man seek for a friend, he can look for him only in the streets, and in the broad ways—that is, either in towns, or in the fields. So will I do,' says the spouse. 'In what way, ordinance, or institution soever, in or by what duty soever, public or private, of communion with others or solitary retiredness, Christ ever was or may be found, or peace obtained, 'I will seek him, and not give over until I come to an enjoyment of him.' And this frame, this resolution, a soul in depths must come to, if ever it expect deliverance. For the most part, men's 'wounds stink, and are corrupt, because of their foolishness,' as the psalmist complains (Ps. 38:5).

They are wounded by sin, and through spiritual sloth they neglect their cure; this weakens them, and disquiets them day by day: yet they endure all, rather than they will come out of their carnal ease, to deal effectually with God in an extraordinary manner. It was otherwise with David, 'Why,' says he, 'Are you so far from helping me, and from the words of my roaring? O my God, I cry in the daytime, and in the night season, and am not silent' (Ps. 22:1–2). What ails the man? Can he not be quiet night nor day? Never silent, never hold his peace? And if he be somewhat disquieted, can he not contain himself, but that he must roar and cry out? Yea, must he 'roar' thus 'all the day long,' as he speaks (Ps. 32:3), and 'groan all the night' (Ps. 6:6)? What is the matter, with all this roaring, sighing, tears, roaring all the day, all night long? Ah! Let him alone, his soul is bitter in him; he is fallen into depths; the Lord is withdrawn from him; trouble is hard at hand; yea, he is full of anxiety on the account of sin; there is no quietness and soundness in him; and he must thus earnestly and restlessly apply himself for relief. Alas! What strangers, for the most part, are men now-a-days to this frame! How little of the workings of this spirit is found amongst us! And is not the reason of it, that we value the world more, and heaven and heavenly things less, than he did? That we can live at a better rate, without a sense of the love of God in Christ, than he could do? And is it not hence that we every day see so many withering professors, that have in a manner lost all communion with God, beyond a little lip-labour or talking; the filthy savour of whose wounds are offensive to all but themselves? And so will they go on, ready to die and perish, rather than with this holy man thus stir up themselves to meet the Lord. Heman was also like to him (Ps. 88:11–12). What sense he had of his depths he declares, 'My soul,' says he, 'is full of troubles; and my life draws nigh to the grave' (v. 3). And what course does he steer in this heavy, sorrowful, and disconsolate condition? Why, says he, 'O LORD God of my salvation, I have cried day and night before you: let my prayer come before you: incline your ear to my cry' (v. 1–2). Day and night he cries to the God of his salvation, and that with earnestness and importunity. This was his business, this was he exercised about all his days.

This is that which is aimed at—if a gracious soul be brought into the depths before mentioned and described, by reason of sin, when the Lord is pleased to lead him forth towards a recovery, he causes him to be vigorous and restless in all the duties whereby he may make application to him for deliverance. Now, wherein this intenseness and earnestness of the soul, in its applications to God, principally consists I shall briefly declare, when I have touched a little upon some considerations and grounds that stir it up thereunto.

### Provoked by the Greatest of Concern

The greatest of men's concerns may well put them on this earnestness. Men do not use to deal with dull and slothful spirits about their greatest concerns. David tells us that he was more concerned in the 'light of God's countenance' than the men of the world could be in their 'corn and wine' (Ps. 4:6–7). Suppose a man of the world should have his house, wherein all his stock and riches are laid up, set on fire, and so the whole be in danger under his eye to be consumed, would he be calm and quiet in the consideration of it? Would he not bestir himself with all his might, and call in all the help he could obtain? And that because his portion, his all, his great concern, lies at stake. And shall the soul be slothful, careless, dull, secure, when fire is put to its eternal concerns—when the light of God's countenance, which is of more esteem to him than the greatest increase of corn and wine can be to the men of the world, is removed from him? It was an argument of prodigious security in Jonah, that he was fast asleep when the ship wherein he was was ready to be cast away for his sake. And will it be thought less in any soul, who, being in a storm of wrath and displeasure from God, sent out into the deep after him, shall neglect it, and sleep, as Solomon says, 'on the top of a mast in the midst of the sea?' How did that poor creature, whose heart was mad on his idols cry out when he was deprived of them! 'You have taken away my gods,' says he, 'and what have I more?' (Judg. 18:24). And shall a gracious soul lose his God through his own folly—the sense of his love, the consolation of his presence—and not with all his might follow hard after him? Peace with God, joy in believing, such souls have formerly obtained. Can they live without them now in their ordinary walking? Can they choose but cry out with Job, 'Oh that it were with us as in former days, when the candle of the Lord was upon our tabernacle?' (Job 29:2–4); and with David, 'O God, restore to me the joy of your salvation' (Ps. 51:12), 'for O my God, I remember former enjoyments, and my soul is cast down within me?' (Ps. 42:6). They cannot live without it. But suppose they might make a sorry shift to pass on in their pilgrimage whilst all is smooth about them, what will they do in the time of outward trials and distresses, when deep calls to deep, and one trouble excites and sharpens another? Nothing then will support them, they know, but that which is wanting to them (as Hab. 3:17–18; Ps. 23:4): so that the greatness of their concern provokes them to the earnestness mentioned.

### With a Living Sense of Spiritual Things

They have a deep sense of these their great concerns. All men are equally concerned in the love of God and pardon of sin. Every one has a soul of the same immortal constitution, equally capable of bliss and woe. But yet we see most men are so stupidly sottish, that they take little notice of these things. Neither the guilt of sin, nor the wrath of God, nor death, nor hell, are thought on or esteemed by them; they are their concerns, but they are not sensible of them. But gracious souls have a quick, living sense of spiritual things.

They have a saving spiritual fight, whereby they are able to discern the true nature of sin and the terror of the Lord: for though they are now supposed to have lost the comforting light of the Spirit, yet they never lose the sanctifying light of the Spirit, the light whereby they are enabled to discern spiritual things in a spiritual manner; this never utterly departs from them. By this they see sin to be 'exceeding sinful' (Rom. 7:13). By this they know 'the terror of the Lord' (2 Cor. 5:11); and that 'it is a fearful thing to fall into the hands of the living God' (Heb. 10:31). By this they discover the excellency of the love of God in Christ, which passes knowledge, the present sense whereof they have lost. By this they are enabled to look within the veil, and to take a view of the blessed consolations which the saints enjoy whose communion with God was never interrupted. This represents to them all the sweetness, pleasure, joy, peace, which in former days they had, whilst God was present with them in love. By this are they taught to value all the fruits of the blood of Jesus Christ, of the enjoyment of many whereof they are at present cut short and deprived. All which, with other things of the like nature and importance, make them very sensible of their concerns.

They remember what it cost them formerly to deal with God about sin; and hence they know it is no ordinary matter they have in hand. They must again to their old work, take the old cup into their hands again. a recovery from depths is as a new conversion.

Ofttimes in it the whole work, as to the soul's apprehension, is gone over afresh. This the soul knows to have been a work of dread, terror, and trouble, and trembles in itself at its new trials.

And the Holy Ghost gives to poor souls a fresh sense of their deep concerns, on purpose that it may be a means to stir them up to these earnest applications to God. The whole work is his, and he carries it on by means suited to the compassing of the end he aims at; and by these means is a gracious soul brought into the frame mentioned. Now, there are sundry things that concur in and to this frame.

### With Continual Thoughtfulness

There is a continual thoughtfulness about the sad condition wherein the soul is in its depths. Being deeply affected with their condition, they are continually ruminating upon it, and pondering it in their minds. So David declares the case to have been with him: 'Your arrows stick fast in me, and your hand presses me sore. There is no soundness in my flesh because of your anger; neither is there any rest in my bones because of my sin. For mine iniquities are gone over mine head: as an heavy burden they are too heavy for me. My wounds stink and are corrupt because of my foolishness. I am troubled; I am bowed down greatly; I go mourning all the day long. I am feeble and sore broken: I have roared by reason of the disquietness of my heart' (Ps. 38:2–6, 8). Restlessness, deep thoughtfulness, disquietness of heart, continual heaviness of soul, sorrow and anxiety of mind, lie at the bottom of the applications we speak of. From these principles their prayers flow out.

David adds, 'Lord, all my desire is before you, and my groaning is not hid from you' (v. 9). This way all his trouble wrought. He prayed out of the abundance of his meditation and grief. Thoughts of their state and condition lie down with such persons, and rise with them, and accompany them all the day long. As Reuben cried, 'The child is not; and I, whither shall I go?' so does such a soul— 'The love of God is not, Christ is not; and I, whither shall I cause my sorrow to go? God is provoked, death is nigh at hand, relief is far away, darkness is about me. I have lost my peace, my joy, my song in the night. What do I think of duties? Can two walk together unless they be agreed? Can I walk with God in them, whilst I have thus made him mine enemy? What do I think of ordinances? Will it do me any good to be at Jerusalem, and not see the face of the King? To live under ordinances, and not to meet in them with the King of saints? May I not justly fear that the Lord will take his Holy Spirit from me until I be left without remedy?' With such thoughts as these are sin-entangled souls exercised, and they lie rolling in their minds in all their applications to God.

### With Importunity & Constancy

We see the application itself consists in and is made by the prayer of faith, or crying to God. Now, this is done with intenseness of mind; which has a twofold fruit or propriety: First, importunity, and secondly, constancy.

It is said of our blessed Saviour, that when he was in his depths about our sins, 'he offered up prayers and supplications, with strong cries and tears' (Heb. 5:7). 'Strong cries and tears' express the utmost intension of spirit. And David expresses it by 'roaring,' as we have seen before; as also by 'sighing, groaning, and panting.' a soul in such a condition lies down before the Lord with sighs, groans, mourning, cries, tears, and roaring, according to the various working of his heart, and its being affected with the things that it has to do; and this produces:

The power of the importunity of faith our Saviour has marvelously set out (Luke 11:5–10; 18:1). Importunate prayer is certainly prevailing; and importunity is, as it were, made up of these two things—frequency of interposition and variety of arguings. You shall have a man that is importunate come to you seven times a day about the same business; and after all, if any new thought come into his mind, though he had resolved to the contrary, he will come again. And there is nothing that can be imagined to relate to the business he has in hand but he will make use of it, and turn it to the furtherance of his plea. So is it in this case. Men will use both frequency of interposition and variety of arguings: 'I cry to you daily' (Ps. 86:3), or rather, all the day. He had but that one business, and he attended it to the purpose. By this means we give God 'no rest' (Isa. 62:7); which is the very character of importunity. Such souls go to God; and they are not satisfied with what they have done, and they go again; and somewhat abides still with them, and they go to him again; and the heart is not yet emptied, they will go again to him, that he may have no rest. What variety of arguments are pleaded with God in this case I could manifest in the same David; but it is known to all. There is not any thing almost that he makes not a plea of—the faithfulness, righteousness, name, mercy, goodness, and kindness of God in Jesus Christ; the concern of others in him, both the friends and foes of God; his own weakness and helplessness, yea, the greatness of sin itself: 'Be merciful to my sin,' says he, 'for it is great.' Sometimes he begins with some arguments of this kind; and then, being a little diverted by other considerations, some new plea is suggested to him by the Spirit, and he returns immediately to his first employment and design—all arguing great intension of mind and spirit.

Constancy also flows from intenseness. Such a soul will not give over until it obtain what it aims at and looks for; as we shall see in our process in opening this psalm.

And this is in general the deportment of a gracious soul in the condition here represented to us. As poor creatures love their peace, as they love their souls, as they tender the glory of God, they are not to be wanting in this duty. What is the reason that controversies hang so long between God and your souls, that it may be you scarce see a good day all your lives? Is it not, for the most part, from your sloth and despondency of spirit? You will not gird up the loins of your minds, in dealing with God, to put them to a speedy issue in the blood of Christ. You go on and off, begin and cease, try and give over; and, for the most part, though your case be extraordinary, content yourselves with ordinary and customary applications to God. This makes you wither, become useless, and pine away in and under your perplexities. David did not so; but after many and many a breach made by sin, yet, through quick, vigorous, restless actings of faith, all was repaired, so that he lived peaceably, and died triumphantly. Up, then, and be doing; let not your 'wounds corrupt because of your folly.' Make thorough work of that which lies before you; be it long, or difficult, it is all one, it must be done, and is attended with safety. What you are like to meet withal in the first place shall next be declared.

# 2

## LORD, WHO SHALL STAND?

---------------------------------------------------------------------

<sup></sup>³ If you, LORD, should mark iniquities,
     O Lord, who shall stand?

The general frame of a gracious soul, in its perplexities about sin, has been declared. Its particular actings, what it does, what it meets withal, are next represented to us.

First, then, in particular, it cries out, 'If you, LORD, should mark iniquities, O Lord, who shall stand?'

There is in the words a supposition, and an inference on that supposition. In the supposition there is, (a) the name of God, that is fixed on as suited to it; and (b) the thing itself supposed. In the inference there is expressed the matter of it, to 'stand;' and the manner of its proposal, wherein two things occur: (a) That it is expressed by way of interrogation. (b) The indefiniteness of that interrogation, 'Who shall stand?'

'If you, LORD.' He here fixes on another name of God, which is JAH—a name, though from the same root with the former, yet seldom used but to intimate and express the terrible majesty of God: 'He rides on the heavens, and is extolled by his name JAH' (Ps. 68:4). He is to deal now with God about the guilt of sin; and God is represented to the soul as great and terrible, that he may know what to expect and look for, if the matter must be tried out according to the demerit of sin.

What, then, says he to JAH? אִם־עֲוֹנוֹת תִּשְׁמָר—'If you should mark iniquities.' שָׁמַר is to observe and keep as in safe custody; to keep, preserve, and watch diligently; so to remark and observe, as to retain that which is observed, to ponder it, and lay it up in the heart. Jacob 'observed' Joseph's dream (Gen. 37:11); that is, he retained the memory of it, and pondered it in his heart.

The marking of iniquities, then, here intended, is God's so far considering and observing of them as to reserve them for punishment and vengeance. In opposition to this marking, he is said not to see sin, to overlook it, to cover it, or remember it no more; that is, to forgive it, as the next verse declares.

I need not show that God so far marks all sins in all persons as to see them, know them, disallow them, and to be displeased with them. This cannot be denied without taking away of all grounds of fear and worship. To deny it is all one as to deny the very being of God; deny his holiness and righteousness, and you deny his existence. But there is a day appointed, wherein all the men of the world shall know that God knew and took notice of all and every one of their most secret sins. There is, then, a double marking of sin in God; neither of which can be denied in reference to any sins, in any persons. The first is physical, consisting in his omniscience, whereunto all things are open and naked. Thus no sin is hid from him; the secretest are before the light of his countenance. All are marked by him. Secondly, moral, in a displicency with or displeasure against every sin; which is inseparable from the nature of God, upon the account of his holiness. And this is declared in the sentence of the law, and that equally to all men in the world. But the marking here intended is that which is in a tendency to animadversion and punishment, according to the tenor of the law.

Not only the sentence of the law, but a will of punishing according to it, is included in it. 'If,' says the psalmist, 'you, the great and dreadful God, who are extolled by the glorious name JAH, should take notice of iniquities, so as to recompense sinners that come to you according to the severity and exigence of your holy law'— what then? It is answered by the matter of the proposal, 'Who can stand?' That is, none can so do. Τὸ γὰρ τίς ἐνταῦθα οὐδείς ἐστιν, says Chrysostom. This 'who,' is none; no man; not one in the world. מִי יַעֲמֹד, '*Quis stabit?*' or '*consistet*'—'Who can stand?' or abide and endure the trial? Every one on this supposition must perish, and that eternally. This the desert of sin, and the curse of the law, which is the rule of this marking of their iniquity, requires. And there is a notable emphasis in the interrogation, which contains the manner of the inference. 'Who can stand?' is more than if he had said, 'None can abide the trial, and escape without everlasting ruin;' for the interrogation is indefinite; not, 'How can I?' but, 'Who can stand?' When the Holy Ghost would set out the certainty and dreadfulness of the perishing of ungodly men, he does it by such a kind of expression, wherein there is a deeper sense intimated into the minds of men than any words can well clothe or declare: 'What shall the end be of them that obey not the gospels' (1 Pet. 4:17). And verse 18, 'Where shall the ungodly and the sinner appear?' So here, 'Who can stand?' There is a deep insinuation of a dreadful ruin as to all with whom God shall so deal as to mark their iniquities (see Ps. 1:5).

The psalmist then addressing himself to deal with God about sin, lays down in the first place, in the general, how things must go, not with himself only, but with all the world, upon the supposition he had fixed: 'This is not my case only; but it is so with all mankind, every one who is partaker of flesh and blood. Whether their guilt answer that which I am oppressed withal or no, all is one; guilty they are all, and all must perish. How much more must that needs be my condition, who have contracted so great a guilt as I have done!' Here, then, he lays a great argument against himself, on the supposition before laid down: 'If none, the holiest, the humblest, the most believing soul, can abide the trial, can endure; how much less can I, who am the chiefest of sinners, the least of saints, who come unspeakably behind them in holiness, and have equally gone beyond them in sin!'

This is the sense and importance of the words. Let us consider how they are expressive of the actings of the soul whose state and condition is here represented to us, and what directions they will afford to us, to give to them who are fallen into the same state.

## Apprehensions of a Sin-Perplexed Soul

What depths the psalmist was in has been declared; in them what resolution he takes upon himself to seek God alone for relief and recovery has been also showed; and what earnestness in general he uses therein. Addressing himself to God in that frame, with that purpose and resolution, the first thing he fixes on in particular is the greatness of his sin and guilt, according to the tenor of the law.

It appears then that, *first*, in a sin-perplexed soul's addresses to God, the first thing that presents itself to him is God's marking sin according to the tenor of the law. The case is the same in this matter with all sorts of sinners, whether before conversion or in relapses and entanglements after conversion. There is a proportion between conversion and recoveries. They are both wrought by the same means and ways, and have both the same effects upon the souls of sinners, although in sundry things they differ, not now to be spoken to. What, then, is spoken on this head may be applied to both sorts—to them that are yet unconverted, and to them who are really delivered from their state and condition; but especially to those who know not whether state they belong to, that is, to all guilty souls. The law will put in its claim to all. It will condemn the sin, and try what it can do against the sinner. There is no shaking of it off; it must be fairly answered, or it will prevail. The law issues out an arrest for the debt; and it is to no purpose to bid the sergeant be gone, or to entreat him to spare. If payment be not procured, and an acquaintance produced, the soul must to prison. 'I am going to God,' says the soul; 'he is great and terrible, a marker of sin, and what shall I say to him?'

This makes him tremble, and cry out, 'O Lord, who shall stand?' so that it appears hence that, *secondly,* serious thoughts of God's marking sin according to the tenor of the law is a thing full of dread and terror to the soul of a sinner. But this is not all; he is not swallowed up in this amazement, crying out only, 'Who can stand?' There is included in the words a thorough, sincere acknowledgment of his own sin and the guilt thereof.

Mentioning the desert of sin, in his own case, he acknowledges his own so that, *thirdly,* sincere sense and acknowledgment for sin, with self-condemnation in the justification of God, is the first peculiar, especial working of a gracious soul rising out of its entanglements. All this is included in these words. He acknowledges both his own guilt and the righteousness of God if he should deal with him according to the demerit of sin.

And these things lie in the words absolutely considered. But the state of the soul here represented carries us on farther. He rests not here, as we shall see in the opening of the next verse, the chief thing aimed at in the whole. And as a transition from the one to the other, that we may still carry on the general design at the entrance laid down, we must take along with us this farther observation:

*Fourthly,* though self-condemnation be an eminent preparation for the discovery of forgiveness in God, yet a poor distressed soul is not to rest in it, nor to rest upon it, but to pass on to the embracing of forgiveness itself.

There is yet a general proposition lying in the words that we may make use of in our passage, and it is this: God's marking of iniquities and man's salvation are everlastingly inconsistent. I mean his marking them in the persons of sinners for the ends before mentioned.

Of some of these I shall farther treat, according as the handling of them conduces to the purpose in hand.

That which I shall begin withal is that which was first laid down, about the effects of serious thoughts concerning God's marking sin according to the tenor of the law; which, as I said, is the first thing that presents itself to a sin-entangled soul in its addresses to God.

But this shall not pass alone. I shall draw the two first observations into one, and make use of the first only in the confirmation of the other; which will express the sense of the words absolutely considered. The third and fourth will lead us on in the progress of the soul towards the relief sought after and proposed.

## DREAD AS GOD MARKS SIN ACCORDING TO THE LAW

That, therefore, which is to be first insisted on comes up to this proposition: In a sin-perplexed soul's addresses to God, the first thing that presents itself to him is God's marking of sin according to the tenor of the law; which of itself is apt to fill the soul with dread and terror.

I shall first somewhat speak to it in this, as considered in itself, and then inquire into the concern of the soul in it, whose condition is here described.

The Lord speaks of some who, when they hear the word of the curse, yet 'bless themselves,' and say they shall have 'peace' (Deut. 29:19). Let men preach and say what they will of the terror of the Lord, they will despise it; which God threatens with utter extermination. And he notes it again as an amazing wickedness, and the height of obdurateness (Jer. 36:24). Generally it is with sinners as it was with Gaal the son of Ebed (Judg. 9), when he was fortifying Sichem against Abimelech. Zebul tells him that Abimelech will come and destroy him. 'Let him come,' says Gaal, 'I shall deal well enough with him. Let him bring forth his army; I fear him not.' But upon the very first appearance of Abimelech's army he trembled for fear (v. 36). Tell obdurate sinners of the wrath of God, and that he will come to plead his cause against them; for the most part they take no notice of what you say, nor have any serious thoughts about it, but go on as if they were resolved they should deal well enough with him. Notwithstanding all their stoutness, a day is coming wherein fearfulness shall surprise them, and make them cry out, 'Who among us shall dwell with devouring fire? Who among us shall dwell with everlasting burnings?' Yea, if the Lord be pleased in this life, in an especial manner, to draw nigh to any of them, they quickly see that their 'hearts cannot endure, nor can their hands be strong' (Ezek. 22:14). Their hands hang down, and their stout hearts tremble like an aspen leaf.

He who first sinned, and had first occasion to have serious thoughts about God's marking of sin, gives us a notable instance of what we have affirmed; and the first in every kind is the measure of all that follows in the same kind. 'He heard the voice of the LORD God' (Gen. 3:8); so he had done before without the least trouble or consternation of spirit. He was made for communion with God; and that he might hear his voice was part of his blessedness. But now says he, 'I heard your voice and was afraid, and hid myself.' He knew that God was coming on the inquest of sin, and he was not able to bear the thoughts of meeting him. Could he have gone into the bowels of the earth from whence he was taken, and have been there hid from God, he would not have failed to have attempted it. Things are now altered with him. In that God whom he loved before as a good, holy, powerful, righteous creator, preserver, benefactor, and rewarder, he saw nothing now but wrath, indignation, vengeance, and terror. This makes him tremble out those dreadful words, 'I heard your voice and was afraid, and hid myself.'

The giving out of the law afterwards evinces what effects the consideration of God's proceeding with sinners according to the tenor of it must needs produce: 'All the people saw the thunder and the lightning, and the voice of the trumpet, and the mountain smoking' (Exod. 20:18–19); as the apostle also describes it (Heb. 12:18). In this manner came forth from the Lord that 'fiery law' (Deut. 33:2); so that all who are concerned in it 'did exceedingly quake and tremble.' And yet all this respects but the severity of the law in general, without the application of it to any soul in particular. There is a solemnity that carries an awe with it in the preparation of an assize to be kept and held by poor worms like ourselves; but the dread of it is peculiar to the malefactors for whose trial and execution all this preparation is made. When a soul comes to think that all this dreadful preparation, this appearance of terrible majesty, these streams of the fiery law, are all pointed towards him, it will make him cry out, 'Lord, who can stand?' And this law is still in force towards sinners, even as it was on the day wherein it was given on mount Sinai. Though Moses grew old, yet his strength never failed; nor has his law, the law given by him, lost any thing of its strength, power, or authority towards sinners. It is still accompanied with thunderings and lightnings, as of old; and it will not fail to represent the terror of the Lord to a guilty soul.

Among the saints themselves I could produce instances to manifest that they have found it to be thus. The cases of Job, David, Heman are known. I shall only consider it in Christ himself. From himself he had no occasion of any discouraging thought, being holy, harmless, undefiled. He fulfilled all righteousness, did his Father's will in all things, and abode in his love. This must needs be attended with the highest peace and most blessed joy. In the very entrance of his trials, he had a full persuasion of a comfortable issue and success; as we may see (Isa. 50:7–9). But yet when his soul was exercised with thoughts of God's marking our iniquities upon him, it was 'sorrowful to death.' He was 'sore amazed, and very heavy' (Mark 14:33–4). His agony; his blood-sweat; his strong cries and supplications; his reiterated prayers, 'If it be possible let this cup pass from me;' his last and dreadful cry, 'My God, my God, why have you forsaken me?'—all manifest what apprehensions he had of what it was for God to mark iniquities. Well may poor sinners cry out, 'Lord, who shall stand?' when the Son of God himself so trembled under the weight of it.

In serious thoughts of God's marking sin, he is represented to the soul under all those glorious, terrible attributes and excellencies which are apt to beget a dread and terror in the hearts of sinners, when they have no relief from any covenant engagements in Christ. The soul looks upon him as the great lawgiver (James 4:12)—able to revenge the breach of it, by destroying body and soul in hell fire; as one terrible in holiness, of purer eyes than to behold iniquity; so also in greatness and in power; the living God, into whose hands it is a fearful thing to fall; as attended with vindictive justice, saying, 'Vengeance belongs to me, I will recompense' (Heb. 10:30). Now, for a soul to consider God, clothed with all these dreadful and terrible excellencies, coming to deal with sinners according to the tenor of his fiery law, it cannot but make him cry out, with Moses, 'I exceedingly fear and quake.'

These things work on their minds the conclusion mentioned before, as asserted in these words—namely, that God's marking of sin according to the tenor of the law, and man's salvation, are utterly inconsistent; a conclusion that must needs shake a soul when pressed under a sense of its own guilt.

### WEIGHING UP GROUNDS FOR HOPE?

When a person who is really guilty, and knows himself to be guilty, is brought to his trial, he has but these four grounds of hope that his safety and his trial may be consistent. He may think that either:

1. The judge will not be able to find out or discover his crimes;
2. That someone will powerfully intercede for him with the judge;
3. That the rule of the law is not so strict as to take notice of his miscarriages; or,
4. That the penalty of it is not so severe but that there may be a way of escape.

Cut him short of his expectations from some, one, or all of these, and all his hopes must of necessity perish. And how is it in this case?

### *'The Judge Will not Discover Crimes'*

Of the Judge we have spoken somewhat already. The present inquiry is, whether any thing may be hid from him or no, and so a door of escape be opened to a sinner? The apostle tells us that 'all things are naked and open to him' (Heb. 4:13); and the psalmist, that 'there is not a thought in our hearts, nor a word in our tongue, but he understands it afar off, and knows it altogether' (Ps. 139:2–4). What the sinner knows of himself that may cause him to fear, that God knows; and what he knows not of himself that deserves his fear, that God knows also: 'He is greater than our hearts, and knows all things' (1 John 3:20). When God shall not only set in order before the sinner the secret sins which he retains some remembrance of, but also brings to mind and represents to him that world of filth and folly which either he never took any real notice of or has utterly forgotten, it will trouble him, yea, confound him.

### 'Someone Will Intercede for Me'

But may not this Judge be entreated to pass by what he knows, and to deal favourably with the sinner? May not an intercessor be obtained to plead in the behalf of the guilty soul? Eli determines this matter, 'If one man sin against another, the judge shall judge him; but if a man sin against the LORD, who shall intreat for him?' (1 Sam. 2:25). 'There is not,' says Job, 'between us מוֹכִיחַ, one that might argue the case, in pleading for me, and so make up the matter, "laying his hand upon us both"' (Job 9:33). We now consider a sinner purely under the administration of the law, which knows nothing of a mediator. In that case, who shall take upon him to intercede for the sinner? Besides that all creatures in heaven and earth are engaged in the quarrel of God against sinners, and besides the greatness and terror of his majesty, that will certainly deter all or any of them from undertaking any such work, what is the request that in this case must be put up to God? Is it not that he would cease to be holy, leave off from being righteous, relinquish his throne, deny himself and his sovereignty, that a rebel, a traitor, his cursed enemy, may live and escape his justice? Is this request reasonable? Is he fit to intercede for sinners that make it? Would he not by so doing prove himself to be the greatest of them? The sinner cannot, then, expect any door of escape to be opened to him; all the world is against him; and the case must be tried out nakedly between God and him.

### 'Mitigating Circumstances Will Save Me'

It may be the rule of the law whereby the sinner is to be tried is not so strict, but that, in the case of such sins as he is guilty of, it may admit of a favourable interpretation; or that the good that he has done may be laid in the balance against his evil, and so some relief be obtained that way. But the matter is quite otherwise. There is no good action of a sinner, though it were perfectly good, that can lie in the balance with, or compensate the evil of, the least sin committed; for all good is due on another account, though no guilt were incurred. And the payment of money that a man owes, that he has borrowed, makes no satisfaction for what he has stole; no more will our duties compensate for our sins. Nor is there any good action of a sinner but it has evil and guilt enough attending it to render itself unacceptable; so that men may well cease from thoughts of their supererogation. Besides, where there is any one sin, if all the good in the world might be supposed to be in the same person, yet, in the indispensable order of our dependence on God, nothing of that good could come into consideration until the guilt of that sin were answered for to the utmost. Now, the penalty of every sin being the eternal ruin of the sinner, all his supposed good can stand him in little stead. And for the law itself, it is an issue of the holiness, righteousness, and wisdom of God; so that there is not any evil so great or small but is forbidden in it, and condemned by it. Hereupon David so states this whole matter, 'Enter not into judgment with your servant, for in your sight shall no man living be justified' (Ps. 118:2)—that is, if things are to be tried out and determined by the law, no sinner can obtain acquitment; as Paul declares the sense of that place to be (Rom. 3:20, Gal. 2:16).

### 'The Sentence Might Be Suspended'

It may be the sentence of the law is not so fierce and dreadful, but that, though guilt be found, there may be yet a way of escape. But the law speaks not one word on this side death to an offender. There is a greatness and an eternity of wrath in the sentence of it; and it is God himself who has undertaken to see the vengeance of it executed. So that, on all these accounts, the conclusion mentioned must needs be fixed in the soul of a sinner that entertains thoughts of drawing nigh to God.

Though what has been spoken may be of general use to sinners of all sorts, whether called home to God or yet strangers to him, yet I shall not insist upon any general improvement of it, because it is intended only for one special end or purpose. That which is aimed at is, to show what are the first thoughts that arise in the heart of a poor entangled soul, when first he begins to endeavour a recovery in a return to God. The law immediately puts in its claim to him and against him; God is represented to him as angry, displeased, provoked; and his terror more or less besets him round about. This fills him with fear, shame, and confusion of face; so that he knows not what to do. These troubles are greater or lesser, according as God sees it best for the poor creature's present humiliation and future safety. What, then, does the sinner? What are his thoughts hereupon? Does he think to fly from God, and to give over all endeavours of recovery? Does he say, 'This God is a holy and terrible God; I cannot serve him; it is to no purpose for me to look for any thing but fury and destruction from him: and therefore I had as good give over as persist in my design of drawing nigh to him?'

It cannot be denied but that in this case thoughts of this nature will be suggested by unbelief, and that sometimes great perplexities arise to the soul by them: but this is not the issue and final product of this exercise of the soul; it produces another effect; it calls for that which is the first particular working of a gracious soul arising out of its sin-entanglements. This is, as was declared, a sincere sense of sin, and acknowledgment of it, with self-condemnation in the justification of God; this is the first thing that a soul endeavouring a recovery from its depths is brought and wrought to. His general resolution, to make serious and thorough work with what he has in hand, was before unfolded. That which, in the next place, we are directed to in these words is, the reflection on itself, upon the consideration of God's marking iniquity, now mentioned. This is faith's great and proper use of the law; the nature whereof shall be farther opened in the next discourse.

## THE ATTITUDE OF AN AWAKENED SOUL

What is the frame of the soul in general that is excited by grace, and resolves in the strength thereof to attempt a recovery out of the depths of sin-entanglements, has been declared. We have also showed what entertainments, in general, such a soul had need to expect, yea, ordinarily shall be sure to meet withal. It may be he goes forth at first like Samson with his locks cut, and thinks he will do as at other times; but he quickly finds his peace lost, his wounds painful, his conscience restless, God displeased, and his whole condition, as the utmost of his own apprehension, hazardous. This fills him with the thoughts expressed in this third verse, and fixes the conclusion in his mind discoursed of before. He finds now that he has the law afresh to deal withal. Thence arises that sense and acknowledgment of sin, that self-condemnation in the justification of God, whereof we now speak. He grows not sullen, stubborn, displeased, and so runs away from God; he does not 'utterly faint,' despond, and give over, he pleads not any thing in his own justification or for the extenuation of his sin and guilt; he quarrels not with, he repines not against, the holiness, severity, and righteousness of the law of God; but reflects wholly on himself, his own unworthiness, guilt, and desert, and in a sense of them lies down at the foot of God, in expectation of his word and sentence.

Three things in this condition we ascribe to such a soul.

## A SINCERE SENSE OF SIN

First, a sincere sense of sin. There is a twofold sense of sin. The one is general and notional; whereby a man knows what sin is, that himself is a sinner, that he is guilty of this or that, these or those sins; only his heart is not affected proportionably to that discovery and knowledge which he has of these things. The other is active and efficacious. The soul being acquainted with the nature of sin, with its own guilt in reference to sin in general, as also to this or that sin, is universally influenced by that apprehension to suitable affections and operations.

Of both these we have an instance in the same person. David, before Nathan's coming to him, had the former; afterwards he had the latter also. It cannot be imagined but that, before the coming of the prophet, he had a general knowledge and sense, not only absolutely of the nature of sin, but also that himself was a sinner, and guilty of those very sins which afterward he was reproved for. To think otherwise is to suppose not only that he was unsainted, but unmanned also and turned into a beast. But yet this wrought not in him any one affection suitable to his condition. And the like may be said of most sinners in the world. But now, when Nathan comes to him, and gives him the latter efficacious sense whereof we speak, we know what effects it did produce.

It is the latter only that is under consideration; and that also is twofold (a) legal, or antecedaneous to conversion; (b) evangelical, and previous to the recovery from depths, whereof we treat. How these two differ, and how they may be discerned one from the other, being both of them in their kind sincere, is not my business to declare.

Now, this last, which we assign as the first duty, work, or acting of a returning soul, is a deep and practical apprehension, wrought in the mind and heart of a believing sinner by the Holy Ghost, of sin and its evils, in reference to the law and love of God, the cross and blood of Christ, the communion and consolation of the Spirit, and all the fruits of love, mercy, or grace that it has been made partaker of, or on gospel ground hoped for.

### *Wrought by the Holy Spirit*

The principal efficient cause of it is the Holy Ghost. He it is who 'convinces of sin' (John 16:8). He works indeed by means—he wrought it in David by the ministry of Nathan, and he wrought it in Peter by the look of Christ—but his work it is; no man can work upon his own soul. It will not spring out of men's rational considerations. Though men may exercise their thoughts about such things, as one would think were enough to break the heart of stones, yet if the Holy Ghost put not forth a peculiar efficacy of his own, this sense of sin will not be wrought or produced. As the waters at the pool of Bethesda were not troubled but when an illapse: angel descended and moved them, no more will the descent, fall heart for sin without a saving illapse of the Holy Ghost.

### Not a Transient Impression

It is deep apprehension of sin and the evils of it. Slight, transient thoughts about them amount not to the sense of which we speak. 'My sorrow,' says David, 'is continually before me' (Ps. 38:17). It pressed him always and greatly. Hence he compares this sense of sin wrought by the Holy Ghost to 'arrows that stick in the flesh' (v. 2); they pain sorely and are always perplexing. Sin, in this sense of it, lays hold on the soul, so that the sinner cannot look up (Ps. 40:12); and it abides with him, making 'his sore run in the night without ceasing' (Ps. 77:2), and deprives the soul of rest. 'My soul,' says he, 'refused to be comforted.' This apprehension of sin lies down and rises with him in whom it is. Transient thoughts, attended with infrequent sighs and ejaculations, little become a returning soul.

### Practical Effects

It is practical. It is not seated only in the speculative part of the mind, hovering in general notions, but it dwells in the practical understanding, which effectually influences the will and affections— such an apprehension as from which sorrow and humiliation are inseparable. The acts of the practical understanding do so necessarily produce together with them suitable acts of the will and affections, that some have concluded that those are indeed proper acts of the will which are usually ascribed to the understanding. It is so in the mind as that the whole soul is cast into the mould and likeness of it; humiliation, sorrow, self-abhorrency, do live and die with it.

## Companions to a Renewed Sense of Sin

THE LAW OF GOD. It has, in the first place, respect to the law of God. There can be no due consideration of sin wherein the law has not its place. The law calls for the sinner, and he willingly gives up his sin to be judged by it. There he sees it to be 'exceeding sinful' (Rom. 7:13). Though a believer be less under the power of the law than others, yet he knows more of the authority and nature of it than others; he sees more of its spirituality and holiness. And the more a man sees of the excellency of the law, the more he sees of the vileness of sin. This is done by a soul in its first endeavour of a recovery from the entanglements of sin. He labours thoroughly to know his disease, that he may be cured. It will do him no good, he knows, to be ignorant of his distemper or his danger. He knows that if his wounds be not searched to the bottom, they will stink and be corrupt. To the law, then, he brings himself and his sin. By that he sees the vileness of the one and the danger of the other. Most men lie still in their depths, because they would willingly escape the first step of their rising. From the bottom of their misery, they would fain at once be at the top of their felicity. The soul managed in this work by the Holy Ghost does not so. He converses with the law, brings his sin to it, and fully hears the sentence of it. When the sin is thoroughly condemned, then he farther takes care of the sinner. As ever you desire to come to rest, avoid not this entrance of your passion to it. Weigh it well, and attend to what the law speaks of your sin and its desert, or you will never make a due application to God for forgiveness. As ever you would have your souls justified by grace, take care to have your sins judged by the law.

THE LOVE OF GOD. There is a respect in it to the love of God; and this breaks the heart of the poor returning sinner. Sorrow from the law shuts itself up in the soul, and strangles it. Sorrow from the thoughts of the love of God opens it, and causes it to flow forth. Thoughts of sinning against the love of God, managed by the Holy Ghost—what shall I say? their effects in the heart are not to be expressed. This made Ezra cry out, 'O my God, I am ashamed and blush to lift up my face to you' (Ezra 9:6); and verse 10, 'What shall we say after this?' After what? Why, all the fruits of love and kindness they had been made partakers of thoughts of love and sin laid together make the soul blush, mourn, be ashamed, and confounded in itself. So Ezekiel 36:31, 'Then shall you remember your own evil ways, and your doings that were not good.' When shall they do so? When thoughts and apprehensions of love shall be brought home to them; and, says he, 'Then shall you loathe yourselves in your own sight.' The soul now calls to mind what love, what kindness, and what mercy, what grace, what patience has been exercised towards it, and whereof it has been made partaker. The thoughts of all these now come in upon him as streams of water. Such mercy, such communion, such privileges, such hopes of glory, such tastes of heaven, such peace, such consolation, such joy, such communications of the Spirit—all to a poor, wretched, cursed, lost, forlorn sinner; and all this despised, neglected! The God of them all provoked, forsaken! 'Ah,' says the soul, 'whither shall I cause my sorrow to go?' This fills him with shame and confusion of face, makes him mourn in secret, and sigh to the breaking of the loins.

THE BLOOD AND CROSS OF CHRIST is also brought to remembrance by the Holy Ghost. 'Ah,' says the soul, 'have I thus requited the wonderful, astonishing love of my Redeemer? Is this the return, the requital, I have made to him? Are not heaven and earth astonished at the despising of that love, at which they are astonished?' This brake Peter's heart upon the look of Christ. Such words as these from Christ will, in this condition, sound in the ears of the soul: 'Did I love you, and leave my glory to become a scorn and reproach for your sake? Did I think my life, and all that was dear to me, too good for you, to save you from the wrath to come? Have I been a wilderness to you, or a land of darkness? What could I have done more for you? When I had nothing left but my life, blood, and soul, they went all for you, that you might live by my death, be washed in my blood, and be saved through my soul's being made an offering for you! And have you thus requited my love, to prefer a lust before me, or by mere sloth and folly to be turned away from me? Go, unkind and unthankful soul, and see if you can find another Redeemer.' This overwhelms the soul, and even drowns it in tears of sorrow. And then the bitterness also of the sufferings of Christ are brought to mind: 'They look on him whom they have pierced, and mourn' (Zech. 12:10). They remember his gall and wormwood, his cry and tears, his agony and sweat, his desertion and anguish, his blood and death, the sharpness of the sword that was in his soul, and the bitterness of the cup that was put into his hand. Such a soul now looks on Christ, bleeding, dying, wrestling with wrath and curse for him, and sees his sin in the streams of blood that issued from his side. And all this increases that sense of sin of which we speak.

THE INDWELLING SPIRIT. It relates to the communion and consolations of the Holy Ghost, with all the privileges and fruits of love we are by him made partakers of. The Spirit is given to believers, upon the promise of Christ, to dwell in them. He takes up their hearts to be his dwelling-place. To what ends and purposes? That he may purify and sanctify them, make them holy, and dedicate them to God; to furnish them with grace and gifts; to interest them in privileges; to guide, lead, direct, comfort them; to seal them to the day of redemption. Now, this Spirit is grieved by sin (Eph. 4:30), and his dwelling-place defiled thereby (1 Cor. 6:19, 3:17). Thoughts hereof greatly sharpen the spiritual sense of sin in a recovering soul. He considers what light, what love, what joy, what consolation, what privileges, it has by him been made partaker of; what motions, warnings, workings to keep it from sin, it has found from him; and says within itself, 'What have I done? Whom have I grieved? Whom have I provoked? What if the Lord should now, for my folly and ingratitude, utterly take his Holy Spirit from me? What if I should have so grieved him that he will dwell in me no more, delight in me no more? What dismal darkness and disconsolation, yea, what utter ruin should I be left to! However, what shame and confusion of face belongs to me for my wretched disingenuity and ingratitude towards him!'

This is the first thing that appears in the returning soul's actings and frame—a sincere sense of sin on the account mentioned, wrought in it by the Holy Ghost. And this a soul in the depths described must come to, if ever it expects or looks for deliverance and a recovery. Let not such persons expect to have a renewed sense of mercy without a revived sense of sin.

## Acknowledgment of Sin

Secondly, from hence proceeds an ingenuous, free, gracious acknowledgment of sin. Men may have a sense of sin, and yet suffer it to lie burning as a fire shut up in their bones, to their continual disquiet, and not be able to come off to a free, soul-opening acknowledgment; yea, confession may be made in general, and mention therein of that very sin wherewith the soul is most entangled, and yet the soul come short of a due performance of this duty.

Consider how the case stood with David: 'When I kept silence, my bones waxed old through my roaring all the day long' (Ps. 32:3). How could David keep silence, and yet roar all the day long? What is that silence which is consistent with roaring? It is a mere negation of that duty which is expressed that is intended: 'I acknowledged my sin to you, and mine iniquity have I not hid' (v. 5). It was not a silence of submission and waiting on God that he intends; that would not have produced a wasting of his spiritual strength, as he complains this silence did: 'My bones waxed old.' Nor yet was it a sullen, stubborn, and contumacious frame that was upon him; but he notes, says Calvin (and he says well), '*Affectum qui medius est inter tolerantiam et contumaciam, vitio et virtuti affinis*'—'An affection between patience and stubbornness, bordering on the one and other.' That is, he had a deep sense of sin; this disquieted and perplexed him all the day long; which he calls his roaring. It weakened and wearied him, making his bones wax old, or his strength decay; yet was he not able to bring his heart to that ingenuous, gracious acknowledgment which, like the lancing of a festered wound, would have given at least some ease to his soul. God's children are ofttimes in this matter like ours. Though they are convinced of a fault, and are really troubled at it, yet they will hardly acknowledge it. So do they. They will go up and down, sigh and mourn, roar all the day long; but an evil and toward frame of spirit, under the power of unbelief and fear, keeps them from this duty.

Now, that this acknowledgment may be acceptable to God, it is required, first, that it be free; then, that it be full.

### Free and Sincere

It must be free, and spiritually ingenuous. Cain, Pharaoh, Ahab, Judas, came all to an acknowledgment of sin; but it was whether they would or no. It was pressed out of them; it did not flow from them. The confession of a person under the convincing terrors of the law or dread of imminent judgments is like that of malefactors on the rack, who speak out that for which themselves and friends must die. What they say, though it be the truth, is a fruit of force and torture, not of any ingenuity of mind. So is it with merely convinced persona. They come not to the acknowledgment of sin with any more freedom. And the reason is, because all sin has shame; and for men to be free to shame is naturally impossible, shame being nature's shrinking from itself and the posture it would appear in. But now the returning soul has never more freedom, liberty, and aptitude of spirit, than when he is in the acknowledgment of those things whereof he is most ashamed. And this is no small evidence that it proceeds from that Spirit which is attended with that liberty; for 'where the Spirit of the Lord is, there is liberty' (2 Cor. 3:17). When David was delivered from his silence, he expresses this frame in the performance of his duty: 'I acknowledged my sin to you, and mine iniquity have I not hid. I said, I will confess my transgressions' (Ps. 32:5). His mouth is now open, and his heart enlarged, and he multiplies one expression upon another to manifest his enlargement. So does a soul rising out of its depths, in this beginning of this address to God. Having the sense of sin before described wrought in him by the Holy Ghost, his heart is made free, and enlarged to an ingenuous acknowledgment of his sin before the Lord. Herein he pours out his soul to God, and has not more freedom in any thing than in dealing about that whereof he is most ashamed.

### Full and Unreserved

Full also it must be. Reserves ruin confession. If the soul have any secret thought of rolling a sweet morsel under its tongue, of a bow in the house of Rimmon, it is like part of the price kept back, which makes the whole robbery instead of an offering. If there be remaining a bitter root of favouring any one lust or sin, of any occasion of or temptation to sin, let a man be as open, free, and earnest as can be imagined in the acknowledgment of all other sins and evils, the whole duty is rendered abominable. Some persons, when they are brought into depths and anguish about any sin, and are thereon forced to the acknowledgment of it, at the same time they are little concerned with their other follies and iniquities, that, it may be, are no less provoking to God than that is from whence their present trouble arises. 'Let not,' as James speaks in another case, 'such a man think that he shall receive any thing of the Lord.' It must be full and comprehensive, as well as free and ingenuous.

And of such importance is the right performance of this duty, that the promise of pardon is ofttimes peculiarly annexed to it, as that which certainly carries along with it the other duties which make up a full return to God (Prov. 28:13; 1 John 1:9). And that place in Job is remarkable, 'He looks upon men, and if any say, I have sinned, and perverted that which was right, and it profited me not; he will deliver his soul from going into the pit, and his life shall see the light' (Job 33:27–8). He shall not only be made partaker of pardon, but of consolation also, and joy in the light of God's countenance.

### SELF-CONDEMNATION

Thirdly, there yet remains self-condemnation with the justification of God, which lies expressly in the words of the verse under consideration; and hereof are two parts.

## Self-abhorrence

Self-abhorrence, or dislike. The soul is now wholly displeased with itself, and reflects upon itself with all affections of regret and trouble. So the apostle declares it to have been with the Corinthians, when their godly sorrow was working in them (2 Cor. 7:11). Among other things, it wrought in them 'indignation and revenge;' or a reflection on themselves with all manner of dislike and abhorrence. In the winding up of the controversy between God and Job, this is the point he rests in. As he had come in general to a free, full, ingenuous acknowledgment of sin (Job 40:4–5), so in particular he gives up his whole contest in this abhorrence of himself, 'I abhor myself, and repent in dust and ashes' (Job 42:6). 'What a vile, wretched creature have I been!' says the soul. 'I blush and am ashamed to think of my folly, baseness, and ingratitude. Is it possible that I should deal thus with the Lord? I abhor, I loathe myself; I would fly anywhere from myself, I am so vile and loathsome—a thing to be despised of God, angels, and men.'

## Self-judgment

There is self-judging in it also. This the apostle invites the Corinthians to, 'If we would judge ourselves, we should not be judged' (1 Cor. 11:31). This is a person pronouncing sentence on himself according to the tenor of the law. The soul brings not only its sin but itself also to the law. It puts itself, as to merit and desert, under the stroke and severity of it. Hence arises a full justification of God in what sentences soever he shall be pleased to pronounce in the case before him.

And these three things which we have passed through compose the frame and first actings of a gracious soul rising from its depths. They are all of them signally expressed in that place where we have a signal recovery exemplified (Hos. 14:1–3). And this makes way for the exaltation of grace, the great thing in all this dispensation aimed at by God (Eph. 1:6). That which he is now doing is to bring the soul to glory in him (1 Cor. 1:31); which is all the return he has from his large and infinitely bountiful expenses of grace and mercy. Now, nothing can render grace conspicuous and glorious until the soul come to this frame. Grace will not seem high until the soul be laid very low. And this also suits or prepares the soul for the receiving of mercy in a sense of pardon, the great thing aimed at on the part of the sinner; and it prepares it for every duty that is incumbent on him in that condition wherein he is. This brings the soul to waiting with diligence and patience. If things presently answer not our expectation, we are ready to think we have done what we can; if it will be no better, we must bear it as we are able—which frame God abhors. The soul in this frame is contented to wait the pleasure of God, as we shall see in the close of this psalm. 'Oh,' says such a one, 'if ever I obtain a sense of love, if ever I enjoy one smile of his countenance more, it is of unspeakable grace. Let him take his own time, his own season; it is good for me quietly to wait, and to hope for his salvation.' And it puts the soul on prayer; yea, a soul in this frame prays always. And there is nothing more evident than that want of a thorough engagement to the performance of these duties is the great cause why so few come clear off from their entanglement all their days. Men heal their wounds slightly; and, therefore, after a new, painful festering, they are brought into the same condition of restlessness and trouble which they were in before.

## Self-condemnation Is not the Goal

The soul is not to be left in the state before described. There is other work for it to apply itself to, if it intend to come to rest and peace. It has obtained an eminent advantage for the discovery of forgiveness; but to rest in that state wherein it is, or to rest upon it, will not bring it into its harbour. Three things we discovered before in the soul's first serious address to God for deliverance—sense of sin, acknowledgment of it, and self-condemnation. Two evils there are which attend men oftentimes when they are brought into that state. Some rest in it, and press no farther; some rest upon it, and suppose that it is all which is required of them. The psalmist avoids both these, and notwithstanding all his pressures reaches out towards forgiveness, as we shall see in the next verse. I shall briefly unfold these two evils, and show the necessity of their avoidance.

### SINFUL DESPONDENCY PROVOKES THE LORD

First, by resting or staying in it, I mean the soul's desponding, through discouraging thoughts that deliverance is not to be obtained. Being made deeply sensible of sin, it is so overwhelmed with thoughts of its own vileness and unworthiness as to sink under the burden. Such a soul is 'afflicted, and tossed with tempest, and not comforted' (Isa. 54:11), until it is quite weary—as a ship in a storm at sea, when all means of contending are gone, men give up themselves to be driven and tossed by the winds and seas at their pleasure. This brought Israel to that state wherein he cried out, 'My way is hid from the LORD, and my judgment is passed over from my God' (Isa. 40:27); and Zion, 'The Lord has forsaken me, and my Lord has forgotten me' (Isa. 49:14). The soul begins secretly to think there is no hope; God regards it not; it shall one day perish; relief is far away, and trouble nigh at hand. These thoughts do so oppress them, that though they forsake not God utterly to their destruction, yet they draw not nigh to him effectually to their consolation.

This is the first evil that the soul in this condition is enabled to avoid. We know how God rebukes it in Zion: 'Zion said, The LORD has forsaken me, and my Lord has forgotten me' (Isa. 49:14). But how foolish is Zion, how froward, how unbelieving in this matter! What ground has she for such sinful despondencies, such discouraging conclusions? 'Can a woman,' says the Lord, 'forget her sucking child, that she should not have compassion on the son of her womb? Yea, they may forget, yet will I not forget you.' The like reproof he gives to Jacob upon the like complaint (Isa. 40:28–31). There is nothing that is more provoking to the Lord, nor more disadvantageous to the soul, than such sinful despondency.

## It Weakens and Disables the Soul

It insensibly weakens the soul, and disenables it both for present duties and future endeavour. Hence some poor creatures mourn, and even pine away in this condition, never getting one step beyond a perplexing sense of sin all their days. Some have dwelt so long upon it, and have so entangled themselves with a multitude of perplexed thoughts, that at length their natural faculties have been weakened and rendered utterly useless; so that they have lost both sense of sin and every thing else. Against some, Satan has taken advantage to cast in so many entangling objections into their minds, that their whole time has been taken up in proposing doubts and objections against themselves; with these they have gone up and down to one and another, and being never able to come to a consistency in their own thoughts, they have spent all their days in a fruitless, sapless, withering, comfortless condition. Some, with whom things come to a better issue, are yet for a season brought to that discomposure of spirit, or are so filled with their own apprehensions, that when the things which are most proper to their condition are spoken to them, they take no impression in the least upon them. Thus the soul is weakened by dwelling too long on these considerations; until some cry with those in Ezekiel 33:10, 'Our sins are upon us, we pine away in them, how should we then live?'

## It Leads to Hard Thoughts of God

This frame, if it abides by itself, will insensibly give countenance to hard thoughts of God, and so to repining and weariness in waiting on him. At first the soul neither apprehends nor fears any such issue. It supposes that it shall condemn and abhor itself and justify God, and that for ever. But when relief comes not in, this resolution begins to weaken. Secret thoughts arise in the heart that God is austere, inexorable, and not to be dealt withal. This sometimes casts forth such complaints as will bring the soul to new complaints before it comes to have an issue of its trials. Here, in humiliation antecedaneous to conversion, many a convinced person perishes. They cannot wait God's season, and perish under their impatience. And what the saints of God themselves have been overtaken withal in their depths and trials, we have many examples and instances. Delight and expectations are the grounds of our abiding with God. Both these are weakened by a conquering, prevailing sense of sin, without some relief from the discovery of forgiveness, though at a distance. And, therefore, our perplexed soul stays not here, but presses on towards that discovery.

### CONVICTION IS NOT CONVERSION

Secondly, there is a resting on this frame that is noxious and hurtful also. Some finding this sense of sin, with those other things that attend it, wrought in them in some measure, begin to think that now all is well, this is all that is of them required. They will endeavour to make a life from such arguments of comfort as they can take from their trouble. They think this a ground of peace, that they have not peace. Here some take up before conversion, and it proves their ruin. Because they are convinced of sin, and troubled about it, and burdened with it, they think it shall be well with them. But were not Cain, Esau, Saul, Ahab, Judas, convinced of sin and burdened with it? Did this profit them? Did it interest them in the promises? Did not the wrath of God overtake them notwithstanding? So is it with many daily; they think their conviction is conversion, and that their sins are pardoned because they have been troubled.

This, then, is that which we reject, which the soul in this condition carefully avoids, so to satisfy itself with its humiliation, as to make that a ground of support and consolation, being thereby kept off from exercising faith for forgiveness.

### *Resting in Remorse Is Self-righteousness*

A fruit of self-righteousness. For a soul to place the spring of its peace or comfort in any thing of its own, is to fall short of Christ and to take up in self. We must not only be 'justified,' but 'glory' in him also (Isa. 45:25). Men may make use of the evidence of their graces, but only as mediums to a farther end; not as the rest of the soul in the least. And this deprives men's very humiliations of all gospel humility. True humility consists more in believing than in being sensible of sin. That is the soul's great self-emptying and abasing; this may consist with an obstinate resolution to scramble for something upon the account of self-endeavours.

### To Be Weary and Heavy Laden Is not Enough

Though evangelical sense of sin be a grace, yet it is not the uniting grace; it is not that which interests us in Christ, not that which peculiarly and in its own nature exalts him. There is in this sense of sin that which is natural and that which is spiritual; or the matter of it and its spirituality. The former consists in sorrow, trouble, self-abasement, dejection, and anxiety of mind, with the like passions. Of these I may say, as the apostle of afflictions, 'They are not joyous, but grievous.' They are such as are accompanied with the aversation of the object which they are conversant about. In their own nature they are no more but the soul's retreat into itself, with an abhorrency of the objects of its sorrow and grief. When these affections are spiritualized, their nature is not changed. The soul in and by them acts according to their nature; and does by them, as such, but retreat into itself, with a dislike of that they are exercised about. To take up here, then, must needs be to sit down short of Christ, whether it be for life or consolation.

Let there be no mistake. There can be no evangelical sense of sin and humiliation where there is not union with Christ (Zech. 12:10). Only in itself and in its own nature it is not availing. Now, Christ is the only rest of our souls; in any thing, for any end or purpose, to take up short of him is to lose it. It is not enough that we be 'prisoners of hope,' but we must 'turn to our stronghold' (Zech. 9:12); not enough that we are 'weary and heavy laden,' but we must 'come to him' (Matt. 11:28–30). It will not suffice that we are weak, and know we are weak, but we must 'take hold on the strength of God' (Isa. 27:4–5).

## *Evangelical Humiliation Pursues God for Pardon*

Indeed, pressing after forgiveness is the very life and power of evangelical humiliation. How shall a man know that his humiliation is evangelical, that his sorrow is according to God? Is it not from hence he may be resolved, that he does not in it as Cain did, who cried his sins were greater than he could bear, and so departed from the presence of God; nor as Judas did, who repented and hanged himself; nor as Felix did—tremble for a while, and then return to his lusts; nor as the Jews did in the prophet, pine away under their iniquities because of vexation of heart? Nor does he divert his thoughts to other things, thereby to relieve his soul in his trouble; nor fix upon a righteousness of his own; nor slothfully lie down under his perplexity, but in the midst of it he plies himself to God in Christ for pardon and mercy. And it is the soul's application to God for forgiveness, and not its sense of sin, that gives to God the glory of his grace.

Thus far, then, have we accompanied the soul in its depths. It is now looking out for forgiveness; which, what it is, and how we come to have an interest in it, the principal matter in this discourse intended, is nextly to be considered.

## 3

## BUT THERE IS FORGIVENESS WITH YOU

---

> ⁴ But there is forgiveness with you,
> that you may be feared.

The state and condition of the soul making application to God in this psalm is recounted (v. 1). It was in the 'depths' not only providential depths of trouble, affliction, and perplexities thereon; but also depths of conscience, distress on the account of sin; as in the opening of those words have been declared.

The application of this soul to God, with restless fervency and earnestness, in that state and condition; its consideration in the first place of the law, and the severity of God's justice in a procedure thereon, with the inevitable ruin of all sinners if God insist on that way of dealing with them, have also been opened and manifested from the foregoing verses.

Being in this estate, perplexed in itself, lost in and under the consideration of God's marking iniquity according to the tenor of the law, that which it fixes on, from whence any relief, stay, or support might be expected in such a condition, is laid down in this verse: 'But there is forgiveness with you, that you may be feared' (v. 4).

I shall first open the words as to their signification and importance; then show the design of the psalmist in them, with reference to the soul whose condition is here represented; and, lastly, propose the general truths contained in them, wherein all our concerns do lie.

'There is forgiveness.' ἱλασμός say the LXX, and Jerome accordingly, '*propitiatio*,' 'propitiation;' which is somewhat more than '*venia*,' or 'pardon,' as by some it is rendered.

הַסְּלִיחָה '*Condonatio ipsa*,' 'Forgiveness itself.' It is from סָלַח, to spare, to pardon, to forgive, to be propitious; and is opposed to חָסַל, a word composed of the same letters varied (which is common in that language), signifying to cut off and destroy.

Now, it is constantly applied to sin, and expresses every thing that concurs to its pardon or forgiveness.

First, it expresses the mind or will of pardoning, or God's gracious readiness to forgive: 'You, Lord, are good, וְסַלָּח, and ready to forgive' (Ps. 86:5), χρηστὸς καὶ ἐπιεικής, 'benign and meek,' or 'sparing, propitious'—of a gracious, merciful heart and nature. So Nehemiah 9:17, 'You are a God סְלִיחוֹת '*propitiationum*,' of propitiations or pardons;' or, as we have rendered it, 'ready to forgive'—'a God of forgivenesses;' or, 'all plenty of them is in your gracious heart,' 'so that you are always ready to make out pardons to sinners' (Isa. 40:7). The word is used again (Dan. 9:9), to the same purpose.

Secondly, it regards the act of pardoning, or actual forgiveness itself: הַסֹּלֵחַ, 'Who forgives all your iniquities' (Ps. 103:3)—'actually discharges you of them;' which place the apostle respecting, renders the word by χαρισάμενος: 'Having freely forgiven you' (for so much the word imports) 'all your trespasses' (Col. 2:13).

And this is the word that God uses in the covenant, in that great promise of grace and pardon (Jer. 31:34).

It is warrantable for us, yea, necessary, to take the word in the utmost extent of its signification and use. It is a word of favour, and requires an interpretation tending towards the enlargement of it. We see it may be rendered ἱλασμός, or 'propitiation;' χάρις, or 'grace;' and '*venia*,' or 'pardon;' and may denote these three things:

1. The gracious, tender, merciful heart and will of God, who is the God of pardons and forgivenesses; or ready to forgive, to give out mercy, to add to pardon.
2. A respect to Jesus Christ, the only ἱλασμός, or propitiation for sin, as he is expressly called (Rom. 3:25; 1 John 2:2). And this is that which interposes between the gracious heart of God and the actual pardon of sinners. All forgiveness is founded on propitiation.
3. It denotes condonation, or actual forgiveness itself, as we are made partakers of it; comprising it both actively, as it is an act of grace in God, and passively, as terminated in our souls, with the deliverance that attends it. In this sense, as it looks downwards and in its effects respects us, it is of mere grace; as it looks upwards to its causes and respects the Lord Christ, it is from propitiation or atonement. And this is that pardon which is administered in the covenant of grace.

Now, as to the place which these words enjoy in this psalm, and their relation to the state and condition of the soul here mentioned, this seems to be their importance:

> O Lord, although this must be granted, that if you should mark iniquities according to the tenor of the law, every man living must perish, and that for ever; yet there is hope for my soul, that even I, who am in the depths of sin-entanglements, may find acceptance with you: for whilst I am putting my mouth in the dust, if so be there may be hope, I find that there is an atonement, a propitiation made for sin, on the account of which you say you have found a ransom, and will not deal with them that come to you according to the severity and exigence of your justice; but are gracious, loving, tender, ready to forgive and pardon, and do so accordingly. *There is forgiveness with you*.

The following words, 'Therefore you shall be feared,' or 'That you may be feared,' though in the original free from all ambiguity, yet are so signally varied by interpreters, that it may not be amiss to take notice of it in our passage.

The Targum has it, 'That you may be seen.' This answers not the word, but it does the sense of the place well enough. God in his displeasure is said to hide himself or his face: 'The LORD hides his face from the house of Jacob' (Isa. 8:17). By forgiveness we obtain again the light of his countenance. This dispels the darkness and clouds that are about him, and gives us a comfortable prospect of his face and favour. 'There is forgiveness with him that he may be seen.' Besides, there is but one letter different in the original words, and that which is usually changed for the other.

The LXX render them Ἕνεκα τοῦ ὀνόματός σου—'For your name's sake,' or 'your own sake;' that is, freely, without any respect to any thing in us. This also would admit of a fair and sound construction, but that there is more than ordinary evidence of the places being corrupted: for the Vulgar Latin, which, as to the Psalms, was translated out of the LXX, renders these words, '*Propter legera tuam*'—'For your law's sake;' which makes it evident that that translator reads the words ἕνεκα τοῦ νόμου σου, and not ὀνόματός, as now we read. Now, though this has in itself no proper sense (for forgiveness is not bestowed for the law's sake), yet it discovers the original of the whole mistake. תּוֹרָא, 'the law,' differs but in one letter from תִּוָּרֵא, 'that you may be feared;' by a mistake whereof this ἕνεκα τοῦ νόμου, 'for your law's sake,' crept into the text. Nor does this any thing countenance the corrupt figment of the novelty of the Hebrew vowels and accents, as though this difference might arise from the LXX using a copy that had none—that is, before their invention, which might occasion mistakes and differences; for this difference is in a letter as well as in the vowels, and therefore there can be no colour for this conceit, unless we say also that they had copies of old with other consonants than those we now enjoy. Bellarmine, in his exposition of this place, endeavours to give countenance to the reading of the Vulgar Latin, 'For your law's sake;' affirming that by the law here, not the law of our obedience is intended, but the law or order of God's dealing with us, that is, his mercy and faithfulness—which is a mere new invention to countenance an old error, which any tolerable ingenuity would have confessed, rather than have justified by so sorry a pretence; for neither is that expression or that word ever used in the sense here by him feigned, nor can it have any such signification.

Jerome renders these words, '*Ut sis terribilis*'—'That you may be dreadful or terrible;' doubtless not according to the intendment of the place. It is for the relieving of the soul, and not for the increasing of its dread and terror, that this observation is made, 'There is forgiveness with you.'

But the words are clear, and their sense is obvious. לְמַעַן תִּוָּרֵא — 'Therefore you shall be feared;' or, 'That you may be feared.'

By the 'fear of the LORD,' in the Old Testament, the whole worship of God, moral and instituted, all the obedience which we owe to him, both for matter and manner, is intended. Whatever we are to perform to God, being to be carried on and performed with reverence and godly fear, by a metonymy of the adjunct, that name is given to the whole. 'That you may be feared,' then, is, 'That you may be served, worshipped; that I, who am ready to faint and give over on the account of sin, may yet be encouraged to, and yet continue in, that obedience which you require at my hands.' And this appears to be the sense of the whole verse, as influenced by and from those foregoing:

> Although, O Lord, no man can approach to you, stand before you, or walk with you, if you should mark their sins and follies according to the tenor of the law, nor could they serve so great and holy a God as you are; yet because I know from your revelation of it that there is also with you, on the account of Jesus Christ the propitiation, pardon and forgiveness, I am encouraged to continue with you, waiting for you, worshipping of you, when, without this discovery, I should rather choose to have rocks and mountains fall upon me, to hide me from your presence. But there is forgiveness with you, and therefore you shall be feared.

The words being thus opened, we may take a full view in them of the state and condition of the soul expressed in this psalm; and that answering the experiences of all who have had any thing to do with God in and about the depths and entanglements of sin.

Having in and from his great depths (v. 1), addressed himself with fervent, redoubled cries, yea, outcries to God, and to him alone, for relief (v. 1–2); having also acknowledged his iniquities, and considered them according to the tenor of the law (v. 3); he confesses himself to be lost and undone for ever on that account (v. 3). But he abides not in the state of self-condemnation and dejection of soul; he says not, 'There is no hope; God is a jealous God, a holy God, I cannot serve him; his law is a fiery law, which I cannot stand before; so that I had as good give over, sit down and perish, as contend any longer!' No; but searching by faith into the discovery that God makes of himself in Christ through the covenant of grace, he finds a stable foundation of encouragement to continue waiting on him, with expectation of mercy and pardon.

From the words unfolded, as they lie in their contexture in the psalm, the ensuing propositions do arise.

First, faith's discovery of forgiveness in God, though it have no present sense of its own peculiar interest therein, is the great support of a sin-perplexed soul.

Secondly, gospel forgiveness, whose discovery is the sole support of sin-distressed souls, relates to the gracious heart or good will of the Father, the God of forgiveness, the propitiation that is made by the blood of the Son, and free condonation or pardon according to the tenor of the covenant of grace.

Thirdly, faith's discovery of forgiveness in God is the sole bottom of adherence to him, in acceptable worship and reverential obedience.

The first of these is that whose confirmation and improvement I principally aim at; and the others only so far as they have coincidence therewith, or may be used in a subserviency to the illustration or demonstration thereof.

In the handling, then, of this truth, that it may be of the more advantage to them whose good is sought and intended in the proposal and management of it, I shall steer this course, and show:

1. That there is not the least encouragement to the soul of a sinner to deal with God without this discovery.

2. That this discovery of forgiveness in God is a matter great, holy, and mysterious; and which very few on gospel abiding grounds do attain to.

3. That yet this is a great, sacred, and certain truth, as from the manifold evidences of it may be made to appear.[1]

4. That this is a stable support to a sin-distressed soul shall be manifested, and the whole applied, according to the several concerns of those who shall consider it.

### No Approach to God without Forgiveness

First, there is not the least encouragement for the soul of a sinner to entertain any thoughts of approaching to God without this discovery. All the rest of the world is covered with a deluge of wrath. This is the only ark whereunto the soul may repair and find rest. All without it is darkness, curse, and terror.

We have an instance and example of it, beyond all exception, in Adam. When he knew himself to be a sinner (and it was impossible for him, as we shall show afterward, to make a discovery of any such thing as forgiveness with God), he laid aside all thoughts of treating with him; the best of his foolish contrivance was for an escape: 'I heard your voice,' says he to God, 'in the garden, and I was afraid, because I was naked; and I hid myself' (Gen. 3:10). Nothing but 'You shall die the death,' sounded in his ears. In the morning of that day, he was made by the hand of God; a few hours before, he had converse and communion with him, with boldness and peace; why, then, does nothing now but fear, flying, and hiding, possess him? Adam had sinned, the promise was not yet given, no revelation made of forgiveness in God; and what other course than that vain and foolish one to fix upon he knew not. No more can any of his posterity, without this revelation. What else any of them has fixed on in this case has been no less foolish than his hiding; and in most, more pernicious. When Cain had received his sentence from God, it is said 'he went out מִלִּפְנֵי יְהוָה, from the presence' or face 'of the LORD' (Gen. 4:16). From his providential

---

1 Owen switches the order and deals with the fourth point first.

presence he could never subduct himself: so the psalmist informs us at large (Ps. 139:7–10). The very heathen knew, by the light of nature, that guilt could never drive men out of the reach of God: '*Quo fugis Encelade? quascunque accesseris oras Sub Jove semper eris.*' They knew that δίκη (the vengeance of God) would not spare sinners, nor could be avoided (Acts 28:4). From God's gracious presence, which he never enjoyed, he could not depart. It was, then, his presence as to his worship, and all outward acts of communion, that he forsook, and departed from. He had no discovery by faith of forgiveness, and therefore resolved to have no more to do with God, nor those who cleaved to him; for it respects his course, and not any one particular action.

This also is stated, 'The sinners in Zion are afraid; fearfulness has surprised the hypocrites. Who among us shall dwell with the devouring fire? Who among us shall dwell with everlasting burnings?' (Isa. 33:14). The persons spoken of are sinners, great sinners, and hypocrites. Conviction of sin and the desert of it was fallen upon them; a light to discern forgiveness they had not; they apprehend God as devouring fire and everlasting burnings only—one that would not spare, but assuredly inflict punishment according to the desert of sin; and thence is their conclusion, couched in their interrogation, that there can be no intercourse of peace between him and them—there is no abiding, no enduring of his presence. And what condition this consideration brings the souls of sinners to, when conviction grows strong upon them, the Holy Ghost declares: 'Wherewith shall I come before the LORD, and bow myself before the high God? Shall I come before him with burnt-offerings, with calves of a year old? Will the LORD be pleased with thousands of rams, or with ten thousands of rivers of oil? Shall I give my first-born for my transgression, the fruit of my body for the sin of my soul?' (Mic. 6:6–7). Sense of sin presses, forgiveness is not discovered (like the Philistines on Saul, Samuel not coming to his direction); and how does the poor creature perplex itself in vain, to find out a way of dealing with God? 'Will a sedulous and diligent observation of his own ordinances and institutions relieve me?' 'Shall I come before him with burnt-offerings, with calves of a year old?' Alas! You are a sinner, and these sacrifices cannot make you 'perfect,' or acquit you (Heb. 10:1). 'Shall I do more than ever he required of any of the sons of men? O that I had "thousands of rams, and ten thousands of rivers of oil" to offer to him!' Alas! if you had all the 'bulls and goats' in the world, 'it is not possible that their blood should take away sins' (v. 4). 'But I have heard of them who have snatched their own children from their mothers' breasts, and cast them into the fire, until they were consumed, so to pacify their consciences in expiating the guilt of their iniquities. Shall I take this course? Will it relieve me? I am ready to part with my 'first-born' into the fire, so I may have deliverance from my 'transgression.' Alas! This never came into the heart of God to approve or accept of. And as it was then, whilst that kind of worship was in force, so is it still as to any duties really to be performed, or imaginarily. Where there is no discovery of forgiveness, they will yield the soul no relief, no support; God is not to be treated upon such terms.

## FORGIVENESS—A RARE ATTAINMENT

Secondly, this discovery of forgiveness in God is great, holy, and mysterious, and which very few on gospel grounds do attain to.

All men, indeed, say there is; most men are persuaded that they think so. Only men in great and desperate extremities, like Cain or Spira, seem to call it into question. But their thoughts are empty, groundless, yea, for the most part wicked and atheistic. Elihu tells us, that to declare this aright to a sinful soul, it is the work of 'a messenger, an interpreter, one among a thousand' (Job 33:23); that is, indeed, of Christ himself. The common thoughts of men about this thing are slight and foolish, and may be resolved into those mentioned by the psalmist (Ps. 1:21). They think that 'God is altogether such an one as themselves;' that, indeed, he takes little or no care about these things, but passes them over as slightly as they do themselves. That, notwithstanding all their pretences, the most of men never had indeed any real discovery of forgiveness, shall be afterward undeniably evinced; and I shall speedily show the difference that is between their vain credulity and a gracious gospel discovery of forgiveness in God. For it must be observed, that by this discovery I intend both the revelation of it made by God and our understanding and reception of that revelation to our own advantage; as shall be showed immediately.

Now, the grounds of the difficulty intimated consist partly in the hinderances that lie in the way of this discovery, and partly in the nature of the thing itself that is discovered; of both which I shall briefly treat.

But here, before I proceed, somewhat must be premised to show what it is that I particularly intend by a discovery of forgiveness. It may, then, be considered two ways:

1. For a doctrinal, objective discovery of it in its truth.
2. An experimental, subjective discovery of it in its power.

In the first sense, forgiveness in God has been discovered ever since the giving out of the first promise: God revealed it in a word of promise, or it could never have been known; as shall be afterward declared. In this sense, after many lesser degrees and advancements of the light of it, it was fully and gloriously brought forth by the Lord Jesus Christ in his own person, and is now revealed and preached in the gospel, and by them to whom the word of reconciliation is committed; and to declare this is the principal work of the ministers of the gospel. Herein lie those unsearchable treasures and riches of Christ, which the apostle esteemed as his chiefest honour and privilege that he was intrusted with the declaration and dispensation of (Eph. 3:8–9). I know by many it is despised, by many traduced, whose ignorance and blindness is to be lamented; but the day is coming which will manifest every man's work of what sort it is. In the latter sense, how it is made by faith in the soul, shall in its proper place be farther opened and made known. Here many men mistake and deceive themselves. Because it is so in the book, they think it is so in them also. Because they have been taught it, they think they believe it. But it is not so; they have not heard this voice of God at any time, nor seen his shape.

It has not been revealed to them in its power. To have this done is a great work.

## Conscience Opposes Forgiveness

First, the constant voice of conscience lies against it. Conscience, if not seared, inexorably condemns and pronounces wrath and anger upon the soul that has the least guilt cleaving to it. Now, it has this advantage, it lies close to the soul, and by importunity and loud speaking it will be heard in what it has to say; it will make the whole soul attend, or it will speak like thunder. And its constant voice is, that where there is guilt there must be judgment (Rom. 2:14–15). Conscience naturally knows nothing of forgiveness; yea, it is against its very trust, work, and office to hear any thing of it. If a man of courage and honesty be intrusted to keep a garrison against an enemy, let one come and tell him that there is peace made between those whom he serves and their enemies, so that he may leave his guard, and set open the gates, and cease his watchfulness; how wary will he be, lest under this pretence he be betrayed! 'No,' says he; 'I will keep my hold until I have express order from my superiors.' Conscience is intrusted with the power of God in the soul of a sinner, with command to keep all in subjection with reference to the judgment to come. It will not betray its trust in believing every report of peace. No; but this it says, and it speaks in the name of God, 'Guilt and punishment are inseparable twins; if the soul sin, God will judge. What tell you me of forgiveness? I know what my commission is, and that I will abide by. You shall not bring in a superior commander, a cross principle, into my trust; for if this be so, it seems I must let go my throne—another lord must come in;' not knowing, as yet, how this whole business is compounded in the blood of Christ. Now, whom should a man believe if not his own conscience, which, as it will not flatter him, so it intends not to affright him, but to speak the truth as the matter requires? Conscience has two works in reference to sin—one to condemn the acts of sin, another to judge the person of the sinner; both with reference to the judgment of God. When forgiveness comes, it would sever and part these employments, and take one of them out of the hand of conscience; it would divide the spoil with this strong one. It shall condemn the fact, or every sin: but it shall no more condemn the sinner, the person of the sinner; that shall be freed from its sentence. Here conscience labours with all its might to keep its whole dominion, and to keep out the power of forgiveness from being enthroned in the soul. It will allow men to talk of forgiveness, to hear it preached, though they abuse it every day; but to receive it in its power, that stands up in direct opposition to its dominion. 'In the kingdom,' says conscience, 'I will be greater than you;' and in many, in the most, it keeps its possession, and will not be deposed.

Nor, indeed, is it an easy work so to deal with it. The apostle tells us that all the sacrifices of the law could not do it (Heb. 10:2): they could not bring a man into that estate wherein he 'should have no more conscience of sin'—that is, conscience condemning the person; for conscience in a sense of sin, and condemnation of it, is never to be taken away. And this can be no otherwise done but by the blood of Christ, as the apostle at large there declares.

It is, then, no easy thing to make a discovery of forgiveness to a soul, when the work and employment which conscience, upon unquestionable grounds, challenges to itself lies in opposition to it. Hence is the soul's great desire to establish its own righteousness, whereby its natural principles may be preserved in their power. Let self-righteousness be enthroned, and natural conscience desires no more; it is satisfied and pacified. The law it knows, and righteousness it knows; but as for forgiveness, it says, 'Whence is it?' to the utmost, until Christ perfects his conquest, there are on this account secret strugglings in the heart against free pardon in the gospel, and fluctuations of mind and spirit about it. Yea, hence are the doubts and fears of believers themselves. They are nothing but the strivings of conscience to keep its whole dominion, to condemn the sinner as well as the sin. More or less it keeps up its pretensions against the gospel whilst we live in this world. It is a great work that the blood of Christ has to do upon the conscience of a sinner; for whereas, as it has been declared, it has a power, and claims a right to condemn both sin and sinner, the one part of this its power is to be cleared, strengthened, made more active, vigorous, and watchful, the other to be taken quite away. It shall now see more sins than formerly, more of the vileness of all sins than formerly, and condemn them with more abhorrency than ever, upon more and more glorious accounts than formerly; but it is also made to see an interposition between these sins and the person of the sinner who has committed them, which is no small or ordinary work.

### The Law Opposes Forgiveness

Secondly, the law lies against this discovery. The law is a beam of the holiness of God himself. What it speaks to us, it speaks in the name and authority of God; and I shall briefly show concerning it these two things: (a) That this is the voice of the law—namely, that there is no forgiveness for a sinner. (b) That a sinner has great reason to give credit to the law in that assertion.

### 'The Soul that Sins, it shall die.'

It is certain that the law knows neither mercy nor forgiveness. The very sanction of it lies wholly against them: 'The soul that sins, it shall die;' 'Cursed is he that continues not in all things in the book of the law to do them' (Deut. 27:26; Gal. 3:10). Hence the apostle pronounces universally, without exception, that they who 'are under the law are under the curse' (Gal. 3:10); and says he, 'The law is not of faith' (v. 12). There is an inconsistency between the law and believing; they cannot have their abode in power together. '"Do this and live;" fail and die,' is the constant, immutable voice of the law. This it speaks in general to all, and this in particular to every one.

### Many Reasons to Listen to the Law

The sinner seems to have manifold and weighty reasons to attend to the voice of this law, and to acquiesce in its sentence.

AN OLD FRIEND. The law is connatural to him; his domestic, his old acquaintance. It came into the world with him, and has grown up with him from his infancy. It was implanted in his heart by nature—is his own reason; he can never shake it off or part with it. It is his familiar, his friend, that cleaves to him as the flesh to the bone; so that they who have not the law written cannot but show forth the work of the law (Rom. 2:14–15), and that because the law itself is inbred to them. And all the faculties of the soul are at peace with it, in subjection to it. It is the bond and ligament of their union, harmony, and correspondency among themselves, in all their moral actings. It gives life, order, motion to them all. Now, the gospel, that comes to control this sentence of the law, and to relieve the sinner from it, is foreign to his nature, a strange thing to him, a thing he has no acquaintance or familiarity with; it has not been bred up with him; nor is there any thing in him to side with it, to make a party for it, or to plead in its behalf. Now, shall not a man rather believe a domestic, a friend, indeed himself, than a foreigner, a stranger, that comes with uncouth principles, and such as suit not its reason at all? (1 Cor. 1:18).

A COMPELLING WITNESS. The law speaks nothing to a sinner but what his conscience assures him to be true. There is a constant concurrence in the testimony of the law and conscience. When the law says, 'This or that is a sin worthy of death,' conscience says, 'It is even so' (Rom. 1:32). And where the law of itself, as being a general rule, rests, conscience helps it on, and says, 'This and that sin, so worthy of death, is the soul guilty of.' 'Then die,' says the law, 'as you have deserved.' Now, this must needs have a mighty efficacy to prevail with the soul to give credit to the report and testimony of the law; it speaks not one word but what he has a witness within himself to the truth of it. These witnesses always agree; and so it seems to be established for a truth that there is no forgiveness.

IRREFUTABLE TESTIMONY. The law, though it speak against the soul's interest, yet it speaks nothing but what is so just, righteous, and equal, that it even forces the soul's consent. So Paul tells us, that men know this voice of the law to be the 'judgment of God' (Rom. 1:32). They know it, and cannot but consent to it, that it is the judgment of God—that is, good, righteous, equal, not to be controlled. And, indeed, what can be more righteous than its sentence? It commands obedience to the God of life and death; promises a reward, and declares that for non-performance of duty, death will be inflicted. On these terms the sinner comes into the world. They are good, righteous, holy; the soul accepts of them, and knows not what it can desire better or more equal. This the apostle insists upon, 'Wherefore the law is holy, and the commandment holy, and just, and good. Was then that which was good made death to me? God forbid. But sin, that it might appear sin, working death in me by that which is good; that sin by the commandment might become exceeding sinful' (Rom. 7:12–13). Wherever the blame falls, the soul cannot but acquit the law, and confess that what it says is righteous and uncontrollably equal. And it is meet things should be so. Now, though the authority and credit of a witness may go very far in a doubtful matter, when there is a concurrence of more witnesses it strengthens the testimony; but nothing is so prevalent to beget belief as when the things themselves that are spoken are just and good, not liable to any reasonable exception. And so is it in this case: to the authority of the law and concurrence of conscience, this also is added, the reasonableness and equity of the thing itself proposed, even in the judgment of the sinner—namely, that every sin shall be punished, and every transgression receive a meet recompense of reward.

IT SPEAKS IN THE NAME OF GOD. But yet farther. What the law says, it speaks in the name and authority of God. What it says, then, must be believed, or we make God a liar. It comes not in its own name, but in the name of him who appointed it. You will say, then, 'Is it so indeed? Is there no forgiveness with God? For this is the constant voice of the law, which you say speaks in the name and authority of God, and is therefore to be believed?' I answer briefly with the apostle, 'What the law speaks, it speaks to them that are under the law.' It does not speak to them that are 'in Christ,' whom the 'law of the Spirit of life has set free from the law of sin and death;' but to them that are 'under the law' it speaks; and it speaks the very truth, and it speaks in the name of God, and its testimony is to be received. It says there is no forgiveness in God, namely, to them that are under the law; and they that shall flatter themselves with a contrary persuasion will find themselves woefully mistaken at the great day.

On these and the like considerations, I say, there seems to be a great deal of reason why a soul should conclude that it will be according to the testimony of the law, and that he shall not find forgiveness. Law and conscience close together, and insinuate themselves into the thoughts, mind, and judgment of a sinner. They strengthen the testimony of one another, and greatly prevail. If any are otherwise minded, I leave them to the trial. If ever God awaken their consciences to a thorough performance of their duty—if ever he open their souls, and let in the light and power of the law upon them—they will find it no small work to grapple with them. I am sure that eventually they prevail so far, that in the preaching of the gospel we have great cause to say, 'Lord, who has believed our report?' We come with our report of forgiveness, but who believes it? By whom is it received? Neither does the light, nor conscience, nor conversation of the most, allow us to suppose it is embraced.

### Human Thinking Rejects Forgiveness

Thirdly, the ingrafted notions that are in the minds of men concerning the nature and justice of God lie against this discovery also. There are in all men by nature indelible characters of the holiness and purity of God, of his justice and hatred of sin, of his invariable righteousness in the government of the world, that they can neither depose nor lay aside; for notions of God, whatever they are, will bear sway and role in the heart, when things are put to the trial.

They were in the heathens of old; they abode with them in all their darkness; as might be manifested by innumerable instances. But so it is in all men by nature. Their inward thought is, that God is an avenger of sin; that it belongs to his rule and government of the world, his holiness and righteousness, to take care that every sin be punished; this is his judgment, which all men know, as was observed before (Rom. 1:32). They know that it is a righteous thing with God to render tribulation to sinners. From thence is that dread and fear which surprises men at an apprehension of the presence of God, or of any thing under him, above them, that may seem to come on his errand. This notion of God's avenging all sin exerts itself secretly but effectually. So Adam trembled, and hid himself. And it was the saying of old, 'I have seen God, and shall die.' When men are under any dreadful providence—thunderings, lightnings, tempests, in darkness—they tremble; not so much at what they see, or hear, or feel, as from their secret thoughts that God is nigh, and that he is a consuming fire.

Now, these inbred notions lie universally against all apprehensions of forgiveness, which must be brought into the soul from without doors, having no principle of nature to promote them. It is true, men by nature have presumptions and common ingrafted notions of other properties of God besides his holiness and justice—as of his goodness, benignity, love of his creatures, and the like; but all these have this supposition inlaid with them in the souls of men, namely, that all things stand between God and his creatures as they did at their first creation. And as they have no natural notion of forgiveness, so the interposition of sin weakens, disturbs, darkens them, as to any improvement of those apprehensions of goodness and benignity which they have. If they have any notion of forgiveness, it is from some corrupt tradition, and not at all from any universal principle that is inbred in nature, such as are those which they have of God's holiness and vindictive justice.

And this is the first ground; from whence it appears that a real, solid discovery of forgiveness is indeed a great work; many difficulties and hindrances lie in the way of its accomplishment.

## FALSE NOTIONS OF FORGIVENESS

Before I proceed to produce and manage the remaining evidences of this truth, because what has been spoken lies obnoxious and open to an objection, which must needs rise in the minds of many, that it may not thereby be rendered useless to them, I shall remove it out of the way, that we may pass on to what remains.

It will, then, be said, 'Does not all this lie directly contrary to our daily experience? Do you not find all men full enough, most too full, of apprehensions of forgiveness with God? What so common as "God is merciful?" Are not the consciences and convictions of the most stifled by this apprehension? Can you find a man that is otherwise minded? Is it not a common complaint, that men presume on it to their eternal ruin? Certainly, then, that which all men do, which every man can so easily do, and which you cannot keep men off from doing, though it be to their hurt, has no such difficulty in it as is pretended.' And on this very account has this weak endeavour to demonstrate this truth been by some laughed to scorn; men who have taken upon them the teaching of others, but, as it seems, had need be taught themselves the very 'first principles of the oracles of God.'

Answer: All this, then, I say, is so, and much more to this purpose may be spoken. The folly and presumption of poor souls herein can never be enough lamented. But it is one thing to embrace a cloud, a shadow, another to have the truth in reality. I shall hereafter show the true nature of forgiveness and wherein it consists, whereby the vanity of this self-deceiving will be discovered and laid open. It will appear in the issue, that, notwithstanding all their pretensions, the most of men know nothing at all, or not any thing to the purpose, of that which is under consideration. I shall, therefore, for the present, in some few observations, show how far this delusion of many differs from a true gospel discovery of forgiveness, such as that we are inquiring after.

### 'God Is Like Ourselves'

First, the common notion of forgiveness that men have in the world is twofold—an atheistic presumption on God, that he is not so just and holy, or not just and holy in such a way and manner, as he is by some represented, is the ground of their persuasion of forgiveness. Men think that some declarations of God are fitted only to make them mad; that he takes little notice of these things; and that what he does he will easily pass by, as, they suppose, better becomes him. 'Come, "let us eat and drink, for tomorrow we shall die."' This is their inward thought, 'The Lord will not do good, neither will he do evil;' which, says the psalmist, is men's thinking that God is such a one as themselves (Ps. 1:21). They have no deep nor serious thoughts of his greatness, holiness, purity, severity, but think that he is like themselves, so far as not to be much moved with what they do. What thoughts they have of sin, the same they think God has. If with them a slight ejaculation be enough to expiate sin, that their consciences be no more troubled, they think it is enough with God that it be not punished. The generality of men make light work of sin; and yet in nothing does it more appear what thoughts they have of God. He that has slight thoughts of sin had never great thoughts of God. Indeed, men's undervaluing of sin arises merely from their contempt of God. All sin's concerns flow from its relation to God; and as men's apprehensions are of God, so will they be of sin, which is an opposition to him. This is the frame of the most of men—they know little of God, and are little troubled about any thing that relates to him. God is not reverenced, sin is but a trifle, forgiveness a matter of nothing; whoso will may have it for asking. But shall this atheistic wickedness of the heart of man be called a discovery of forgiveness? Is not this to make God an idol? He who is not acquainted with God's holiness and purity, who knows not sin's desert and sinfulness, knows nothing of forgiveness.

### 'GOD WILL FORGIVE ME; THAT'S HIS JOB'

From the doctrine of the gospel commonly preached and made known, there is a general notion begotten in the minds of men that God is ready to forgive. Men, I say, from hence have a doctrinal apprehension of this truth, without any real, satisfactory foundation of that apprehension as to themselves. This they have heard, this they have been often told; so they think, and so they resolved to do. a general persuasion hereof spreads itself over all to whom the sound of the gospel comes. It is not fiducially resolved into the gospel, but is an opinion growing out of the report of it.

Some relief men find by it in the common course of their conversation, in the duties of worship which they do perform, as also in their troubles and distresses, whether internal and of conscience, or external and of providence, so that they resolve to retain it.

### HOW TO IDENTIFY FALSE NOTIONS OF FORGIVENESS

And this is that which I shall briefly speak to, and therein manifest the differences between this common prevailing apprehension of forgiveness, and faith's discovery of it to the soul in its power.

### *Loose and General*

That which we reject is loose and general; not fixed, ingrafted, or planted on the mind. So is it always where the minds of men receive things only in their notion and not in their power. It wants fixedness and foundation; which defects accompany all notions of the mind that are only retained in the memory, not implanted in the judgment. They have general thoughts of it, which they use as occasion serves. They hear that God is a merciful God, and as such they intend to deal with him. For the true bottom, rise, and foundation of it—whence or on what account the pure and holy God, who will do no iniquity, the righteous God, whose judgment it is that they that commit sin are worthy of death, should yet pardon iniquity, transgression, and sin—they weigh it not, they consider it not; or, if they do, it is in a slight and notional way, as they consider the thing itself. They take it for granted so it is, and are never put seriously upon the inquiry how it comes to be so; and that because indeed they have no real concern in it. How many thousands may we meet withal who take it for granted that forgiveness is to be had with God, that never yet had any serious exercise in their souls about the grounds of it, and its consistency with his holiness and justice! But those that know it by faith have a sense of it fixed particularly and distinctly on their minds. They have been put upon an inquiry into the rise and grounds of it in Christ; so that on a good and unquestionable foundation they can go to God and say, 'There is forgiveness with you.' They see how and by what means more glory comes to God by forgiveness than by punishing of sin; which is a matter that the other sort of men are not at all solicitous about. If they may escape punishment, whether God have any glory or no, for the most part they are indifferent.

## Superficial

The first apprehension arises without any trial upon inquiry in the consciences of them in whom it is. They have not, by the power of their convictions and distresses of conscience, been put to make inquiry whether this thing be so or no. It is not a persuasion that they have arrived to in a way of seeking satisfaction to their own souls. It is not the result of a deep inquiry after peace and rest. It is antecedent to trial and experience, and so is not faith, but opinion; for although faith be not experience, yet it is inseparable from it, as is every practical habit. Distresses in their consciences have been prevented by this opinion, not removed. The reason why the most of men are not troubled about their sins to any purpose, is from a persuasion that God is merciful and will pardon; when indeed none can really, on a gospel account, ordinarily, have that persuasion, but those who have been troubled for sin, and that to the purpose. So is it with them that make this discovery by faith. They have had conflicts in their own spirits, and, being deprived of peace, have accomplished a diligent search whether forgiveness were to be obtained or no. The persuasion they have of it, be it more or less, is the issue of a trial they have had in their own souls, of an inquiry how things stood between God and them as to peace and acceptation of their persons. This is a vast difference. The one sort might possibly have had trouble in their consciences about sin, had it not been for their opinion of forgiveness. This has prevented or stifled their convictions; not healed their wounds, which is the work of the gospel; but kept them from being wounded, which is the work of security. Yea, here lies the ruin of the most of them who perish under the preaching of the gospel. They have received the general notion of pardon; it floats in their minds, and presently presents itself to their relief on all occasions. Does God at any time, in the dispensation of the word, under an affliction, upon some great sin against their ruling light, begin to deal with their consciences? — before their conviction can ripen or come to any perfection, before it draw nigh to its perfect work, they choke it, and heal their consciences with this notion of pardon. Many a man, between the assembly and his dwelling-house, is thus cured. You may see them go away shaking their heads, and striking on their breasts, and before they come home be as whole as ever. 'Well, God is merciful, there is pardon,' has wrought the cure. The other sort have obtained their persuasion as a result of the discovery of Christ in the gospel, upon a full conviction. Trials they have had, and this is the issue.

### Flippant Towards God

The one which we reject works no love to God, no delight in him, no reverence of him, but rather a contempt and commonness of spirit in dealing with him. There are none in the world that deal worse with God than those who have an ungrounded persuasion of forgiveness. And if they do fear him, or love him, or obey him in any thing, more or less, it is on other motives and considerations, which will not render any thing they do acceptable, and not at all on this. As he is good to the creation, they may love, as he is great and powerful, they may fear him; but sense of pardon, as to any such ends or purposes, has no power upon them. Carnal boldness, formality, and despising of God, are the common issues of such a notion and persuasion. Indeed, this is the generation of great sinners in the world; men who have a general apprehension, but not a sense of the special power of pardon, openly or secretly, in fleshly or spiritual sins, are the great sinners among men. Where faith makes a discovery of forgiveness, all things are otherwise. Great love, fear, and reverence of God, are its attendants. Mary Magdalene loved much, because much was forgiven. Great love will spring out of great forgiveness. 'There is forgiveness with you,' says the psalmist, 'that you may be feared.' No unbeliever does truly and experimentally know the truth of this inference. But so it is when men 'fear the LORD, and his goodness' (Hos. 3:5). I say, then, where pardoning mercy is truly apprehended, where faith makes a discovery of it to the soul, it is endeared to God, and possessed of the great springs of love, delight, fear, and reverence (Ps. 116:1, 5–7).

### Little Antipathy Towards Sin

This notional apprehension of the pardon of sin begets no serious, thorough hatred and detestation of sin, nor is prevalent to a relinquishment of it; nay, it rather secretly insinuates into the soul encouragements to a continuance in it. It is the nature of it to lessen and extenuate sin, and to support the soul against its convictions. So Jude tells us, that some 'turn the grace of God into lasciviousness' (v. 4); and says he, 'They are "ungodly men;" let them profess what they will, they are ungodly men.' But how can they turn the grace of our God into lasciviousness? Is grace capable of a conversion into lust or sin? Will what was once grace ever become wantonness? It is objective, not subjective grace, the doctrine, not the real substance of grace, that is intended. The doctrine of forgiveness is this grace of God, which may be thus abused. From hence do men who have only a general notion of it habitually draw secret encouragements to sin and folly. Paul also lets us know that carnal men, coming to a doctrinal acquaintance with gospel grace, are very apt to make such conclusions (Rom. 6:1). And it will appear at the last day how unspeakably this glorious grace has been perverted in the world. It would be well for many if they had never heard the name of forgiveness. It is otherwise where this revelation is received indeed in the soul by believing (Rom. 6:14). Our being under grace, under the power of the belief of forgiveness, is our great preservative from our being under the power of sin. Faith of forgiveness is the principle of gospel obedience (Tit. 2:11–12).

## No Lasting Rest and Contentment

The general notion of forgiveness brings with it no sweetness, no rest to the soul. Flashes of joy it may, abiding rest it does not. The truth of the doctrine fluctuates to and fro in the minds of those that have it, but their wills and affections have no solid delight nor rest by it. Hence, notwithstanding all that profession that is made in the world of forgiveness, the most of men ultimately resolve their peace and comfort to themselves. As their apprehensions are of their own doing, good or evil, according to their ruling light, whatever it be, so as to peace and rest are they secretly tossed up and down. Every one in his several way pleases himself with what he does in answer to his own convictions, and is disquieted as to his state and condition, according as he seems to himself to come short thereof. To make a full life of contentation upon pardon, they know not how to do it. One duty yields them more true repose than many thoughts of forgiveness. But faith finds sweetness and rest in it; being thereby apprehended, it is the only harbour of the soul. It leads a man to God as good, to Christ as rest. Fading evanid joys do ofttimes attend the one; but solid delight, with constant obedience, are the fruits only of the other.

evanid: liable to vanish

## Founded on Self-righteousness

Those who have the former only take up their persuasion on false grounds, though the thing itself be true; and they cannot but use it to false ends and purposes, besides its natural and genuine tendency. For their grounds, they will be discovered when I come to treat of the true nature of gospel forgiveness. For the end, it is used generally only to fill up what is wanting. Self-righteousness is their bottom; and when that is too short or narrow to cover them, they piece it out by forgiveness. Where conscience accuses, this must supply the defect. Faith lays it on its proper foundation, of which afterwards also; and it uses it to its proper end—namely, to be the sole and only ground of our acceptance with God. That is the proper use of forgiveness, that all may be of grace; for when the foundation is pardon, the whole superstructure must needs be grace. From what has been spoken it is evident that, notwithstanding the pretences to the contrary, insinuated in the objection now removed, it is a great thing to have gospel forgiveness discovered to a soul in a saving manner.

## True Gospel Forgiveness

The difficulties that lie in the way of faith's discovery of forgiveness, whence it appears to be a matter of greater weight and importance than it is commonly apprehended to be, have been insisted on in the foregoing discourse. There is yet remaining another ground of the same truth. Now, this is taken from the nature and greatness of the thing itself discovered—that is, of forgiveness. To this end I shall show what it is, wherein it consists, what it comprises and relates to, according to the importance of the second proposition before laid down.

I do not in this place take forgiveness, strictly and precisely, for the act of pardoning; nor shall I dispute what that is, and wherein it consists. Consciences that come with sin-entanglements to God know nothing of such disputes. Nor will this expression, 'There is forgiveness with God,' bear any such restriction as that it should regard only actual condonation or pardon. That which I have to do is to inquire into the nature of that pardon which poor, convinced, troubled souls seek after, and which the Scripture proposes to them for their relief and rest. And I shall not handle this absolutely neither, but in relation to the truth under consideration—namely, that it is a great thing to attain to a true gospel discovery of forgiveness.

## Its Relation to the Gracious Heart of the Father

First, as was showed in the opening of the words, the forgiveness inquired after has relation to the gracious heart of the Father. Two things I understand hereby: (a) the infinite goodness and graciousness of his nature; (b) the sovereign purpose of his will and grace.

### In the Infinite Goodness of His Nature

There is considerable in it, the infinite goodness of his nature. Sin stands in a contrariety to God. It is a rebellion against his sovereignty, an opposition to his holiness, a provocation to his justice, a rejection of his yoke, a casting off, what lies in the sinner, of that dependence which a creature has on its Creator. That God, then, should have pity and compassion on sinners, in every one of whose sins there is all this evil, and inconceivably more than we can comprehend, it argues an infinitely gracious, good, and loving heart and nature in him; for God does nothing but suitably to the properties of his nature, and from them. All the acts of his will are the effects of his nature.

Now, whatever God proposes as an encouragement for sinners to come to him, that is of, or has a special influence into, the forgiveness that is with him; for nothing can encourage a sinner as such, but under this consideration, that it is, or it respects, forgiveness. That this graciousness of God's nature lies at the head or spring, and is the root from whence forgiveness grows, is manifest from that solemn proclamation which he made of old of his name, and the revelation of his nature therein (for God assuredly is what by himself he is called): 'The LORD, The LORD God, merciful and gracious, long-suffering, and abundant in goodness and truth, keeping mercy for thousands, forgiving iniquity and transgression and sin' (Exod. 34:6–7). His forgiving of iniquity flows from hence, that in his nature he is merciful, gracious, long-suffering, abundant in goodness. Were he not so, infinite in all these, it were in vain to look for forgiveness from him. Having made this known to be his name, and thereby declared his nature, he in many places proposes it as a relief, a refuge for sinners, an encouragement to come to him, and to wait for mercy from him: 'They that know your name will put their trust in you' (Ps. 9:10). It will encourage them so to do; others have no foundation of their confidence. But if this name of God be indeed made known to us by the Holy Ghost, what can hinder why we should not repair to him and rest upon him? So Isaiah 50:10, 'Who is among you that fears the LORD, that obeys the voice of his servant, that walks in darkness, and has no light? Let him trust in the name of the LORD, and stay upon his God.' Not only sinners, but sinners in great distress are here spoken to. Darkness of state or condition, in the Scripture, denotes every thing of disconsolation and trouble. To be, then, in darkness, where yet there is some light, some relief, though darkness be predominant, is sad and disconsolate; but now, not only to be, but also to walk, that is, to continue a course in darkness, and that with no light, no discovery of help or relief—this seems an overwhelming condition: yet sinners in this estate are called 'to trust in the name of the LORD.' I have showed before that nothing but forgiveness, or that which influences it and encourages to an expectation of it, is of any use to a sinner, much more one in so great distress upon the account of sin; yet is such a one here sent only to the name of the Lord, wherein his gracious heart and nature is revealed. That, then, is the very fountain and spring of forgiveness. And this is that which John would work a sense of upon our souls where he tells us that 'God is love' (1 John 4:8), or one of an infinitely gracious, tender, good, compassionate, loving nature. Infinite goodness and grace is the soil wherein forgiveness grows. It is impossible this flower should spring from any other root. Unless this be revealed to the soul, forgiveness is not revealed. To consider pardon merely as it is terminated on ourselves, not as it flows from God, will bring neither profit to us nor glory to God.

And this also (which is our design in hand) will make it appear that this discovery of forgiveness whereof we speak is indeed no common thing—is a great discovery. Let men come, with a sense of the guilt of sin, to have deep and serious thoughts of God, they will find it no such easy and light matter to have their hearts truly and thoroughly apprehensive of this loving and gracious nature of God in reference to pardon. It is an easy matter to say so in common; but the soul will not find it so easy to believe it for itself. What has been spoken before concerning the ingrafted notions that are in the minds of men about the justice, holiness, and severity of God, will here take place. Though men profess that God is gracious, yet that aversation which they have to him and communion with him does abundantly manifest that they do not believe what they say and profess: if they did, they could not but delight and trust in him, which they do not; for 'They that know his name will put their trust in him.' So said the slothful servant in the gospel, 'I knew that you were austere, and not for me to deal withal.' It may be he professed otherwise before, but that lay in his heart when it came to the trial. But this, I say, is necessary to them to whom this discovery is to be made, even a spiritual apprehension of the gracious, loving heart and nature of God. This is the spring of all that follows; and the fountain must needs be infinitely sweet from whence such streams do flow. He that considers the glorious fabric of heaven and earth, with the things in them contained, must needs conclude that they were the product of infinite wisdom and power; nothing less or under them could have brought forth such an effect. And he that really considers forgiveness, and looks on it with a spiritual eye, must conclude that it comes from infinite goodness and grace. And this is that which the hearts of sinners are exercised about when they come to deal for pardon: 'You, Lord, are good, and ready to forgive' (Ps. 86:5); 'You are a God ready to pardon, gracious and merciful, slow to anger, and of great kindness' (Neh. 9:17); and 'Who is a God like to you, that pardons iniquity?...because he delights in mercy' (Mic. 7:18). And God encourages them hereunto wherever he says that he forgives sins and blots out iniquities for his own sake or his name's sake; that is, he will deal with sinners according to the goodness of his own gracious nature. So Hosea 11:9, 'I will not execute the fierceness of mine anger, I will not return to destroy Ephraim: for I am God, and not man.' Were there no more mercy, grace, compassion to be showed in this case than it is possible should be treasured up in the heart of a man, it would be impossible that Ephraim should be spared; but says he, 'I am God, and not man.' Consider the infinite largeness, bounty, and goodness of the heart of God, and there is yet hope. When a sinner is in good earnest seeking after forgiveness, there is nothing he is more solicitous about than the heart of God towards him—nothing that he more labours to have a discovery of; there is nothing that sin and Satan labour more to hide from him. This he rolls in his mind, and exercises his thoughts about; and if ever that voice of God, 'Fury is not in me' (Isa. 27:4), sound in his heart, he is relieved from his great distresses. And the fear of our hearts in this matter our Saviour seems to intend the prevention or a removal of: 'I say not to you, that I will pray the Father for you; for the Father himself loves you' (John 16:26–7). They had good thoughts of the tender heart and care of Christ himself, the mediator, towards them; but what is the heart of the Father? What acceptance shall they find with him? Will Christ pray that they may find favour with him? Why, says he, as to the love of his heart, 'There is no need of it; "for the Father himself loves you."' If this, then, belongs to forgiveness, as whoever has sought for it knows that it does, it is certainly no common discovery to have it revealed to us.

To have all the clouds and darkness that are raised by sin between us and the throne of God dispelled; to have the fire, and storms, and tempests, that are kindled and stirred up about him by the law removed; to have his glorious face unveiled, and his holy heart laid open, and a view given of those infinite treasures and stores of goodness, mercy, love, and kindness which have had an unchangeable habitation therein from all eternity; to have a discovery of these eternal springs of forbearance and forgiveness—is that which none but Christ can accomplish and bring about (John 17:6).

## *In His Sovereign Purpose*

This is not all. This eternal ocean, that is infinitely satisfied with its own fullness and perfection, does not naturally yield forth streams for our refreshment. Mercy and pardon do not come forth from God as light does from the sun or water from the sea, by a necessary consequence of their natures, whether they will or no. It does not necessarily follow that any one must be made partaker of forgiveness because God is infinitely gracious; for may he not do what he will with his own? 'Who has first given to him, that it should be recompensed to him again?' (Rom. 11:35). All the fruits of God's goodness and grace are in the sole keeping of his own sovereign will and pleasure. This is his great glory: 'Show me your glory,' says Moses. 'And he said, I will make all my goodness pass before you, and I will proclaim the name of the Lord before you; and I will be gracious to whom I will be gracious' (Exod. 33:18–19). Upon that proclamation of the name of God, that he is merciful, gracious, long-suffering, abundant in goodness, some might conclude that it could not be otherwise with any but well—he is such a one as that men need scarce be beholding to him for mercy. 'Nay,' says he; 'but this is my great glory, that "I will be gracious to whom I will be gracious."' There must be an interposition of a free act of the will of God to deal with us according to this his abundant goodness, or we can have no interest therein. This I call the purpose of his grace, or 'The good pleasure which he has purposed in himself' (Eph. 1:9); or, as it is termed, 'The good pleasure of his will,' that he has purposed 'to the praise of his glorious grace' (Eph. 1:5–6). This free and gracious pleasure of God, or purpose of his will to act towards sinners according to his own abundant goodness, is another thing that influences the forgiveness of which we treat. Pardon flows immediately from a sovereign act of free grace. This free purpose of God's will and grace for the pardoning of sinners is indeed that which is principally intended when we say, 'There is forgiveness with him;' that is, he is pleased to forgive, and so to do is agreeable to his nature. Now, the mystery of this grace is deep; it is eternal, and therefore incomprehensible. Few there are whose hearts are raised to a contemplation of it. Men rest and content themselves in a general notion of mercy, which will not be advantageous to their souls. Freed they would be from punishment, but what it is to be forgiven they inquire not. So what they know of it they come easily by, but will find in the issue it will stand them in little stead. But these fountains of God's actings are revealed, that they may be the fountains of our comforts.

Now, of this purpose of God's grace there are several acts, all of them relating to gospel forgiveness.

HE SENT HIS SON TO PROCURE FORGIVENESS. There is his purpose of sending his Son to be the great means of procuring, of purchasing forgiveness. Though God be infinitely and incomprehensibly gracious, though he purpose to exert his grace and goodness toward sinners, yet he will so do it, do it in such a way, as shall not be prejudicial to his own holiness and righteousness. His justice must be satisfied, and his holy indignation against sin made known. Wherefore he purposes to send his Son, and has sent him, to make way for the exercise of mercy; so as no way to eclipse the glory of his justice, holiness, and hatred of sin. Better we should all eternally come short of forgiveness than that God should lose any thing of his glory. This we have, 'God set him forth to be a propitiation through faith in his blood, to declare his righteousness for the remission of sins that are past' (Rom. 3:25). The remission of sins is the thing aimed at; but this must be so brought about as that therein not only the mercy but the righteousness of God may be declared, and therefore must it be brought forth by a propitiation, or making of an atonement in the blood of Christ (so John 3:16; 1 John 4:9; Rom. 5:8).

This, I say, also lies in the mystery of that forgiveness that is administered in the gospel—it comes forth from this eternal purpose of making way by the blood of Christ to the dispensation of pardon. And this greatly heightens the excellency of this discovery. Men who have slight thoughts of God, whose hearts were never awed with his dread or greatness, who never seriously considered his purity and holiness, may think it no great matter that God should pardon sin, but do they consider the way whereby it is to be brought about? — even by the sending of his only Son, and that to die, as we shall see afterward. Neither was there any other way whereby it might be done.

Let us now lay aside common thoughts, assent upon reports and tradition, and rightly weigh this matter. Doubtless we shall find it to be a great thing, that forgiveness should be so with God as to be made out to us (we know somewhat what we are) by sending his only Son to die. Oh, how little is this really believed, even by them who make a profession of it! And what mean thoughts are entertained about it when men seek for pardon! Immunity from punishment is the utmost that lies in the aims and desires of most, and is all that they are exercised in the consideration of, when they deal with God about sin. Such men think, and will do so, that we have an easy task in hand — namely, to prove that there is forgiveness in God; but this ease lies in their own ignorance and darkness. If ever they come to search after it indeed, to inquire into the nature, reasons, causes, fountains, and springs of it, they will be able to give another account of these things. Christ is the centre of the mystery of the gospel, and forgiveness is laid up in the heart of Christ, from the love of the Father; in him are all the treasures of it hid.

And surely it is no small thing to have the heart of Christ revealed to us. When believers deal about pardon, their faith exercises itself about this, that God, with whom the soul has to do, has sent the Lord Christ to die for this end, that it may be freely given out. General notions of impunity they dwell not on, they pass not for; they have a closer converse with God than to be satisfied with such thoughts. They inquire into the graciousness of his nature, and the good pleasure of his will, the purpose of his grace; they ponder and look into the mystery of his wisdom and love in sending his Son. If these springs be not clear to them, the streams will yield them but little refreshment. It is not enough that we seek after salvation, but we are to inquire and search diligently into the nature and manner of it. These are the things that 'the angels desire to' bow down and 'look into' (1 Pet. 1:11–12). And some think if they have got a form of words about them, they have gotten a sufficient comprehension of them! It is doubtless one reason why many who truly believe do yet so fluctuate about forgiveness all their days, that they never exercised faith to look into the springs of it, its eternal fountains, but have merely dwelt on actual condonation. However, I say, these things lie utterly out of the consideration of the common pretenders to an acquaintance with the truth we have in hand.

HE ELECTS THOSE WHO WILL BE PARDONED. There is another sovereign act, of God's will to be considered in this matter, and that is his eternal designation of the persons who shall be made partakers of this mercy. He has not left this thing to hazard and uncertainties, that it should, as it were, be unknown to him who should be pardoned and who not. Nay, none ever are made partakers of forgiveness but those whom he has eternally and graciously designed thereunto: so the apostle declares it (Eph. 1:5–7). The rise is his eternal predestination; the end, the glory of his grace; the means, redemption in the blood of Christ; the thing itself, forgiveness of sins. None ever are or can be made partakers thereof but by virtue of this act of God's will and grace; which thereupon has a peculiar influence into it, and is to be respected in the consideration of it. I know this may be abused by pride, profaneness, and unbelief, and so may the whole work of God's grace—and so it is, even the blood of Christ in an especial manner; but in its proper place and use it has a signal influence into the glory of God and the consolation of the souls of men.

There are also other acts of this purpose of God's grace, as of giving sinners to Christ and giving sinners an interest in Christ, which I shall not insist upon, because the nature of them is sufficiently discovered in that one explained already.

## ITS RELATION TO THE BLOOD OF CHRIST

Secondly, forgiveness has respect to the propitiation made in and by the blood of Christ the Son of God. This was declared in the opening of the words. Indeed, here lies the knot and centre of gospel forgiveness. It flows from the cross, and springs out of the grave of Christ.

Thus Elihu describes it, 'God is gracious to him, and says, Deliver him from going down to the pit: I have found a ransom' (Job 33:24). The whole of what is aimed at lies in these words:

1. There is God's gracious and merciful heart towards a sinner: 'He is gracious to him.'
2. There is actual condonation itself, of which we shall treat afterward: 'He says, Deliver him from going down to the pit.'
3. There is the centre of the whole, wherein God's gracious heart and actual pardon do meet; and that is the ransom, the propitiation or atonement that is in the blood of Christ, of which we speak: 'I have found a ransom.'

The same is expressed, 'My righteous servant shall justify many; for he shall bear their iniquities' (Isa. 53:11). Of the justification of sinners, absolution or pardon is the first part. This arises from Christ's bearing their iniquities. Therein he 'finished the transgression, made an end of sins, and made reconciliation for iniquity' (Dan. 9:24). Even all the sacrifices, and so consequently the whole worship of the Old Testament, evinced this relation between forgiveness and blood-shedding; whence the apostle concludes that 'without shedding of blood is no remission' (Heb. 9:22)—that is, all pardon arises from blood-shedding, even of the blood of the Son of God; so that we are said 'in him to have redemption, even the forgiveness of sins' (Eph. 1:7). Our redemption in his blood is our forgiveness: not that we are all actually pardoned in the blood of his cross, for thereunto must be added gospel condonation, of which afterward; but thereby it is procured, the grant of pardon is therein sealed, and security given that it shall in due time be made out to us. To which purpose is that discourse of the apostle (Rom. 3:24–6). The work there mentioned proceeds from grace, is managed to the interest of righteousness, is carried on by the blood of Christ, and issues in forgiveness. Now, the blood of Christ relates variously to the pardon of sin.

### His Blood Procures Pardon

Pardon is purchased and procured by it. Our redemption is our forgiveness, as the cause contains the effect. No soul is pardoned but with respect to the blood of Christ as the procuring cause of that pardon. Hence he is said to have 'washed us in his blood' (Rev. 1:5); 'by himself to have purged our sins' (Heb. 1:3); 'by one offering' to have taken away sin, and to have 'perfected for ever them that are sanctified' (Heb. 10:14); to be the ransom and 'propitiation for our sins' (1 John 2:2); to have 'made an end of sins' (Dan. 9:24); and to have 'made reconciliation for the sins of the people' (Heb. 2:17). God has enclosed his rich stores of pardon and mercy in the blood of Jesus.

### Pardon Ratified

Because in his blood the promise of pardon is ratified and confirmed, so that nothing is wanting to our complete forgiveness but our pleading the promise by faith in him, 'All the promises of God in him are yea, and in him Amen' (2 Cor. 1:20); that is, faithfully, and irrevocably, and immutably established. And therefore the apostle having told us that this is the covenant of God, that he would be 'merciful to our sins and iniquities' (Heb. 8:12), he informs us that in the undertaking of Christ this covenant is become a testament (Heb. 9:15–17); so ratified in his blood, that mercy and forgiveness of sin is irrevocably confirmed to us therein.

### Acquittal & Discharge

Because he has in his own person, as the head of the church, received an acquitment for the whole body. His personal discharge, upon the accomplishment of his work, was a pledge of the discharge which was in due time to be given to his whole mystical body. Peter tells us that it was impossible he should be detained by death (Acts 2:24). And why so? Because death being penally inflicted on him, when he had paid the debt he was legally to be acquitted. Now, for whom and in whose name and stead he suffered, for them and in their name and stead he received this acquitment.

### Forgiveness Is Now at Christ's Disposal

Because upon his death, God the Father has committed to him the whole management of the business of forgiveness: he now gives 'repentance' and the 'forgiveness of sins' (Acts 5:31). It is Christ that forgives us (Col. 3:13). All forgiveness is now at his disposal, and he pardons whom he will, even all that are given to him of the Father, not casting out any that come to God by him. He is intrusted with all the stores of his Father's purpose and his own purchase; and thence tells us that 'all things that the Father has are his' (John 16:15).

---

In all these respects does forgiveness relate to the blood of Christ. Mercy, pardon, and grace could find no other way to issue forth from the heart of the Father but by the heart-blood of the Son; and so do they stream to the heart of the sinner.

Two things are principally to be considered in the respect that forgiveness has to the blood of Christ: (a) The way of its procurement; (b) The way of its administration by him. The first is deep, mysterious, dreadful. It was by his blood, the blood of the cross, the travail of his soul, his undergoing wrath and curse. The other is gracious, merciful, and tender; whence so many things are spoken of his mercifulness and faithfulness, to encourage us to expect forgiveness from him.

This also adds to the mysterious depths of forgiveness, and makes its discovery a great matter. The soul that looks after it in earnest must consider what it cost. How light do most men make of pardon! What an easy thing is it to be acquainted with it! And no very hard matter to obtain it! But to hold communion with God, in the blood of his Son, is a thing of another nature than is once dreamed of by many who think they know well enough what it is to be pardoned. 'God be merciful,' is a common saying; and as common to desire he would be so 'for Christ's sake.' Poor creatures are cast into the mould of such expressions, who know neither God, nor mercy, nor Christ, nor any thing of the mystery of the gospel. Others look on the outside of the cross. To see into the mystery of the love of the Father, working in the blood of the Mediator; to consider by faith the great transaction of divine wisdom, justice, and mercy therein—how few attain to it! To come to God by Christ for forgiveness, and therein to behold the law issuing all its threats and curses in his blood, and losing its sting, putting an end to its obligation to punishment, in the cross; to see all sins gathered up in the hands of God's justice, and made to meet on the Mediator, and eternal love springing forth triumphantly from his blood, flourishing into pardon, grace, mercy, forgiveness—this the heart of a sinner can be enlarged to only by the Spirit of God.

### ITS RELATION TO THE PROMISE OF THE GOSPEL

Thirdly, there is in forgiveness free condonation, discharge, or pardon, according to the tenor of the gospel; and this may be considered two ways:

1. As it lies in the promise itself; and so it is God's gracious declaration of pardon to sinners, in and by the blood of Christ, his covenant to that end and purpose, which is variously proposed, according as he knew needful for all the ends and purposes of ingenerating faith, and communicating that consolation which he intends therein. This is the law of his grace, the declaration of the mystery of his love, before insisted on.

2. There is the bringing home and application of all this mercy to the soul of a sinner by the Holy Ghost, wherein we are freely forgiven all our trespasses (Col. 2:13).

*Where Does Faith Fix Itself?*

Gospel forgiveness I say, respects all these things, these principles; they have all an influence into it. And that which makes this more evident (wherewith I shall close this consideration of the nature of it), is, that faith, in its application of itself to God about and for forgiveness, does distinctly apply itself to and close with sometimes one of these severally and singly, sometimes another, and sometimes jointly takes in the consideration of them all expressly. Not that at any time it fixes on any or either of them exclusively to the others, but that eminently it finds some special encouragement at some season, and some peculiar attractive, from some one of them, more than from the rest; and then that proves an inlet, a door of entrance, to the treasures that are laid up in the rest of them. Let us go over the severals by instances.

ON THE NATURE OF GOD. Sometimes faith fixes upon the name and infinite goodness of the nature of God, and draws out forgiveness from thence. So does the psalmist: 'You, Lord, are good and ready to forgive' (Ps. 86:5). He rolls himself, in the pursuit and expectation of pardon, on the infinite goodness of the nature of God. 'You are a God of pardons' (Neh. 9:17), or ready to forgive — of an infinite gracious, loving nature — not severe and wrathful; and this is that which we are encouraged to (Isa. 50:10), to stay on the name of God, as in innumerable other places.

And thus faith often finds a peculiar sweetness and encouragement in and from the consideration of God's gracious nature. Sometimes this is the first thing it fixes on, and sometimes the last that it rests in. And ofttimes it makes a stay here, when it is driven from all other holds; it can say, however it be, 'Yet God is gracious;' and at least make that conclusion which we have from it, 'God is gracious and merciful; who knows but he will return' (Joel 2:13–14). And when faith has well laid hold on this consideration, it will not easily be driven from its expectation of relief and forgiveness even from hence.

ON THE SOVEREIGNTY OF GOD'S WILL. Sometimes the soul by faith addresses itself in a peculiar manner to the sovereignty of God's will, whereby he is gracious to whom he will be gracious, and merciful to whom he will be merciful; which, as was showed, is another considerable spring or principle of forgiveness. This way David's faith steered him in his great strait and perplexity: 'If I shall find favour in the eyes of the LORD, he will bring me again. But if he thus say, I have no delight in you; behold, here am I, let him do to me as seems good to him' (2 Sam. 15:25–6). That which he has in consideration is whether God has any delight in him or no; that is, whether God would graciously remit and pardon the great sin against which at that time he manifests his indignation. Here he lays himself down before the sovereign grace of God, and awaits patiently the discovery of the free act of his will concerning him; and at this door, as it were, enters into the consideration of those other springs of pardon which faith inquires after and closes withal. This sometimes is all the cloud that appears to a distressed soul, which after a while fills the heavens by the addition of the other considerations mentioned, and yields plentiful refreshing showers. And this condition is a sin-entangled soul ofttimes reduced to in looking out for relief—it can discover nothing but this, that God is able, and can, if he graciously please, relieve and acquit him. All other supports, all springs of relief, are shut up or hid from him. The springs, indeed, may be nigh, as that was to Hagar, but their eyes are withheld that they cannot see them. Wherefore they cast themselves on God's sovereign pleasure, and say with Job, "'Though he slay us, yet will we trust in him;" we will not let him go. In ourselves we are lost, that is unquestionable. How the Lord will deal with us we know not; we see not our signs and tokens any more. Evidences of God's grace in us, or of his love and favour to us, are all out of sight. To a present special interest in Christ we are strangers; and we lie every moment at the door of eternity. What course shall we take? What way shall we proceed? If we abide at a distance from God, we shall assuredly perish. "Who ever hardened himself against him and prospered?" Nor is there the least relief to be had but from and by him, "for who can forgive sins but God?" We will, then, bring our guilty souls into his presence, and attend the pleasure of his grace; what he speaks concerning us, we will willingly submit to.' And this sometimes proves an anchor to a tossed soul, which, though it gives it not rest and peace, yet it saves it from the rock of despair. Here it abides until light do more and more break forth upon it.

ON THE MEDIATION OF CHRIST. Faith dealing about forgiveness does commonly eye, in a particular manner, its relation to the mediation and blood of Christ. So the apostle directs, 'If any man sin, we have an advocate with the Father, Jesus Christ the righteous: and he is the propitiation for our sins' (1 John 2:1–2). If any one has sinned, and is in depths and entanglements about it, what course shall he take, how shall he proceed, to obtain deliverance? Why, he must apply to God for pardon. But what shall he rely upon to encourage him in his so doing? Says the apostle, 'Consider by faith the atonement and propitiation made for sin by the blood of Christ, and that he is still pursuing the work of love to the suing out of pardon for us; and rest your soul thereon.' This, I say, most commonly is that which faith in the first place immediately fixes on.

ON THE PARDON OF SIN. Faith eyes actual pardon or condonation. So God proposes it as a motive to farther believing: 'I have blotted out, as a thick cloud, your transgressions, and, as a cloud, your sins: return to me; for I have redeemed you' (Isa. 44:22). Actual pardon of sin is proposed to faith as an encouragement to a full returning to God in all things (2 Sam. 23:5). And the like may be said of all the other particulars which we have insisted on. There is not any of them but will yield peculiar relief to a soul dealing with God about forgiveness, as having some one special concern or other of forgiveness inwrapped in them—only, as I said, they do it not exclusively, but are the special doors whereby believing enters into the whole. And these things must be spoken to afterward.

Let us now take along with us the end for which all these consider-ations have been insisted on. It is to manifest that a real discovery of gospel forgiveness is a matter of greater consequence and importance than at first proposal, it may be, it appeared to some to be. Who is not in hopes, in expectation of pardon? Who think not that they know well enough at least what it is, if they might but obtain it? But men may have general thoughts of impunity, and yet be far enough from any saving acquaintance with gospel mercy.

## Only Faith Discovers Forgiveness

For a close of this discourse, I shall only add what is included in that proposition which is the foundation of the whole—namely, that this discovery of forgiveness is and can be made to faith alone. The nature of it is such as that nothing else can discover it or receive it. No reasonings, no inquiries of the heart of man can reach to it. That guess or glimpse which the heathens had of old of somewhat so called, and which false worshippers have at present, is not the forgiveness we insist upon, but a mere imagination of their own hearts.

This the apostle informs us, 'The righteousness of God is' (in the gospel) 'revealed from faith to faith' (Rom. 1:17). Nothing but faith has any thing to do with it. It is that righteousness of God whereof he speaks that consists in the forgiveness of sins by the blood of Christ, declared in the gospel. And this is revealed from the faith of God in the promise to the faith of the believer—to him that mixes the promise with faith. And again more fully, 'Eye has not seen, nor ear heard, neither have entered into the heart of man, the things which God has prepared for them that love him' (1 Cor. 2:9). The ways whereby we may come to the knowledge of any thing are, by the seeing of the eye or hearing of the ear, or the reasonings and meditations of the heart; but now none of these will reach to the matter in hand—by none of these ways can we come to an acquaintance with the things of the gospel that are prepared for us in Christ. How, then, shall we obtain the knowledge of them? That he declares, 'God has revealed them to us by his Spirit' (v. 10). Now, it is faith only that receives the revelations of the Spirit; nothing else has to do with them.

To give evidence to this, we may consider that this great mystery, (a) is too deep, (b) is too great, for aught else to discover; and, (c) that nothing else but faith is suited to the making of this discovery.

### *It Is Unfathomable to Human Reason*

It is too deep and mysterious to be fathomed and reached by any thing else. Reason's line is too short to fathom the depths of the Father's love, of the blood of the Son, and the promises of the gospel built thereon, wherein forgiveness dwells. Men cannot by their rational considerations launch out into these deeps, nor draw water by them from these 'wells of salvation.' Reason stands by amazed, and cries, 'How can these things be?' It can but gather cockleshells, like him of old, at the shore of this ocean, a few criticisms upon the outward letter, and so bring an evil report upon the land, as did the spies. All it can do is but to hinder faith from venturing into it, crying, 'spare yourself; this attempt is vain, these things are impossible.' It is among the things that faith puts off and lays aside when it engages the soul into this great work. This, then, that it may come to a discovery of forgiveness, causes the soul to deny itself and all its own reasonings, and to give up itself to an infinite fullness of goodness and truth. Though it cannot go to the bottom of these depths, yet it enters into them, and finds rest in them. Nothing but faith is suited to rest, to satiate, and content itself in mysterious, bottomless, unsearchable depths. Being a soul-emptying, a reason-denying grace, the more it meets withal beyond its search and reach, the more satisfaction it finds. 'This is that which I looked for,' says faith, 'even for that which is infinite and unsearchable, when I know that there is abundantly more beyond me that I do not comprehend, than what I have attained to; for I know that nothing else will do good to the soul.' Now, this is that which really puzzles and overwhelms reason, rendering it useless. What it cannot compass, it will neglect or despise. It is either amazed and confounded, and dazzled like weak eyes at too great a light; or fortifying of itself by inbred pride and obstinacy, it concludes that this preaching of the cross, of forgiveness from the love of God, by the blood of Christ, is plain folly, a thing not for a wise man to take notice of or to trouble himself about: so it appeared to the wise Greeks of old (1 Cor. 1:23). Hence, when a soul is brought under the power of a real conviction of sin, so as that it would desirously be freed from the galling entanglements of it, it is then the hardest thing in the world to persuade such a soul of this forgiveness. Any thing appears more rational to it—any self-righteousness in this world, any purgatory hereafter.

The greatest part of the world of convinced persons have forsaken forgiveness on this account; masses, penances, merits, have appeared more eligible. Yea, men who have no other desire but to be forgiven do choose to close with any thing rather than forgiveness. If men do escape these rocks, and resolve that nothing but pardon will relieve them, yet it is impossible for them to receive it in the truth and power of it, if not enabled by faith thereunto. I speak not of men that take it up by hearsay, as a common report, but of those souls who find themselves really concerned to look after it. When they know it is their sole concern, all their hope and relief; when they know that they must perish everlastingly without it; and when it is declared to them in the words of truth and soberness—yet they cannot receive it. What is the reason of it? What staves off these hungry creatures from their proper food? Why, they have nothing to lead them into the mysterious depths of eternal love, of the blood of Christ, and promises of the gospel. How may we see poor deserted souls standing every day at the side of this pool, and yet not once venture themselves into it all their days!

### It Is Too Great to Comprehend

It is too great for any thing else to discover. Forgiveness is a thing chosen out of God from all eternity, to exalt and magnify the glory of his grace; and it will be made appear to all the world at the day of judgment to have been a great thing. When the soul comes in any measure to be made sensible of it, it finds it so great, so excellent and astonishable, that it sinks under the thoughts of it. It has dimensions, a length, breadth, depth, and height, that no line of the rational soul can take or measure. There is 'exceeding greatness' in it (Eph. 1:19). That is a great work which we have prescribed (Eph. 3:19), even 'to know the love of Christ, which passes knowledge.' Here, I suppose, reason will confess itself at a stand and an issue; to know that which passes knowledge is none of its work. 'It cannot be known,' says reason; and so ends the matter. But this is faith's proper work, even to know that which passes knowledge; to know that, in its power, virtue, sweetness, and efficacy, which cannot be thoroughly known in its nature and excellency; to have, by believing, all the ends of a full comprehension of that which cannot be fully comprehended. Hence it is said to be the ὑπόστασις of 'things not seen' (Heb. 11:1), their subsistence; though in themselves absent, yet faith gives them a present subsistence in the soul. So it knows things that pass knowledge; by mixing itself with them, it draws out and communicates their benefit to the soul.

From all which is evident what in the third place was proposed, of faith's being only suited to be the means of this discovery; so that I shall not need farther to insist thereon.

### The Benefit of Discovering Forgiveness in God

Fourthly, there yet remains a brief confirmation of the position I at first laid down and thus cleared, before I come to the improvement of the words, especially aimed at. I say, then, this discovery of forgiveness in God is a great support for a sin-entangled soul, although it has no special persuasion of its own particular interest therein. Somewhat is supposed in this assertion, and somewhat affirmed.

#### Assurance of Forgiveness Is Possible

It is supposed that there may be a gracious persuasion and assurance of faith in a man concerning his own particular interest in forgiveness. a man may, many do, believe it for themselves, so as not only to have the benefit of it but the comfort also. Generally, all the saints mentioned in Scripture had this assurance, unless it were in the case of depths, distresses, and desertions, such as that in this psalm. David expresses his confidence of the love and favour of God to his own soul hundreds of times; Paul does the same for himself: 'Christ loved me, and gave himself for me' (Gal. 2:20); 'There is laid up for me a crown of righteousness, which the Lord, the righteous judge, shall give me at that day' (2 Tim. 4:8). And that this boasting in the Lord and his grace was not an enclosure to himself he shows (Rom. 8:38–9).

Nothing can be more vain than what is usually pleaded to remove this sheet-anchor of the saints' consolation—namely, that no man's particular name is in the promise. It is not said to this or that man by name that his sins are forgiven him; but the matter is far otherwise. To think that it is necessary that the names whereby we are known among ourselves, and are distinguished here one from another, should be written in the promise, that we may believe in particular every child of God is in the promise, is a fond conceit. And believing makes it very legible to him. Yea, we find by experience that there is no need of argumentation in this case. The soul, by a direct act of faith, believes its own forgiveness, without making inferences or gathering conclusions; and may do so upon the proposition of it to be believed in the promise. But I will not digress from my work in hand, and, therefore, shall only observe one or two things upon the supposition laid down.

### Every Believer Should Labour for Assurance

It is the duty of every believer to labour after an assurance of a personal interest in forgiveness, and to be diligent in the cherishing and preservation of it when it is attained. The apostle exhorts us all to it, 'Let us draw near in full assurance of faith' (Heb. 10:22); that is, of our acceptance with God through forgiveness in the blood of Jesus. This he plainly discourses of; and this principle of our faith and confidence he would have us to hold fast to the end (Heb. 3:14). It is no small evil in believers not to be pressing after perfection in believing and obedience. Ofttimes some sinful indulgence to self, or the world, or sloth, is the cause of it.

Hence few come up to gospel assurance. But yet most of our privileges, and upon the matter all our comforts, depend on this one thing. a little by the way, to encourage to this duty, I shall desire you to consider both whence this assurance is produced and what it produces—what it is the fruit of, and what fruit it bears.

It is, in general, the product of a more plentiful communication of the Spirit than ordinary, as to a sense and participation of the choice fruits of the death of Christ, procured for those who are justified by their acceptance of the atonement. It flourishes not without his sealing, witnessing, establishing, and shedding abroad the love of God in our hearts (see Rom. 5:1–5). And what believer ought not to long for and press after the enjoyment of these things? Nay, to read of these things in the gospel, not experiencing them in our own hearts, and yet to sit down quietly on this side of them, without continual pressing after them, is to despise the blood of Christ, the Spirit of grace, and the whole work of God's love. If there are no such things, the gospel is not true; if there are, if we press not after them, we are despisers of the gospel. Surely he has not the Spirit who would not have more of him, all of him that is promised by Christ. These things are the 'hundredfold' that Christ has left us in the world to counterpoise our sorrows, troubles, and losses; and shall we be so foolish as to neglect our only abiding riches and treasures—in particular, as it is the product of an exercised, vigorous, active faith? That our faith should be such always, in every state and condition, I suppose it our duty to endeavour. Not only our comforts but our obedience also depends upon it. The more faith that is true and of the right kind, the more obedience; for all our obedience is the obedience of faith.

For its own fruit, and what it produces, they are the choicest actings of our souls towards God—as love, delight, rejoicing in the Lord, peace, joy, and consolation in ourselves, readiness to do or suffer, cheerfulness in so doing. If they grow not from this root, yet their flourishing wholly depends upon it; so that surely it is the duty of every believer to break through all difficulties in pressing after this particular assurance. The objections that persons raise against themselves in this case may be afterward considered.

### *Negligence and Sloth Deprives Us of Assurance*

In ordinary dispensations of God towards us, and dealings with us, it is mostly our own negligence and sloth that we come short of this assurance. It is true it depends in a peculiar manner on the sovereignty of God. He is as absolute in giving peace to believers as in giving grace to sinners. This takes place and may be proposed as a relief in times of trial and distress. He creates light and causes darkness, as he pleases. But yet, considering what promises are made to us, what encouragements are given us, what love and tenderness there is in God to receive us, I cannot but conclude that ordinarily the cause of our coming short of this assurance is where I have fixed it. And this is the first thing that is supposed in the foregoing assertion.

### FORGIVENESS WITHOUT ASSURANCE IS POSSIBLE

It is supposed that there is or may be a saving persuasion or discovery of forgiveness in God, where there is no assurance of any particular interest therein, or that our own sins in particular are pardoned. This is that which has a promise of gracious acceptance with God, and is therefore saving: 'Who is among you that fears the LORD, that obeys the voice of his servant, that walks in darkness, and has no light? Let him trust in the name of the LORD, and stay upon his God' (Isa. 50:10). Here is the fear of the Lord and obedience, with a blessed encouragement to rest in God and his all-sufficiency, yet no assurance nor light, but darkness, and that walked in or continued in for a long season; for he cannot walk in darkness, meet with nothing but darkness, without any beam or ray of light, as the words signify, who is persuaded of the love of God in the pardon of his sins. And yet the faith of such a one, and his obedience springing from it, have this gracious promise of acceptance with God. And innumerable testimonies to this purpose might be produced, and instances in great plenty. I shall only tender a little evidence to it, in one observation concerning the nature of faith, and one more about the proposal of the thing to be believed, or forgiveness.

### A Safe yet Sometimes Uncomfortable Pilgrimage

Faith is called, and is, a cleaving to the Lord: 'You that cleaved,' or adhered, 'to the LORD' (Deut. 4:4); that is, who believed, 'Cleaved,' or adhered, 'to the LORD your God' (Josh. 23:8). The same word is used also in the New Testament: 'He exhorted them all, that with purpose of heart they would cleave to the Lord' (Acts 11:23), or continue steadfast in believing. It is also often expressed by trusting in the Lord, rolling our burden, or casting our care upon him, by committing ourselves or our ways to him. Now, all this goes no farther than the soul's resignation of itself to God, to be dealt withal by him according to the tenor of the covenant of grace, ratified in the blood of Christ. This a soul cannot do, without a discovery of forgiveness in God; but this a soul may do, without a special assurance of his own interest therein. This faith, that thus adheres to God, that cleaves to him, will carry men to conclude that it is their duty and their wisdom to give up the disposal of their souls to God, and to cleave and adhere to him as revealed in Christ, waiting the pleasure of his will. It enables them to make Christ their choice; and will carry men to heaven safely, though it may be at some seasons not very comfortably.

### The Gospel's First Proposal

The revelation and discovery of forgiveness that is made in the gospel evidences the same truth. The first proposal of it or concerning it is not to any man that his sins are forgiven. No; but it is only that there is redemption and forgiveness of sins in Christ. So the apostle lays it down, 'Be it known to you therefore, men and brethren, that through this man is preached to you the forgiveness of sins: and by him all that believe are justified from all things, from which you could not be justified by the law of Moses.' All this may be believed without a man's assurance of his own personal interest in the things mentioned. Now, where they are believed with the faith the gospel requires, that faith is saving, and the root of gospel, acceptable obedience. The ransom, I say, the atonement by Christ, the fullness of the redemption that is in him, and so forgiveness in his blood for believers, from the good will, grace, and love of the Father, is the first gospel discovery that a sinner in a saving manner closes withal. Particular assurance arises or may arise afterward; and this also is supposed in the assertion.

### FORGIVENESS WITHOUT ASSURANCE NOT TO BE DESPISED

Secondly, that which is affirmed in it is, that a discovery of forgiveness in God, without any particular assurance of personal interest therein, is a great support to a sin-entangled soul. And let no man despise the day of this small thing; small in the eyes of some, and those good men also, as if it did not deserve the name of faith. Now, as has been made to appear, this discovery of forgiveness is the soul's persuasion, on gospel grounds, that however it be with him, and whatever his state and condition be, or is like to be, yet that God in his own nature is infinitely gracious, and that he has determined, in a sovereign act of his will from eternity, to be gracious to sinners, and that he has made way for the administration of forgiveness by the blood of his Son, according as he has abundantly manifested and declared in the promises of the gospel. 'However it be with me, yet thus it is with God; there is forgiveness with him.' This is the first thing that a soul in its depths rises up to; and it is a support for it, enabling it to all present duties until consolation come from above.

Thus has it been to and with the saints of old: 'Asshur shall not save us; we will not ride upon horses: neither will we say any more to the work of our hands, You are our gods: for in you the fatherless finds mercy' (Hos. 14:3). a solemn renunciation we have of all other helps, reliefs, or assistances, civil or religious, that are not God's; thereon a solemn resolution, in their great distress, of cleaving to God alone—both which are great and blessed effects of faith. What is the bottom and foundation of this blessed resolution?— namely, that proposition, 'In you the fatherless finds mercy;' that is, 'There is forgiveness with you for helpless sinners.' This lifted up their hearts in their depths, and supported them in waiting to the receiving of the blessed promises of mercy, pardon, grace, and holiness, which ensue in the next verses. Until they came home to them in their efficacy and effects, they made a life on this, 'In you the fatherless finds mercy.'

The state and condition of things seem to lie yet lower in that proposal we have, 'Rend your heart, and not your garments, and turn to the LORD your God: for he is gracious and merciful, slow to anger, and of great kindness, and repents him of the evil. Who knows if he will return and repent, and leave a blessing?' (Joel 2:13–14). That which is proposed to the faith of those here spoken to is, that the Lord is gracious and merciful—that there is forgiveness in him. The duty they are provoked to hereupon is gospel repentance. The assent to the proposition demanded, as to their own interest, amounts but to this, 'Who knows but that the LORD may return, and leave a blessing?' or, 'deal with us according to the manifestation he has made of himself, that he is merciful and gracious.' This is far enough from any comfortable persuasion of a particular interest in that grace, mercy, or pardon. But yet, says the prophet, 'Come but thus far, and here is a firm foundation of dealing with God about farther discoveries of himself in a way of grace and mercy.' When a soul sees but so much in God as to conclude, 'Well, who knows but that he may return, and have mercy upon me also?' it will support him, and give him an entrance into farther light.

The church in the Lamentations gives a sad account of her state and condition in this matter; for she makes that hard conclusion against herself, 'My strength and my hope is perished from the LORD …Also when I cry and shout, he shuts out my prayer' (Lam. 3:18, 8). So far is she from a comfortable persuasion of a particular interest in mercy and acceptance, that, under her pressures and in her temptations, she is ready positively to determine on the other side, namely, that she is rejected and cast off for ever. What course, then, shall she take? Shall she give over waiting on God, and say, 'There is no hope?' 'No,' says she, 'I will not take that way; for "It is good that a man should both hope and quietly wait for the salvation of God" (v. 26). But yet there seems small encouragement for her so to do if things be with her as was expressed. 'Things, indeed,' says she, 'are very sad with me. "My soul has them still in remembrance, and is bowed down in me" (v. 20); but yet somewhat "I recall to mind, and therefore have I hope" (v. 21) — "It is of the LORD's mercy that we are not consumed, because his compassions fail not" (v. 22). There is mercy and never-failing compassion in God, so that though my own present condition be full of darkness, and I see no deliverance, yet I purpose still to abide waiting on him. Who knows what those infinite stores and treasures of mercy and relief that are with him may at length afford to me?' And many instances of the like kind may be added.

### Benefits Accompanying Forgiveness without Assurance

We may observe, by the way, how far this relief extends itself, and what it enables the soul to.

SELF-RESIGNATION TO GOD'S GRACIOUS WILL. The soul is enabled thereby to resign itself to the disposal of sovereign grace in self-abhorrency, and a renunciation of all other ways of relief: 'He puts his mouth in the dust, if so be there may be hope' (Lam. 3:29). 'What God will,' is his language. Here he lies at his disposal, humble, broken, but abiding his pleasure. 'Though he slay me,' says Job, 'yet will I trust in him' (Job 13:15); —'It is all one how he deals with me; whatever be the event, I will abide cleaving to him. I will not think of any other way of extricating myself from my distress. I will neither fly like Jonah, nor hide like Adam, nor take any other course for deliverance.' Says the soul, '"God is a God that hides himself" from me (Isa. 45:15); "I walk in darkness and have no light" (Isa. 50:10). "My flesh fails and my heart falls" (Ps. 73:26); so that I am overwhelmed with trouble. "Mine iniquities have taken such hold on me that I cannot look up" (Ps. 40:12). "The LORD has forsaken me, and my Lord has forgotten me" (Isa. 49:14). Every day am I in dread and terror, and I am ready utterly to faint, and no relief can I obtain. What, then, shall I do? Shall I "curse God and die?" or cry, "This evil is of the LORD; why should I wait for him any longer?" Shall I take the course of the world, and, seeing it will be no better, be wholly regardless of my latter end? No; I know, whatever my lot and portion be, that there is forgiveness with God. This and that poor man trusted in him; they cried to him, and were delivered. So did David in his greatest distress; he encouraged his heart in the Lord his God (2 Sam. 15:25–6). It is good for me to cast myself into his arms. It may be he will frown; it may be he is wroth still: but all is one, this way I will go. As it seems good to him to deal with me, so let it be.' And unspeakable are the advantages which a soul obtains by this self-resignation, which the faith treated of will infallibly produce.

EXPECTANT WAITING FOR THE LORD. It extends itself to a resolution of waiting in the condition wherein the soul is. This the church comes to, 'It is good that a man should both hope and quietly wait for the salvation of the LORD' (Lam. 3:26) —'I will not give over my expectation, I will not make haste nor limit God; but I will lie at his feet until his own appointed time of mercy shall come.' Expectation and quietness make up waiting. These the soul attains to with this support. It looks upwards, 'as a servant that looks to the hands of his master,' still fixed on God, to see what he will do, to hear what he will speak concerning him; missing no season, no opportunity wherein any discovery of the will of God may be made to him. And this he does in quietness, without repining or murmuring, turning all his complaints against himself and his own vileness, that has cut him short from a participation of that fullness of love and grace which is with God. That this effect also attends this faith will fully appear in the close of the psalm.

DILIGENT USE OF MEANS. It supports to waiting in the use of all means for the attainment of a sense of forgiveness, and so has its effect in the whole course of our obedience. 'There is forgiveness with you, that you may be feared.' To fear the Lord, is an expression comprehensive of his whole worship and all our duty. 'This I am encouraged to, in my depths,' says the psalmist, 'because there is forgiveness with you. I will abide in all duties, in all the ways of your worship, wherein you may be found.' And however it be for a while, the latter end of that soul, who thus abides with God, will be peace.

### Discovering Forgiveness in God Nurtures Assurance

Let us, then, next see by what ways and means it yields this support.

#### It Begets Love for God

It begets a liking of God in the soul, and consequently some love to him. The soul apprehends God as one infinitely to be desired and delighted in by those who have a share in forgiveness. It cannot but consider him as good and gracious, however its own estate be hazardous. 'Yet God is good to Israel, to such as are of a clean heart. As for me, my feet were almost gone; my steps had well nigh slipped' (Ps. 73:1–2) —'However the state stands with me, yet I know that God is good, good to Israel; and therewith shall I support myself.' When once this ground is got upon the soul, that it considers God in Christ as one to be delighted in and loved, great and blessed effects will ensue:

1. Self-abhorrency and condemnation, with resignation of all to God, and permanency therein, do certainly attend it.
2. Still, somewhat or other in God will be brought to mind to relieve it under faintings, some new springs of hope will be every day opened.
3. And the soul will be insensibly wrought upon to delight itself in dealing with God.

Though, in its own particular, it meets with frownings, chidings, and repulses, yet this still relieves him, that God is so as has been declared; so that he says, 'However it be, yet God is good; and it is good for me to wait upon him.' Without this discovery the soul likes not God, and whatever it does with respect to him, it is because it dares do no otherwise, being overawed with his terror and greatness; and such obedience God may have from devils.

### It Clears Obstacles in the Way

It removes sundry overwhelming difficulties that lie in the soul's way before it close with this discovery of forgiveness.

DREAD OF GOD. It takes away all these hinderances that were formerly insisted on from the greatness, holiness, and severity of God, the inexorableness and strictness of the law, and the natural actings of conscience rising up against all hopes of forgiveness. All these are by this faith removed, and taken out of the way. Where this faith is, it discovers not only forgiveness, as has been showed, but also the true nature of gospel forgiveness; it reveals it as flowing from the gracious heart of the Father, through the blood of the Son. Now, this propitiation in the blood of the Son removes all these difficulties, even antecedently to our special sense of an interest therein. It shows how all the properties of God may be exalted and the law fulfilled, and yet forgiveness given out to sinners. And herein lies no small advantage to a soul in its approaches to God. All those dreadful apprehensions of God, which were wont to beset him in the first thoughts of coming to him, are now taken out of the way, so that he can quietly apply himself to his own particular concerns before him.

THE GREATNESS OF SIN. In particular, it removes the overwhelming consideration of the unspeakable greatness of sin. This presses the soul to death, when once the heart is possessed with it. Were not their sins so great, such as no heart can imagine or tongue declare, it might possibly be well with them, say distressed sinners. They are not so troubled that they are sinners, as that they are great sinners; not that these and those sins they are guilty of, but that they are great sins, attended with fearful aggravations. Otherwise they could deal well enough with them. Now, though this discovery free men not from the entanglement of their sins as theirs, yet it does from the whole entanglement of their sins as great and many. This consideration may be abstracted. The soul sees enough in God to forgive great sins, though it does not as yet to forgive his sins. That great sins shall be pardoned, this discovery puts out of question. Whether his sins shall be pardoned is now all the inquiry. Whatever any faith can do, that this faith will do, unless it be the making of particular application of the things believed to itself. The soul, then, can no longer justly be troubled about the greatness of sin; the infiniteness of forgiveness that he sees in God will relieve him against it. All that remains is, that it is his own sin about which he has to deal; whereof afterwards. These and the like difficulties are removed by it.

## It Encourages Us to Live as Christians

It gives some life in and encouragement to duty. And that, first, to duty as duty. Eyeing God by faith, in such a fullness of grace, the soul cannot but be encouraged to meet him in every way of duty, and to lay hold upon him thereby—every way leading to him, as leading to him, must be well liked and approved of. And, secondly, to all duties. And herein lies no small advantage. God is oftentimes found in duties, but in what, or of what kind, he will be found of any one in particular, is uncertain. This faith puts the soul on all: so it did the spouse in the parallel to that in hand (S. of S. 3:2–4). Now, what support may be hence obtained is easily apprehended—support not from them or by them, but in them, as the means of intercourse between God and the soul.

### SUPPORTS TO SPIRITUAL LIFE

From these effects of this discovery of forgiveness in God three things will ensue, which are sufficient to maintain the spiritual life of the soul.

## *Resolve to Abide with God*

A resolution to abide with God, and to commit all to him. This the word, as was observed, teaches us: 'There is forgiveness with you, and therefore you shall be feared'—'Because this I found, this I am persuaded of, therefore I will abide with him in the way of his fear and worship.' This our Saviour calls to, '"Abide in me;" except you do so you can bear no fruit' (John 15:4). So the Lord, representing his taking of the church to himself under the type of the prophet's taking an adulteress in vision, does it on these terms, 'You shall abide for me many days; you shall not play the harlot, and you shall not be for another man: so will I also be for you' (Hos. 3:3). Now, this abiding with God intimates two things: (a) Oppositions, solicitations, and temptations to the contrary. (b) Forbearing to make any other choice, as to that end for which we abide with God.

AGAINST OPPOSITION. It argues oppositions. To abide, to be stable and permanent, is to be so against oppositions. Many discouragements are ready to rise up in the soul against it: in fears especially that it shall not hold out, that it shall be rejected at last, that all is naught and hypocritical with it, that it shall not be forgiven, that God indeed regards it not, and therefore it may well enough give over its hopes, which seems often as the giving up of the ghost; [these] will assault it. Again, oppositions arise from corruptions and temptations to sin, contrary to the life of faith; and these often proceed to a high degree of prevalency, so that the guilt contracted upon them is ready to cast the soul quite out of all expectation of mercy. 'I shall one day perish by these means,' says the soul, 'if I am not already lost.'

But now, where faith has made this discovery of forgiveness, the soul will abide with God against all these discouragements and oppositions. It will not leave him, it will not give over waiting for him. So David expresses the matter in the instance of himself: 'But as for me, my feet were almost gone; my steps had well-nigh slipped' (Ps. 73:2); and, 'Verily I have cleansed my heart in vain' (v. 13). But yet, after all his conflicts, this at last he comes to,

'Though "my flesh and my heart fails" (v. 26), yet "It is good for me to draw near to God" (v. 28)—I will yet abide with God; I will not let go his fear nor my profession. Although I walk weakly, lamely, unevenly, yet I will still follow after him.' As it was with the disciples, when many, upon a strong temptation, went back from Christ, and walked no more with him, 'Jesus said to them, Will you also go away?' to which Peter replies, in the name of the rest of them, 'Lord, to whom shall we go? You have the words of eternal life' (John 6:66–8)—'It is thus and thus with me,' says the soul; 'I am tossed and afflicted, and not comforted; little life, little strength, real guilt, many sins, and much disconsolation.' 'What then?' says God by his word; 'will you also go away?' 'No,' says the soul; 'there is forgiveness with you; you have the words of eternal life, and therefore I will abide with you.'

REJECTING ANY OTHER CHOICE. This abiding with God argues a forbearance of any other choice. Whilst the soul is in this condition, having not attained any evidences of its own special interest in forgiveness, many lovers will be soliciting of it to play the harlot by taking them into its embraces. Both self-righteousness and sin will be very importunate in this matter. The former tenders itself as exceeding useful to give the soul some help, assistance, and support in its condition. 'Samuel does not come,' says Saul, 'and the Philistines invade me; I will venture and offer sacrifice myself, contrary to the law.' The promise does not come to the soul for its particular relief; it has no evidence as to an especial interest in forgiveness. Temptation invades the mind: 'Try yourself,' says it, 'to take relief in somewhat of your own providing.' And this is to play the harlot from God. To this purpose self-righteousness variously disguises itself, like the wife of Jeroboam when she went to the prophet. Sometimes it appears as duty, sometimes as signs and tokens; but its end is to get somewhat of the faith and trust of the soul to be fixed upon it. But when the soul has indeed a discovery of forgiveness, it will not give ear to these solicitations. 'No,' says it; 'I see such a beauty, such an excellency, such a desirableness and suitableness to my wants and condition, in that forgiveness that is with God, that I am resolved to abide in the gospel desire and expectation of it all the days of my life; here my choice is fixed, and I will not alter.' And this resolution gives glory to the grace of God. When the soul, without an evidence of an interest in it, yet prefers it above that which, with many reasonings and pretences, offers itself as a present relief to it, hereby is God glorified, and Christ exalted, and the spiritual life of the soul secured.

### A Resolve to Wait on God for Consolation

This discovery of forgiveness in God, with the effects of it before mentioned, will produce a resolution of waiting on God for peace and consolation in his own time and way. 'He that believes shall not make haste' (Isa. 28:16). Not make haste, to what? Not to the enjoyment of the thing believed. Haste argues precipitation and impatience; this the soul that has this discovery is freed from, resolving to wait the time of God's appointment for peace and consolation. God, speaking of his accomplishment of his promises, says, 'I the LORD will hasten it' (Isa. 9:22). Well, then, if God will hasten it, may not we hasten to it? 'Nay,' says he, 'I will hasten it, but in its time.' All oppositions and impediments considered, it shall be hastened, but in its time, its due time, its appointed time. And this the soul is to wait for; and so it will. As when Jacob had seen the beauty of Rachel, and loved her, he was contented to wait seven years for the enjoyment of her to be his wife, and thought no time long, no toil too hard, that he might obtain her; so the soul having discovered the beauty and excellency of forgiveness as it is with God, as it is in his gracious heart, in his eternal purpose, in the blood of Christ, in the promise of the gospel, is resolved to wait quietly and patiently for the time wherein God will clear up to it

*Even one experimental embrace of [forgiveness], even at the hour of death, does well deserve the waiting and obedience of the whole course of a man's life.*

its own personal interest therein. Even one experimental embrace of it, even at the hour of death, does well deserve the waiting and obedience of the whole course of a man's life.

And this the psalmist manifests to have been the effect produced in his heart and spirit; for upon this discovery of forgiveness in God, he resolved both to wait upon him himself, and encourages others so to do.

### Preparation for Consolation

This prepares the soul for the receiving of that consolation and deliverance out of its pressures, by an evidence of a special interest in forgiveness, which it waits for.

LOOKING FOR GOOD NEWS FROM A FAR COUNTRY. For this makes men to hearken after it. It makes the soul like the merchant who has great riches, all his wealth, in a far country, which he is endeavouring to bring home safe to him. If they come, he is well provided for; if they miscarry, he is lost and undone. This makes him hearken after tidings that they are safe there; and, as Solomon says, 'Good news,' in this case, 'from a far country, is as cold waters to a thirsty soul' (Prov. 25:25) — full of refreshment. Though he cannot look upon them as his own yet absolutely, because he has them not in possession, he is glad they are safe there. So is it with the soul. These riches that it so values are as to its apprehensions in a far country. So is the promise, that 'he shall behold the land that is very far off' (Isa. 33:17). He is glad to hear news that they are safe, to hear forgiveness preached, and the promises insisted on, though he cannot as yet look upon them as his own. The merchant rests not here, but he hearkens with much solicitousness after the things that should bring home his riches, especially if they have in them his all. Hence such ships are called ships of desire (Job 9:26). Such a man greatly desires the speeding of them to their port. He considers the wind and the weather, all the occasions, and inconveniences, and dangers of the way; and blame him not—his all is at stake. The soul does so in like manner: it hearkens after all the ways and means whereby this forgiveness may be particularly brought home to it; is afraid of sin and of temptation, glad to find a fresh gale of the Spirit of grace, hoping that it may bring in his return from the land of promise. This prepares the heart for a spiritual sense of it when it is revealed.

VALUING THE DESIRED GIFT. It so prepares the soul, by giving it a due valuation of the grace and mercy desired. The merchantman in the gospel was not prepared to enjoy the pearl himself, until it was discovered to him to be of great price; then he knew how to purchase it, procure it, and keep it. The soul having, by this acting of faith, upon the discovery of forgiveness insisted on, come to find that the pearl hid in the field is indeed precious, is both stirred up to seek after possession of it, and to give it its due. Says such a soul, 'How excellent, how precious is this forgiveness that is with God! Blessed, yea, ever blessed, are they who are made partakers of it! What a life of joy, rest, peace, and consolation do they lead! Had I but their evidence of an interest in it, and the spiritual consolation that ensues thereon, how would I despise the world and all the temptations of Satan, and rejoice in the Lord in every condition!' And this apprehension of grace also exceedingly prepares and fits the soul for a receiving of a blessed sense of it, so as that God may have glory thereby.

SEEING THE GLORY OF FORGIVENESS. It fits the soul, by giving a right understanding of it, of its nature, its causes, and effects. At the first the soul goes no farther but to look after impunity, or freedom from punishment, any way. 'What shall I do to be saved?' is the utmost it aims at. 'Who shall deliver me? How shall I escape?' And it would be contented to escape any way—by the law, or the gospel, all is one, so it may escape. But upon this discovery of forgiveness treated of, which is made by faith of adherence to God, a man plainly sees the nature of it, and that it is so excellent that it is to be desired for its own sake. Indeed, when a soul is brought under trouble for sin, it knows not well what it would have. It has an uneasiness or disquietment that it would be freed from—a dread of some evil condition that it would avoid. But now the soul can tell what it desires, what it aims at, as well as what it would be freed from. It would have an interest in eternal love;

have the gracious kindness of the heart of God turned towards itself—a sense of the everlasting purpose of his will shed abroad in his heart; have an especial interest in the precious blood of the Son of God, whereby atonement is made for him; and that all these things be testified to his conscience in a word of promise mixed with faith. These things he came for; this way alone he would be saved, and no other. It sees such a glory of wisdom, love, and grace in forgiveness, such an exaltation of the love of Christ in all his offices, in all his undertaking, especially in his death, sacrifice, and blood-shedding, whereby he procured or made reconciliation for us, that it exceedingly longs after the participation of them.

All these things, in their several degrees, will this discovery of forgiveness in God, without an evidence of an especial interest therein, produce. And these will assuredly maintain the spiritual life of the soul, and keep it up to such an obedience as shall be accepted of God in Christ. Darkness, sorrow, storms, they in whom it is may meet withal; but their eternal condition is secured in the covenant of God—their souls are bound up in the bundle of life.

## The True Concept of Believing

From what has been spoken, we may make some inferences in our passage concerning the true notion of believing.

### Many Pretend to Believe

These effects ascribed to this faith of forgiveness in God, and always produced by it, make it evident that the most of them who pretend to it, who pretend to believe that there is forgiveness with God, do indeed believe no such thing. Although I shall, on set purpose, afterward evince this, yet I cannot here utterly pass it by. I shall, then, only demand of them who are so forward in the profession of this faith that they think it almost impossible that any one should not believe it, what effects it has produced in them, and whether they have been by it enabled to the performance of the duties before mentioned? I fear with many, things on the account of their pretended faith are quite otherwise. They love sin the more for it, and God never the better. Supposing that a few barren words will issue the controversy about their sins, they become insensibly to have slight thoughts of sin and of God also. This persuasion is not of him that calls us. Poor souls, your faith is the devil's greatest engine for your ruin; the highest contempt of God, and Christ, and forgiveness also, that you can be guilty of; a means to let you down quietly into hell; the Pharisees' Moses, trusted in, and [yet] will condemn you. As none is saved but by faith, so you, if it were not for your faith (as you call it), might possibly be saved. If a man's gold prove counterfeit, his jewels painted glass, his silver lead or dross, he will not only be found poor when he comes to be tried, and want the benefit of riches, but have withal a fearful aggravation of his poverty by his disappointment and surprisal. If a man's faith, which should be more precious than gold, be found rotten and corrupt, if his light be darkness, how vile is that faith, how great is that darkness! Such, it is evident, will the faith of too many be found in this business.

### MANY HAVE NOT LAID THE FOUNDATION

The work we are carrying on is the raising of a sin-entangled soul out of its depths; and this we have spoken to is that which must give him his first relief. Commonly, when souls are in distress, that which they look after is consolation. What is it that they intend thereby? That they may have assurance that their sins are forgiven them, and so be freed from their present perplexities. What is the issue? Some of them continue complaining all their days, and never come to rest or peace, so far do they fall short of consolation and joy; and some are utterly discouraged from attempting any progress in the ways of God. What is the reason hereof? Is it not that they would fain be finishing their building, when they have not laid the foundation? They have not yet made thorough work in believing forgiveness with God, and they would immediately be at assurance in themselves. Now, God delights not in such a frame of spirit:

1. It is selfish. The great design of faith is to 'give glory to God' (Rom. 4:20). The end of God's giving out forgiveness is the 'praise of his glorious grace' (Eph. 1:6). But let a soul in this frame have peace in itself, it is very little solicitous about giving glory to God. He cries like Rachel, 'Give me children, or I die'—'Give me peace, or I perish.' That God may be honoured, and the forgiveness he seeks after be rendered glorious, it is cared for in the second place, if at all. This selfish earnestness, at first to be thrusting our hand in the side of Christ, is that which he will pardon in many, but accepts in none.

2. It is impatient. Men do thus deport themselves because they will not wait. They do not care for standing afar off for any season with the publican. They love not to submit their souls to lie at the foot of God, to give him the glow of his goodness, mercy, wisdom, and love, in the disposal of them and their concerns. This waiting comprises the universal subjection of the soul to God, with a resolved judgment that it is meet and right that we, and all we desire and aim at, should be at his sovereign disposal. This gives glory to God—a duty which the impatience of these poor souls will not admit them to the performance of. And both these arise:

3. From weakness. It is weak. It is weakness in any condition, that makes men restless and weary. The state of adherence is as safe a condition as the state of assurance; only, it has more combats and wrestling attending it. It is not, then, fear of the event, but weakness and weariness of the combat, that makes men anxiously solicitous about a deliverance from that state before they are well entered into it.

Let, then, the sin-entangled soul remember always this way, method, and order of the gospel, that we have under consideration. First, exercise faith on forgiveness in God; and when the soul is fixed therein, it will have a ground and foundation whereon it may stand securely in making application of it to itself. Drive this principle, in the first place, to a stable issue upon gospel evidences, answer the objections that lie against it, and then you may proceed.

In believing, the soul makes a conquest upon Satan's territories. Do, then, as they do who are entering on an enemy's country—secure the passages, fortify the strongholds as you go on, that you be not cut off in your progress. Be not as a ship at sea, which passes on, and is no more possessed or master of the water it has gone through than of that whereunto it is not yet arrived. But so it is with a soul that fixes not on these foundation principles: he presses forwards, and the ground crumbles away under his feet, and so he wilders away all his days in uncertainties. Would men but lay this principle well in their souls, and secure it against assaults, they might proceed, though not with so much speed as some do, yet with more safety. Some pretend at once to fall into full assurance; I wish it prove not a broad presumption in the most. It is to no purpose for him to strive to fly who cannot yet go—to labour to come to assurance in himself who never well believed forgiveness in God.

4

## 'THERE IS FORGIVENESS'—THE EVIDENCE

---

Now, that we may be enabled to fix this persuasion against all opposition, that which in the next place I shall do is, to give out such unquestionable evidences of this gospel truth as the soul may safely build and rest upon; and these contain the confirmation of the principal proposition before laid down.

### The Wrong Place to Look for Proof

First, the things that are spoken or to be known of God are of two sorts.

### The Light of Nature

Natural and necessary; such as are his essential properties, or the attributes of his nature, his goodness, holiness, righteousness, omnipotence, eternity, and the like. These are called, τὸ γνωστὸν τοῦ θεοῦ (Rom. 1:19)—'That which may be known of God.' And there are two ways, as the apostle there declares, whereby that which he there intimates of God may be known — (1.) By the inbred light of nature: φανερόν ἐστιν ἐν αὐτοῖς (v. 19) — 'It is manifest in themselves,' in their own hearts; they are taught it by the common conceptions and presumptions which they have of God by the light of nature. From hence do all mankind know concerning God that he is, that he is eternal, infinitely powerful, good, righteous, holy, omnipotent. There needs no special revelation of these things, that men may know them. That, indeed, they may be known savingly, there is; and, therefore, they that know these things by nature do also believe them on revelation: 'He that comes to God must believe that he is, and that he is a rewarder' (Heb. 11:6), though men know God by the light of nature, yet they cannot come to God by that knowledge. (2.) These essential properties of the nature of God are revealed by his works. So the apostle in the same place, 'The invisible things of God from the creation of the world are clearly seen, being understood by the things that are made, even his eternal power and Godhead' (Rom. 1:20, see also Ps. 19:1–3). And this is the first sort of things that may be known of God.

### Inbred Notions of the Acts of God

There are the free acts of his will and power, or his free, eternal purposes, with the temporal dispensations that flow from them. Now, of this sort is the forgiveness that we are inquiring after. It is not a property of the nature of God, but an act of his will and a work of his grace. Although it has its rise and spring in the infinite goodness of his nature, yet it proceeds from him, and is not exercised but by an absolute, free, and sovereign act of his will. Now, there is nothing of God or with him of this sort that can be any ways known but only by especial revelation.

### In the Heart of Man

There is no inbred notion of the acts of God's will in the heart of man; which is the first way whereby we come to the knowledge of any thing of God. Forgiveness is not revealed by the light of nature. Flesh and blood, which nature is, declares it not; by that means 'no man has seen God at any time' (John 1:18)—that is, as a God of mercy and pardon, as the Son reveals him. Adam had an intimate acquaintance, according to the limited capacity of a creature, with the properties and excellencies of the nature of God. It was implanted in his heart, as indispensably necessary to that natural worship which, by the law of his creation, he was to perform. But when he had sinned, it is evident that he had not the least apprehension that there was forgiveness with God. Such a thought would have laid a foundation of some farther treaty with God about his condition. But he had no other design but of flying and hiding himself (Gen. 3:10); so declaring that he was utterly ignorant of any such thing as pardoning mercy. Such, and no other, are all the first or purely natural conceptions of sinners—namely, that it is δικαίωμα τοῦ θεοῦ, 'the judgment of God' (Rom. 1:32), that sin is to be punished with death. It is true, these conceptions in many are stifled by rumours, reports, traditions, that it may be otherwise; but all these are far enough from that revelation of forgiveness which we are inquiring after.

### In the Works of Creation

The consideration of the works of God's creation will not help a man to this knowledge, that there is forgiveness with God. The apostle tells us what it is of God that his works reveal, 'even his eternal power and Godhead' (Rom. 1:20), or the essential properties of his nature, but no more; not any of the purposes of his grace, not any of the free acts of his will, not pardon and forgiveness. Besides, God made all things in such an estate and condition—namely, of rectitude, integrity, and uprightness (Eccles. 7:29)—that it was impossible they should have any respect to sin, which is the corruption of all, or to the pardon of it, which is their restitution, whereof they stood in no need. There being no such thing in the world as a sin, nor any such thing supposed to be, when all things were made of nothing, how could any thing declare or reveal the forgiveness of it?

## *In the Works of God's Providence*

No works of God's providence can make this discovery. God has, indeed, borne testimony to himself and his goodness in all ages, from the foundation of the world, in the works of his providence: so Acts 14:15–17:

> We preach to you that you should turn from these vanities to the living God, which made heaven, and earth, and the sea, and all things that are therein: who in times past suffered all nations to walk in their own ways. Nevertheless he left not himself without witness, in that he did good, and gave us rain from heaven, and fruitful seasons, filling our hearts with food and gladness.

Οὐκ ἀμάρτυρον ἑαυτὸν ἀφῆκεν—'He left not himself without witness;' that is, by the works of his providence, there recounted, he thus far bare testimony to himself, that he is, and is good, and does good, and rules the world; so that they were utterly inexcusable, who, taking no notice of these works of his, nor the fruits of his goodness, which they lived upon, turned away after τὰ μάταια, 'vain things,' as the apostle there calls the idols of the Gentiles. But yet these things did not discover pardon and forgiveness; for still God suffered them to go on in their own ways, and winked at their ignorance. So again, Acts 17:23–7:

> Whom you ignorantly worship, him declare I to you. God that made the world and all things therein, seeing that he is Lord of heaven and earth, dwells not in temples made with hands; neither is worshipped with men's hands, as though he needed any thing, seeing he gives to all life, and breath, and all things; and has made of one blood all nations of men for to dwell on all the face of the earth (where, by the way, there is an allusion to that of Gen. 11:8, 'The LORD scattered them abroad upon the face of all the earth') and has determined the times before appointed, and the bounds of their habitation; that they should seek the Lord, if haply they might feel after him, and find him, though he be not far from every one of us.

By arguments taken from the works of God, both of creation and providence, the apostle proves the being and the properties of God; yea, he lets them know with whom he had to do, that God designed by his works so far to reveal himself to them as the true and living God, the maker and governor of all things, as that they ought to have inquired more diligently after him, and not to look on him alone as the 'unknown God' who alone might be known, all their idols being vain and nothing. But of the discovery of pardon and forgiveness in God by these ways and means he speaks not; yea, he plainly shows that this was not done thereby: for the great call to saving repentance is by the revelation of forgiveness. But now, by these works of his providence, God called not the Gentiles to saving repentance. No; says he, 'He suffered them to walk still in their own ways' (Acts 14:16), 'and winked at the times of their ignorance; but now'—that is, by the word of the gospel—'commands them to repent' (Acts 17:30).

## GOD'S DEALING WITH SINNING ANGELS

Secondly, whereas there had been one signal act of God's providence about sin, when man first fell into the snares of it, it was so far from the revealing forgiveness in God, that it rather severely intimated the contrary. This was God's dealing with sinning angels. The angels were the first sinners, and God dealt first with them about sin. And what was his dealing with them the Holy Ghost tells us, Ἀγγέλων ἁμαρτησάντων οὐκ ἐφείσατο- 'He spared not the sinning angels' (2 Pet. 2:4). 'He spared them not;' it is the same word which he uses where he speaks of laying all our iniquities on Christ, he undergoing the punishment due to them: Οὐκ ἐφείσατο—'He spared him not' (Rom. 8:32); that is, he laid on him the full punishment that by the curse and sanction of the law was due to sin. So he dealt with the angels that sinned: 'He spared them not,' but inflicted on them the punishment due to sin, shutting them up under chains of darkness for the judgment of the great day. Hitherto, then, God keeps all thoughts of forgiveness in his own eternal bosom; there is not so much as the least dawning of it upon the world. And this was at first no small prejudice against any thoughts of forgiveness. The world is made; sin enters by the most glorious part of the creation, whose recovery by pardon might seem to be more desirable, but not the least appearance of it is discovered. Thus it was 'from the beginning of the world hid in God' (Eph. 3:9).

### The Law God Gave to Adam

Thirdly, God gave to man a law of obedience immediately upon his creation; yea, for the main of it, he implanted it in him by and in his creation. This law it was supposed that man might transgress. The very nature of a law prescribed to free agents, attended with threatenings and promises of reward, requires that supposition. Now, there was not annexed to this law, or revealed with it, the least intimation of pardon to be obtained if transgression should ensue. We have this law, 'In the day you eat you shall surely die' (Gen. 2:17)—'Dying you shall die;' or 'bring upon yourself assuredly the guilt of death temporal and eternal.' There God leaves the sinner, under the power of that commination. Of forgiveness or pardoning mercy there is not the least intimation. To this very day that law, which was then the whole rule of life and acceptance with God, knows no such thing. 'Dying you shall die, O sinner,' is the precise and final voice of it.

### Preliminary Considerations

From these previous considerations, added to what was formerly spoken, some things preparatory to the ensuing discourse may be inferred.

### Forgiveness Is a Rare Discovery

That it is a great and rare thing to have forgiveness in God discovered to a sinful soul. a thing it is that, as has been showed, conscience and law, with the inbred notions that are in the heart of man about God's holiness and vindictive justice, do lie against; a matter whereof we have no natural presumption, whereof there is no common notion in the mind of man; a thing which no consideration of the works of God, either of creation or providence, will reveal, and which the great instance of God's dealing with sinning angels renders deep, admirable, and mysterious. Men who have common and slight thoughts of God, of themselves, of sin, of obedience, of the judgment to come, of eternity—that feed upon the ashes of rumours, reports, hearsays, traditions, without looking into the reality of things—may and do take this to be an ordinary and acknowledged truth, easy to be entertained, which upon the matter no man disbelieves. But convinced sinners, who make a trial of these things as running into eternity, have other thoughts of them. And as to that which, it is pretended, every one believes, we have great cause to cry out, 'Lord, who has believed our report? to whom has the arm of the Lord been revealed?'

### The Foundation of Our Communion with God

That the discovery of forgiveness in God, being a matter of so great difficulty, is a thing precious and excellent, as being the foundation of all our communion with God here, and of all undeceiving expectation of our enjoyment of him hereafter. It is a pure gospel truth, that has neither shadow, footstep, nor intimation elsewhere. The whole creation has not the least obscure impression of it left thereon.

### A Matter for Serious and Diligent Enquiry

It is undoubtedly greatly incumbent on us to inquire diligently, as the prophets did of old, into this salvation; to consider what sure evidences faith has of it, such as will not, as cannot fail us. To be slight and common in this matter, to take it up at random, is an argument of an unsound, rotten heart. He that is not serious in his inquiry into the revelation of this matter, is serious in nothing wherein God or his soul is concerned. The Holy Ghost knows what our frame of heart is, and how slow we are to receive this blessed truth in a gracious, saving manner. Therefore does he confirm it to us with such weighty considerations as, 'God, willing more abundantly to shew to the heirs of promise the immutability of his counsel, confirmed it by an oath: that by two immutable things, in which it was impossible for God to lie, we might have strong consolation' (Heb. 6:17–18). It is of forgiveness of sin that the apostle treats; as has been made evident by the description of it before given. Now, to give evidence hereunto, and to beget a belief of it in us, he first engages a property of God's nature in that business. He with whom we deal is ἀψευδὴς (as Tit. 1:2), the God that cannot lie, that cannot deceive or be deceived: it is impossible it should be so with him. Now, as this extends itself in general to all the words and works of God, so there is peculiarly in this, whereof he treats, τὸ ἀμετάθετον τῆς βουλῆς—an especial 'immutability of his counsel' (Heb. 6:17). Men may think that although there be words spoken about forgiveness, yet it is possible it may be otherwise.' 'No,' says the apostle; 'it is spoken by God, and it is impossible he should lie.' Yea, but upon the manifold provocations of sinners, he may change his mind and thoughts therein. 'No,' says the apostle; 'there is a peculiar immutability in his counsel concerning the execution of this thing: there can be no change in it.' But how does this appear, that indeed this is the counsel of his will? 'Why,' says he, 'he has declared it by his word, and that given in a way of promise: which, as in its own nature it is suited to raise an expectation in him or them to whom it is made or given, so it requires exact faithfulness in the discharge and performance of it which God on his part will assuredly answer. But neither is this all; but that no place might be left for any cavilling objection in this matter, ἐμεσίτευσεν ὅρκῳ, "he interposed himself by an oath".' Thus we have this truth deduced from the veracity of God's nature, one of his essential excellencies; established in the immutable purpose of his will; brought forth by a word of promise; and confirmed by God's interposing himself against all occasions of exception (so to put an end to all strife about it) by an oath, swearing by himself that so it should be. I have mentioned this only to show what weight the Holy Ghost lays upon the delivery of this great truth, and thence how deeply it concerns us to inquire diligently into it and after the grounds and evidences which may be tendered of it; which, among others, are these that follow:

## HOW GOD DEALT WITH OUR FIRST PARENTS

The first discovery of forgiveness in God (and which I place as the first evidence of it) was made in his dealing with our first parents after their shameful sin and fall. Now, to make it appear that this is an evidence that carries along with it a great conviction, and is such as faith may securely rest upon and close withal, the ensuing observations are to be considered.

## THE FIRST SIN—THE GREATEST SIN

The first sin in the world was, on many accounts, the greatest sin that ever was in the world. It was the sin, as it were, of human nature, wherein there was a conspiracy of all individuals: '*Omnes eramus unus ille homo*'—'In that one man, or that one sin, we all sinned' (Rom. 5:12). It left not God one subject, as to moral obedience, on the earth, nor the least ground for any such to be to eternity. When the angels sinned, the whole race or kind did not prevaricate. 'Thousand thousands' of them, and 'ten thousand times ten thousand,' continued in their obedience (Dan. 7:10). But here all and every individual of mankind (He only excepted which was not then in Adam)were embarked in the same crime and guilt. Besides, it disturbed the government of God in and over the whole creation. God had made all things, in number, weight, and measure, in order and beauty; pronouncing himself concerning his whole work that it was טוֹב מְאֹד, 'exceeding beautiful and good' (Gen. 1:31). Much of this beauty lay in the subordination of one thing to another, and of all to himself by the mediation and interposition of man, through whose praises and obedience the rest of the creation, being made subject to him, was to return their tribute of honour and glory to God. But all this order was destroyed by this sin, and the very 'creation made subject to vanity' (Rom. 8:20); on which and the like accounts, it might be easily made to appear that it was the greatest sin that ever was in the world.

## MAN KNEW WHAT HE DESERVED

Man, who had sinned, subscribed in his heart and conscience to the righteous sentence of the law. He knew what he had deserved, and looked for nothing but the immediate execution of the sentence of death upon him. Hence he meditates not a defence, expects no pardon, stays not for a trial, but flies and hides, and attempts an escape: 'I was afraid,' says he, 'and hid myself' (Gen. 3:10); than which never were there words of greater horror in the world, nor shall be until the day of judgment. Poor creature! He was full of expectation of the vengeance due for a broken covenant.

## GOD HAD DECLARED HOW HE WOULD DEAL WITH SIN

God had newly declared in the sinning angels what his justice required, and how he could deal with sinning man, without the least impeachment of his government, holiness, or goodness (2 Pet. 2:4).

## NOTHING WITHOUT GOD COULD HALT HIS WRATH

There was nothing without God himself that should move him in the least, so much as to suspend the execution of his wrath for one moment. He had not done so with the angels. All things lay now under wrath, curse, confusion, and disorder; nothing was left good, lovely, or desirable in his eye. As in the first creation, that which was first brought forth from nothing was תהו וָבֹהוּ, 'without form, and void,' empty of all order and beauty—nothing was in it to induce or move God to bring forth all things in the glory that ensued, but the whole design of it proceeded from his own infinite goodness and wisdom—so was it now again. There was an emptiness and vanity brought by sin upon the whole creation. Nothing remained that might be a motive to a merciful restoration, but all is again devolved on his sovereignty. All things being in this state and condition, wherein all doors stood open to the glory of God's justice in the punishing of sin, nothing remaining without him to hold his hand in the least, the whole creation, and especially the sinner himself, lying trembling in expectation of a dreadful doom, what now comes forth from him? The blessed word which we have, 'The seed of the woman shall break the serpent's head' (Gen. 3:15). It is full well known that the whole mystery of forgiveness is wrapped up in this one word of promise. And the great way of its coming forth from God, by the blood of the Messiah, whose heel was to be bruised, is also intimated. And this was the first discovery that ever was made of forgiveness in God. By a word of pure revelation it was made, and so faith must take it up and receive it. Now, this revelation of forgiveness with God in this one promise was the bottom of all that worship that was yielded to him by sinners for many ages; for we have showed before, that without this no sinner can have the least encouragement to approach to him. And this will continue to the end of the world as a notable evidence of the truth in hand, a firm foundation for faith to rest and build upon. Let a sinner seriously consider the state of things as they were then in the world, laid down before, and then view God coming forth with a word of pardon and forgiveness, merely from his own love and those counsels of peace that were between the Father and the Son, and he cannot but conclude, under his greatest difficulties, that yet 'there is forgiveness with God, that he may be feared.' Let now the law and conscience, let sin and Satan, stand forth and except against his evidence. Enough may be spoken from it, whatever the particular case be about which the soul has a contest with them, to put them all to silence.

## The Institution of Sacrifices

God revealed this sacred truth by his institution of sacrifices. Sacrifices by blood do all of them respect atonement, expiation, and consequently forgiveness. It is true, indeed, they could not themselves take away sin, nor make them perfect who came to God by them (Heb. 10:1); but yet they undeniably evince the taking away of sin, or the forgiveness of it, by what they did denote and typify. I shall, therefore, look back into their rise and intendment.

### Appointed by God

The original and first spring of sacrifices is not in the Scripture expressly mentioned, only the practice of the saints is recorded. But it is certain, from infallible Scripture evidences, that they were of God's immediate institution and appointment. God never allowed that the will or wisdom of man should be the spring and rule of his worship. That solemn word wherewith he fronts the command that is the rule of his worship, לֹא תַעֲשֶׂה־לְךָ—'You shall not make for yourself,' which is the life of the command (that which follows being an explanation and confirmation of the law itself by instances), cuts off all such pretences, and is as a flaming sword, turning every way to prevent men's arbitrary approaches to God's institutions. God will not part with his glory of being the only lawgiver, as to the whole concern of his worship, or any part of it, to any of the sons of men.

### After Sin Came into the World

Neither is the time of their institution mentioned. Some of the Papists dispute (as there are a generation of philosophical disputers amongst them, by whom their tottering cause is supported) that there should have been sacrifices in paradise, if a man had not sinned. But as, in all their opinions, our first inquiry ought to be, What do they get by this or that? Their whole religion being pointed to their carnal interest, so we may in particular do it upon this uncouth assertion, which is perfectly contradictious to the very nature and end of most sacrifices—namely, that they should be offered where there is no sin. Why, they hope to establish hence a general rule, that there can be no true worship of God, in any state or condition, without a sacrifice. What, then, I pray? Why, then it is evident that the continual sacrifice of the mass is necessary in the church, and that without it there is no true worship of God; and so they are quickly come home to their advantage and profit—the mass being that inexhaustible spring of revenue which feeds their pride and lust throughout the world. But there is in the church of Christ an altar still, and a sacrifice still, which they have rejected for the abominable figment of their mass—namely, Christ himself, as the apostle informs us (Heb. 13:10). But as the sacrifices of beasts could not have been before the entrance of sin, so it may be evidenced that they were instituted from the foundation of the world—that is, presently after the entrance of sin. Christ is called 'The Lamb of God' (John 1:29), which he was in reference to the sacrifices of old (as 1 Pet. 1:18–19); whence he is represented in the church as a 'Lamb slain' (Rev. 5:6), or giving out the efficacy of all sacrifices to his church. Now, he is said to be a 'Lamb slain from the foundation of the world' (Rev. 13:8), which could not be unless some sacrifice, prefiguring his being slain, had been then offered; for it denotes not only the efficacy of his mediation, but the way. Besides, the apostle tells us that 'without shedding of blood there was no remission' (Heb. 9:22)—that is, God, to demonstrate that all pardon and forgiveness related to the blood of Christ from the foundation of the world, gave out no word of pardon but by and with blood. Now, I have showed before that he revealed pardon in the first promise; and therefore there ensued thereon the shedding of blood and sacrifices; and thereby that testament or covenant 'was dedicated with blood' also (v. 18). Some think that the beasts, of whose skins God made garments for Adam, were offered in sacrifices. Nor is the conjecture vain; yea, it seems not to want a shadow of a gospel mystery, that their nakedness, which became their shame upon their sin (whence the pollution and shame of sin is frequently so termed), should be covered with the skins of their sacrifices: for in the true sacrifice there is somewhat answerable thereunto; and the righteousness of him whose sacrifice takes away the guilt of our sin is called our clothing, that hides our pollution and shame.

## THE GREATEST PART OF OLD TESTAMENT WORSHIP

That after the giving of the law, the greatest, most noble, and solemn part of the worship of God consisted in sacrifices. And this kind of worship continued, with the approbation of God, in the world about four thousand years; that is, from the entrance of sin until the death of the Messiah, the true sacrifice, which put an end to all that was typical

These things being premised, we may consider what was the mind and aim of God in the institution of this worship. One instance, and that of the most solemn of the whole kind, will resolve us in this inquiry. 'Two kids of the goats' are taken for 'an offering for sin' (Lev. 16:5). Consider only (that we do not enlarge on particulars) how one of them was dealt withal (v. 20–22):

> He shall bring the live goat: and Aaron shall lay both his hands upon the head of the live goat, and confess over him all the iniquities of the children of Israel, and all their transgressions in all their sins, putting them upon the head of the goat, and shall send him away by the hand of a fit man into the wilderness: and the goat shall bear upon him all their iniquities to a land not inhabited.

Let us see to what end is all this solemnity, and what is declared thereby. Wherefore should God appoint poor sinful men to come together, to take a goat or a lamb, and to confess over his head all their sins and transgressions, and to devote him to destruction under that confession? Had men invented this themselves, it had been a matter of no moment; but it was an institution of God, which he bound his church to the observation of upon the penalty of his highest displeasure. Certainly this was a solemn declaration that there is forgiveness with him. Would that God who is infinitely good, and so will not, who is infinitely true, holy, and faithful, and so cannot deceive, call men out, whom he loved, to a solemn representation of a thing wherein their chiefest, their eternal concern lies, and suffer them to feed upon ashes? Let men take heed that they mock not God; for of a truth God mocks not man until he be finally rejected by him. For four thousand years together, then, did God declare by sacrifices that there is forgiveness with him, and led his people by them to make a public representation of it in the face of the world. This is a second uncontrollable evidence of the truth asserted, which may possibly be of use to souls that come indeed deeply and seriously to deal with God; for though the practice be ceased, yet the instruction intended in them continues.

## THE PRESCRIPTION OF REPENTANCE

God's appointment of repentance to sinners reveals that there is forgiveness in himself. I say, the prescription of repentance is a revelation of forgiveness. After the angels had sinned, God never once called them to repentance. He would not deceive them, but let them know what they were to look for at his hands; he has no forgiveness for them, and therefore would require no repentance of them. It is not, nor ever was, a duty incumbent on them to repent. Nor is it so to the damned in hell. God requires it not of them, nor is it their duty. There being no forgiveness for them, what should move them to repent? Why should it be their duty so to do? Their eternal anguish about sin committed has nothing of repentance in it. Assignation then, of repentance is a revelation of forgiveness. God would not call upon a sinful creature to humble itself and bewail its sin if there were no way of recovery or relief; and the only way of recovery from the guilt of sin is pardon. So Job 33:27-8, 'He looks upon men, and if any say, I have sinned, and perverted that which was right, and it profited me not; he will deliver his soul from going into the pit, and his life shall see the light.' In the foregoing verses he declares the various ways that God used to bring men to repentance. He did it by dreams (v. 15-16); by afflictions (v. 19); by the preaching of the word (v. 23). What, then, does God aim at in and by all these various ways of teaching? It is to cause man to say, 'I have sinned, and perverted that which was right.' It is to bring him to repentance. What now if he obtain his end, and comes to that which is aimed at? Why, then, there is forgiveness for him, as is declared (v. 28).

To improve this evidence, I shall confirm, by some few obvious considerations, these two things: 1. That the prescription of repentance does indeed evince that there is forgiveness with God. 2. That every one in whom there is repentance wrought towards God, may certainly conclude that there is forgiveness with God for him.

## TRUE REPENTANCE LAYS HOLD OF FORGIVENESS

No repentance is acceptable with God but what is built or leans on the faith of forgiveness. We have a cloud of witnesses to this truth in the Scripture. Many there have been, many are recorded who have been convinced of sin, perplexed about it, sorry for it, that have made open confession and acknowledgment of it, that, under the pressing sense of it, have cried out even to God for deliverance, and yet have come short of mercy, pardon, and acceptance with God. The cases of Cain, Pharaoh, Saul, Ahab, Judas, and others, might be insisted on. What was wanting, that made all that they did abominable? Consider one instance for all. It is said of Judas that he repented: Μεταμεληθεὶς (Matt. 27:3), 'He repented himself.' But wherein did this repentance consist?

1. He was convinced of his sin in general: Ἥμαρτον, says he— 'I have sinned' (v. 4).
2. He was sensible of the particular sin whereof he stood charged in conscience before God. 'I have,' says he, 'betrayed innocent blood'—'I am guilty of blood, innocent blood, and that in the vilest manner, by treachery.' So that he comes—
3. To a full and open confession of his sin.
4. He makes restitution of what he was advantaged by his sin, 'He brought again the thirty pieces of silver' (v. 3)—all testifying a hearty sorrow that spirited the whole.

Methinks now Judas' repentance looks like the young man's obedience, who cried out, 'All these things have I done; is there any thing yet lacking?' Yea, one thing was wanting to that young man—he had no true faith nor love to God all this while; which vitiated and spoiled all the rest of his performances. One thing also is wanting to this repentance of Judas—he had no faith of forgiveness in God; that he could not believe; and, therefore, after all this sorrow, instead of coming to him, he bids him the utmost defiance, and goes away and hangs himself.

Indeed, faith of forgiveness, as has been showed, has many degrees. There is of them that which is indispensably necessary to render repentance acceptable. What it is in particular I do not dispute. It is not an assurance of the acceptance of our persons in general. It is not that the particular sin wherewith, it may be, the soul is perplexed, is forgiven. a general, so it be a gospel discovery that there is forgiveness in God, will suffice. The church expresses it, 'In you the fatherless finds mercy' (Hos. 14:3); and 'Who knows but he will return and repent?' (Joel 2:14). 'I have this ground,' says the soul, 'God is in himself gracious and merciful; the fatherless, the destitute and helpless, that come to him by Christ, find mercy in him. None in heaven and earth can evince but that he may return to me also.' Now, let a man's convictions be never so great, sharp, wounding; his sorrow never so abundant, overflowing, abiding; his confession never so full, free, or open—if this one thing be wanting, all is nothing but what tends to death.

### The Call to Repent is Founded on Forgiveness

To prescribe repentance as a duty to sinners, without a foundation of pardon and forgiveness in himself, is inconsistent with the wisdom, holiness, goodness, faithfulness, and all other glorious excellencies and perfections of the nature of God.

### *God Cannot Lie*

The apostle lays this as the great foundation of all consolation, that God cannot lie or deceive (Heb. 6:18). And again, he engages the faithfulness and veracity of God to the same purpose: 'God, who cannot lie, has promised it' (Tit. 1:2). Now, there is a lie, a deceit, in things as well as in words, he that does a thing which in its own nature is apt to deceive them that consider it, with an intention of deceiving them, is no less a liar than he which affirms that to be true which he knows to be false. There is a lie in actions as well as in words. The whole life of a hypocrite is a lie; so says the prophet of idolaters, there is 'a lie in their right hand' (Isa. 44:20).

## Repenting Is for Sinners

The proposal of repentance is a thing fitted and suited in its own nature to beget thoughts in the mind of a sinner that there is forgiveness with God. Repenting is for sinners only. 'I come not,' says our Saviour, 'to call the righteous, but sinners to repentance.' It is for them, and them only. It was no duty for Adam in Eden, it is none for the angels in heaven, nor for the damned in hell. What, then, may be the language of this appointment? 'O sinners, come and deal with God by repentance.' Does it not openly speak forgiveness in God? And, if it were otherwise, could men possibly be more frustrated or deceived? Would not the institution of repentance be a lie? Such a delusion may proceed from Satan, but not from Him who is the fountain of goodness, holiness, and truth. His call to repentance is a full demonstration of his readiness to forgive (Acts 17:30–31). It is true, many do thus deceive themselves: they raise themselves to an expectation of immunity, not on gospel grounds; and their disappointment is a great part of their punishment. But God deceives none; whoever comes to him on his proposal of repentance shall find forgiveness. It is said of some, indeed, that 'he will laugh at their calamity, and mock when their fear comes' (Prov. 1:26). He will aggravate their misery, by giving them to see what their pride and folly has brought them to. But who are they? Only such as refuse his call to repentance, with the promises of the acceptation annexed.

## Those Called to Repent Cannot Question Forgiveness

There is, then, no cause why those who are under a call to repentance should question whether there be forgiveness in God or no.

This concerns my second proposition. 'Come,' says the Lord to the souls of men, 'leave your sinful ways, turn to me; humble yourselves with broken and contrite heart.' 'Alas!' say poor convinced sinners, 'we are poor, dark, and ignorant creatures; or we are old in sin, or greater sinners or backsliders, or have fallen often into the same sins; can we expect there should be forgiveness for us?' Why, you are under God's invitation to repentance; and to disbelieve forgiveness is to call the truth, holiness, and faithfulness of God into question. If you will not believe forgiveness, pretend what you please, it is in truth because you hate repentance. You do but deceive your souls, when you pretend you come not up to repentance because you cannot believe forgiveness; for in the very institution of this duty God engages all his properties to make it good that he has pardon and mercy for sinners.

## God's Call to Repentance Is Sincere

Much less cause is there to doubt of forgiveness where sincere repentance is in any measure wrought. No soul comes to repentance but upon God's call; God calls none but whom he has mercy for upon their coming. And as for those who sin against the Holy Ghost, as they shut themselves out from forgiveness, so they are not called to repentance.

## Scriptural Declarations

God expressly declares in the Scripture that the forgiveness that is with him is the foundation of his prescribing repentance to man. One instance may suffice: 'Let the wicked forsake his way' (Isa. 55:7) (רָשָׁע, 'a perverse wicked one') וְאִישׁ אָוֶן, 'and the man of iniquity his thoughts: and let him return to the LORD, and he will have mercy; and to our God, for יַרְבֶּה לִסְלוֹחַ, he will multiply to pardon.' You see to whom he speaks—to men perversely wicked, and such as make a trade of sinning. What does he call them to? Plainly, to repentance, to the duty we have insisted on. But what is the ground of such an invitation to such profligate sinners? Why, the abundant forgiveness and pardon that is with him, superabounding to what the worst of them can stand in need of (as Rom. 5:20).

And this is another way whereby God has revealed that there is forgiveness with him; and an infallible bottom for faith to build upon in its approaches to God it is. Nor can the certainty of this evidence be called into question but on such grounds as are derogatory to the glory and honour of God. And this connection of repentance and forgiveness is that principle from whence God convinces a stubborn, unbelieving people that all his ways and dealings with sinners are just and equal (Ezek. 18:25). And should there be any failure in it, they could not be so. Every soul, then, that is under a call to repentance, whether out of his natural condition or from any backsliding into folly after conversion, has a sufficient foundation to rest on as to the pardon he inquires after. God is ready to deal with him on terms of mercy. If, out of love to sin or the power of unbelief, he refuse to close with him on these terms, his condemnation is just. And it will be well that this consideration be well imprinted on the minds of men. I say, notwithstanding the general presumptions that men seem to have of this matter, yet these principles of it ought to be inculcated.

Such is the atheism that lies lurking in the hearts of men by nature, that, notwithstanding their pretences and professions, we have need to be pressing upon them evidences of the very being and essential properties of God. In so doing, we have the assistance of inbred notions in their own minds, which they cannot eject, to help to carry on the work. How much more is this necessary in reference to the free acts of the will of God, which are to be known only by mere revelation! Our word had need to be 'line upon line;' and yet, when we have done, we have cause enough to cry out, as was said, 'Lord, who has believed our report? And to whom has the arm of the Lord been revealed?'

What was spoken before of the obstacles that lie in the way, hindering souls from a saving reception of this truth, ought to be remembered. Those who have no experience of them between God and their souls seem to be ignorant of the true nature of conscience, law, gospel, grace, sin, and forgiveness.

Many who are come to a saving persuasion of it, yet having not received it upon clear and unquestionable grounds, and so not knowing how to resolve their faith of it into its proper principles, are not able to answer the objections that lie against it in their own consciences, and so do miserably fluctuate about it all their days. These had need to have these principles inculcated on them. Were they pondered aright, some might have cause to say, with the Samaritans, who first gave credit to the report of the woman (John 4): they had but a report before, but now they find all things to be according to it, yea, to exceed it. a little experience of a man's own unbelief, with the observation that may easily be made of the uncertain progresses and fluctuations of the spirits of others, will be a sufficient conviction of the necessity of the work we are engaged in.

## WHY SO MANY ARGUMENTS?

But it will yet be said, that it is needless to multiply arguments and evidences in this case, the truth insisted on being granted as one of the fundamental principles of religion. As it is not, then, by any called in question, so it does not appear that so much time and pains is needful for the confirmation of it; for what is granted and plain needs little confirmation. But several things may be returned in answer hereunto; all which may at once be here pleaded for the multiplication of our arguments in this matter.

### *To Encourage Belief*

That it is generally granted by all is no argument that it is effectually believed by many. Sundry things are taken for granted in point of opinion that are not so believed as to be improved in practice. We have in part showed before, and shall afterward undeniably evince, that there are very few that believe this truth with that faith that will interest them in it and give them the benefit of it. And what will it avail any of us that there is forgiveness of sin with God, if our sins be not forgiven? No more than that such or such a king is rich, whilst we are poor and starving. My aim is not to prove it as an opinion or a mere speculative truth, but so to evidence it in the principles of its being and revelation as that it may be believed; whereon all our blessedness depends.

## A Fundamental Truth

It needs never the less confirmation because it is a plain fundamental truth, but rather the more; and that because both of the worth and weight of it. 'This is a faithful saying,' says the apostle, 'worthy of all acceptation, that Jesus Christ came into the world to save sinners.' So I say of this, which, for the substance of it, is the same with that. It is worthy of all acceptation, namely, that there is forgiveness with God; and therefore ought it to be fully confirmed, especially whilst we make use of no other demonstrations of it but those only which God has furnished us withal to that purpose: and this he would not have done, but that he knew them needful for us. And for the plainness of this truth, it is well if it be so to us. This I know, nothing but the Spirit of God can make it so. Men may please themselves and others sometimes with curious notions, and make them seem to be things of great search and attainment, which, when they are well examined, it may be they are not true; or if they are, are yet of a very little consequence or importance. It is these fundamental truths that have the mysteries of the wisdom and grace of God inwrapped in them; which whoso can unfold aright, will show himself 'a workman that needs not be ashamed.' These still waters are deep; and the farther we dive into them, the greater discovery shall we make of their depths. And many other sacred truths there are whose mention is common, but whose depths are little searched and whose efficacy is little known.

## They Concern Multitudes

We multiply these evidences, because they are multitudes that are concerned in them. All that do believe, and all that do not believe, are so—those that do believe, that they may be established; and those that do not believe, that they may be encouraged so to do.

Among both these sorts, some evidences may be more profitable and useful, one to one, some to another. It may be, amongst all, all will be gathered up, that no fragments be lost. They are all, I hope, instruments provided by the Holy Ghost for this end; and by this ordinance do we endeavour to put them into his hand, to be made effectual as he will. One may reach one soul, another another, according to his pleasure. One may be of use to establishment, another to consolation, a third to encouragement, according as the necessities of poor souls do require. However, God, who has provided them, knows them all to be needful.

### Different Arguments Help Different People

They are so, also, upon the account of the various conditions wherein the spirits of believers themselves may be. One may give help to the same soul at one season, another at another; one may secure the soul against a temptation, another stir it up to thankfulness and obedience,

These things have I spoken, that you may not think we dwell too long on this consideration. And I pray God that your consolation and establishment may abound in the reading of these meditations, as I hope they have not been altogether without their fruit in their preparation.

### God's Pleasure with His Saints

Let us, then, in the fourth place, as a fourth evidence of this truth, consider those, both under the Old Testament and the New, concerning whom we have the greatest assurance that God was well pleased with them, and that they are now in the enjoyment of him. And this argument to this purpose the apostle insists upon, and presses from sundry instances. How many does he there reckon up who of old 'obtained a good report,' and 'this testimony, that they pleased God!' (Heb. 11:2, 5). 'All these inherited the promises' through believing—that is, obtained the 'forgiveness of sins' for whereas 'by nature they were children of wrath,' and 'under the curse' as well as others, obtaining an infallible interest in the favour of God, and this testimony, 'that they pleased him,' it could no otherwise be; for without this, on a just account, every one of them would have continued in the state wherein Adam was when he 'heard the voice of God, and was afraid.' Wherefore, it being evident that some persons, in all generations, have enjoyed the friendship, love, and favour of God in this world, and at their departure out of it have entered into glory, it makes it evident that there is forgiveness of sin with him; without which these things could not be.

Let us, after the example of the apostle, mention some particular instances in this matter. Look to Abraham: he was the 'friend of God,' and walked with God. God made a solemn covenant with him, and takes it for his memorial throughout all generations that he is the 'God of Abraham.' And he is doubtless now at rest with God. Our Saviour calls the place or condition into which blessed souls are gathered, 'Abraham's bosom.' He is at rest with whom others are at rest.

The condition was the same with Isaac and Jacob. They also are in heaven, being alive to and with God. Our Saviour proves it from the tenor of the covenant: 'I am the God of Abraham, and the God of Isaac, and the God of Jacob. God is not the God of the dead, but of the living' (Matt. 22:32). They are yet alive, alive to God, and with him by virtue of the covenant; or, after their death, God would not be said to be their God. This is the force of our Saviour's argument in that place, that after their death God was still their God. Then death had not reached their whole persons. They were still alive with God in heaven; and their bodies, by virtue of the same covenant, were to be recovered out of the dust.

The same is the state with David. He was a 'man after God's own heart,' that did his will and fulfilled all his pleasure. And although he died, and his body saw corruption, yet he is not lost; he is with God in heaven. Hence he ended his days triumphantly, in a full apprehension of eternal rest, beyond what could in this world be attained, and that by virtue of the covenant; for these are the last words of David, 'Although my house be not so with God, yet he has made with me an everlasting covenant,' ascertaining to him sure and eternal mercies (2 Sam. 23:5).

Peter also is in heaven. Christ prayed for him that his faith should not fail; and in his death he glorified God (John 21:19). So is Paul; he also is in heaven. He knew that when he was dissolved he should be with Christ.

Here, then, 'we are compassed about with a cloud of witnesses.'

## The Saints Above Were All Sinners

It is most certain that they were all sinners. They were all so by nature; for therein there is no difference between any of the children of men. And personally they were sinners also. They confessed so of themselves, and some of the sins of all of them stand upon record. Yea, some of them were great sinners, or guilty of great and signal miscarriages; some before their conversion, as Abraham, who was an idolater (Josh. 24:2–3), and Paul, who was a persecutor and a blasphemer; some after their conversion; some in sins of the flesh against their obedience, as David; and some in sins of profession against faith, as Peter. Nothing, then, is more evident than that no one of them came to rest with God but by forgiveness. Had they never been guilty of any one sin, but only what is left upon record concerning them in holy writ, yet they could be saved no other way; for he that transgresses the law in any one point is guilty of the breach of the whole (James 2:10).

What shall we now say? Do we think that God has forgiveness only for this or that individual person? No man questions but that all these were pardoned. Was it by virtue of any especial personal privilege that was peculiar to them? Whence should any such privilege arise, seeing by nature they were no better than others, nor would have been so personally had not they been delivered from sin, and prepared for obedience by grace, mercy, and pardon? Wherefore, they all obtained forgiveness by virtue of the covenant, from the forgiveness which is with God. And this is equally ready for others who come to God the same way that they did; that is, by faith and repentance.

### SOME WERE GREAT SINNERS

Many of those concerning whom we have the assurance mentioned were not only sinners but great sinners, as was said; which must be also insisted on, to obviate another objection. For some may say, that although they were sinners, yet they were not such sinners as we are; and although they obtained forgiveness, yet this is no argument that we shall do so also, who are guilty of other sins than they were, and those attended with other aggravations than theirs were. To which I say, that I delight not in aggravating, no, nor yet in repeating, the sins and faults of the saints of God of old. Not only the grace of God, but the sins of men have by some been turned into lasciviousness, or been made a cloak for their lusts. But yet, for the ends and purposes for which they are recorded by the Holy Ghost, we may make mention of them. That they may warn us of our duty, that we take heed lest we also fall, that they may yield us a relief under our surprisals, are they written. So, then, where the mention of them tends to the advancement of sovereign grace and mercy, which is the case in hand, we may insist on them. I think, then, that, without mention of particulars, I may safely say that there is no sin, no degree of sin, no aggravating circumstance of sin, no kind of continuance in sin (the only sin excepted), but that there are those in heaven who have been guilty of them.

### *Pardon for All Sorts of Sinners*

It may be, yet some will say that they have considered the sins and falls of Lot, David, Peter, Paul, and the thief himself on the cross, and yet they find not their own condition exemplified, so as to conclude that they shall have the same success with them.

I am not showing that this or that man shall be pardoned, but only demonstrating that there is forgiveness with God, and that for all sorts of sins and sinners; which these instances do assuredly confirm. And, moreover, they manifest that if other men are not pardoned, it is merely because they make not that application for forgiveness which they did.

Yet by the way, to take off this objection also, consider what the apostle says in particular concerning the several sorts of sinners that obtained mercy: 'Be not deceived: neither fornicators, nor idolaters, nor adulterers, nor effeminate, nor abusers of themselves with mankind, nor thieves, nor covetous, nor drunkards, nor revilers, nor extortioners, shall inherit the kingdom of God. And such were some of you: but you are washed, but you are sanctified, but you are justified' (1 Cor. 6:9–11). Hell can scarce, in no more words, yield us a sadder catalogue. Yet some of all these sorts were justified and pardoned.

Suppose this enumeration of sins does not reach the condition of the soul, because of some especial aggravation of its sin not expressed; let such a one add that of our Saviour: 'I say to you, all manner of sin and blasphemy shall be forgiven to men, but the blasphemy against the Holy Ghost' (Matt. 12:31). They are not, they shall not be, all actually remitted and pardoned to all men; but they are all pardonable to those that seek to obtain pardon for them according to the gospel. There is with God forgiveness for them all. Now, certainly there is no sin, but only that excepted, but it comes within the compass of 'All manner of sin and blasphemy;' and so, consequently, some that have been guilty of it are now in heaven.

### A Cloud of Witnesses

We take it for a good token and evidence of a virtuous healing water, when, without fraud or pretence, we see the crutches of cured cripples and impotent persons hung about it as a memorial of its efficacy. And it is a great demonstration of the skill and ability of a physician, when many come to a sick person and tell him 'We had the same distemper with you—it had the same symptoms, the same effects; and by his skill and care we are cured.' 'Oh!' says the sick man, 'bring him to me, I will venture my life in his hand.' Now, all the saints of heaven stand about a sin-sick soul; for in this matter 'we are compassed about with a cloud of witnesses' (Heb. 12:1). And what do they bear witness to? What say they to a poor guilty sinner? 'As you are, so were we; so guilty, so perplexed, so obnoxious to wrath, so fearing destruction from God.'

'And what way did you steer, what course did you take, to obtain the blessed condition wherein now you are?'

Say they, 'We went all to God through Christ for forgiveness; and found plenty of grace, mercy, and pardon in him for us all.'

The rich man in the parable thought it would be a great means of conversion if one should 'rise from the dead' and preach; but here we see that all the saints departed and now in glory do jointly preach this fundamental truth, that 'there is forgiveness with God.'

Poor souls are apt to think that all those whom they read or hear of to be gone to heaven, went thither because they were so good and so holy. It is true many of them were eminently and exemplarily so in their generations, all of them were so according to their degrees and measures; for 'without holiness no man can see God,' and it is our duty to labour to be like to them in holiness, if ever we intend to be so in happiness and glory; but yet not one of them, not any one that is now in heaven, Jesus Christ alone excepted, did ever come thither any other way but by forgiveness of sin; and that will also bring us thither, though we come short of many of them in holiness and grace.

And this evidence of forgiveness I the rather urge, because I find the apostle Paul doing of it eminently in his own person (1 Tim. 1:12–16):

> I thank Christ Jesus our Lord, who has enabled me, for that he counted me faithful, putting me into the ministry; who was before a blasphemer, and a persecutor, and injurious: but I obtained mercy, because I did it ignorantly in unbelief. And the grace of our Lord was exceeding abundant with faith and love which is in Christ Jesus. This is a faithful saying, and worthy of all acceptation, that Christ Jesus came into the world to save sinners; of whom I am chief. Howbeit for this cause I obtained mercy, that in me first Jesus Christ might shew forth all long-suffering, for a pattern to them which should hereafter believe on him to life everlasting.

'A great sinner,' says he, 'the chiefest of sinners I was;' which he manifests by some notable instances of his sin. 'I was,' says he, 'a blasphemer'—the highest sin against God; 'a persecutor'—the highest sin against the saints; 'injurious'—the highest wickedness towards mankind. 'But,' says he, 'I obtained mercy, I am pardoned;' and that with a blessed effect; first, that he should after all this be so accounted faithful as to be put into the ministry; and then that the grace of our Lord Jesus Christ in him and towards him was exceeding abundant. And what was the reason, what was the cause, that he was thus dealt withal? Why, it was that he might be a pattern, an evidence, an argument, that there was grace, mercy, forgiveness, to be had for all sorts of sinners that would believe to life everlasting.

To conclude, then, this evidence—Every one who is now in heaven has his pardon sealed in the blood of Christ. All these pardons are, as it were, hanged up in the gospel; they are all enrolled in the promises thereof, for the encouragement of them that stand in need of forgiveness to come and sue out theirs also. Fear not, then, the guilt of sin, but the love of it and the power of it. If we love and like sin better than forgiveness, we shall assuredly go without it. If we had but rather be pardoned in God's way than perish, our condition is secure.

## God's Patience Towards the World

The same is evident from the patience of God towards the world, and the end of it For the clearing hereof we may observe:

### After Adam's Fall

That upon the first entrance of sin and breach of that covenant which God had made with mankind in Adam, he might immediately have executed the threatened curse, and have brought eternal death upon them that sinned. Justice required that it should be so, and there was nothing in the whole creation to interpose so much as for a reprieve or a respite of vengeance. And had God then sent sinning man, with the apostate angels that induced him into sin, immediately into eternal destruction, he would have been glorified in his righteousness and severity by and among the angels that sinned not. Or he could have created a new race of innocent creatures to have worshipped him and glorified him for his righteous judgment, even as the elect at the last day shall do for the destruction of ungodly men.

### THROUGHOUT HISTORY

God has not taken this course. He has continued the race of mankind for a long season on the earth; he has watched over them with his providence, and exercised exceeding patience, forbearance, and long-suffering towards them. Thus the apostle Paul at large discourses on (Acts 14:15–17, 17:24–30, as also Rom. 2:4). And it is open and manifest in their event. The whole world is every day filled with tokens of the power and patience of God; every nation, every city, every family is filled with them.

### CONSTANTLY ABUSED

That there is a common abuse of this patience of God visible in the world in all generations. So it was of old: God saw it to be so, and complained of it (Gen. 6:5–6). All the evil, sin, wickedness, that has been in the world, which no heart can conceive, no tongue can express, has been all an abuse of this patience of God. This, with the most, is the consequent of God's patience and forbearance. Men count it a season to fulfil all the abominations that their evil hearts can suggest to them, or Satan draw them into a combination with himself in. This the state of things in the world proclaims, and every one's experience confirms.

### MORE THAN SUFFERANCE

Let us, therefore, consider what is the true and proper end of this patience of God towards the world, enduring it in sin and wickedness for so long a season, and suffering one generation to be multiplied after another. Shall we think that God has no other design in all this patience towards mankind, in all generations, but merely to suffer them, all and every one, without exception, to sin against him, dishonour him, provoke him, that so he may at length everlastingly destroy them all? It is confessed that this is the consequent, the event of it with the most, through their perverse wickedness, with their love of sin and pleasure. But is this the design of God—his only design? Has he no other purpose but merely to forbear them a while in their folly, and then to avenge himself upon them? Is this his intendment, not only towards those who are obstinate in their darkness, ignorance, and rebellion against him, whose 'damnation is just, and sleeps not,' but also towards those whom he stirs up by his grace to seek after a remedy and deliverance from the state of sin and death? God forbid; yea, such an apprehension would be contrary to all those notions of the infinite wisdom and goodness of God which are ingrafted upon our hearts by nature, and which all his works manifest and declare. Whatever, therefore, it be, this cannot be the design of God in his patience towards the world. It cannot be but that he must long since have cut off the whole race of mankind, if he had no other thoughts and purposes towards them.

## REACHES ALL FOR THE SAKE OF SOME

If this patience of God has any other intention towards any, any other effect upon some, upon any, that is to be reckoned the principal end of it, and for the sake whereof it is evidently extended to some others, consequentially to all. For those concerning whom God has an especial design in his patience, being to be brought forth in the world after the ordinary way of mankind, and that in all ages during the continuance of the world, from the beginning to the end thereof, the patience which is extended to them must also of necessity reach to all in that variety wherein God is pleased to exercise it. The whole world, therefore, is continued under the patience of God and the fruits of it, for the sake of some that are in it.

### POINTS TO GOD'S WILLINGNESS TO FORGIVE

Let us, therefore, see what is the end of this patience, and what it teaches us. Now, it can have no end possible but only that before rejected, unless there be forgiveness of sins with God. Unless God be ready and willing to forgive the sins of them that come to him according to his appointment, his patience is merely subservient to a design of wrath, anger, severity, and a resolution to destroy. Now, this is an abomination once to suppose, and would reflect unspeakable dishonour upon the holy God. Let a man but deal thus, and it is a token of as evil an habit of mind, and perverse, as any can befall him. Let him bear with those that are in his power in their faults, for no other end or with no other design but that he may take advantage to bring a greater punishment and revenge upon them; and what more vile affection, what more wretched corruption of heart and mind, can he manifest? And shall we think that this is the whole design of the patience of God? God forbid.

It may be objected 'That this argument is not cogent, because of the instance that lies against it in God's dealing with the angels that sinned. It is evident that they fell into their transgression and apostasy before mankind did so, for they led and seduced our first parents into sin; and yet God bears with them, and exercises patience towards them, to this very day, and will do so to the consummation of all things, when they shall be cast into the fire 'prepared for the devil and his angels;' and yet it is granted that there is no forgiveness in God for them: so that it does not necessarily follow that there is so for man, because of his patience towards them.

### 'But God Is Patient with Fallen Angels'

I answer, that this must be more fully spoken to when we come to remove that great objection against this whole truth which was mentioned before, taken from God's dealing with the sinning angels, whom he spared not. At present two or three observations will remove it out of our way.

ANGELS DO NOT MULTIPLY. The case is not the same with the sinning angels and the race of mankind in all generations. There are no other angels in this condition, but only those individuals who first sinned in their own persons. They are not, in the providence and patience of God, multiplied and increased in ensuing times and seasons, but they continue the same individual persons who first sinned, and no more; so that immediate execution of the whole punishment due to their sin would not have prevented any increase of them. But now with man it is otherwise; for God continues his patience towards them to the production of millions of other persons, who were not actually in the first sin. Had not God so continued his forbearance, their being, and consequently their sin and misery, had been prevented; so that the case is not the same with sinning angels and men.

GOD IS NOT PATIENT WITH FALLEN ANGELS. Indeed God exercises no patience toward the angels that sinned, and that because he had no forgiveness for them. So Peter tells us, 'God spared not the angels that sinned, but cast them down to hell, and delivered them into chains of darkness' (2 Pet. 2:4). Immediately upon their sin they were cast out of the presence of God, whose vision and enjoyment they were made for, and which they received some experience of; and they were cast into hell, as the place of their ordinary retention and of their present anguish, under the sense of God's curse and displeasure. And although they may some of them be permitted to compass the earth, and to walk to and fro therein, to serve the ends of God's holy, wise providence, and so to be out of their prison, yet they are still in their chains; for they were delivered to chains of darkness, to be kept to the last judgment. And in these things they lie actually under the execution of the curse of God, so that there is indeed no patience exercised towards them. If a notorious malefactor or murderer be committed to a dungeon, and kept bound with iron chains to prevent his escape, until the appointed day of his solemn judgment and execution, without the least intention to spare him, none will say there is patience exercised towards him, things being disposed only so as that his punishment may be secure and severe. And such is the case, such is the condition of the angels that sinned; who are not, therefore, to be esteemed objects of God's patience.

THEIR PUNISHMENT IS NOT DELAYED FOR THEIR SAKES. The reason why the full and final punishment of these angels is reserved and respited to the appointed season is not for their own sakes, their good, benefit, or advantage at all, but merely that the end of God's patience towards mankind might be accomplished. When this is once brought about they shall not be spared a day, an hour, a moment. So that God's dispensation towards them is nothing but a mere withholding the infliction of the utmost of their punishment, until he has accomplished the blessed ends of his patience towards mankind.

### 'God's Patience Is Subservient to His Wrath'

But you will say, secondly, 'Is it not said that God, willing to shew his wrath, and to make his power known, endures with much long-suffering the vessels of wrath fitted to destruction?' (Rom. 9:22); so that it seems that the end of God's endurance and long-suffering, to some at least, is only their fitting to destruction.

1. It is one thing to endure with much long-suffering, another thing to exercise and declare patience. The former only intimates God's withholding for a season of that destruction which he might justly inflict, which we speak not of; the other denotes an acting in a way of goodness and kindness for some especial end.
2. The next verse declares the great end of God's patience, and answers this objection: 'That he might make known the riches of his glory on the vessels of mercy, which he had afore prepared to glory' (v. 23). This is the great end of God's patience, which whilst he is in the pursuit of towards the vessels of mercy, he endures others with much long-suffering and forbearance. This, then, is fully evident, that there could be no sufficient reason assigned of the patience

of God towards sinners, but that there is forgiveness prepared for them that come to him by Christ.

And this the Scripture clearly testifies to (2 Pet. 3:9). The question is, what is the reason why God forbears the execution of his judgment upon wicked and ungodly men? Some would have it that God is slack, that is, regardless of the sins of men, and takes no notice of them. 'No,' says the apostle; 'God has another design in his patience and long-suffering.' What is this? 'It is to manifest that he is not willing we should perish.' That is it which we have proved; for our freedom from destruction is by repentance, which necessarily infers the forgiveness of sin. So Paul tells us that in the gospel is declared what is the end of God's patience and forbearance: 'It is,' says he, 'the remission of sins' (Rom. 3:25).

Let us, therefore, also mind this evidence in the application of ourselves to God for pardon. It is certain that God might have taken us from the womb, and have cast us into utter darkness; and in the course of our lives we have been guilty of such provocations as God might justly have taken the advantage of to glorify his justice and severity in our ruin; but yet we have lived thus long, in the patience and forbearance of God. And to what end has he thus spared us, and let pass those advantages for our destruction that we have put into his hand? Is it not that he might by his patience give us leave and space to get an interest in that forgiveness which he thus testifies to be in himself? Let us, then, be encouraged by it to use it to the end and purpose for which it is exercised towards us. You that are yet in doubt of your condition, consider that the patience of God was extended to you this day, this very day, that you might use it for the obtaining of the remission of your sins. Lose not this day, nor one day more, as you love your souls; for woeful will be their condition who shall perish for despising or abusing the patience of God.

## SAINTS' FAITH AND EXPERIENCE IN THIS WORLD

The faith and experience of the saints in this world give in testimony to this truth; and we know that their record in this matter is true. Let us, then, ask of them what they believe, what they have found, what they have experience of, as to the forgiveness of sin. This God himself directs and leads us to by appealing to our own experience, whence he shows us that we may take relief and support in our distresses: 'Have you not known? Have you not heard?' (Isa. 40:28)—' Have not you yourself, who now cries out that you are lost and undone because God has forsaken you, found and known by experience the contrary, from his former dealings with you?' And if our own experiences may confirm us against the workings of our unbelief, so may those of others also. And this is that which Eliphaz directs Job to, 'Call now, if there be any that will answer you; and to which of the saints will you look?' (Job 5:1). It is not a supplication to them for help that is intended, but an inquiry after their experience in the case in hand, wherein he wrongfully thought they could not justify Job. וְאֶל־מִי מִקְּדֹשִׁים תִּפְנֶה, 'To which of the saints, on the right hand or left, will you have regard in this matter?' Some would foolishly hence seek to confirm the invocation of the saints departed; when, indeed, if they were intended, it is rather forbidden and discountenanced than directed to. But the קְדוֹשִׁים here are the קְדוֹשִׁים אֲשֶׁר־בָּאָרֶץ (Ps. 16:3), 'The saints that are in the earth,' whose experiences Job is directed to inquire into and after. David makes it a great encouragement to waiting upon God, as a God hearing prayer, that others had done so and found success: 'This poor man cried, and the LORD heard him, and saved him out of all his troubles' (Ps. 34:6). If he did so, and had that blessed issue, why should not we do so also? The experiences of one are often proposed for the confirmation and establishment of others. So the same David: 'Come,' says he, 'and hear, all you that fear God, and I will declare what he has done for my soul.' He contents not himself to mind them of the word, promises, and providence of God, which he does most frequently; but he will give them the encouragement and support also of his own experience. So Paul tells us that he 'was comforted of God in all his tribulation, that he might be able to comfort them which are in any trouble, by the comfort wherewith he himself was comforted of God' (2 Cor. 1:4); that is, that he might be able to communicate to them his own experience of God's dealing with him, and the satisfaction and assurance that he found therein. So also he proposes the example of God's dealing with him in the pardon of his sins as a great motive to others to believe (1 Tim. 1:13–16). And this mutual communication of satisfying experiences in the things of God, or of our spiritual sense and evidence of the power, efficacy, and reality of gospel truths, being rightly managed, is of singular use to all sorts of believers. So the same great apostle acquaints us in his own example, 'I long to see you, that I may impart to you some spiritual gift, to the end you may be established; that is, that I may be comforted together with you, by the mutual faith both of you and me' (Rom. 1:11–12). He longed not only to be instructing of them, in the pursuit of the work of the ministry committed to him, but to confer also with them about their mutual faith, and what experiences of the peace of God in believing they had attained.

We have in our case called in the testimony of the saints in heaven, with whom those on earth do make up one family, even that one family in heaven and earth which is called after the name of the Father of our Lord Jesus Christ (Eph. 3:14–15). And they all agree in their testimony, as becomes the family and children of God. But those below we may deal personally with; whereas we gather the witness of the other only from what is left upon record concerning them. And for the clearing of this evidence sundry things are to be observed.

## PROFESSION WITHOUT POWER

Men living under the profession of religion, and not experiencing the power, virtue, and efficacy of it in their hearts, are, whatever they profess, very near to atheism, or at least exposed to great temptations thereunto. If 'they profess they know God, but in works deny him,' they are 'abominable, and disobedient, and to every good work reprobate' (Tit. 1:16). Let such men lay aside tradition and custom, let them give up themselves to a free and a rational consideration of things, and they will quickly find that all their profession is but a miserable self-deceiving, and that, indeed, they believe not one word of the religion which they profess: for of what their religion affirms to be in themselves they find not any thing true or real; and what reason have they, then, to believe that the things which it speaks of that are without them are one jot better? If they have no experience of what it affirms to be within them, what confidence can they have of the reality of what it reveals to be without them? John tells us that 'he who says he loves God whom he has not seen, and does not love his brother whom he has seen, is a liar.' Men who do not things of an equal concern to them wherein they may be tried, are not to be believed in what they profess about greater things, whereof no trial can be had. So he that believes not, who experiences not, the power of that which the religion he professes affirms to be in him, if he says that he believes other things which he can have no experience of, he is a liar. For instance, he that professes the gospel avows that the death of Christ crucifies sin; that faith purifies the heart; that the Holy Ghost quickens and enables the soul to duty; that God is good and gracious to all that come to him; that there is precious communion to be obtained with him by Christ; that there is great joy in believing. These things are plainly, openly, frequently insisted on in the gospel. Hence the apostle presses men to obedience on the account of them; and, as it were, leaves them at liberty from it if they were not so (Phil. 2:1–2). Now, if men have lived long in the profession of these things, saying that they are so, but indeed find nothing of truth, reality, or power in them, have no experience of the effects of them in their own hearts or souls, what stable ground have they of believing any thing else in the gospel whereof they cannot have experience? a man professes that the death of Christ will mortify sin and subdue corruption; why does he believe it? Because it is so affirmed in the gospel. How, then, does he find it to be so? Has it this effect upon his soul, in his own heart? Not at all; he finds no such thing in him. How, then, can this man believe that Jesus Christ is the Son of God because it is affirmed in the gospel, seeing that he finds no real truth of that which it affirms to be in himself? So our Saviour argues, 'If I have told you earthly things, and you believe not, how will you believe if I tell you heavenly things?' (John 3:12)—'If you believe not the doctrine of regeneration, which you ought to have experience of, as a thing that is wrought in the hearts of men on the earth, how can you assent to those heavenly mysteries of the gospel which at first are to be received by a pure act of faith, without any present sense or experience?'

Of all dangers, therefore, in profession, let professors take heed of this—namely, of a customary, traditional, or doctrinal owning such truths as ought to have their effects and accomplishment in themselves, whilst they have no experience of the reality and efficacy of them. This is plainly to have a form of godliness, and to deny the power thereof. And of this sort of men do we see many turning atheists, scoffers, and open apostates. They find in themselves that their profession was a lie, and that in truth they had none of those things which they talked of; and to what end should they continue longer in the avowing of that which is not? Besides, finding those things which they have professed to be in them not to be so, they think that what they have believed of the things that are without them are of no other nature; and so reject them altogether.

You will say, then, 'What shall a man do who cannot find or obtain an experience in himself of what is affirmed in the word? He cannot find the death of Christ crucifying sin in him, and he cannot find the Holy Ghost sanctifying his nature, or obtain joy in believing; what shall he, then, do? Shall he not believe or profess those things to be so, because he cannot obtain a blessed experience of them?' I answer, our Saviour has perfectly given direction in this case: 'If any man will do his will, he shall know of the doctrine, whether it be of God, or whether I speak of myself' (John 7:17). Continue in following after the things revealed in the doctrine of the gospel, and you shall have a satisfactory experience that they are true, and that they are of God. Cease not to act faith on them, and you shall find their effects; for 'then shall we know, if we follow on to know the LORD' (Hos. 6:3). Experience will ensue upon permanency in faith and obedience; yea, the first act of sincere believing will be accompanied with such a taste, will give the soul so much experience, as to produce a firm adherence to the things believed. And this is the way to 'prove what is that good, and acceptable, and perfect will of God,' which is revealed to us (Rom. 12:2).

PROFESSION WITH POWER

Where there is an inward, spiritual experience of the power, reality, and efficacy of any supernatural truth, it gives great satisfaction, stability, and assurance to the soul. It puts the soul out of danger or suspicion of being deceived, and gives it to have the testimony of God in itself. So the apostle tells us, 'He that believes on the Son of God has the witness in himself' (1 John 5:10). He had discoursed of the manifold testimony that is given in heaven by all the holy persons of the Trinity, and on earth by grace and ordinances, to the forgiveness of sin and eternal life to be obtained by Jesus Christ. And this record is true, firm, and stable, an abiding foundation for souls to rest upon, that will never deceive them. But yet all this while it is without us—it is that which we have no experience of in ourselves; only we rest upon it because of the authority and faithfulness of them that gave it. But now he that actually believes, he has the testimony in himself; he has by experience a real evidence and assurance of the things testified to—namely, 'That God has given to us eternal life, and this life is in his Son' (v. 11). Let us, then, a little consider wherein this evidence consists, and from whence this assurance arises. To this end some few things must be considered.

*The Doctrine of the Gospel Begets the Form*

That there is a great answerableness and correspondency between the heart of a believer and the truth that he believes. As the word is in the gospel, so is grace in the heart; yea, they are the same thing variously expressed: 'You have obeyed from the heart,' εἰς ὃν παρεδόθητε τύπον διδαχῆς, 'that form of doctrine which was delivered you' (Rom. 6:17). As our translation does not, so I know not how in so few words to express that which is emphatically here insinuated by the Holy Ghost. The meaning is, that the doctrine of the gospel begets the form, figure, image, or likeness of itself in the hearts of them that believe, so they are cast into the mould of it. As is the one, so is the other. The principle of grace in the heart and that in the word are as children of the same parent, completely resembling and representing one another. Grace is a living word, and the word is figured, limned grace. As is regeneration, so is a regenerate heart; as is the doctrine of faith, so is a believer. And this gives great evidence to and assurance of the things that are believed: 'As we have heard, so we have seen and found it.' Such a soul can produce the duplicate of the word, and so adjust all things thereby.

### What a Believer Is

That the first original expression of divine truth is not in the word, no, not as given out from the infinite abyss of divine wisdom and veracity, but it is first hid, laid up, and expressed in the person of Christ. He is the ἀρχέτυπος, the first pattern of truth, which from him is expressed in the word, and from and by the word impressed in the hearts of believers: so that as it has pleased God that all the treasures of wisdom and knowledge should be in him, dwell in him, have their principal residence in him (Col. 2:3); so the whole word is but a revelation of the truth in Christ, or an expression of his image and likeness to the sons of men. Thus we are said to learn 'the truth as it is in Jesus' (Eph. 4:21). It is in Jesus originally and really; and from him it is communicated to us by the word. We are thereby taught and do learn it, for thereby, as the apostle proceeds, 'we are renewed in the spirit of our mind, and do put on the new man, which after God is created in righteousness and true holiness' (v. 23–4). First, the truth is in Jesus, then it is expressed in the word; this word learned and believed becomes grace in the heart, every way answering to the Lord Christ his image, from whom this transforming truth did thus proceed. Nay, this is carried by the apostle yet higher, namely, to God the Father himself, whose image Christ is, and believers his through the word: 'We all, with open face beholding as in a glass the glory of the Lord, are changed into the same image from glory to glory, as by the Spirit of the Lord' (2 Cor. 3:18); 'God, who commanded the light to shine out of darkness, has shined in our hearts, to give the light of the knowledge of the glory of God in the face of Jesus Christ' (2 Cor. 4:6). The first pattern or example of all truth and holiness is God himself; hereof 'Christ is the image' (v. 4). Christ is the image of God, 'The brightness of his glory, and the express image of his person' (Heb. 1:3); 'The image of the invisible God' (Col. 1:15). Hence we are said to 'see the glory of God in the face of Jesus Christ;' because he being his image, the love, grace, and truth of the Father are represented and made conspicuous in him: for we are said to 'behold it in his face,' because of the open and illustrious manifestation of the glory of God in him. And how do we behold this glory? In a glass—'As in a glass;' that is, in the gospel, which has the image and likeness of Christ, who is the image of God, reflected upon it and communicated to it. So have we traced truth and grace from the person of the Father to the Son as a mediator, and thence transfused into the word. In the Father it is essentially; in Jesus Christ originally and exemplarily; and in the word as in a transcript or copy. But does it abide there? No; God by the word of the gospel 'shines in our hearts' (2 Cor. 4:6). He irradiates our minds with a saving light into it and apprehension of it. And what thence ensues? The soul of a believer is 'changed into the same image' by the effectual working of the Holy Ghost (2 Cor. 3:18); that is, the likeness of Christ implanted on the word is impressed on the soul itself, whereby it is renewed into the image of God, whereunto it was at first created. This brings all into a perfect harmony. There is not, where gospel truth is effectually received and experienced in the soul, only a consonancy merely between the soul and the word, but between the soul and Christ by the word, and the soul and God by Christ. And this gives assured establishment to the soul in the things that it believes. Divine truth so conveyed to us is firm, stable, and immovable; and we can say of it in a spiritual sense, '"That which we have heard, that which we have seen with our eyes, which we have looked upon, and our hands have handled, of the Word of life," we know to be true.' Yea, a believer is a testimony to the certainty of truth in what he is, much beyond what he is in all that he says. Words may be pretended; real effects have their testimony inseparably annexed to them.

### The Experience of the Saints on Earth

Hence it appears that there must needs be great assurance of those truths which are thus received and believed; for hereby are 'the senses exercised to discern both good and evil' (Heb. 5:14). Where there is a spiritual sense of truth, of the good and evil that is in doctrines, from an inward experience of what is so good, and from thence an aversation to the contrary, and this obtained διὰ τὴν ἕξιν, by reason of a habit or an habitual frame of heart, there is strength, there is steadfastness and assurance. This is the teaching of the unction, which will not, which cannot, deceive. Hence many of old and of late that could not dispute could yet die for the truth. He that came to another, and went about to prove by sophistical reasonings that there was no such thing as motion, had only this return from him, who either was not able to answer his cavilling or unwilling to put himself to trouble about it—he arose, and, walking up and down, gave him a real confutation of his sophistry. It is so in this case. When a soul has a real experience of the grace of God, of the pardon of sins, of the virtue and efficacy of the death of Christ, of justification by his blood, and peace with God by believing; let men, or devils, or angels from heaven, oppose these things, if it cannot answer their sophisms, yet he can rise up and walk—he can, with all holy confidence and assurance, oppose his own satisfying experience to all their arguings and suggestions. a man will not be disputed out of what he sees and feels; and a believer will abide as firmly by his spiritual sense as any man can by his natural.

This is the meaning of that prayer of the apostle, 'That your hearts might be comforted, being knit together in love, and to all riches of the full assurance of understanding, to the acknowledgment of the mystery of God, and of the Father, and of Christ' (Col. 2:2). Understanding in the mysteries of the gospel they had; but he prays that, by a farther experience of it, they might come to the 'assurance of understanding.' To be true, is the property of the doctrine itself; to be certain or assured, is the property of our minds. Now, this experience does so unite the mind and truth, that we say, 'such a truth is most certain;' whereas certainty is indeed the property of our minds or their knowledge, and not of the truth known. It is certain to us; that is, we have an assured knowledge of it by the experience we have of it. This is the assurance of understanding here mentioned. And he farther prays that we may come to the 'riches' of this assurance—that is, to an abundant, plentiful assurance; and that εἰς ἐπίγνωσιν, 'to the acknowledgment of the mystery of God,' owning it from a sense and experience of its excellency and worth.

And this is in the nature of all gospel truths—they are fitted and suited to be experienced by a believing soul. There is nothing in them so sublime and high, nothing so mysterious, nothing so seemingly low and outwardly contemptible, but that a gracious soul has experience of an excellency, reality, power, and efficacy in it all. For instance, look on that which concerns the order and worship of the gospel. This seems to many to be a mere external thing, whereof a soul can have no inward sense or relish. Notions there are many about it, and endless contentions, but what more? Why, let a gracious soul, in simplicity and sincerity of spirit, give up himself to walk with Christ according to his appointment, and he shall quickly find such a taste and relish in the fellowship of the gospel, in the communion of saints, and of Christ amongst them, as that he shall come up to such riches of assurance in the understanding and acknowledgment of the ways of the Lord, as others by their disputing can never attain to. What is so high, glorious, and mysterious as the doctrine of the ever-blessed Trinity? Some wise men have thought meet to keep it veiled from ordinary Christians, and some have delivered it in such terms as that they can understand nothing by them. But take a believer who has tasted how gracious the Lord is, in the eternal love of the Father, the great undertaking of the Son in the work of mediation and redemption, with the almighty work of the Spirit creating grace and comfort in the soul; and has had an experience of the love, holiness, and power of God in them all; and he will with more firm confidence adhere to this mysterious truth, being led into it and confirmed in it by some few plain testimonies of the word, than a thousand disputers shall do who only have the notion of it in their minds. Let a real trial come, and this will appear. Few will be found to sacrifice their lives on bare speculations. Experience will give assurance and stability.

We have thus cleared the credit of the testimony now to be improved. It is evident, on these grounds, that there is a great certainty in those truths whereof believers have experience. Where they communicate their power to the heart, they give an unquestionable assurance of their truth; and when that is once realized in the soul, all disputes about it are put to silence.

These things being so, let us inquire into the faith and experience of the saints on the earth as to what they know of the truth proposed to confirmation, namely, that there is forgiveness with God. Let us go to some poor soul that now walks comfortably under the light of God's countenance, and say to him, 'Did we not know you some while since to be full of sadness and great anxiety of spirit; yea, sorrowful almost to death, and bitter in soul?'

'Yes,' says he, 'so it was, indeed. My days were consumed with mourning, and my life with sorrow; and I walked heavily, in fear and bitterness of spirit, all the day long.'

'Why, what ailed you, what was the matter with you, seeing as to outward things you were in peace?'

'The law of God had laid hold upon me and slain me. I found myself thereby a woeful sinner, yea, overwhelmed with the guilt of sin. Every moment I expected tribulation and wrath from the hand of God; my sore ran in the night and ceased not, and my soul refused comfort.'

'How is it, then, that you are thus delivered, that you are no more sad? Where have you found ease and peace? Have you been by any means delivered, or did your trouble wear off and depart of its own accord?'

'Alas, no! Had I not met with an effectual remedy, I had sunk and everlastingly perished.'

'What course did you take?'

'I went to Him by Jesus Christ against whom I have sinned, and have found him better to me than I could expect or ever should have believed, had not he overpowered my heart by his Spirit. Instead of wrath, which I feared, and that justly, because I had deserved it, he said to me in Christ, 'Fury is not in me.' For a long time I thought it impossible that there should be mercy and pardon for me, or such a one as I. But he still supported me, sometimes by one means, sometimes by another; until, taking my soul near to himself, he caused me to see the folly of my unbelieving heart, and the vileness of the hard thoughts I had of him, and that, indeed, there is with him forgiveness and plenteous redemption. This has taken away all my sorrows, and given me quietness, with rest and assurance.'

'But are you sure, now, that this is so? May you not possibly be deceived?'

Says the soul, 'I have not the least suspicion of any such matter; and if at any time aught arises to that purpose, it is quickly overcome.'

'But how are you confirmed in this persuasion?'

'That sense of it which I have in my heart; that sweetness and rest which I have experience of; that influence it has upon my soul; that obligation I find laid upon me by it to all thankful obedience; that relief, support, and consolation that it has afforded me in trials and troubles, in the mouth of the grave and entrances of eternity—all answering what is declared concerning these things in the word—will not suffer me to be deceived. I could not, indeed, receive it until God was pleased to speak it to me; but now let Satan do his utmost, I shall never cease to bear this testimony, that there is mercy and forgiveness with him.'

How many thousands may we find of these in the world, who have had such a seal of this truth in their hearts, as they can not only securely lay down their lives in the confirmation of it, if called thereunto, but also do cheerfully and triumphantly venture their eternal concerns upon it! Yea, this is the rise of all that peace, serenity of mind, and strong consolation, which in this world they are made partakers of.

Now this is to me, on the principles before laid down, an evidence great and important. God has not manifested this truth to the saints, thus copied it out of his word, and exemplified it in their souls, to leave them under any possibility of being deceived.

## The Institution of Religious Worship

God's institution of religious worship, and honour therein to be rendered to him by sinners, is another evidence that there is forgiveness with him. I have instanced before in one particular of worship to this purpose—namely, in that of sacrifices; but therein we intended only their particular nature and signification, how they declared and manifested reconciliation, atonement, and pardon. That now aimed at is, to show how all the worship that God has appointed to us, and all the honour which we give to his holy majesty thereby, is built upon the same foundation—namely, a supposition of forgiveness—and is appointed to teach it, and to ascertain us of it; which shall briefly be declared.

### To Glorify God

That the general end of all divine and religious worship is to raise to God a revenue of glory out of the creation. Such is God's infinite natural self-sufficiency, that he stands in need of no such glory and honour. He was in himself no less infinitely and eternally glorious before the creation of all or any thing whatever, than he will be when he shall be encompassed about with the praises of all the works of his hands. And such is his absolute perfection, that no honour given to him, no admiration of him, no ascription of glory and praise, can add any thing to him. Hence says the psalmist, 'My goodness does not extend to you' (Ps. 16:2)—'It does not so reach you as to add to you, to profit you, as it may do the saints that are on earth.' As he in Job 22:2–3, 'Can a man be profitable to God, as he that is wise may be profitable to himself? Is it any pleasure to the Almighty, that you are righteous? Or is it gain to him, that you make your ways perfect?' There is no doubt but that it is well-pleasing to God that we should be righteous and upright; but we do him not a pleasure therein, as though he stood in need of it, or it were advantage or gain to him. And again, Job 35:7, 'If you be righteous, what do you give him? Or what does he receive at your hand?' And the reason of all this the apostle gives us, 'Of him, and through him, and to him, are all things' (Rom. 11:36). Being the first sovereign cause and last absolute end of all things, every way perfect and self-sufficient, nothing can be added to him: or, as the same apostle speaks, 'God that made the world and all things therein, seeing that he is Lord of heaven and earth, is not worshipped with men's hands, as though he needed any thing, seeing he gives to all life, and breath, and all things' (Acts 17:24–5); as he himself pleads at large (Ps. 50:7–13).

## God Chooses What He Will Receive as Worship

Wherefore, all the revenue of glory that God will receive by his worship depends merely on his own voluntary choice and appointment. All worship, I say, depends now on the sovereign will and pleasure of God. It is true there is a natural worship due from rational creatures by the law of their creation. This was indispensably and absolutely necessary at first. The very being of God and order of things required that it should be so. Supposing that God had made such creatures as we are, it could not be but that moral obedience was due to him—namely, that he should be believed in, trusted, and obeyed, as the first cause, last end, and sovereign Lord of all. But the entrance of sin, laying the sinner absolutely under the curse of God, utterly put an end to this order of things. Man was now to have perished immediately, and an end to be put to the law of this obedience. But here, in the sovereign will of God, an interposition was made between sin and the sentence, and man was respited from destruction. All worship following hereon, even that which was before natural, by the law of creation, is now resolved into an arbitrary act of God's will.

And to this end is all worship designed—namely, to give glory to God. For as God has said that 'he will be sanctified in all that draw nigh him'—that is, in his worship—and that therein 'he will be glorified' (Lev. 10:3); and that 'he that offers him praise,' that is, performs any part of his worship and service—'glorifies him' (Ps. 50:23): so the nature of the thing itself declares that it can have no other end. By this he has all his glory, even from the inanimate creation.

## FALLEN ANGELS ARE NOT CALLED TO WORSHIP

Consider that God has not prescribed any worship of himself to the angels that sinned. They are, indeed, under his power, and he uses them as he pleases, to serve the ends of his holy providence. Bounds he prescribes to them by his power, and keeps them in dread of the full execution of his wrath; but he requires not of them that they should believe in him. They believe, indeed, and tremble. They have a natural apprehension of the being, power, providence, holiness, and righteousness of God, which is inseparable from their natures; and they have an expectation from thence of that punishment and vengeance which is due to them, which is inseparable from them as sinners; and this is their faith: but to believe in God—that is, to put their trust in him, to resign up themselves to him—God requires it not of them. The same is the case with them also as to love, and fear, and delight—all inward affections, which are the proper worship of God. These they have not, nor does God any longer require them in them. They eternally cast them off in their first sin. And where these are not, where they are not required, where they cannot be, there no outward worship can be prescribed or appointed; for external instituted worship is nothing but the way that God assigns and chooses us to express and exercise the inward affections of our minds towards him. He rules the fallen angels '*per nuturn providentim*,' not '*verbum praecepti.*'

Now, as God dealt with the angels, so also would he have dealt with mankind, had he left them all under the curse, without remedy or hope of relief. As he does with them—he eternally satisfies himself in that revenue of glory which arises to him in their punishment—so also he would have done with these, had there been no forgiveness with him for them. He would not have required them to fear, love, or obey him, or have appointed to them any way of worship whereby to express such affections towards him; for to what end should he have done it? What righteousness would admit that service, duty, and obedience should be prescribed to them who could not, ought not to have any expectation or hope of acceptance or reward? This is contrary to the very first notion which God requires in us of his nature: for 'he that comes to God must believe that he is, and that he is a rewarder of them that diligently seek him' (Heb. 11:6); which would not be so should he appoint a voluntary worship, and not propose a reward to the worshippers.

## GOD'S CALL TO WORSHIP DECLARES FORGIVENESS

It is evident that God, by the prescription of a worship to sinners, fully declares that there is forgiveness with him for them.

### *He Accepts the Worship of His People*

He manifests thereby that he is willing to receive a new revenue of glory from them. This, as we have proved, is the end of worship. This he would never have done but with a design of accepting and rewarding his creatures; for do we think that he will be beholding to them? That he will take and admit of their voluntary, reasonable service, according to his will and command, without giving them a reward, yea, and such a one as their obedience holds no proportion to? No such thing would become his infinite self-sufficiency, goodness, and bounty. This the wife of Manoah well pleads: 'If,' says she, 'the LORD were pleased to kill us, he would not have received a burnt-offering and a meat-offering at our hands' (Judg. 13:23). His acceptance of worship from us is an infallible demonstration that he will not execute against us the severity of the first curse. And this is clearly evidenced in the first record of solemn instituted worship performed by sinners: 'The LORD had respect to Abel and to his offering' (Gen. 4:4). Some think that

God gave a visible pledge of his acceptance of Abel and his offering. It may be it was by fire from heaven; for how else should Cain so instantly know that his brother and his offering were accepted, but that he and his were refused? However it were, it is evident that what testimony God gave of the acceptance of his offering, the same he gave concerning his person; and that in the first place he had respect to Abel, and then to his offering. And therefore the apostle says that thereby 'he obtained witness that he was righteous' (Heb. 11:4) — that is, the witness or testimony of God himself. Now, this was in the forgiveness of his sins, without which he could neither be righteous nor accepted, for he was a sinner. This God declared by acceptance of his worship. And thus we also, if we have any testimony of God's acceptance of us in any part of his worship, should employ it to the same end. Has God enlarged our hearts in prayer? Has he given us an answer to any of our supplications? Has he refreshed our hearts in the preaching and dispensation of the word, or any other ordinance? We are not to rest in the particular about which our communion with him has been; our doing so is the cause why we lose our experiences; they lie scattered up and down, separated from their proper root, and so are easily lost: but this is that which we should first improve such particular experiences in the worship of God to — namely, that God has pardoned our sins, and accepted our persons thereon; for without that, none of our worship or service would please him or be accepted with him.

### He Deals with Us on New Terms

Hereby God lets us know that he deals with us upon new terms, so that, notwithstanding sin, we may enjoy his love and favour. For this we have the engagement of his truth and veracity, and he cannot deceive us. But yet by this command of his for his worship we should be deceived, if there were no forgiveness with him; for it gives us encouragement to expect, and assurance of finding, acceptance with him, which without it cannot be obtained. This, then, God declares by his institution of and command for his worship—namely, that there is nothing that shall indispensably hinder those who give up themselves to obedience of God's commands from enjoying his love and favour, and communion with him.

### He Is the Author of Biblical Worship

For matter of fact, it is known and confessed that God has appointed a worship for sinners to perform All the institutions of the Old and New Testament bear witness hereunto. God was the author of them. And men know not what they do when either they neglect them or would be intermixing their own imaginations with them. What can the mind of man conceive or invent that may have any influence into this matter, to secure the souls of believers of their acceptance with God? Is there any need of their testimony to the truth, faithfulness, and goodness of God? These things he has taken upon himself. This, then, is that which is to be fixed on our souls upon our first invitation to religious worship—namely, that God intends a new revenue of glory from us, and therefore declares that there is a way for the taking away of our sins, without which we can give no glory to him by our obedience; and this is done only by forgiveness.

#### ORDINANCES THAT SPECIFICALLY CONFIRM FORGIVENESS

There are some ordinances of worship appointed for this very end and purpose, to confirm to us the forgiveness of sin, especially in that worship which is instituted by the Lord Jesus under the New Testament. I shall instance in one or two.

### Baptism

The ordinance of baptism. This was accompanied with the dawning of the gospel in the ministry of John the Baptist; and he expressly declared, in his sermons upon it, that it was instituted of God to declare the 'remission of sins' (Mark 1:4).

It is true the Lord Christ submitted to that ordinance and was baptized by John, who had no sin; but this belonged to the obedience which God required of him, as for our sakes he was made under the law. He was to observe all ordinances and institutions of the worship of God, not for any need he had in his own person of the especial ends and significations of some of them; yet, as he was our sponsor, surety, and mediator, standing in our stead in all that he so did, he was to yield obedience to them, that so he might 'fulfil all righteousness' (Matt. 3:15). So was he circumcised, so he was baptized, both which had respect to sin, though absolutely free from all sin in his own person; and that because he was free from no obedience to any command of God.

But, as was said, baptism itself, as appointed to be an ordinance of worship for sinners to observe, was a declaration of that forgiveness that is with God. It was so in its first institution. God calls a man in a marvellous and miraculous manner; gives him a ministry from heaven; commands him to go and baptize all those who, confessing their sins, and professing repentance of them, should come to him to have a testimony of forgiveness. And as to the especial nature of this ordinance, he appoints it to be such as to represent the certainty and truth of his grace in pardon to their senses by a visible pledge. He lets them know that he would take away their sin, wherein their spiritual defilement consists, even as water takes away the outward filth of the body; and that hereby they shall be saved, as surely as Noah and his family were saved in the ark swimming upon the waters (1 Pet. 3:20). Now, how great a deceit must needs in this whole matter have been put upon poor sinners, if it were not infallibly certain that they might obtain forgiveness with God!

After the entrance of this ordinance in the ministry of John, the Lord Christ takes it into his own hand, and commands the observation of it to all his disciples. I dispute not now who are the proper immediate objects of it; whether they only who actually can make profession of their faith, or believers with their infant seed. For my part, I believe that all whom Christ loves and pardons are to be made partakers of the pledge thereof. And the sole reason which they of old insisted on why the infants of believing parents should not be baptized was, because they thought they had no sin; and therein we know their mistake. But I treat not now of these things. Only this I say is certain, that in the prescription of this ordinance to his church, the great intention of the Lord Christ was to ascertain to us the forgiveness of sins. And sinners are invited to a participation of this ordinance for that end, that they may receive the pardon of their sins; that is, an infallible pledge and assurance of it (Acts 2:38). And the very nature of it declares this to be its end, as was before intimated. This is another engagement of the truth, and faithfulness, and holiness of God, so that we cannot be deceived in this matter.

'There is,' says God, 'forgiveness with me.'

Says the soul, 'How, Lord, shall I know, how shall I come to be assured of it? For by reason of the perpetual accusations of conscience, and the curse of the law upon the guilt of my sin, I find it a very hard matter for me to believe. Like Gideon, I would have a token of it.'

'Why, behold,' says God, 'I will give you a pledge and a token of it, which cannot deceive you. When the world of old had been overwhelmed with a deluge of waters by reason of their sins, and those who remained, though they had just cause to fear that the same judgment would again befall them or their posterity, because they saw there was like to be the same cause of it, the thoughts and imaginations of the hearts of men being evil still, and that continually; to secure them against these fears, I told them that I would destroy the earth no more with water, and I gave them a token of my faithfulness therein by placing my bow in the cloud. And have I failed them? Though the sin and wickedness of the world has been, since that day, unspeakably great, yet mankind is not drowned again, nor ever shall be. I will not deceive their expectation from the token I have given them. Wherever, then, there is a word of promise confirmed with a token, never fear a disappointment. But so is this matter. I have declared that there is forgiveness with me; and, to give you assurance thereof, I have ordained this pledge and sign as a seal of my word, to take away all doubts and suspicion of your being deceived. As the world shall be drowned no more, so neither shall they who believe come short of forgiveness.'

And this is the use which we ought to make of this ordinance. It is God's security of the pardon of our sins, which we may safely rest in.

## The Lord's Supper

The same is the end of that other great ordinance of the church, the supper of the Lord. The same thing is therein confirmed to us by another sign, pledge, token, or seal. We have shown before what respect gospel forgiveness has to the death or blood of Jesus Christ. That is the means whereby for us it is procured, the way whereby it comes forth from God, to the glory of his righteousness and grace; which afterward must be more distinctly insisted on. This ordinance, therefore, designed and appointed on purpose for the representation and calling to remembrance of the death of Christ, with the communication of the benefits thereof to them that believe, principally intends our faith and comfort in the truth under consideration. And, therefore, in the very institution of it, besides the general end before mentioned, which had been sufficient for our security, there is moreover added an especial mention of the forgiveness of sin; for so speaks our Saviour, in the institution of it for the use of the church to the end of the world: 'This is my blood of the new testament, which is shed for many for the remission of sins' (Matt. 26:28). As if he had said, 'The end for which I have appointed the observance of this duty and service to you is, that I may testify thereby to you that by my blood, the sacrifice of myself, and the atonement made thereby, I have purchased for you the remission of your sins; which you shall assuredly be made partakers of.' And more I shall not add to this consideration, because the death of Christ, respected in this ordinance, will again occur to us.

## Church Order, Assemblies, and Worship

What is the end of all church-order, assemblies, and worship? What is a church? Is it not a company of sinners gathered together, according to God's appointment, to give glory and praise to him for pardoning grace, for the forgiveness of sins, and to yield him that obedience which he requires from us on the account of his having so dealt with us? This is the nature, this is the end of a church. He that understands it not, he that uses it not to that end, does but abuse that great institution. And such abuse the world is full of. Some endeavour to make their own secular advantages by the pretence of the church; some discharge the duty required in it with some secret hopes that it shall be their righteousness before God; some answer only their light and convictions in an empty profession. This alone is the true end, the true use of it— we assemble ourselves to learn that there is forgiveness with God through Christ; to pray that we may be made partakers of it; to bless and praise God for our interest in it; to engage ourselves to that obedience which he requires upon the account of it. And were this constantly upon our minds and in our designs, we might be more established in the faith of it than, it may be, the most of us are.

### COMMANDS TO PRAY FOR PARDON

One particular instance more of this nature shall conclude this evidence—God has commanded us, the Lord Christ has taught us, to pray for the pardon of sin; which gives us unquestionable security that it may be attained, that it is to be found in God. For the clearing whereof observe.

### 'Forgive Us Our Debts'

That the Lord Christ, in the revelation of the will of God to us, as to the duty that he required at our hands, has taught and instructed us to pray for the forgiveness of sin. It is one of the petitions which he has left on record for our use and imitation in that summary of all prayer which he has given us: 'Forgive us our debts' (Matt. 6:12) our trespasses, our sins. Some contend that this is a form of prayer to be used in the prescript limited words of it. All grant that it is a rule for prayer, comprising the heads of all necessary things that we are to pray for, and obliging us to make supplications for them. So, then, upon the authority of God, revealed to us by Jesus Christ, we are bound in duty to pray for pardon of sins or forgiveness.

### Not to Pray for Forgiveness Is Blasphemy and Sin

On this supposition it is the highest blasphemy and reproach of God imaginable, to conceive that there is not forgiveness with him for us. Indeed, if we should go upon our own heads, without his warranty and authority, to ask any thing at his hand, we might well expect to meet with disappointment; for what should encourage us to any such boldness? But now, when God himself shall command us to come and ask any thing from him—so making it thereby our duty, and that the neglect thereof should be our great sin and rebellion against him—to suppose he has not the thing in his power to bestow on us, or that his will is wholly averse from so doing, is to reproach him with want of truth, faithfulness, and holiness, and not to be God. For what sincerity can be in such proceedings? Is it consistent with any divine excellency? Could it have any other end but to deceive poor creatures? Either to delude them if they do pray according to his command, or to involve them in farther guilt if they do not? God forbid any such thoughts should enter into our hearts.

### God Promises to Hear

To put this whole matter out of the question, God has promised to hear our prayers, and in particular those which we make to him for the forgiveness of sin. So our Saviour has assured us that what we ask in his name it shall be done for us. And he has, as we have showed, taught us to ask this very thing of God as our heavenly Father—that is, in his name; for in and through him alone is he a Father to us. I need not insist on particular promises to this purpose; they are, as you know, multiplied in the Scriptures.

---

What has been spoken may suffice to establish our present argument, namely, that God's prescription of religious worship to sinners undeniably proves that with him there is forgiveness; especially considering that the principal parts of the worship so prescribed and appointed by him are peculiarly designed to confirm us in the faith thereof.

And this is the design of the words that we do insist upon: 'There is forgiveness with you, that you may be feared.' The fear of God, as we have showed, in the Old Testament, frequently expresses, not that gracious affection of our minds which is distinctly so called, but that whole worship of God, wherein that and all other gracious affections towards God are to be exercised. Now, the psalmist tells us that the foundation of this fear or worship, and the only motive and encouragement for sinners to engage in it and give up themselves to it, is this, that there is forgiveness with God. Without this no sinner could fear, serve, or worship him. This, therefore, is undeniably proved by the institution of this worship, which was proposed to confirmation.

The end of all these things, as we shall afterward at large declare, is to encourage poor sinners to believe, and to evidence how inexcusable they will be left who, notwithstanding all this, do, through the power of their lusts and unbelief, refuse to come to God in Christ that they may be pardoned. Yea, the laying open of the certainty and fullness of the evidence given to this truth makes it plain and conspicuous whence it is that men perish in and for their sins. Is it for want of mercy, goodness, grace, or patience in God? Is it through any defect in the mediation of the Lord Christ? Is it for want of the mightiest encouragements and most infallible assurances that with God there is forgiveness? Not at all; but merely on the account of their own obstinacy, stubbornness, and perverseness. They will not come to this light, yea, they hate it, because their deeds are evil. They will not come to Christ, that they may have life. It is merely darkness, blindness, and love of sin that brings men to destruction. And this is laid open, and all pretences and excuses are removed, and the shame of men's lusts made naked, by the full confirmation of this truth which God has furnished us withal.

Take heed, you that hear or read these things; if they are not mixed with faith, they will add greatly to your misery. Every argument will be your torment. But these considerations must be insisted on afterward.

Moreover, if you will take into your minds what has been delivered in particular concerning the nature and end of the worship of God which you attend to, you may be instructed in the use and due observation of it. When you address yourselves to it, remember that this is that which God requires of you who are sinners; that this he would not have done but with thoughts and intention of mercy for sinners. Bless him with all your souls that this is laid as the foundation of all that you have to do with him. You are not utterly cast off because you are sinners. Let this support and warm your hearts when you go to hear, to pray, or any duty of worship. Consider what is your principal work in the whole. You are going to deal with God about forgiveness, in the being, causes, consequents, and effects of it. Hearken what he speaks, declares, or reveals about it; mix his revelation and promises with faith. Inquire diligently into all the obedience and thankfulness, all those duties of holiness and righteousness, which he justly expects from them who are made partakers of it. So shall you observe the worship of God to his glory and your own advantage.

## THE NEW COVENANT

Another evidence hereof may be taken from the making, establishing, and ratifying of the new covenant. That God would make a new covenant with his people is often promised, often declared (see, among other places, Jer. 31:31–2). And that he has done so accordingly the apostle at large manifests (Heb. 8:8–12). Now, herein sundry things to our present purpose may be considered.

## ANY COVENANT BETWEEN GOD AND MAN IS A MARVEL

First, it is supposed that God had before made another covenant with mankind. With reference hereunto is this said to be a new one. It is opposed to another that was before it, and in comparison whereof that is called old and this said to be new, as the apostle speaks expressly in the place before mentioned. Now, a covenant between God and man is a thing great and marvellous, whether we consider the nature of it or the ends of it. In its own nature it is a convention, compact, and agreement for some certain ends and purposes between the holy Creator and his poor creatures. How infinite, how unspeakable must needs the grace and condescension of God in this matter be! For what is poor miserable man, that God should set his heart upon him—that he should, as it were, give bounds to his sovereignty over him, and enter into terms of agreement with him? For whereas before he was a mere object of his absolute dominion, made at his will and for his pleasure, and on the same reasons to be crushed at any time into nothing; now he has a bottom and ground given him to stand upon, whereon to expect good things from God upon the account of his faithfulness and righteousness. God in a covenant gives those holy properties of his nature to his creature, as his hand or arm for him to lay hold upon, and by them to plead and argue with him. And without this a man could have no foundation for any intercourse or communion with God, or of any expectation from him, nor any direction how to deal with him in any of his concerns. Great and signal, then, was the condescension of God, to take his poor creature into covenant with himself; and especially will this be manifest if we consider the ends of it, and why it is that God thus deals with man. Now, these are no other than that man might serve him aright, be blessed by him, and be brought to the everlasting enjoyment of him—all to his glory. These are the ends of every covenant that God takes us into with himself; and these are 'the whole of man' [Eccles. 12:13]. No more is required of us in a way of duty, no more can be required by us to make us blessed and happy, but what is contained in them. That we might live to God, be accepted with him, and come to the eternal fruition of him, is the whole of man, all that we were made for or are capable of; and these are the ends of every covenant that God makes with men, being all comprised in that solemn word, that 'he will be their God, and they shall be his people.'

## COVENANT ABROGATION REQUIRES MOMENTOUS CAUSE

Secondly, this being the nature, this the end of a covenant, there must be some great and important cause to change, alter, and abrogate a covenant once made and established—to lay aside one covenant and to enter into another. And yet this the apostle says expressly that God had done (Heb. 8:13), and proves it, because himself calls that which he promised a new covenant: which undeniably confirms two things: first, that the other was become old; and, secondly, that being become so, it was changed, altered, and removed. I know the apostle speaks immediately of the old administration of the covenant under the Old Testament of Mosaical institutions; but he does so with reference to that revival which in it was given to the first covenant made with Adam: for in the giving of the law, and the curse wherewith it was accompanied, which were immixed with that administration of the covenant, there was a solemn revival and representation of the first covenant and its sanction, whereby it had life and power given it to keep the people in bondage all their days. And the end of the abolition, or taking away of the legal administration of the covenant, was merely to take out of God's dealing with his people all use and remembrance of the first covenant. As was said, therefore, to take away, disannul, and change a covenant so made, ratified, and established betwixt God and man, is a matter that must be resolved into some cogent, important, and indispensable cause. And this will the more evidently appear if we consider:

### The First Covenant Was Good

In general, that the first covenant was good, holy, righteous, and equal. It was such as became God to make, and was every way the happiness of the creature to accept of. We need no other argument to prove it holy and good than this, that God made it. It was the effect of infinite holiness, wisdom, righteousness, goodness, and grace; and therefore in itself was it every way perfect, for so are all the works of God. Besides, it was such as man, when through his own fault he cannot obtain any good by it, and must perish everlastingly by virtue of the curse of it, yet cannot but subscribe to its righteousness and holiness. The law was the rule of it; therein is the tenor of it contained. Now, says the apostle, 'Whatever becomes of the sin and the sinner, "the law is holy, and the commandment is holy, and just, and good"' (Rom. 7:12)—holy in itself and its own nature, as being the order and constitution of the most holy God; just and equal with reference to us, such as we have no reason to complain of, or repine against the authority of; and the terms of it are most righteous. And not only so, but it is good also; that which, notwithstanding the appearance of rigour and severity which it is accompanied withal, had in it an exceeding mixture of goodness and grace, both in the obedience constituted in it and the reward annexed to it; as might be more fully manifested were that our present work.

### Good in Its Demands & Promises

In particular, it was good, holy, and righteous in all the commands of it, in the obedience which it required.

And two things there were that rendered it exceeding righteous in reference to its precepts or commands. First, that they were all suited to the principles of the nature of man created by God, and in the regular acting whereof consisted his perfection. God in the first covenant required nothing of man, prescribed nothing to him, but what there was a principle for the doing and accomplishing of it ingrafted and implanted on his nature, which rendered all those commands equal, holy, and good; for what need any man complain of that which requires nothing of him but what he is from his own frame and principles inclined to? Secondly, all the commands of it were proportionate to the strength and ability of them to whom they were given. God in that covenant required nothing of any man but what he had before enabled him to perform, nothing above his strength or beyond his power; and thence was it also righteous.

Secondly, it was exceeding good, holy, and righteous, upon the account of its promises and rewards. 'Do this,' says the covenant; 'this which you are able to do, which the principles of your nature are fitted for and inclined to.' Well, what shall be the issue thereof? Why, 'Do this, and live.' Life is promised to obedience, and that such a life as, both for the present and future condition of the creature, was accompanied with every thing that was needful to make it blessed and happy. Yea, this life having in it the eternal enjoyment of God, God himself, as a reward, was exceedingly above whatever the obedience of man could require as due, or have any reason, on any other account but merely of the goodness of God, to expect.

### God's Glory Manifested in any Outcome

There was provision in that covenant for the preservation and manifestation of the glory of God, whatever was the event on the part of man. This was provided for in the wisdom and righteousness of God. Did man continue in his obedience, and fulfil the terms of the covenant, all things were laid in subserviency. to the eternal glory of God in his reward. Herein would he for ever have manifested and exalted the glory of his holiness, power, faithfulness, righteousness, and goodness. As an almighty Creator and Preserver, as a faithful God and righteous Rewarder, would he have been glorified. On supposition, on the other side, that man by sin and rebellion should transgress the terms and tenor of this covenant, yet God had made provision that no detriment to his glory should ensue thereon; for by the constitution of a punishment proportionable in his justice to that sin and demerit, he had provided that the glory of his holiness, righteousness, and veracity, in his threatenings, should be exalted, and that to all eternity. God would have lost no more glory and honour by the sin of man than by the sin of angels, which, in his infinite wisdom and righteousness, is become a great theatre of his eternal glory; for he is no less excellent in his greatness and severity than in his goodness and power.

Wherefore, we may now return to our former inquiry: All things being thus excellently and admirably disposed, in infinite wisdom and holiness, in this covenant, the whole duty and blessedness of man being fully provided for, and the glory of God absolutely secured upon all events, what was the reason that God left not all things to stand or fall according to the terms of it? Wherefore does he reject and lay aside this covenant, and promise to make another, and do so accordingly? Certain it is that he might have continued it with a blessed security to his own glory; and he 'makes all things for himself, even the wicked for the day of evil.'

God himself shows what was the only and sole reason of this dispensation (Heb. 8:7–13). The sum of it is this: Notwithstanding the blessed constitution of the first covenant, yet there was no provision for the pardon of sin, no room or place for forgiveness in it; but on supposition that man sinned, he was in that covenant left remediless. God had not in it revealed that there was any such thing as forgiveness with him; nor had any sinner the least hope or grounds of expectation from thence of any such thing in him. Die he must, and perish, and that without remedy or recovery. 'Now,' says God, 'this must not be. Mercy, goodness, grace, require another state of things. This covenant will not manifest them; their effects will not be communicated to poor sinners by it. Hence,' says he, 'it is faulty, that is, defective. I will not lose the glory of them, nor shall sinners be unrelieved by them. And, therefore, although I may strictly tie up all mankind to the terms of this, yet I will make another covenant with them, wherein they shall know and find that there is forgiveness with me, that they may fear me.'

Now, next to the blood of Christ, whereby this covenant was ratified and confirmed, this is the greatest evidence that can possibly be given that there is forgiveness with God. To what end else does God make this great alteration in the effects of his will, in his way of dealing with mankind? As forgiveness of sin is expressly contained in the tenor and words of the covenant, so set it aside, and it will be of no more use or advantage than the former; for as this covenant is made directly with sinners, nor was there any one in the world when God made it that was not a sinner, nor is it of use to any but sinners, so is forgiveness of sins the very life of it.

Hence we may see two things. First, the greatness of forgiveness, that we may learn to value it; and, secondly, the certainty of it, that we may learn to believe it.

### The Greatness of Forgiveness

First, the greatness of it. God would not do so great a thing as that mentioned but for a great, the greatest end. Had it not been a matter of the greatest importance to the glory of God and the good of the souls of men, God would not for the sake of it have laid aside one covenant and made another. We may evidently see how the heart of God was set upon it, how his nature and will were engaged in it. All this was done that we might be pardoned. The old glorious fabric of obedience and rewards shall be taken down to the ground, that a new one may be erected for the honour and glory of forgiveness. God forbid that we should have slight thoughts of that which was so strangely and wonderfully brought forth, wherein God had as it were embarked his great glory! Shall all this be done for our sakes, and shall we undervalue it or disesteem it? God forbid. God could, if I may so say, more easily have made a new world of innocent creatures, and have governed them by the old covenant, than have established this new one for the salvation of poor sinners; but then, where had been the glory of forgiveness? It could never have been known that there was forgiveness with him. The old covenant could not have been preserved and sinners pardoned. Wherefore, God chose rather to leave the covenant than sinners unrelieved, than grace unexalted and pardon unexercised.

Prize it as you prize your souls; and give glory to God for it, as all those that believe will do to eternity.

### The Certainty of Forgiveness

Secondly, for the security of it, that we may believe it. What greater can be given? God deceives no man, no more than he is deceived. And what could God, that cannot lie, do more to give us satisfaction herein than he has done? Would you be made partakers of this forgiveness? Go to God, spread before him this whole matter; plead with him that he himself has so far laid aside the first covenant, of his own gracious will, as to make a new one, and that merely because it had no forgiveness in it. This he has made on purpose that it might be known that there is forgiveness in him. And shall not we now be made partakers of it? Will he now deny that to us which he has given such assurance of, and raised such expectations concerning it? Nothing can here wrong us, nothing can ruin us, but unbelief. Lay hold on this covenant, and we shall have pardon. This God expresses (Isa. 27:4–5). Will we continue on the old bottom of the first covenant? All that we can do thereon is but to set thorns and briers in the way of God, to secure ourselves from his coming against us and upon us with his indignation and fury. Our sins are so, and our righteousness is no better. And what will be the issue? Both they and we shall be trodden down, consumed, and burnt up. What way, then, what remedy is left to us? Only this of laying hold on the arm and strength of God in that covenant wherein forgiveness of sin is provided. Therein alone he says, 'Fury is not in me.' And the end will be that we shall have peace with him, both here and for ever.

## THE OATH OF GOD

The oath of God engaged and interposed in this matter is another evidence of the truth insisted on. Now, because this is annexed to the covenant before mentioned, and is its establishment, I shall pass it over the more briefly. And in it we may consider:

## THE NATURE OF THE OATH

First, the nature of the oath of God. The apostle tells us that 'He sware by himself;' and he gives this reason of it, 'Because he had no greater to swear by' (Heb. 6:13). An oath for the confirmation of any thing is an invocation of a supreme power that can judge of the truth that is spoken, and vindicate the breach of the engagement. This God has none other but himself: 'Because he could swear by no greater, he sware by himself.' Now, this God does—First, by express affirmation that he has so sworn by himself, which was the form of the first solemn oath of God, 'By myself have I sworn, says the LORD' (Gen. 22:16). The meaning whereof is, 'I have taken it upon myself as I am God; or let me not be so, if I perform not this thing.' And this is expressed by his soul: 'The LORD of hosts has sworn by his soul' (Jer. 51:14); that is, 'by himself,' as we render the words. Secondly, God does it by the especial interposition of some such property of his nature as is suited to give credit and confirmation to the word spoken—as of his holiness, 'I have sworn by my holiness' (Ps. 89:35, so also Amos 4:2); sometimes by his life, 'As I live, says the LORD' (חַי־אָנִי, 'I live, says God'), 'it shall be so;' and sometimes by his name (Jer. 44:26). God as it were engages the honour and glory of the properties of his nature for the certain accomplishment of the things mentioned. And this is evident from the manner of the expression, as in that place of Psalm 89:35, 'Once have I sworn by my holiness that I will not lie to David.' So we; in the original the words are elliptical: 'If I lie to David;' that is, 'Let me not be so, nor be esteemed to be so, if I lie to David.'

## THE END OF HIS OATH

Secondly, the end of his oath. God does not give it to make his word or promise sure and steadfast, but to give assurance and security to us of their accomplishment. Every word of God is sure and certain, truth itself, because it is his; and he might justly require of us the belief of it without any farther attestation: but yet, knowing what great objections Satan and our own unbelieving hearts will raise against him promises, at least as to our own concern in them, to confirm our minds, and to take away all pretences of unbelief, he interposes his oath in this matter. What can remain of distrust in such a case? If there be a matter in doubt between men, and an oath be interposed in the confirmation of that which is called in question, it is 'an end,' as the apostle tells us, 'unto them of all strife' (Heb. 6:16). How much more ought it to be so on the part of God, when his oath is engaged! And the apostle declares this end of his oath; it is 'to show the immutability of his counsel' (v. 17). His counsel was declared before in the promise; but now some doubt or strife may arise whether, on one occasion or other, God may not change his counsel, or whether he has not changed it with such conditions as to render it useless to us. In what case soever it be, to remove all doubts and suspicions of this nature, God adds his oath, manifesting the unquestionable immutability of his counsel and promises. What, therefore, is thus confirmed is ascertained to the height of what any thing is capable of; and not to believe it is the height of impiety.

### UNSPEAKABLE CONDESCENSION

Thirdly, in this interposition of God by an oath there is unspeakable condescension of grace, which is both an exceeding great motive to faith and a great aggravation of unbelief; for what are we, that the holy and blessed God should thus condescend to us, as, for our satisfaction and surety, to engage himself by an oath? One said well of old, *'Felices nos quorum causa Deus jurat! O infelices, si nec juranti Deo credimus;'*—'It is an inestimable advantage that God should for our sakes engage himself by his oath. So it will be our misery if we believe him not when he swears to us.' What can we now object against what is thus confirmed? What pretence, colour, or excuse can we have for our unbelief? How just, how righteous, how holy must their destruction be, who, upon this strange, wonderful, and unexpected warranty, refuse to set to their seal that God is true!

### 'AS I LIVE'

These things being premised, we may consider how variously God has engaged his oath that there is forgiveness with him. First, he swears that he has no pleasure in the death of a sinner, but rather that he repent and live: 'As I live, says the Lord, I have no pleasure in the death of the wicked' (Ezek. 33:11). Now, without forgiveness in him every sinner must die, and that without remedy. Confirming, therefore, with his oath that it is his will the sinner should return, repent, and live, he does in the first place swear by himself that there is forgiveness with him for these sinners that shall so repent and turn to him.

Again, whereas the great means he has appointed for the forgiveness of sins is by the mediation of the Lord Christ, as we shall afterward show, he has on several occasions confirmed his purpose in him, and the counsel of his will, by his oath. By this oath be promised him to Abraham and David of old; which proved the foundation of the church's stability in all generations, and also of their security and assurance of acceptance with him (see Luke 1:73-5). And in his taking upon him that office whereby in an especial manner the forgiveness of sins was to be procured—namely, of his being a priest to offer sacrifice, to make an atonement for sinners—he confirmed it to him, and him in it, by his oath: 'He was not made a priest without an oath' (Heb. 7:20). And to what end? Namely, that he might be 'a surety of a better testament' (v. 22). And what was that better testament? Why, that which brought along with it the 'forgiveness of sins' (Heb. 8:12-13). So that it was forgiveness which was so confirmed by the oath of God.

Farther: the apostle shows that the great original promise made to Abraham being confirmed by the oath of God, all his other promises were in like manner confirmed; whence he draws that blessed conclusion which we have (Heb. 6:17-18): 'As to every one,' says he, 'that flees for refuge to the hope that is set before him'—that is, who seeks to escape the guilt of sin, the curse and the sentence of the law, by an application of himself to God in Christ for pardon—'He has the oath of God to secure him that he shall not fall thereof.' And thus are all the concerns of the forgiveness of sin testified to by the oath of God; which we have manifested to be the highest security in this matter that God can give or that we are capable of.

## THE NAME OF GOD

Another foundation of this truth, and infallible evidence of it, may be taken from that especial name and title which God takes to himself in this matter; for he owns the name of 'The God of pardons,' or 'The God of forgiveness.' So is he called, אֱלוֹהַּ סְלִיחוֹת (Neh. 9:17). We have rendered the words, 'You are a God ready to pardon;' but they are, as was said, 'You are a God of pardons,' 'forgiveness,' or' propitiations.' That is his name, which he owns, which he accepts of the ascription of to himself; the name whereby he will be known. And to clear this evidence, we must take in some considerations of the name of God and the use thereof.

### GOD REVEALS HIMSELF BY HIS NAME

The name of God is that whereby he reveals himself to us, whereby he would have us know him and own him. It is something expressive of his nature or properties which he has appropriated to himself. Whatever, therefore, any name of God expresses him to be, that he is, that we may expect to find him; for he will not deceive us by giving himself a wrong or a false name. And on this account he requires us to trust in his name, because he will assuredly be found to us what his name imports. Resting on his name, flying to his name, calling upon his name, praising his name, things so often mentioned in the Scripture, confirm the same to us. These things could not be our duty if we might be deceived in so doing. God is, then, and will be, to us what his name declares.

## GOD REVEALS HIMSELF BY AN APPROPRIATE NAME

On this ground and reason God is said then first to be known by
any name, when those to whom he reveals himself do, in an especial
manner, rest on that name by faith, and have that accomplished
towards them which that name imports, signifies, or declares. And
therefore God did not, under the Old Testament, reveal himself to
any by the name of the Father of Jesus Christ or the Son incarnate,
because the grace of it to them was not to be accomplished. 'God
having provided some better thing for us, that they without us
should not be made perfect,' they were not intrusted with the full
revelation of God by all his blessed names. Neither does God call
us to trust in any name of his, however declared or revealed, unless
he gives it us in an especial manner, by way of covenant, to rest
upon. So he speaks, 'I appeared to Abraham, to Isaac, and to Jacob
בְּאֵל שַׁדָּי, by the name of God Almighty, but by my name Jehovah
was I not known to them' (Exod. 6:3). It is certain that both these
names of God, El-shaddai and Jehovah, were known among his
people before. In the first mention we have of Abraham's addressing
himself to the worship of God, he makes use of the name Jehovah:
'He built an altar to Jehovah' (Gen. 12:7). And so afterward not only
does Moses make use of that name in the repetition of the story,
but it was also of frequent use amongst them. Whence, then, is it
said that God appeared to them by the name of El-shaddai, but not
by the name of Jehovah? The reason is, because that was the name
which God gave himself in the solemn confirmation of the covenant
with Abraham (Gen. 17:1): אֲנִי־אֵל שַׁדַּי—'I am El-shaddai,' 'God
Almighty,' 'God All-sufficient.' And when Isaac would pray for the
blessing of the covenant on Jacob, he makes use of that name (Gen.
28:3), 'God Almighty bless you.' He invocates that name of God
which was engaged in the covenant made with his father Abraham
and himself. That, therefore, we may with full assurance rest on
the name of God, it is not only necessary that God reveal that
name to be his, but also that he give it out to us for that end and

purpose, that we might know him thereby, and place our trust and confidence in him according to what that name of his imports. And this was the case wherever he revealed himself to any in a peculiar manner by an especial name. So he did to Jacob, 'I am the LORD God of Abraham your father, and the God of Isaac' (Gen. 28:13), assuring him, that as he dealt faithfully in his covenant with his fathers, Abraham and Isaac, so also he would deal with him. And, 'I am the God of Bethel' (Gen. 31:13) — 'He who appeared to you there, and blessed you, and will continue so to do.' But when the same Jacob comes to ask after another name of God, he answers him not; as it were commanding him to live by faith on what he was pleased to reveal.

Now, then, God had not made himself known to Abraham, and Isaac, and Jacob by his name Jehovah, because he had not peculiarly called himself to them by that name, nor had engaged it in his covenant with them, although it were otherwise known to them. They lived and rested on the name of God Almighty, as suited to their support and consolation in their wandering, helpless condition, before the promise was to be accomplished. But now, when God came to fulfil his promises, and to bring the people, by virtue of his covenant, into the land of Canaan, he reveals himself to them by, and renews his covenant with them in, the name of Jehovah. And hereby did God declare that he came to give stability and accomplishment to his promises; to which end they were now to live upon this name of Jehovah, in an expectation of the fulfilling of the promises, as their fathers did on that of God Almighty, in an expectation of protection from him in their wandering state and condition. Hence this name became the foundation of the Judaical church, and ground of the faith of them who did sincerely believe in God therein. And it is strangely fallen out, in the providence of God, that since the Jews have rejected the covenant of their fathers, and are cast out of the covenant for their unbelief, they have utterly forgot that name of God. No Jew in the world knows what it is, nor how to pronounce it or make mention of it. I know themselves and others pretend strange mysteries in the letters and vowels of that name, which make it ineffable; but the truth is, being cast out of that covenant which was built and established on that name, in the just judgment of God, through their own blindness and superstition, they are no more able to make mention of it or to take it into their mouths. It is required, then, that the name of God be given to us as engaged in covenant, to secure our expectation that he will be to us according to his name.

### EVERY NAME CONFIRMED IN JESUS CHRIST

All the whole gracious name of God, every title that he has given himself, every ascription of honour to himself that he has owned, is confirmed to us (unto as many as believe) in Jesus Christ. For as he has declared to us the whole name of God (John 17:6), so not this or that promise of God, but all the promises of God are in him yea and amen. So that, as of old, every particular promise that God made to the people served especially for the particular occasion on which it was given, and each name of God was to be rested on as to that dispensation whereunto it was suited to give relief and confidence—as the name of El-shaddai to Abraham, Isaac, and Jacob, and the name Jehovah to Moses and the people; so now, by Jesus Christ, and in him, every particular promise belongs to all believers in all their occasions, and every name of God whatever is theirs also, at all times, to rest upon and put their trust in. Thus, the particular promise made to Joshua, at his entrance into Canaan, to encourage and strengthen him in that great enterprise of conquering the land, is by the apostle applied to all believers in all their occasions whatever: 'I will never leave you, nor forsake you' (Heb. 13:5). So likewise does every name of God belong now to us, as if it had in a particular manner been engaged in covenant to us, and that because the whole covenant is ratified and confirmed to us by Jesus Christ (2 Cor. 6:18, 7:1). This, then, absolutely secures to us an interest in the name of God insisted on, the God of forgiveness, as if it had been given to every one of us to assure us thereof.

### 'The God of Forgiveness'

God takes this name, 'The God of forgiveness,' to be his in a peculiar manner, as that whereby he will be distinguished and known. He appropriates it to himself, as expressing that which the power and goodness of no other can extend to. 'There are lords many, and gods many,' says the apostle (1 Cor. 8:5) — λεγόμενοι θεοί, some that are called so, such as some account so to be. How is the true God distinguished from these gods by reputation? He is so by this name; he is the God of pardons: 'Who is a God like to you, that pardons iniquity?' (Mic. 7:18). This is his prerogative; herein none is equal to him, like him, or a sharer with him. 'Who is a God like to you, that may be called a God of pardons?' The vanities of the nations cannot give them this rain; they have no refreshing showers of mercy and pardon in their power. Neither angels, nor saints, nor images, nor popes, can pardon sin. By this name he distinguishs himself from them all.

To be known by this name is the great glory of God in this world. When Moses desired to see the glory of God, the Lord tells him that 'he could not see his face' (Exod. 33:18–20). The face of God, or the gracious majesty of his Being, his essential glory, is not to be seen of any in this life; we cannot see him as he is. But the glorious manifestation of himself we may behold and contemplate. This we may see as the back parts of God; that shadow of his excellencies which he casts forth in the passing by us in his works and dispensations. This Moses shall see. And wherein did it consist? Why, in the revelation and declaration of this name of God: 'The LORD passed by before him, and proclaimed, The LORD, The LORD God, merciful and gracious, long-suffering, and abundant in goodness and truth, keeping mercy for thousands, forgiving iniquity and transgression and sin' (Exod. 34:6–7). To be known by this name, to be honoured, feared, believed as that declares him, is the great glory of God. And shall this fail us? Can we be deceived trusting in it, or expecting that we shall find him to be what his name declares? God forbid.

Let us lay together these considerations, and we shall find that they will give us another stable foundation of the truth insisted on, and a great encouragement to poor sinful souls to draw nigh to God in Christ for pardon. God has no name but what he gives to himself; nor is it lawful to know him or call him otherwise. As he calls himself, so is he; what his name imports, so is his nature.

Every name also of God is engaged in Jesus Christ in the covenant, and is proposed to us to place our trust and confidence in. Now, this is his name and his memorial, even 'The God of forgiveness.' By this he distinguishes himself from all others, and expresses it as the principal title of his honour, or his peculiar glory. According to this name, therefore, all that believe shall assuredly find 'there is forgiveness with him.'

## The Nature of God

The consideration of the essential properties of the nature of God, and what is required to the manifestation of them, will afford us farther assurance. Let us to this end take in the ensuing observations.

### Eternally Glorious

First, God being absolutely perfect and absolutely self-sufficient, was eternally glorious, and satisfied with and in his own holy excellencies and perfections, before and without the creation of all or any thing by the putting forth or the exercise of his almighty power. The making, therefore, of all things depends on a mere sovereign act of the will and pleasure of God. So the whole creation makes its acknowledgment: 'You are worthy, O Lord, to receive glory and honour and power: for you have created all things, and for your pleasure they are and were created' (Rev. 4:11, 5:12). God could have omitted all this great work without the least impeachment of his glory. Not one holy property of his nature would have been diminished or abated in its eternal glory by that omission. This, then, depended on a pure act of his will and choice.

## He Made All Things for Himself

Secondly, on supposition that God would work *'ad extra,'* by his power produce any thing without himself, it was absolutely necessary that himself should be the end of his so doing. For as before the production of all things, there was nothing that could be the end why any of them should be brought forth out of nothing, or towards which they should be disposed; so God, being an infinite agent in wisdom, and understanding, and power, he could have no end in his actings but that also which is infinite. It is therefore natural and necessary to God to do all things for himself. It is impossible he should have any other end. And he has done so accordingly, 'The Lord has made all things for himself' (Prov. 16:4). He aimed at himself in all that he did; there being no other infinite good for him to make his object and his end but himself alone.

## He Can Add Nothing to Himself

Thirdly, this doing things, all things for himself, cannot intend an addition or accruement thereby of any new real good to himself. His absolute eternal perfection and all-sufficiency render this impossible. God does not become more powerful, great, wise, just, holy, good, or gracious, by any of his works, by any thing that he does. He can add nothing to himself. It must therefore be the manifestation and declaration of the holy properties of his nature that he intends and designs in his works, and there are two things required hereunto.

### He Acts to Make His Power Known

That he make them known; that by ways suited to his infinite wisdom he declares that such properties do belong to him, as also what is the nature of them, according as the creature is able to apprehend.

So he does things 'to make his power known,' to show his power, and to declare his name through the earth (Rom. 9:17, 22). So it was said that by the works of creation, τὸ γνωστὸν τοῦ θεοῦ, 'that which may be known of God is manifest' (Rom. 1:19–20). And what is that? Even the natural, essential properties of his being, 'his eternal power and Godhead.' To this head are referred all those promises of God that he would glorify himself, and the prayers of his saints that he would do so, and the attestations given to it in the Scripture that he has done so. He has made known his wisdom, holiness, power, goodness, self-sufficiency, and the like perfections of his nature.

*He Acts that He May Receive Praise & Glory*

That he attain an ascription, an attribution of praise and glory to himself upon their account. His design is 'to be admired in all them that believe' (2 Thess. 1:10); that is, that upon an apprehension of his excellencies which he has revealed, and as he has revealed them, they should admire, adore, applaud, glorify, and praise him; worship, believe in, and trust him in all things; and endeavour the enjoyment of him as an eternal reward. And this is also threefold.

INTERPRETATIVE. So the inanimate and brute creatures ascribe to God the glory of his properties, even by what they are and do. By what they are in their beings, and their observation of the law and inclination of their nature, they give to God the glory of that wisdom and power whereby they are made, and of that sovereignty whereon they depend. Hence, nothing more frequent in the praises of God of old, than the calling of the inanimate creatures, heaven and earth, winds, storms, thunder, and the beasts of the field, to give praise and glory to God; that is, by what they are they do so, inasmuch as from the impression of God's glorious excellencies in their effects upon them, they are made known and manifest.

INVOLUNTARY IN SOME RATIONAL CREATURES. Sinning men and angels have no design, no will, no desire to give glory to God. They do their utmost endeavour to the contrary, to hate him, reproach and blaspheme him. But they cannot yet cast off the yoke of God. In their minds and consciences they are forced, and shall be for ever, to acknowledge that God is infinitely holy, infinitely wise, powerful, and righteous. And he has the glory of all these properties from them in their very desires that he were otherwise. When they would that God were not just to punish them, powerful to torment them, wise to find them out, holy to be displeased with their lusts and sins, they do at the same time, in the same thing, own, acknowledge, and give to God the glory of his being, justice, wisdom, power, and holiness. When, therefore, God has made known his properties, the ascription of glory to him on their account is to rational creatures natural and unavoidable.

VOLUNTARY IN TRUE WORSHIPPERS. It is voluntary, in the reasonable service, worship, fear, trust, obedience of angels and men. God having revealed to them the properties of his nature, they acknowledge, adore them, and place their confidence in them, and thereby glorify him as God. And this glorifying of God consists in three things:

1. In making the excellencies of God revealed to us the principle and chief object of all the moral actings of our souls, and of all the actings of our affections. To fear the Lord and his goodness, and to fear him for his goodness; to trust in his power and faithfulness; to obey his authority; to delight in his will and grace; to love him above all, because of his excellencies and beauty; this is to glorify him.

2. To pray for, and to rejoice in, the ways and means whereby he will or has promised farther to manifest or declare these properties of his nature and his glory in them. What is the reason why we pray for, long for, the accomplishment of the promises of God toward his saints, of his threatenings towards his enemies, of the fulfilling of the glorious works of his power and grace that yet remain to be done, of the coming of the kingdom of Christ, of the approach of glory? Is it not chiefly and principally that the glorious excellencies of God's nature may be made more manifest, be more known, more exalted—that God may appear more as he is, and as he

has declared himself to be? This is to give glory to God. So likewise our joy, rejoicing, and satisfaction in any of the ways and works of God; it is solely on this account, that in them, God in his properties—that is, his power, wisdom, holiness, and the like—is revealed, declared, and made known.

3. In their joint actual celebration of his praises; which, as it is a duty of the greatest importance, and which we are, indeed, of all others most frequently exhorted to and most earnestly called upon for; so in the nature of it, it consists in our believing, rejoicing expression of what God is and what he does—that is, our admiring, adoring, and blessing him, because of his holiness, goodness, and the rest of his properties, and his works of grace and power suitable to them. This it is to praise God (Rev. 5).

## WE KNOW ONLY WHAT HE IS PLEASED TO REVEAL

Fourthly, observe that none of these properties of God can be thus manifested and known, nor himself be glorified for them, but by his declaration of them, and by their effects. We know no more of God than he is pleased to reveal to us. I mean not mere revelation by his word, but any ways or means, whether by his word, or by his works, or by impressions from the law of nature upon our hearts and minds. And whatever God thus declares of himself, he does it by exercising, putting forth, and manifesting the effects of it. So we know his power, wisdom, goodness, and grace, namely, by the effects of them, or the works of God that proceed from them and are suited to them. And whatever is in God that is not thus made known, we cannot apprehend, nor glorify God on the account of it. God, therefore, doing all things, as has been showed, for the glory of these his properties, he so reveals them and makes them known.

## HE REVEALS HIS PROPERTIES IN FITTING ACTS

Fifthly, upon this design of God, it is necessary that he should reveal and make known all the attributes and properties of his nature, in works and effects peculiarly proceeding from them and answering to them, that he might be glorified in them; and which, as the event manifests, he has done accordingly. For what reason can be imagined why God will be glorified in one essential excellency of his nature and not in another? Especially must this be affirmed of those properties of the nature of God which the event manifests his principal glory to consist in and arise from, and the knowledge whereof is of the greatest use, behoof, and benefit to the children of men, in reference to his design towards them.

### Properties Revealed in Their Effects After Creation

Sixthly, these things being so, let us consider how it stands in reference to that which is under consideration. God, in the creation of all things, glorified or manifested his greatness, power, wisdom, and goodness, with many other properties of the like kind. But his sovereignty, righteousness, and holiness, how are they declared hereby? Either not at all, or not in so evident a manner as is necessary, that he might be fully glorified in them or for them. What, then, does he do? Leave them in darkness, veiled, undiscovered, satisfying himself in the glory of those properties which his work of creation had made known? Was there any reason why he should do so, designing to do all things for himself and for his own glory? Wherefore he gives his holy law as a rule of obedience to men and angels. This plainly reveals his sovereignty or authority over them, his holiness and righteousness in the equity and purity of things he required of them: so that in and by these properties also he may be glorified. As he made all things for himself—that is, the manifestation of his greatness, power, wisdom, and goodness; so he gave the law for himself—that is, the manifestation of his authority, holiness, and righteousness.

But is this all? Is there not remunerative justice in God, in a way of bounty? Is there not vindictive justice in him, in a way of severity? There is so; and in the pursuit of the design mentioned they also are to be manifested, or God will not be glorified in them. This, therefore, he did also, in the rewards and punishments that he annexed to the law of obedience that he had prescribed. To manifest his remunerative justice, he promised a reward in a way of bounty, which the angels that sinned not were made partakers of; and in the penalty threatened, which sinning angels and men incurred, he revealed his vindictive justice in a way of severity. So are all these properties of God made known by their effects, and so is God glorified in them or on their account.

## MERCY, GRACE, AND PATIENCE

But, after all this, are there no other properties of his nature, divine excellencies that cannot be separated from his being, which by none of these means are so much as once intimated to be in him? It is evident that there are; such are mercy, grace, patience, long-suffering, compassion, and the like. Concerning which observe—

### Not Revealed Apart from Sinners

That where there are no objects of them, they cannot be declared, or manifested, or exercised. As God's power or wisdom could not be manifest if there were no objects of them, no more can his grace or mercy. If never any stand in need of them, they can never be exercised, and consequently never be known. Therefore were they not revealed, neither by the creation of all things, nor by the law or its sanction, nor by the law written in our hearts; for all these suppose no objects of grace and mercy. For it is sinners only, and such as have made themselves miserable by sin, that they can be exercised about.

### Supremely Expressive of Divine Beauty

There are no excellencies of God's nature that are more expressive of divine goodness, loveliness, and beauty than these are—of mercy, grace, long-suffering, and patience; and, therefore, there is nothing that God so requires our likeness to him, in our conformity to his image, as in these—namely, mercy, grace, and readiness to forgive. And the contrary frame in any he does of all things most abhor: 'They shall have judgment without mercy, who shewed no mercy.' And, therefore, it is certain that God will be glorified in the manifestation of these properties of his nature.

### *Only Known in the Pardon of Sin*

These properties can be no otherwise exercised, and consequently no otherwise known, but only in and by the pardon of sin; which puts it beyond all question that there is forgiveness with God. God will not lose the glory of these his excellencies: he will be revealed in them, he will be known by them, he will be glorified for them; which he could not be if there were not forgiveness with him. So that here comes in not only the truth but the necessity of forgiveness also.

## GOD'S SENDING OF HIS SON

In the next place we shall proceed to that evidence which is the centre wherein all the lines of those foregoing do meet and rest— the fountain of all those streams of refreshment that are in them— that which animates and gives life and efficacy to them. This lies in God's sending of his Son. The consideration hereof will leave no pretence or excuse to unbelief in this matter.

To make this evidence more clear and legible, as to what is intended in it, we must consider—First, what was the rise of this sending we speak of. Secondly, who it was that was sent. Thirdly, how, or in what manner he was sent. Fourthly, to what end and purpose.

### THE SOURCE OF THE SENDING—THE COUNSEL OF PEACE

First, the rise and spring of it is to be considered. It came forth from the eternal mutual consent and counsel of the Father and the Son: 'The counsel of peace shall be between them both' (Zech. 6:13). It is of Christ, the Branch, of whom he speaks. 'He shall build the temple of the LORD; and he shall bear the glory, and shall sit and rule upon his throne; and he shall be a priest upon his throne: and the counsel of peace shall be between them both'—that is, between God the Father, who sends him, and himself. There lay the counsel of peace-making between God and man, in due time accomplished by him who is 'our peace' (Eph. 2:14): so he speaks, 'Then I was by him, as one brought up with him: and I was daily his delight, rejoicing always before him; rejoicing in the habitable part of his earth; and my delights were with the sons of men' (Prov. 8:30–31). They are the words of the Wisdom, that is, of the Son of God. When was this done? 'Then I was by him.' Why, 'before the mountains were settled, while as yet he had not made the earth, nor the fields;' that is, before the creation of the world, or from eternity (v. 25–6). But how then could he 'rejoice in the habitable part of the earth?' And how could his 'delights be with the sons of men,' seeing as yet they were not? I answer, it was the counsel of peace towards them before mentioned, in the pursuit whereof he was to be sent to converse amongst them on the earth. He rejoiced in the fore-thoughts of his being sent to them, and the work he had to do for them. Then, with his own consent and delight, was he 'fore-ordained' to his work, even 'before the foundation of the world' (1 Pet. 1:20), and received of the Father 'the promise of eternal life, even before the world began' (Tit. 1:2); that is, to be given to sinners by way of forgiveness through his blood.

So is this whole counsel expressed (Ps. 40:7–8)—whence it is made use of by the apostle—'Then said I, Lo, I come: in the volume of the book it is written of me, I delight to do your will, O my God. Your law is in the midst of my heart' (Heb. 10:5–7). There is the will of the Father in this matter, and the law of its performance; and there is the will of the Son in answer thereunto, and his delight in fulfilling that law which was prescribed to him.

Let us now consider to what purpose was this eternal counsel of peace, this agreement of the Father and Son from eternity, about the state and condition of mankind. If God would have left them all to perish under the guilt of their sins, there had been no need at all of any such thoughts, design, or counsel. God had given to them a law righteous and holy, which if they transgressed, he had threatened them with eternal destruction. Under the rule, disposal, and power of this law, he might have righteously left them to stand or fall, according to the verdict and sentence thereof. But now he assures us, he reveals to us, that he had other thoughts in this matter; that there were other counsels between the Father and the Son concerning us; and these such as the Son was delighted in the prospect of his accomplishment of them. What can these thoughts and counsels be, but about a way for their deliverance? Which could no otherwise be but by the forgiveness of sins; for whatever else be done, yet if God mark iniquities, there is none can stand. Hearken, therefore, poor sinner, and have hope. God is consulting about your deliverance and freedom. And what cannot the wisdom and grace of the Father and Son effect and accomplish? And to this end was the Son sent into the world; which is the second thing proposed to consideration.

### The Only Begotten of the Father

Secondly, whom did God send about this business? The Scripture lays great weight and emphasis on this consideration, faith must do so also: 'God so loved the world, that he gave his only-begotten Son' (John 3:16); so, 'In this was manifested the love of God towards us, because that God sent his only-begotten Son into the world, that we might live through him' (1 John 4:9). And again, 'Herein is love, not that we loved God, but that he loved us, and sent his Son to be the propitiation for our sins' (v. 10). And who is this that is thus sent, and called the only-begotten Son of God? Take a double description of him, one out of the Old Testament and another from the New; the first from Isaiah 9:6, 'Unto us a child is born, to us a son is given: and the government shall be upon his shoulder: and his name shall be called Wonderful, Counsellor, The mighty God, The everlasting Father, The Prince of Peace;' the other from Hebrew 1:2–3, 'God has spoken to us by his Son, whom he has appointed heir of all things, by whom also he made the worlds; who being the brightness of his glory, and the express image of his person, and upholding all things by the word of his power, when he had by himself purged our sins, sat down on the right hand of the Majesty on high.' This is he who was sent. In nature he was glorious, even 'over all, God blessed for ever;' – in answerableness to the Father, 'the brightness of his glory, and the express image of his person,' possessed of all the same essential properties with him, so that what we find in him we may be assured of in the Father also; for he that has seen him has seen the Father, who is in him; in power omnipotent, for he made all things, and 'upholding all things,' with an unspeakable facility, 'by the word of his power;' in office exalted over all, sitting 'on the right hand of the Majesty on high;' in name, 'The mighty God, The everlasting Father' so that whatever he came about he will assuredly accomplish and fulfil; for what should hinder or let this mighty one from perfecting his design?

Now, this consideration raises our evidence to that height as to give an unquestionable assurance in this matter. Here is a near and a particular object for faith to be exercised about and to rest in. Wherefore did this glorious Son of God come and tabernacle amongst poor sinners? 'We beheld the glory of the eternal Word, the glory of the only-begotten of the Father, and he was made flesh καὶ ἐσκήνωσεν, and pitched his tabernacle amongst us' (John 1:14). To what end? It was no other but to work out and accomplish the eternal counsel of peace towards sinners before mentioned; to procure for them, and to declare to them, the forgiveness of sin. And what greater evidence, what greater assurance can we have, that there is forgiveness with God for us? He himself has given it as a rule, that what is done by giving an only-begotten or an only-beloved son gives assured testimony of reality and sincerity in the thing that is confirmed by it. So he says to Abraham, 'Now I know that you fear God, seeing that you have not withheld your son, your only son, from me' (Gen. 22:12). This way it may be known, or no way. And they are blessed conclusions that faith may make from this consideration: 'Now I know that there is forgiveness with God, seeing he has not withheld his Son, his only Son, that he might accomplish it.' To this purpose the apostle teaches us to reason, 'He that spared not his own Son, but delivered him up for us all, how shall he not with him also freely give us all things?' (Rom. 8:32).

What farther can any soul desire? What ground remains for unbelief to stand upon in this matter? Is there any thing more to be done herein? It was to manifest that there is forgiveness with him, and to make way for the exercise of it, that God sent his Son, that the Son of God came into the world, as will afterwards more fully appear.

### In the Likeness of Sinful Flesh

Thirdly, to this sending of the Son of God to this purpose, there is evidence and security added from the manner wherein he was sent. How was this? Not in glory, not in power—not in an open discovery of his eternal power and Godhead. Had it been so, we might have thought that he had come merely to manifest and glorify himself in the world; and this he might have done without thoughts of mercy or pardon towards us. But he came quite in another manner: he was seen in the 'likeness of sinful flesh' (Rom. 8:3); in 'the form of a servant' (Phil. 2:7); being 'made of a woman, made under the law' (Gal. 4:4). What he endured, suffered, underwent in that state and condition, is in some measure known to us all. All this could not be merely and firstly for himself. All that he expected at the close of it was, to be 'glorified with that glory which he had with the Father before the world was' (John 17:5). It must, then, be for our sakes. And for what? To save and deliver us from that condition of wrath at present, and future expectation of vengeance, which we had cast ourselves into by sin; that is, to procure for us the forgiveness of sin. Had not God designed pardon for sin, he would never have sent his Son in this manner to testify it; and he did it because it could no other way be brought about, as has been declared. Do we doubt whether there be forgiveness with God or no? Or whether we shall obtain it if we address ourselves to him for to be made partakers of it? Consider the condition of his Son in the world—review his afflictions, poverty, temptation, sorrows, sufferings—then ask our souls, 'To what end was all this?'

And if we can find any other design in it, any other reason, cause, or necessity of it, but only and merely to testify and declare that there is forgiveness with God, and to purchase and procure the communication of it to us, let us abide in and perish under our fears. But if this be so, we have sufficient warranty to assure our souls in the expectation of it.

## THE PURPOSE

Fourthly, besides all this, there ensues upon what went before, that great and wonderful issue in the death of the Son of God. This thing was great and marvellous, and we may a little inquire into what it was that was designed therein. And hereof the Scripture gives us a full account.

### To Make Atonement for Sin

That he died to make atonement for sin, or 'reconciliation for iniquity' (Dan. 9:24). He 'gave his life a ransom for the sins of many' (Matt. 20:28; 1 Tim. 2:6). He was in it 'made sin,' that others 'might be made the righteousness of God in him' (2 Cor. 5:21; Rom. 8:3). Therein he 'bare our sins in his own body on the tree' (1 Pet. 2:24). This was the state of this matter. Notwithstanding all the love, grace, and condescension before mentioned, yet our sins were of that nature, and so directly opposite to the justice and holiness of God, that unless atonement were made and a price of redemption paid, there could be no pardon, no forgiveness obtained. This, therefore, he undertook to do, and that by the sacrifice of himself; answering all that was prefigured by and represented in the sacrifices of old, as the apostle largely declares (Heb. 10:5–10). And herein is the forgiveness that is in God copied out and exemplified so clearly and evidently, that he that cannot read it will be cursed to eternity. Yea, and let him be accursed; for what can be more required to justify God in his eternal destruction? He that will not believe his grace, as testified and exemplified in the blood of his Son, let him perish without remedy.

### He Answered the Curse of the Law

The curse and sentence of the law lies on record against sinners. It puts in its demands against our acquittance, and lays an obligation upon us to punishment: and God will not reject nor destroy his law; unless it be answered, there is no acceptance for sinners. This, therefore, in the next place, his death was designed to. As he satisfied and made atonement by it to justice (that was the fountain, spring, and cause of the law), so he fulfilled and answered the demands of the law as it was an effect of the justice of God (so Rom. 8:1–4). He suffered 'in the likeness of sinful flesh, that the righteousness of the law might be fulfilled' and answered. He answered 'the curse of the law' when he was 'made a curse for us' (Gal. 3:13); and so became, as to the obedience of the law, 'the end of the law for righteousness to them that do believe' (Rom. 10:3–4). And as to the penalty that it threatened, he bore it, removed it, and took it out of the way. So has he made way for forgiveness through the very heart of the law; it has not one word to speak against the pardon of them that do believe.

### He Destroyed Satan's Dominion

Sinners are under the power of Satan. He lays a claim to them; and by what means shall they be rescued from his interest and dominion? This also his death was designed to accomplish: for as he was 'manifested to destroy the works of the devil' (1 John 3:8), so 'through death he destroyed him that had the power of death' (Heb. 2:14); that is, to despoil him of his power, to destroy his dominion, to take away his plea to sinners that believe; as we have at large elsewhere declared.

And by all these things, with many other concerns of his death that might be instanced in, we are abundantly secured of the forgiveness that is with God, and of his willingness that we should be made partakers thereof.

## He Lives Again

Fifthly, is this all? Did his work cease in his death? Did he no more for the securing of the forgiveness of sins to us, but only that he died for them? Yes; he lives also after death, for the same end and purpose. This Son of God, in that nature which he assumed to expiate sin by death, lives again after death, to secure to us and to complete the forgiveness of sins. And this he does two ways:

1. Being raised from that death which he underwent, to make atonement for sin, by the power and good will of God, he evidences and testifies to us that he has fully performed the work he undertook, and that in our behalf, and for us, he has received a discharge. Had he not answered the guilt of sin by his death, he had never been raised from it.
2. He lives after death a mediatory life, to make intercession for us, that we may receive the forgiveness of sin, as also himself to give it out to us; which things are frequently made use of to encourage the souls of men to believe, and therefore shall not at present be farther insisted on.

## God's Greatest Work

Thus, then, stands this matter—that mercy might have a way to exercise itself in forgiveness, with a consistency to the honour of the righteousness and law of God, was the Son of God so sent, for the ends and purposes mentioned. Now, herein consists the greatest work that God did ever perform, or ever will. It was the most eminent product of infinite wisdom, goodness, grace, and power; and herein do all the excellencies of God shine forth more gloriously than in all the works of his hands. Let us, then, wisely ponder and consider this matter; let us bring our own souls, with their objections, to this evidence, and see what exception we have to lay against it. I know nothing will satisfy unbelief. The design of it is, to make the soul find that to be so hereafter which it would persuade it of here—namely, that there is no forgiveness in God. And Satan, who makes use of this engine, knows full well that there is none for them who believe there is none, or rather will not believe that there is any; for it will, at the last day, be to men according to their faith or unbelief. He that believes aright, and he that believes not that forgiveness is with God, as to their own particulars, shall neither of them be deceived. But what is it that can be reasonably excepted against this evidence, this foundation of our faith in this matter? God has not sent his Son in vain; which yet he must have done, as we have showed, had he not designed to manifest and exercise forgiveness towards sinners. Wherefore, to confirm our faith from hence, let us make a little search into these things in some particular inquiries.

### Why Did Christ Die?

Seeing the Son of God died in that way and manner that he did, according to the determinate counsel and will of God, wherefore did he do so, and what aimed he at therein?

It is plain that he died for our sins (Rom 4:25); that is, 'to make reconciliation for the sins of the people' (Heb. 2:17–18). This Moses and the prophets, this the whole Scripture, testifies to. And without a supposal of it, not one word of it can be aright believed; nor can we yield any due obedience to God without it.

### What Did God Do to Him?

What, then, did God do to him? What was in transaction between God as the Judge of all, and him that was the Mediator of the church?

God indeed 'laid on him the iniquity of us all' (Isa. 53:6)—all the sins of all the elect; yea, he made him 'a curse for us' (Gal. 3:13); and making him a 'sin-offering,' or 'an offering for sin,' he 'condemned sin in the flesh' (Rom. 8:3, 2 Cor. 5:21): so that all that which the justice or law of God had to require about the punishment due to sin was all laid and executed on him.

### What Did Christ Do in His Death?

What, then, did Christ do in his death? What did he aim at and design? What was his intention in submitting to and undergoing the will of God in these things?

'He bare our sins in his own body on the tree' (1 Pet. 2:24); 'he took our sins upon him,' undertook to answer for them, to pay our debts, to make an end of the difference about them between God and sinners (Dan. 9:24). His aim undoubtedly was, by all that he underwent and suffered, so to make atonement for sin as that no more could on that account be expected.

### Did Christ Satisfy Divine Justice?

Had God any more to require of sinners on the account of sin, that his justice might be satisfied, his holiness vindicated, his glory exalted, his honour be repaired, than what he charged on Christ? Did he lay somewhat of the penalty due to sin on him, execute some part of the curse of the law against him, and yet reserve some wrath for sinners themselves?

No, doubtless he came to do the whole will of God (Heb. 10:7, 9); and God spared him not any thing that in his holy will he had appointed to be done to sin (Rom. 8:32). He would never have so dealt with his Son, to have made a half-work of it; nor is the work of making satisfaction for sin such as that any, the least part of it, should ever be undertaken by another. Nothing is more injurious or blasphemous against God and Christ than the foolish imagination among the Papists of works satisfactory for the punishment due to sin or any part of it; as also is their purgatory pains to expiate any remaining guilt after this life. This work of making satisfaction for sin is such as no creature in heaven or earth can put forth a hand to. It was wholly committed to the Son of God, who alone was able to undertake it, and who has perfectly accomplished it; so that God now says, 'Fury is not in me…he that will lay hold on my strength that he may have peace, he shall have peace' (Isa. 27:4–5).

### Did Christ Succeed?

What, then, became of the Lord Christ in his undertaking? Did he go through with it? Or did he faint under it? Did he only testify his love, and show his good will for our deliverance? Or did he also effectually pursue it, and not faint, until he had made a way for the exercise of forgiveness?

It was not possible that he should be detained by 'the pains of death' (Acts 2:24). He knew beforehand that he should be carried through his work, that he should not be forsaken in it, nor faint under it (Isa. 50:5–9). And God has given this unquestionable evidence of his discharge of the debt of sin to the utmost, in that he was acquitted from the whole account when he was raised from the dead; for he that is given up to prison, upon the sentence of the law, for the debt of sin, shall not be freed until he have paid the utmost farthing. This, therefore, he manifested himself to have done, by his resurrection from the dead.

### What Has Become of Him Now?

What, then, is now become of him? Where is he, and what does he? Has he so done his work and laid it aside, or does he still continue to carry it on until it be brought to its perfection?

It is true, he was dead, but he is alive, and lives for ever; and has told us that 'because he lives we shall live also,' and that because this is the end of his mediatory life in heaven: 'He ever lives to make intercession for us' (Heb. 7:25–7); and to this end, that the forgiveness of sin, which he has procured for us, may be communicated to us, that we might be partakers of it, and live for ever.

What ground is left of questioning the truth in hand? What link of this chain can unbelief break in or upon? If men resolve, notwithstanding all this evidence and assurance that is tendered to them thereof, that they will not yet believe that there is forgiveness with God, or will not be encouraged to attempt the securing of it to themselves, or also despise it as a thing not worth the looking after; it is enough for them that declare it, that preach these things, that they are a sweet savour to God in them that perish as well as in them that are saved. And I bless God that I have had this opportunity to bear testimony to the grace of God in Christ; which if it be not received, it is because 'the god of this world has blinded the eyes of men, that the light of the gospel of the glory of God should not shine into their minds.' But Christ will be glorified in them that believe on these principles and foundations.

## GOD REQUIRES US TO FORGIVE ONE ANOTHER

Another evidence of the same truth may be taken from hence, that God requires forgiveness in us, that we should forgive one another; and therefore, doubtless, there is forgiveness with him for us. The sense of this consideration to our present purpose will be manifest in the ensuing observations.

### MANY TESTIMONIES

First, it is certain that God has required this of us. The testimonies hereof are many and known, so that they need not particularly to be repeated or insisted on (see Luke 17:3-4; Eph. 4:32; Matt. 18:23 to the end). Only, there are some things that put a singular emphasis upon this command, manifesting the great importance of this duty in us, which may be marked.

#### *A Requisite for Acceptable Prayer*

That our Saviour requires us to carry a sense of our integrity and sincerity in the discharge of this duty along with us in our addresses to God in prayer. Hence, he teaches and enjoins us to pray or plead for the forgiveness of our debts to God (that is, our sins or trespasses against him, which make us debtors to his law and justice), even 'as we forgive them that so trespass against us' as to stand in need of our forgiveness (Matt. 6:12). Many are ready to devour such as are not satisfied that the words of that rule of prayer which he has prescribed to us are to be precisely read or repeated every day. I wish they would as heedfully mind that prescription which is given us herein for that frame of heart and spirit which ought to be in all our supplications; it might possibly abate of their wrath in that and other things. But here is a rule for all prayer, as all acknowledge; as also of the things that are requisite to make it acceptable. This, in particular, is required, that before the Searcher of all hearts, and in our addresses to him, in our greatest concerns, we profess our sincerity in the discharge of this duty, and do put our obtaining of what we desire upon that issue. This is a great crown that is put upon the head of this duty, that which makes it very eminent, and evidences the great concern of the glory of God and our own souls therein.

We may observe, that no other duty whatever is expressly placed in the same series, order, or rank with it; which makes it evident that it is singled out to be professed as a token and pledge of our sincerity in all other parts of our obedience to God. It is by Christ himself made the instance for the trial of our sincerity in our universal obedience; which gives no small honour to it. The apostle puts great weight on the fifth commandment, 'Honour your father and mother;' because it 'is the first commandment with promise' (Eph. 6:2). All the commandments, indeed, had a promise, 'Do this, and live,' life was promised to the observance of them all; but this is the first that had a peculiar promise annexed to it, and accompanying of it. And it was such a promise as had a peculiar foundation through God's ordinance in the thing itself. It is, that the parents should prolong the lives of their children that were obedient. יַאֲרִכוּן יָמֶיךָ (Exod. 20:12) —'They shall prolong your days;' that is, by praying for their prosperity, blessing them in the name of God, and directing them in those ways of obedience whereby they might live and possess the land. And this promise is now translated from the covenant of Canaan into the covenant of grace; the blessing of parents going far towards the interesting their children in the promise thereof, and so prolonging their days to eternity, though their days in this world should be of little continuance. So it is said of our Saviour that 'he should see his seed, and prolong his days' (Isa. 53:10); which has carried over that word, and that which is signified by it, to eternal things. But this by the way. As the singular promise made to that command renders it singular, so does this especial instancing in this duty in our prayer render it also; for though, as all the commandments had a promise, so we are to carry a testimony with us of our sincerity in universal obedience in our addresses to God, yet the singling out of this instance renders it exceeding remarkable, and shows what a value God puts upon it, and how well he is pleased with it.

That God requires this forgiveness in us upon the account of the forgiveness we receive from him; which is to put the greatest obligation upon us to it that we are capable of, and to give the strongest and most powerful motive possible to its performance (see Eph. 4:32).

## More Expressly Required in the New Testament

That this duty is more directly and expressly required in the New Testament than in the Old. Required then it was, but not so openly, so plainly, so expressly as now. Hence we find a different frame of spirit between them under that dispensation and those under that of the New Testament. There are found amongst them some such reflections upon their enemies, their oppressors, persecutors, and the like, as although they were warranted by some actings of the Spirit of God in them, yet, being suited to the dispensation they were under, do no way become us now, who, by Jesus Christ, receive 'grace for grace.' So Zechariah, when he died, cried, 'The LORD look upon, and require;' but Stephen, dying in the same cause and manner, said, 'Lord, lay not this sin to their charge.' Elijah called for fire from heaven; but our Saviour reproves the least inclination in his disciples to imitate him therein. And the reason of this difference is, because forgiveness in God is under the New

Testament far more clearly (especially in the nature and cause of it) discovered in the gospel, which has brought life and immortality to light, than it was under the law; for all our obedience, both in matter and manner, is to be suited to the discoveries and revelation of God to us.

### A Condition of Obtaining Pardon

This forgiveness of others is made an express condition of our obtaining pardon and forgiveness from God (Matt. 6:14–15); and the nature hereof is expressly declared (Matt. 18:23–35). Such evangelical conditions we have not many. I confess they have no causal influence into the accomplishment of the promise; but the non-performance of them is a sufficient bar against our pretending to the promise, a sufficient evidence that we have no pleadable interest in it. Our forgiving of others will not procure forgiveness for ourselves; but our not forgiving of others proves that we ourselves are not forgiven. And all these things do show what weight God himself lays on this duty.

### THE CHARACTERISTIC OF A GOOD MAN

Secondly, observe that this duty is such as that there is nothing more comely, useful, or honourable to, or praiseworthy in, any, than a due performance of it. To be morose, implacable, inexorable, revengeful, is one of the greatest degeneracies of human nature. And no men are commonly, even in this world, more branded with real infamy and dishonour, amongst wise and good men, than those who are of such a frame, and do act accordingly. To remember injuries, to retain a sense of wrongs, to watch for opportunities of revenge, to hate and be maliciously perverse, is to represent the image of the devil to the world in its proper colours; he is the great enemy and self-avenger. On the other side, no grace, no virtue, no duty, no ornament of the mind or conversation of man, is in itself so lovely, so comely, so praiseworthy, or so useful to mankind, as are meekness, readiness to forgive, and pardon. This is that principally which renders a man a good man, for whom one would even dare to die. And I am sorry to add that this grace or duty is recommended by its rarity. It is little found amongst the children of men. The consideration of the defect of men herein, as in those other fundamental duties of the gospel—in self-denial, readiness for the cross, and forsaking the world—is an evidence, if not of how little sincerity there is in the world, yet at least it is of how little growing and thriving there is amongst professors.

## The Mark of a True Christian

Thirdly, that there is no grace, virtue, or perfection in any man, but what is as an emanation from the divine goodness and bounty, so expressive of some divine excellencies or perfection—somewhat that is in God, in a way and manner infinitely more excellent. We were created in the image of God. Whatever was good or comely in us was a part of that image; especially the ornaments of our minds, the perfections of our souls. These things had in them a resemblance of, and a correspondency to, some excellencies in God, whereunto, by the way of analogy, they may be reduced. This being, for the most part, lost by sin, a shadow of it only remaining in the faculties of our souls and that dominion over the creatures which is permitted to men in the patience of God, the recovery that we have by grace is nothing but an initial renovation of the image of God in us (Eph. 4:24). It is the implanting upon our natures those graces which may render us again like to him. And nothing is grace or virtue but what so answers to somewhat in God. So, then, whatever is in us of this kind is in God absolutely, perfectly, in a way and manner infinitely more excellent.

Let us now, therefore, put these things together – God requires of us that there should be forgiveness in us for those that do offend us, forgiveness without limitation and bounds. The grace hereof he bestows on his saints, sets a high price upon it, and manifests many ways that he accounts it among the most excellent of our endowments, one of the most lovely and praiseworthy qualifications of any person. What, then, shall we now say? Is there forgiveness with him or no? 'He that planted the ear, shall he not hear? He that formed the eye, shall he not see?' He that thus prescribes forgiveness to us, that bestows the grace of it upon us, is there not forgiveness with him? It is all one as to say, 'Though we are good, yet God is not; though we are benign and bountiful, yet he is not.' He that finds this grace wrought in him in any measure, and yet fears that he shall not find it in God for himself, does therein and so far prefer himself above God; which is the natural effect of cursed unbelief.

But the truth is, were there not forgiveness with God, forgiveness in man would be no virtue, with all these qualities that incline thereto—such are meekness, pity, patience, compassion, and the like; which what were it but to set loose human nature to rage and madness? For as every truth consists in its answerableness to the prime and eternal Verity, so virtue consists not absolutely nor primarily in a conformity to a rule of command, but in a correspondence to the first absolute perfect being and its perfections.

# 5

## FORGIVENESS AND UNBELIEVERS

The arguments and demonstrations foregoing have, we hope, undeniably evinced the great truth we have insisted on; which is the life and soul of all our hope, profession, religion, and worship. The end of all this discourse is to lay a firm foundation for faith to rest upon in its addresses to God for the forgiveness of sins, as also to give encouragements to all sorts of persons so to do. This end remains now to be explained and pressed; which work yet before we directly close withal, two things are farther to be premised. And the first is, to propose some of those adjuncts of, and considerations about, this forgiveness, as may both encourage and necessitate us to seek out after it; and to mix the testimonies given to it and the promises of it with faith, to our benefit and advantage.

The other is, to show how needful all this endeavour is, upon the account of that great unbelief which is in the most in this matter.

### Forgiveness Becomes God

As to the first of these, then, we may consider, first, that this forgiveness that is with God is such as becomes him; such as is suitable to his greatness, goodness, and all other excellencies of his nature; such as that therein he will be known to be God. What he says concerning some of the works of his providence, 'Be still, and know that I am God,' may be much more said concerning this great effect of his grace. Still your souls, and know that he is God. It is not like that narrow, difficult, halving, and manacled forgiveness that is found amongst men, when any such thing is found amongst them; but it is full, free, boundless, bottomless, absolute, such as becomes his nature and excellencies. It is, in a word, forgiveness that is with God, and by the exercise whereof he will be known so to be. And hence:

### His Thoughts Are not Our Thoughts

God himself really separates and distinguishes his forgiveness from any thing that our thoughts and imaginations can reach to; and that because it is his, and like himself. It is an object for faith alone, which can rest in that which it cannot comprehend. It is never safer than when it is, as it were, overwhelmed with infiniteness. But set mere rational thoughts or the imaginations of our minds at work about such things, and they fall inconceivably short of them. They can neither conceive of them aright nor use them to their proper end and purpose. Were not forgiveness in God somewhat beyond what men could imagine, no flesh could be saved. This himself expresses (Isa. 55:7–9):

> Let the wicked forsake his way, and the unrighteous man his thoughts: and let him return to the LORD, and he will have mercy upon him; and to our God, for he will abundantly pardon. For my thoughts are not your thoughts, neither are your ways my ways, says the LORD. For as the heavens are higher than the earth, so are my ways higher than your ways, and my thoughts than your thoughts.

They are, as is plain in the context, thoughts of forgiveness and ways of pardon whereof he speaks. These our apprehensions come short of; we know little or nothing of the infinite largeness of his heart in this matter. He that he speaks of is רָשָׁע, 'an impiously wicked man,' and אִישׁ אָוֶן, 'a man of deceit and perverse wickedness;' he whose design and course is nothing but a lie, sin, and iniquity; such a one as we would have little or no hopes of—that we would scarce think it worth our while to deal withal about—a hopeless conversion; or can scarce find in our hearts to pray for him, but are ready to give him up as one profligate and desperate. But let him turn to the Lord, and he shall obtain forgiveness.

But how can this be? Is it possible there should be mercy for such a one?

Yes; for the Lord יַרְבֶּה לִסְלוֹחַ, 'will multiply to pardon.' He has forgiveness with him to outdo all the multiplied sins of any that turn to him and seek for it.

But this is very hard, very difficult for us to apprehend. This is not the way and manner of men. We deal not thus with profligate offenders against us.

'True,' says God; 'but "your ways are not my ways." I do not act in this matter like to you, nor as you are accustomed to do.'

How then shall we apprehend it? How shall we conceive of it?

'You can never do it by your reason or imaginations; "for as the heavens are above the earth, so are my thoughts," in this matter, "above your thoughts."'

This is an expression to set out the largest and most inconceivable distance that may be. The creation will afford no more significant expression or representation of it. The heavens are inconceivably distant from the earth, and inconceivably glorious above it. So are the thoughts of God: they are not only distant from ours, but have a glory in them also that we cannot rise up to. For the most part, when we come to deal with God about forgiveness, we hang in every brier of disputing, quarrelsome unbelief. This or that circumstance or aggravation, this or that unparalleled particular, bereaves us of our confidence. Want of a due consideration of him with whom we have to do, measuring him by that line of our own imaginations, bringing him down to our thoughts and our ways, is the cause of all our disquietments. Because we find it hard to forgive our pence, we think he cannot forgive talents. But he has provided to obviate such thoughts in us: 'I will not execute the fierceness of mine anger, I will not return to destroy Ephraim: for I AM GOD, AND NOT MAN' (Hos. 11:9). Our satisfaction in this matter is to be taken from his nature. Were he a man, or as the sons of men, it were impossible that, upon such and so many provocations, he should turn away from the fierceness of his anger. But he is God. This gives an infiniteness and an inconceivable boundlessness to the forgiveness that is with him, and exalts it above all our thoughts and ways. This is to be lamented — presumption, which turns God into an idol, ascribes to that idol a greater largeness in forgiveness than faith is able to rise up to when it deals with him as a God of infinite excellencies and perfections. The reasons of it, I confess, are obvious. But this is certain, no presumption can falsely imagine that forgiveness to itself from the idol of its heart, as faith may in the way of God find in him and obtain from him.

### HAVE YOU NOT KNOWN?

For God engages his infinite excellencies to demonstrate the greatness and boundlessness of his forgiveness. He proposes them to our consideration to convince us that we shall find pardon with him suitable and answerable to them (Isa. 40:27–31):

> Why do you say, O Jacob, and speak, O Israel, My way is hid from the LORD, and my judgment is passed over from my God? Have you not known? Have you not heard, that the everlasting God, the LORD, the Creator of the ends of the earth, faints not, neither is weary? There is no searching of his understanding. He gives power to the faint; and to them that have no might he increases strength. Even the youths shall faint and be weary, and the young men shall utterly fall: but they that wait upon the LORD shall renew their strength; they shall mount up with wings as eagles; they shall run, and not be weary; and they shall walk, and not faint.

The matter in question is, whether acceptance with God, which is only by forgiveness, is to be obtained or no. This, sinful Jacob either despairs of, or at least desponds about. But says God, 'My thoughts are not as your thoughts' in this matter. And what course does he take to convince them of their mistake therein? What argument does he make use of to free them from their unbelief, and to rebuke their fears? Plainly, he calls them to the consideration of himself, both who and what he is with whom they had to do, that they might expect acceptance and forgiveness such as did become him. Minding them of his power, his immensity, his infinite wisdom, his unchangeableness, all the excellencies and properties of his nature, he demands of them whether they have not just ground to expect forgiveness and grace above all their thoughts and apprehensions, because answering the infinite largeness of his heart, from whence it proceeds.

And Moses manages this plea for the forgiveness of that people under a high provocation, and a most severe threatening of their destruction thereon (Num. 14:17–18). He pleads for pardon in such a way and manner as may answer the great and glorious properties of the nature of God, and which would manifest an infiniteness of power and all-sufficiency to be in him.

This, I say, is an encouragement in general to believers. We have, as I hope, upon unquestionable grounds, evinced that there is forgiveness with God; which is the hinge on which turns the issue of our eternal condition. Now this is like himself; such as becomes him; that answers the infinite perfections of his nature; that is exercised and given forth by him as God. We are apt to narrow and straiten it by our unbelief, and to render it unbecoming of him. He less dishonours God (or as little), who, being wholly under the power of the law, believes that there is no forgiveness with him, none to be obtained from him, or does not believe it that so it is, or is so to be obtained—for which he has the voice and sentence of the law to countenance him—than those who, being convinced of the principles and grounds of it before mentioned, and of the truth of the testimony given to it, do yet, by straitening and narrowing of it, render it unworthy of him whose excellencies are all infinite, and whose ways on that account are incomprehensible. If, then, we resolve to treat with God about this matter (which is the business now in hand), let us do it as it becomes his greatness; that is, indeed, as the wants of our souls do require. Let us not entangle our own spirits by limiting his grace. The father of the child possessed with a devil, being in a great agony when he came to our Saviour, cries out, 'If you can do any thing, have compassion on us, and help us,' (Mark 9:22). He would fain be delivered, but the matter was so great that he questioned whether the Lord Christ had either compassion or power enough for his relief. And what did he obtain hereby? Nothing but the retarding of the cure of his child for a season; for our Saviour holds him off until he had instructed him in this matter. Says he, 'If you can believe, all things are possible to him that believes' (v. 23)—'Mistake not; if your child be not cured, it is not for want of power or pity in me, but of faith in you. My power is such as renders all things possible, so that they be believed.' So it is with many who would desirously be made partakers of forgiveness. If it be possible, they would be pardoned; but they do not see it possible. Why, where is the defect? God has no pardon for them, or such as they are; and so it may be they come finally short of pardon. What! Because God cannot pardon them? It is not possible with him? Not at all; but because they cannot, they will not believe, that the forgiveness that is with him is such as that it would answer all the wants of their souls, because it answers the infinite largeness of his heart. And if this does not wholly deprive them of pardon, yet it greatly retards their peace and comfort. God does not take it well to be limited by us in any thing, least of all in his grace. This he calls a tempting of him, a provoking temptation: 'They turned back and tempted God, and limited the Holy One of Israel' (Ps. 78:41). This he could not bear with. If there be any pardon with God, it is such as becomes him to give. When he pardons, he will 'abundantly pardon.' Go with your half-forgiveness, limited, conditional pardons, with reserves and limitations, to the sons of men; it may be it may become them, it is like themselves—that of God is absolute and perfect, before which our sins are as a cloud before the east wind and the rising sun. Hence he is said to do this work with his whole heart and his whole soul, χαρίζεσθαι, 'freely,' bountifully, largely to indulge and forgive to us our sins, and 'to cast them into the depths of the sea' (Mic. 7:19), into a bottomless ocean—an emblem of infinite mercy. Remember this, poor souls, when you are to deal with God in this matter: 'All things are possible to them that do believe.'

## FORGIVENESS GLORIFIES GOD

Secondly, this forgiveness is in or with God, not only so as that we may apply ourselves to it if we will, for which he will not be offended with us, but so also as that he has placed his great glory in the declaration and communication of it; nor can we honour him more than by coming to him to be made partakers of it, and so to receive it from him. For the most part, we are, as it were, ready rather to steal forgiveness from God, than to receive from him as one that gives it freely and largely. We take it up and lay it down as though we would be glad to have it, so God did not, as it were, see us take it; for we are afraid he is not willing we should have it indeed. We would steal this fire from heaven, and have a share in God's treasures and riches almost without his consent: at least, we think that we have it from him 'ægrè,' with much difficulty; that it is rarely given, and scarcely obtained; that he gives it out ἑκών ἀέκοντί γε θύμῳ, with a kind of unwilling willingness—as we sometimes give alms without cheerfulness; and that he loses so much by us as he gives out in pardon. We are apt to think that we are very willing to have forgiveness, but that God is unwilling to bestow it, and that because he seems to be a loser by it, and to forego the glory of inflicting punishment for our sins; which of all things we suppose he is most loath to part withal. And this is the very nature of unbelief. But indeed things are quite otherwise. He has in this matter, through the Lord Christ, ordered all things in his dealings with sinners, 'to the praise of the glory of his grace' (Eph. 1:6). His design in the whole mystery of the gospel is to make his grace glorious, or to exalt pardoning mercy. The great fruit and product of his grace is forgiveness of sinners. This God will render himself glorious in and by. All the praise, glory, and worship that he designs from any in this world is to redound to him by the way of this grace, as we have proved at large before. For this cause spared he the world when sin first entered into it; for this cause did he provide a new covenant when the old was become unprofitable; for this cause did he send his Son into the world. This has he testified by all the evidences insisted on. Would he have lost the praise of his grace, nothing hereof would have been done or brought about.

We can, then, no way so eminently bring or ascribe glory to God as by our receiving forgiveness from him, he being willing thereunto upon the account of its tendency to his own glory, in that way which he has peculiarly fixed on for its manifestation. Hence the apostle exhorts us to 'come boldly to the throne of grace' (Heb. 4:16); that is, with the confidence of faith, as he expounds 'boldness' (Heb. 10:19–22). We come about a business wherewith he is well pleased; such as he delights in the doing of, as he expresses himself, 'The LORD your God in the midst of you is mighty; he will save, he will rejoice over you with joy; he will rest in his love, he will joy over you with singing' (Zeph. 3:17). This is the way of God's pardoning; he does it in a rejoicing, triumphant manner, satisfying abundantly his own holy soul therein, and resting in his love. We have, then, abundant encouragement to draw nigh to the throne of grace, to be made partakers of what God is so willing to give out to us.

And to this end serves also the oath of God, before insisted on — namely, to root out all the secret reserves of unbelief concerning God's unwillingness to give mercy, grace, and pardon to sinners (see Heb. 6:17–18, where it is expressed). Therefore, the tendency of our former argument is, not merely to prove that there is forgiveness with God, which we may believe and not be mistaken, but which we ought to believe; it is our duty so to do. We think it our duty to pray, to hear the word, to give alms, to love the brethren, and to abstain from sin; and if we fall in any of these, we find the guilt of them reflected upon our conscience, to our disquietment: but we scarce think it our duty to believe the forgiveness of our sins. It is well, it may be, we think, with them that can do it; but we think it not their fault who do not. Such persons may be pitied, but, as we suppose, not justly blamed, no, not by God himself. Whose conscience almost is burdened with this as a sin, that he does not, as he ought, believe the forgiveness of his sins? And this is merely because men judge it not their duty so to do; for a non-performance of a duty, apprehended to be such, will reflect on the conscience a sense of the guilt of sin. But now what can be required to make any thing a duty to us that is wanting in this matter? For:

1. There is forgiveness with God, and this manifested, revealed, declared. This manifestation of it is that which makes it the object of our faith. We believe things to be in God and with him, not merely and formally because they are so, but because he has manifested and revealed them so to be (1 John 1:2). What he so declares it is our duty to believe, or we frustrate the end of his revelation.

2. We are expressly commanded to believe, and that upon the highest promises and under the greatest penalties. This command is that which makes believing formally a duty. Faith is a grace, as it is freely wrought in us by the Holy Ghost; the root of all obedience and duties, as it is radically fixed in the heart; but as it is commanded, it is a duty. And these commands, you know, are several ways expressed, by invitations, exhortations, propositions; which all have in them the nature of commands, which take up a great part of the books of the New Testament.

3. It is a duty, as we have showed, of the greatest concern to the glory of God.

4. Of the greatest importance to our souls here and hereafter. And these things were necessary to be added, to bottom our ensuing exhortations upon.

### Most Men Do not Believe Forgiveness

That which should now ensue is the peculiar improvement of this truth, all along aimed at—namely, to give exhortations and encouragements to believing; but I can take few steps in this work, wherein methinks I do not hear some saying, 'Surely all this is needless. Who is there that does not believe all that you go about to prove? And so these pains are spent to little or no purpose? I shall, therefore, before I persuade any to it, endeavour to show that they do it not already. Many, I say, the most of men who live under the dispensation of the gospel, do woefully deceive their own souls in this matter. They do not believe what they profess themselves to believe, and what they think they believe. Men talk of 'fundamental errors;' this is to me the most fundamental error that any can fall into, and the most pernicious. It is made up of these two parts:

1. They do not indeed believe forgiveness.
2. They suppose they do believe it, which keeps them from seeking after the only remedy.

Both these mistakes are in the foundation, and do ruin the souls of them that live and die in them. I shall, then, by a brief inquiry, put this matter to a trial. By some plain rules and principles may this important question, whether we do indeed believe forgiveness or no, be answered and decided. But to the resolution intended, I shall premise two observations.

Men in this case are very apt to deceive themselves. Self-love, vain hopes, liking of lust, common false principles, sloth, unwillingness to self-examination, reputation with the world, and it may be in the church, all vigorously concur to men's self-deceivings in this matter. It is no easy thing for a soul to break through all these, and all self-reasonings that rise from them, to come to a clear judgment of its own acting in dealing with God about forgiveness. Men also find a common presumption of this truth, and its being an easy relief against gripings of conscience and disturbing thoughts about sin, which they daily meet withal. Aiming, therefore, only at the removal of trouble, and finding their present imagination of it sufficient thereunto, they never bring their persuasion to the trial.

As men are apt to do thus, so they actually do so; they do deceive themselves, and know not that they do so. The last day will make this evident, if men will no sooner be convinced of their folly. When our Saviour told his disciples that one of them twelve should betray him, though it were but one of twelve that was in danger, yet every one of the twelve made a particular inquiry about himself. I will not say that one in each twelve is here mistaken; but I am sure the truth tells us that 'many are called, but few are chosen.' They are but few who do really believe forgiveness. Is it not, then, incumbent on every one to be inquiring in what number he is likely to be found at the last day? Whilst men put this inquiry off from themselves, and think or say, 'It may be the concern of others, it is not mine,' they perish, and that without remedy. Remember what poor Jacob said when he had lost one child, and was afraid of the loss of another: 'If I be bereaved of my children, I am bereaved' (Gen. 43:14). As if he should have said, 'If I lose my children, I have no more to lose; they are my all. Nothing worse can befall me in this world. Comfort, joy, yea, life and all, go with them.' How much more may men say in this case, 'If we are deceived here, we are deceived; all is lost. Hope, and life, and soul, all must perish, and that for ever!' There is no help or relief for them who deceive themselves in this matter. They have found out a way to go quietly down into the pit.

Now, these things are premised only that they may be incentives to self-examination in this matter, and so render the ensuing considerations useful. Let us, then, address ourselves to them.

### GOSPEL TRUTH

In general, this is a gospel truth; yea, the great fundamental and most important truth of the gospel. It is the turning-point of the two covenants, as God himself declares (Heb. 8:7–13). Now, a very easy consideration of the ways and walkings of men will satisfy us as to this inquiry, whether they do indeed believe the gospel, the covenant of grace, and the fundamental principles of it. Certainly their ignorance, darkness, blindness, their corrupt affections, and worldly conversations, their earthly-mindedness, and open disavowing of the spirit, ways, and yoke of Christ, speak no such language. Shall we think that proud, heady, worldly self-seekers, haters of the people of God and his ways, despisers of the Spirit of grace and his work, sacrificers to their own lusts, and such like, do believe the covenant of grace or remission of sins? God forbid we should entertain any one thought of so great dishonour to the gospel! Wherever that is received or believed it produces other effects (Tit. 2:11–12; Isa. 11:6–9). It 'teaches men to deny all ungodliness and worldly lusts.' It changes their hearts, natures, and ways. It is not such a barren, impotent, and fruitless thing as such an apprehension would represent it.

### BELIEVE FORGIVENESS IN GOD—OBTAIN FORGIVENESS

They that really believe forgiveness in God do thereby obtain forgiveness. Believing gives an interest in it; it brings it home to the soul concerned. This is the inviolable law of the gospel. Believing and forgiveness are inseparably conjoined. Among the evidences that we may have of any one being interested in forgiveness, I shall only name one—they prize and value it above all the world. Let us inquire what esteem and valuation many of those have of forgiveness, who put it out of all question that they do believe it. Do they look upon it as their treasure, their jewel, their pearl of price? Are they solicitous about it? Do they often look and examine whether it continues safe in their possession or no? Suppose a man have a precious jewel laid up in some place in his house; suppose it be to him as the poor widow's two mites, all her substance or living—will he not carefully ponder on it? Will he not frequently satisfy himself that it is safe? We may know that such a house, such fields or lands, do not belong to a man, when he passes by them daily and takes little or no notice of them. Now, how do most men look upon forgiveness? What is their common deportment in reference to it? Are their hearts continually filled with thoughts about it? Are they solicitous concerning their interest in it? Do they reckon that whilst that is safe all is safe with them? When it is, as it were, laid out of the way by sin and unbelief, do they give themselves no rest until it be afresh discovered to them? Is this the frame of the most of men? The Lord knows it is not. They talk of forgiveness, but esteem it not, prize it not, make no particular inquiries after it. They put it to an ungrounded venture whether ever they be partakers of it or no. For a relief against some pangs of conscience it is called upon, or else scarce thought of at all.

Let not any so minded flatter themselves that they have any acquaintance with the mystery of gospel forgiveness.

## EASY BELIEVERS

Let it be inquired of them who pretend to this persuasion how they came by it, that we may know whether it be of Him who calls us or no; that we may try whether they have broken through the difficulties, in the entertaining of it, which we have manifested abundantly to lie in the way of it.

When Peter confessed our Saviour to be 'the Christ, the Son of the living God,' he told him that 'flesh and blood did not reveal that to him, but his Father who is in heaven' (Matt. 16:17). It is so with them who indeed believe forgiveness in God: 'flesh and blood has not revealed it to them;' it has not been furthered by any thing within them or without them, but all lies in opposition to it. 'This is the work of God, that we believe' (John 6:29); a great work, the greatest work that God requires of us. It is not only a great thing in itself (the grace of believing is a great thing), but it is great in respect of its object, or what we have to believe, or forgiveness itself. The great honour of Abraham's faith lay in this, that deaths and difficulties lay in the way of it (Rom. 4:18–20). But what is a dead body and a dead womb to an accusing conscience, a killing law, and apprehensions of a God terrible as a consuming fire? All which, as was showed, oppose themselves to a soul called to believe forgiveness.

What, now, have the most of men, who are confident in the profession of this faith, to say to this thing? Let them speak clearly, and they must say that indeed they never found the least difficulty in this matter; they never doubted of it, they never questioned it, nor do know any reason why they should do so. It is a thing which they have so taken for granted as that it never cost them an hour's labour, prayer, or meditation about it. Have they had secret reasonings and contendings in their hearts about it? No. Have they considered how the objections that lie against it may be removed. Not at all. But is it so, indeed, that this persuasion is thus bred in you, you know not how? Are the corrupted natures of men and the gospel so suited, so complying? Is the new covenant grown so connatural to flesh and blood? Is the greatest secret that ever was revealed from the bosom of the Father become so familiar and easy to the wisdom of the flesh? Is that which was folly to the wise Greeks, and a stumbling-block to the wonder-gazing Jews, become, on a sudden, wisdom and a plain path to the same principles that were in them? But the truth of this matter is, that such men have a general, useless, barren notion of pardon, which Satan, presumption, tradition, common reports, and the customary hearing of the word, have furnished them withal; but for that gospel discovery of forgiveness whereof we have been speaking, they are utterly ignorant of it and unacquainted with it. To convince such poor creatures of the folly of their presumption, I would but desire them to go to some real believers that are or may be known to them. Let them be asked whether they came so easily by their faith and apprehensions of forgiveness or no. 'Alas!' says one, 'these twenty years have I been following after God, and yet I have not arrived to an abiding cheering persuasion of it.' 'I know what it cost me, what trials, difficulties, temptations I wrestled with, and went through withal, before I obtained it,' says another. 'What I have attained to has been of unspeakable mercy; and it is my daily prayer that I may be preserved in it by the exceeding greatness of the power of God, for I continually wrestle with storms that are ready to drive me from my anchor.' a little of this discourse may be sufficient to convince poor, dark, carnal creatures of the folly and vanity of their confidence.

## How Did You Come to Believe?

There are certain means whereby the revelation and discovery of this mystery is made to the souls of men. By these they do obtain it, or they obtain it not. The mystery itself was a secret, hidden in the counsel of God from eternity; nor was there any way whereby it might be revealed but by the Son of God, and that is done in the word of the gospel. If, then, you say you know it, let us inquire how you came so to do, and by what means it has been declared to you. Has this been done by a word of truth—by the promise of the gospel? Was it by preaching of the word to you, or by reading of it, or meditating upon it? Or did you receive it from and by some seasonable word of or from the Scriptures spoken to you? Or has it insensibly gotten ground upon your hearts and minds, upon the strivings and conflicts of your souls about sin, from the truth wherein you had been instructed in general? Or by what other ways or means have you come to that acquaintance with it whereof you boast? You can tell how you came by your wealth, your gold and silver; you know how you became learned, or obtained the knowledge of the mystery of your trade, who taught you in it, and how you came by it. There is not any thing wherein you are concerned but you can answer these inquiries in a reference to it. Think it, then, no great matter if you are put to answer this question also: By what way or means came you to the knowledge of forgiveness which you boast of? Was it by any of those before mentioned, or some other? If you cannot answer distinctly to these things, only you say you have heard it and believed it ever since you can remember (so those said that went before you, so they say with whom you do converse; you never met with any one that called it into question, nor heard of any, unless it were one or two despairing wretches), it will be justly questioned whether you have any portion in this matter or no. If uncertain rumours, reports, general notions, lie at the bottom of your persuasion, do not suppose that you have any communion with Christ therein.

### HAVE YOU MORE THAN A GENERAL BELIEF?

Of them who profess to believe forgiveness, how few are there who indeed know what it is! They believe, they say; but as the Samaritans worshipped—they 'know not what.' With some, a bold presumption, and crying 'Peace, peace,' goes for the belief of forgiveness. a general apprehension of impunity from God, and that they are sinners, yet they shall not be punished, passes with others at the same rate. Some think they shall prevail with God by their prayers and desires to let them alone, and not cast them into hell.

One way or other to escape the vengeance of hell, not to be punished in another world, is that which men fix their minds upon. But is this that forgiveness which is revealed in the gospel? That which we have been treating about? The rise and spring of our forgiveness is in the heart and gracious nature of God, declared by his name. Have you inquired seriously into this? Have you stood at the shore of that infinite ocean of goodness and love? Have your souls found support and relief from that consideration? And have your hearts leaped within you with the thoughts of it? Or, if you have never been affected in an especial manner herewithal, have you bowed down your souls under the consideration of that sovereign act of the will of God that is the next spring of forgiveness; that glorious acting of free grace, that when all might justly have perished, all having sinned and come short of his glory, God would yet have mercy on some? Have you given up yourselves to this grace? Is this any thing of that you do believe? Suppose you are strangers to this also; what communion with God have you had about it in the blood of Christ? We have showed how forgiveness relates thereunto; how way is made thereby for the exercise of mercy, in a consistency with the glory and honour of the justice of God and of his law; how pardon is procured and purchased thereby; with the mysterious reconciliation of love and law, and the new disposal of conscience in its work and duty by it. What have you to say to these things? Have you seen pardon flowing from the heart of the Father through the blood of the Son? Have you looked upon it as the price of his life and the purchase of his blood? Or have you general thoughts that Christ died for sinners, and that on one account or other forgiveness relates to him, but are strangers to the mystery of this great work? Suppose this also; let us go a little farther, and inquire whether you know any thing that yet remains of the like importance in this matter? Forgiveness, as we have showed, is manifested, tendered, exhibited in the covenant of grace and promises of the gospel. The rule of the efficacy of these is, that they be 'mixed with faith' (Heb. 4:2). It is well if you are grown up hereunto; but you that are strangers to the things before mentioned are no less to this also. Upon the matter, you know not, then, what forgiveness is, nor wherein it consists, nor whence it comes, nor how it is procured, nor by what means given out to sinners. It is to no purpose for such persons to pretend that they believe that whereunto, either notionally or practically, or both, they are such utter strangers.

## HAVE YOU BEEN CONVICTED OF YOUR SIN?

Another inquiry into this matter regards the state and condition wherein souls must be before it be possible for them to believe forgiveness. If there be such an estate, and it can be evinced that very many of the pretenders concerning whom we deal were never brought into it, it is then evident that they neither do nor can believe forgiveness, however they do and may delude their own souls.

It has been showed that the first discovery that was made of pardoning grace was to Adam, presently after the fall. What was then his state and condition? How was he prepared for the reception of this great mystery in its first discovery? That seems to be a considerable rule of proceeding in the same matter. That which is first in any kind is a rule to all that follows. Now, what was Adam's condition when the revelation of forgiveness was first made to him? It is known from the story. Convinced of sin, afraid of punishment, he lay trembling at the foot of God: then was forgiveness revealed to him. So the psalmist states it, 'If you, LORD, should mark iniquities, O Lord, who shall stand?' (Ps. 130:3). Full of thoughts he is of the desert of sin, and of inevitable and eternal ruin, in case God should deal with him according to the exigence of the law. In that state is the great support of forgiveness with God suggested to him by the Holy Ghost. We know what work our Saviour had with the Pharisees on this account. 'Are we,' say they, 'blind also?' 'No,' says he; 'you say you see, "therefore your sin remains"' (John 9:40–41); 'It is to no purpose to talk of forgiveness to such persons as you are; you must of necessity abide in your sins. I came not to call such righteous persons as you are, but sinners to repentance; who not only are so, as you are also, and that to the purpose, but are sensible of their being so, and of their undone condition thereby. "The whole have no need of the physician, but the sick." Whilst you are seeming righteous and whole, it is to no end to tell you of forgiveness; you cannot understand it nor receive it.' It is impossible, then, that any one should, in a due manner, believe forgiveness in God, unless in a due manner he be convinced of sin in himself. If the fallow ground be not broken up, it is to no purpose to sow the seed of the gospel. There is neither life, power, nor sweetness in this truth, unless a door be opened for its entrance by conviction of sin.

Let us, then, on this ground also, continue our inquiry upon the ordinary boasters of their skill in this mystery. You believe there is forgiveness with God? Yes. But have you been convinced of sin? Yes. You know that you are sinners well enough. Answer, then, but once more as to the nature of this conviction of sin which you have. Is it not made up of these two ingredients; 1. a general notion that you are sinners, as all men also are; 2. Particular troublesome reflections upon yourselves, when on any eruption of sin conscience accuses, rebukes, condemns? You will say, 'Yes; what would you require more?' This is not the conviction we are inquiring after: that is a work of the Spirit by the word; this you speak of, a mere natural work, which you can no more be without than you can cease to be men. This will give no assistance to the receiving of forgiveness. But, it may be, you will say you have proceeded farther than so, and these things have had an improvement in you. Let us, then, a little try whether your process has been according to the mind of God, and so whether this invincible bar in your way be removed or no; for although every convinced person do not believe forgiveness, yet no one who is not convinced does so. Have you, then, been made sensible of your condition by nature, what it is to be alienated from the life of God, and to be obnoxious to his wrath? Have you been convinced of the universal enmity that is in your hearts to the mind of God, and what it is to be at enmity against God? Has the unspeakable multitude of the sins of your lives been set in order by the law before you? And have you considered what it is for sinners as you are to have to deal with a righteous and a holy God? Has the Holy Ghost wrought a serious recognition in your hearts of all these things, and caused them to abide with you and upon you? If you will answer truly, you must say, many of you, that indeed you have not been so exercised. You have heard of these things many times, but to say that you have gone through with this work, and have had experience of them, that you cannot do. Then, I say, you are strangers to forgiveness, because you are strangers to sin. But and if you shall say that you have had thoughts to this purpose, and are persuaded that you have been thoroughly convinced of sin, I shall yet ask you one question more: What effects has your conviction produced in your hearts and lives? Have you been filled with perplexities and consternation of spirit thereupon? Have you had fears, dreads, or terrors, to wrestle withal? It may be you will say, 'No;' nor will I insist upon that inquiry. But this I deal with you in: has it filled you with self-loathing and abhorrency, with self-condemnation and abasement? If it will do any thing, this it will do. If you come short here, it is justly to be feared that all your other pretences are of no value. Now, where there is no work of conviction there is no faith of forgiveness, whatever is pretended. And how many vain boasters this sword will cut off is evident.

## DO YOU LIVE IN SIN?

We have yet a greater evidence than all these. Men live in sin, and therefore they do not believe forgiveness of sin. Faith in general 'purifies the heart' (Acts 15:9); our 'souls are purified in obeying the truth' (1 Pet. 1:22). And the life is made fruitful by it: 'Faith works by works' (James 2:22) and makes itself perfect by them. And the doctrine concerning forgiveness has a special influence into all holiness: 'The grace of God that brings salvation, teaches us that denying ungodliness and worldly lusts, we should live soberly, righteously, and godly, in this present world' (Tit. 2:11–12). And that is the grace whereof we speak. No man can, then, believe forgiveness of sin without a detestation and relinquishment of it. The ground of this might be farther manifested, and the way of the efficacy of faith of forgiveness to a forsaking of sin, if need were; but all that own the gospel must acknowledge this principle. The real belief of the pardon of sin is prevalent with men not to live longer in sin.

But now, what are the greatest number of those who pretend to receive this truth? Are their hearts purified by it? Are their consciences purged? Are their lives changed? Do they 'deny ungodliness and worldly lusts?' Does forgiveness teach them so to do? Have they found it effectual to these purposes? Whence is it, then, that there is such a bleating and bellowing to the contrary amongst them?

Some of you are drunkards, some of you swearers, some of you unclean persons, some of you liars, some of you worldly, some of you haters of all the ways of Christ, and all his concerns upon the earth; proud, covetous, boasters, self-seekers, envious, wrathful, back-biters, malicious, praters, slanderers, and the like. And shall we think that such as these believe forgiveness of sin? God forbid. Again; some of you are dark, ignorant, blind, utterly unacquainted with the mystery of the gospel, nor do at all make it your business to inquire into it. Either you hear it not at all, or negligently, slothfully, customarily, to no purpose. Let not such persons deceive their own souls; to live in sin and yet to believe the forgiveness of sin is utterly impossible. Christ will not be a minister of sin, nor give his gospel to be a doctrine of licentiousness for your sakes; nor shall you be forgiven that you may be delivered to do more abominations, God forbid.

If any shall say that they thank God they are no such publicans as those mentioned, they are no drunkards, no swearers, no unclean persons, nor the like, so that they are not concerned in this consideration (their lives and their duties give another account of them), then yet consider farther, that the Pharisees were all that you say of yourselves, and yet the greatest despisers of forgiveness that ever were in the world; and that because they hated the light, on this account, that their deeds were evil. And for your duties you mention, what, I pray, is the root and spring of them? Are they influenced from this faith of forgiveness you boast of or no? May it not be feared that it is utterly otherwise? You do not perform them because you love the gospel, but because you fear the law. If the truth were known, I doubt it would appear that you get nothing by your believing of pardon but an encouragement to sin. Your goodness, such as it is, springs from another root. It may be, also, that you ward yourselves by it against the strokes of conscience or the guilt of particular sins; this is as bad as the other. It is as good be encouraged to sin to commit it, as be encouraged under sin so as to be kept from humiliation for it. None under heaven are more remote from the belief of grace and pardon than such persons are; all their righteousness is from the law, and their sin in a great measure from the gospel.

## ALL OF GRACE?

They that believe forgiveness in a due manner, believe it for the ends and purposes for which it is revealed of God. This will farther improve and carry on the former consideration. If God reveals any thing for one end and purpose, and men use it quite to another, they do not receive the word of God, nor believe the thing revealed, but steal the word and delude their own souls.

Let us, then, weigh to what ends and purposes this forgiveness was first revealed by God, for which also its manifestation is still continued in the gospel. We have showed before who it was to whom this revelation was first made, and what condition he was in when it was so made to him. a lost, wretched creature, without hope or help he was; how he should come to obtain acceptance with God he knew not. God reveals forgiveness to him by Christ to be his all. The intention of God in it was, that a sinner's all should be of grace (Rom. 11:6). If any thing be added to it for the same end and purpose, then 'grace is no more grace.' Again; God intended it as a new foundation of obedience, of love, and thankfulness. That men should love because forgiven, and be holy because pardoned, as I have showed before—that it might be the righteousness of a sinner, and a spring of new obedience in him, all to the praise of grace—were God's ends in its revelation.

Our inquiry, then, is, whether men do receive this revelation as to these ends, and use it for these purposes, and these only? I might evince the contrary, by passing through the general abuses of the doctrine of grace which are mentioned in the Scripture and common in the world; but it will not be needful. Instead of believing, the most of men seem to put a studied despite on the gospel. They either proclaim it to be an unholy and polluted way, by turning its grace into lasciviousness, or a weak and insufficient way, by striving to twist it in with their own righteousness; both which are an abomination to the Lord.

From these and such other considerations of the like importance as might be added, it is evident that our word is not in vain, nor the exhortation which is to be built upon it. It appears that notwithstanding the great noise and pretences to this purpose that are in the world, they are but few who seriously receive this fundamental truth of the gospel—namely, that there is forgiveness with God. Poor creatures sport themselves with their own deceivings, and perish by their own delusions.

## An Exhortation to Unbelievers

We shall now proceed to the direct uses of this great truth; for having laid our foundation in the word that will not fail, and having given, as we hope, sufficient evidence to the truth of it, our last work is to make that improvement of it to the good of the souls of men which all along was aimed at. The persons concerned in this truth are all sinners whatever. No sort of sinners are unconcerned in it, none are excluded from it. And we may cast them all under two heads.

First, such as never yet sincerely closed with the promise of grace, nor have ever yet received forgiveness from God in a way of believing. These we have already endeavoured to undeceive, and to discover those false presumptions whereby they are apt to ruin and destroy their own souls. These we would guide now into safe and pleasant paths, wherein they may find assured rest and peace.

Secondly, others there are who have received it, but being again entangled by sin, or clouded by darkness and temptations, or weakened by unbelief, know not how to improve it to their peace and comfort. This is the condition of the soul represented in this psalm, and which we shall therefore apply ourselves to in an especial manner in its proper place.

Our exhortation, then, is to both—to the first, that they would receive it, that they may have life; to the latter, that they would improve it, that they may have peace—to the former, that they would not overlook, disregard, or neglect so great salvation as is tendered to them; to the latter, that they would stir up the grace of God that is in them, to mix with the grace of God that is declared to them.

I shall begin with the first sort—those who are yet utter strangers from the covenant of grace, who never yet upon saving grounds believed this forgiveness, who never yet once tasted of gospel pardon. Poor sinners! This word is to you.

Be it that you have heard or read the same word before, or others like to it, to the same purpose—it may be often, it may be a hundred times—it is your concern to hear it again; God would have it so; the testimony of Jesus Christ is thus to be accomplished. This 'counsel of God' we must 'declare,' that we may be 'pure from the blood of all men' (Acts 20:26–7); and that not once or twice, but in preaching the word we must be 'instant in season, out of season; reproving, rebuking, exhorting with all long-suffering and doctrine' (2 Tim. 4:2). And for you, woe to you when God leaves thus speaking to you! When he refuses to exhort you any more, woe to you! This is God's departure from any person or people, when he will deal with them no more about forgiveness; and says he, 'Woe to them when I depart from them!' (Hos. 9:12). O that God, therefore, would give to such persons seeing eyes and hearing ears, that the word of grace may never more be spoken to them in vain!

Now, in our exhortation to such persons, we shall proceed gradually, according as the matter will bear, and the nature of it requires. Consider, therefore:

## There Are Terms of Peace

First, that notwithstanding all your sins, all the evil that your own hearts know you to be guilty of, and that hidden mass or evil treasure of sin which is in you, which you are not able to look into; notwithstanding that charge that lies upon you from your own consciences, and that dreadful sentence and curse of the law which you are obnoxious to; notwithstanding all the just grounds that you have to apprehend that God is your enemy, and will be so to eternity; yet there are terms of peace and reconciliation provided and proposed between him and your souls. This, in the first place, is spoken out by the word we have insisted on. Whatever else it informs us of, this it positively asserts—namely, that there is a way whereby sinners may come to be accepted with God; for 'there is forgiveness with him, that he may be feared.' And we hope that we have not confirmed it by so many testimonies, by so many evidences, in vain. Now, that you may see how great a privilege this is, and how much your concern lies in it.

### Especially for You

Consider that this belongs to you in an especial manner; it is your peculiar advantage.

It is not so with the angels that sinned. There were never any terms of peace or reconciliation proposed to them, nor ever shall be, to eternity. There is no way of escape provided for them. Having once sinned, as you have done a thousand times, God 'spared them not, but cast them down to hell, and delivered them into chains of darkness, to be reserved to judgment' (2 Pet. 2:4).

It is not so with them that are dead in their sins, if but one moment past. Ah! How would many souls who are departed, it may be not an hour since, out of this world, rejoice for an interest in this privilege, the hearing of terms of peace, once more, between God and them! But their time is past, their house is left to them desolate. As the tree falls, so it must lie: 'It is appointed to men once to die, and after this the judgment' (Heb. 9:27). After death there are no terms of peace, nothing but judgment. 'The living, the living,' he alone is capable of this advantage.

It is not so with them to whom the gospel is not preached. God suffers them to walk in their own ways, and calls them not thus to repentance. The terms of reconciliation which some fancy to be offered in the shining of the sun and falling of the rain, never brought souls to peace with God. Life and immortality are brought to light only by the gospel. This is your privilege who yet live, and yet have the word sounding in your ears.

It is not thus with them who have sinned against the Holy Ghost, though yet alive, and living where the word of forgiveness is preached. God proposes to them no terms of reconciliation. 'Blasphemy against him,' says Christ, 'shall not be forgiven' (Matt. 12:31). There is no forgiveness for such sinners; and we, if we knew them, ought not to pray for them (1 John 5:16). Their sin is 'unto death.' And what number may be in this condition God knows.

This word, then, is to you; these terms of peace are proposed to you. This is that which in an especial manner you are to apply yourselves to; and woe to you if you should be found to have neglected it at the last day!

### Proposed by God

Wherefore, consider, by whom these terms are proposed to you, and by whom they were procured for you. By whom are they proposed? Who shall undertake to umpire the business, the controversy between God and sinners? No creature, doubtless, is either meet or worthy to interpose in this matter—I mean, originally on his own account; for 'who has known the mind of the Lord, or who has been his counsellor?' Wherefore, it is God himself who proposes these terms; and not only proposes them, but invites, exhorts, and persuades you to accept of them. This the whole Scriptures testify to. It is fully expressed (2 Cor. 5:18–20). He has provided them, he has proposed them, and makes use only of men, of ministers, to act in his name. And excuse us if we are a little earnest with you in this matter. Alas! Our utmost that we can, by zeal for his glory or compassion to your souls, raise our thoughts, minds, spirits, words to, comes infinitely short of his own pressing earnestness herein (see Isa. 4:1–4). Oh, infinite condescension! Oh, blessed grace! Who is this that thus bespeaks you? He against whom you have sinned, of whom you are justly afraid; he whose laws you have broken, and whose name you have dishonoured; he who needs not you, nor your love, nor your friendship, nor your salvation! It is he who proposes to you these terms of reconciliation and peace! Consider the exhortation of the apostle upon this consideration: 'see that you do not refuse him that speaks from heaven' (Heb. 12:25). It is God that speaks to you in this matter, and he speaks to you from heaven. And he does therein forego all the advantage that he has against you for your destruction. Woe would be to your souls, and that for ever, if you should refuse him.

### Procured by the Son of God

By whom were these terms procured for you? And by what means? Do not think that this matter was brought about by chance, or by an ordinary undertaking. Remember that the proposal made to you this day cost no less than the price of the blood of the Son of God. It is the fruit of the travail of his soul. For this he prayed, he wept, he suffered, he died. And shall it now be neglected or despised by you? Will you yet account the blood of the covenant to be a common thing? Will you exclude yourselves from all benefit of the purchase of these terms, and only leave your souls to answer for the contempt of the price whereby they were purchased?

### Still on Offer

Consider that you are sinners, great sinners, cursed sinners; some of you, it may be, worse than innumerable of your fellow-sinners were who are now in hell. God might long since have cast you off everlastingly from all expectation of mercy, and have caused all your hopes to perish; or he might have left you alive, and yet have refused to deal with you any more. He could have caused your sun to go down at noon-day, and have given you darkness instead of vision. He could respite your lives for a season, and yet 'swear in his wrath that you should never enter into his rest.' It is now otherwise. How long it may be so, nor you nor I know any thing at all. God only knows what will be your time, what your continuance. We are to speak whilst it is called 'To-day.' And this is that for the present which I have to offer to you—God declares that there is forgiveness with him, that your condition is not desperate nor helpless. There are yet terms of peace proposed to you. Methinks it cannot but seem strange that poor sinners should not at the least stir up themselves to inquire after them. When a poor man had sold himself of old and his children to be servants, and parted with the land of his inheritance to another, because of his poverty, with what heart do you think did he hear the sound of the trumpet when it began to proclaim the year of jubilee, wherein he and all his were to go out at liberty, and to return to his possession and inheritance? And shall not poor servants of sin, slaves to Satan, that have forfeited all their inheritance in this world and that which is to come, attend to any proclamation of the year of rest, of the acceptable year of the Lord? And this is done in the tender of terms of peace with God in this matter. Do not put it off; this belongs to you; the great concern of your souls lies in it. And it is a great matter.

### A Matter of Great Joy

For consider, that when the angels came to bring the news of the birth of our Lord Jesus, they say, 'We bring you good tidings of great joy, which shall be to all people' (Luke 2:10). What are these joyful tidings? What was the matter of this report? Why, 'This day is born a Saviour, Christ the Lord' (v. 11). It is only this, 'A Saviour is born; a way of escape is provided,' and farther they do not proceed. Yet this they say is a matter of 'great joy;' as it was indeed. It is so to every burdened, convinced sinner, a matter of unspeakable joy and rejoicing. Oh, blessed words! 'A Saviour is born!' This gives life to a sinner, and opens 'a door of hope in the valley of Achor,' the first rescue of a sin-distressed soul. Upon the matter, it was all that the saints for many ages had to live upon; and that not in the enjoyment, but only the expectation. They lived on that word, 'The seed of the woman shall break the serpent's head;' that is, a way of deliverance is provided for sinners. This with all 'diligence they inquired into' (1 Pet. 1:10–12); and improved it to their eternal advantage. As of old, Jacob, when he saw the waggons that his son Joseph had sent to bring him to him, it is said his spirit 'revived;' so did they upon their obscure discovery of a way of forgiveness. They looked upon the promise of it as that which God had sent to bring them to him; and they saw the day of the coming of Christ in it, and rejoiced. How much more have sinners now reason so to do, when the substance of the promise is exhibited, and the news of his coming proclaimed to them! This, then, is a great matter— namely, that terms of peace and reconciliation are proposed, in that it is made known that there is forgiveness with God. Upon these considerations, then, we pursue that exhortation which we have in hand.

### No Room for Delay or Excuses

If any of you were justly condemned to a cruel and shameful death, and lay trembling in the expectation of the execution of it, and a man designed for that purpose should come to him and tell him that there were terms propounded on which his life might be spared, only he came away like Ahimaaz before he heard the particulars. Would it not be a reviving to him? Would he not cry out, 'Pray, inquire what they are; for there is not any thing so difficult which I will not undergo to free myself from this miserable condition?' Would it not change the whole frame of the spirit of such a man, and, as it were, put new life into him? But now, if, instead hereof, he should be froward, stubborn, and obstinate, take no notice of the messenger, or say, 'Let the judge keep his terms to himself,' without inquiring what they are, that he would have nothing to do with them. Would not such a person be deemed to perish deservedly? Does he not bring a double destruction upon himself—first of deserving death by his crimes, and then by refusing the honest and good way of delivery tendered to him? I confess it oftentimes falls out that men may come to inquire after these terms of peace, which, when they are revealed, they like them not, but, with the young man in the gospel, they go away sorrowful: the cursed wickedness and misery of which condition, which befalls many convinced persons, shall be spoken to afterwards; at present I speak to them who never yet attended in sincerity to these terms, nor seriously inquired after them. Think you what you please of your condition and of yourselves, or choose whether you will think of it or no—pass your time in a full regardlessness of your present and future estate—yet, indeed, thus it is with you as to your eternal concerns: you lie under the sentence of a bitter, shameful, and everlasting death; you have done so in the midst of all your jollity, ever since you came into this world; and you are in the hand of Him who can, in the twinkling of an eye, destroy both body and soul in hell-fire. In this state and condition men are sent on purpose to let you know that there are terms of peace, there is yet a way of escape for you; and that you may not avoid the issue aimed at, they tell you that God, that cannot lie, has commanded them to tell you so. If you question the truth of what they say, they are ready to produce their warrant under God's own hand and seal. Here, then, is no room for tergiversation or excuses. Certainly, if you have any care of your eternal estate, if you have any drop of tender blood running in your veins towards your own souls, if you have any rational considerations dwelling in your minds, if all be not defaced and obliterated through the power of lust and love of sin, you cannot but take yourselves to be unspeakably concerned in this proposal. But now, if, instead hereof, you give up yourselves to the power of unbelief, the will of Satan, the love of your lusts and this present world, so as to take no notice of this errand or message from God, nor once seriously to inquire after the nature and importance of the terms proposed, can you escape? Shall you be delivered? Will your latter end be peace? The Lord knows it will be otherwise with you, and that to eternity.

So the apostle assures us, 'If our gospel be hid, it is hid to them that are lost: in whom the god of this world has blinded the minds of them that believe not, lest the light of the glorious gospel of Christ, who is the image of God, should shine to them' (2 Cor. 4:3–4). If you receive not this word, if it be hid from you, it is from the power and efficacy of Satan upon your minds. And what will be the end? Perish you must and shall, and that for ever.

Remember the parable of our Saviour: 'What king, going to make war against another king, sits not down first, and consults whether he be able with ten thousand to meet him that comes against him with twenty thousand? Or else, while the other is yet a great way off, he sends an ambassage, and desires conditions of peace' (Luke 14:31–2). That which he teaches in this parable is, the necessity that lies on us of making peace with God, whom we have provoked, and justly made to be our enemy; as also our utter impotency to resist and withstand him when he shall come forth in a way of judgment and vengeance against us. But here lies a difference in this matter, such as is allowed in all similitudes. Amongst men at variance, it is not his part who is the stronger, and secure of success, to send to the weaker, whom he has in his power, to accept of terms of peace. Here it is otherwise: God, who is infinitely powerful, justly provoked, and able to destroy poor sinners in a moment, when now he is not very far off, but at the very door, sends himself an ambassage with conditions of peace. And shall he be refused by you? Will you yet neglect his offers? How great, then, will be your destruction!

Hear, then, once more, poor sin-hardened, senseless souls, you stout-hearted, that are far from righteousness. Is it nothing to you that the great and holy God, whom you have provoked all your days, and whom you yet continue to provoke—who has not the least need of you or your salvation—who can, when he pleases, eternally glorify himself in your destruction—should of his own accord send to you, to let you know that he is willing to be at peace with you on the terms he had prepared? The enmity began on your part, the danger is on your part only, and he might justly expect that the message for peace should begin on your part also; but he begins with you. And shall he be rejected? The prophet well expresses this, 'Thus says the Lord GOD, the Holy One of Israel; In returning and rest shall you be saved; in quietness and in confidence shall be your strength: and you would not' (Isa. 30:15). The love and condescension that is in these words, on the one hand, on the part of God, and the folly and ingratitude mentioned in them on the other hand, is inexpressible. They are fearful words, 'But you would not.' Remember this against another day. As our Saviour says, in the like manner, to the Jews, 'You will not come to me, that you might have life.' Whatever is pretended, it is will and stubbornness that lie at the bottom of this refusal.

Wherefore, that either you may obtain advantage by it, or that the way of the Lord may be prepared for the glorifying of himself upon you, I shall leave this word before all them that hear or read it, as the testimony which God requires to be given to his grace.

There are terms of peace with God provided for and tendered to you. It is yet called today; harden not your hearts like them of old, who could not enter into the rest of God by reason of unbelief (Heb. 3:19). Some of you, it may be, are old in sins and unacquainted with God; some of you, it may be, have been great sinners, scandalous sinners; and some of you, it may be, have reason to apprehend yourselves near the grave, and so also to hell; some of you, it may be, have your consciences disquieted and galled; and it may be some of you are under some outward troubles and perplexities, that cause you a little to look about you; and some of you, it may be, are in the madness of your natural strength and lusts—'your breasts are full of milk and your bones of marrow,' and your hearts of sin, pride, and contempt of the ways of God. All is one: this word is to you all; and I shall only mind you that 'it is a fearful thing to fall into the hands of the living God.' You hear the voice or read the words of a poor worm; but the message is the message, and the word is the word, of Him who shakes heaven and earth. Consider, then, well what you have to do, and what answer you will return to Him who will not be mocked.

But you will say, 'Why, what great matter is there that you have in hand? Why is it urged with so much earnestness? We have heard the same words a hundred times over. The last Lord's day such a one, or such a one, preached to the same purpose; and what need it be insisted on now again with so much importunity?'

But is it so, indeed, that you have thus frequently been dealt withal, and do yet continue in an estate of irreconciliation? My heart is pained for you, to think of your woeful and almost remediless condition. If 'he that being often reproved, and yet hardens his neck, shall suddenly be destroyed, and that without remedy' (Prov. 29:1), how much more will he be so who, being often invited to peace with God, yet hardens his heart, and refuses to treat with him! Methinks I hear his voice concerning you: 'Those mine enemies, they shall not taste of the supper that I have prepared.' Be it, then, that the word in hand is a common word to you, you set no value upon it—then take your way and course in sin; stumble, fall, and perish. It is not so slight a matter to poor convinced sinners, that tremble at the word of God. These will prize it and improve it. We shall follow, then, that counsel, 'Give strong drink to him that is ready to perish, and wine to those that be of heavy hearts' (Prov. 31:6). We shall tender this new wine of the gospel to poor, sad-hearted, conscience-distressed sinners—sinners that are ready to perish: to them it will be pleasant; they will drink of it and forget their poverty, and remember their misery no more. It shall take away all their sorrow and sadness, when you shall be drunk with the fruit of your lusts, and spew, and lie down and not rise again.

But now, if any of you shall begin to say in your hearts that you would willingly treat with God—'Oh that the day were come wherein we might approach to him! Let him speak what he pleases, and propose what terms he pleases, we are ready to hear.'

### Pleasing Terms

Secondly, that the terms provided for you, and proposed to you, are equal, holy, righteous, yea, pleasant and easy. This being another general head of our work in hand, before I proceed to the farther explication and confirmation of it, I shall educe one or two observations from what has been delivered on the first.

See here on what foundation we preach the gospel. Many

disputes there are whether Christ died for all individuals of mankind or no. If we say, 'No, but only for the elect, who are some of all sorts;' some then tell us we cannot invite all men promiscuously to believe. But why so? We invite not men as all men, no man as one of all men, but all men as sinners; and we know that Christ died for sinners. But is this the first thing that we are, in the dispensation of the gospel, to propose to the soul of a sinner under the law, that Christ died for him in particular? Is that the beginning of our message to him? Were not this a ready way to induce him to conclude, 'Let me, then, continue in sin, that grace may abound?' No; but this is in order of nature our first work, even that which we have had in hand; this is the 'beginning of the gospel of Jesus Christ;' this is 'the voice of one crying in the wilderness, Prepare the way of the Lord.' 'There is a way of reconciliation provided. "God is in Christ reconciling the world to himself." There is a way of acceptance; there is forgiveness with him to be obtained.' At this threshold of the Lord's house does the greatest part of men to whom the gospel is preached fall and perish, never looking in to see the treasures that are in the house itself, never coming into any such state and condition wherein they have any ground or bottom to inquire whether Christ died for them in particular or no. They believe not this report, nor take any serious notice of it. This was the ministry of the Baptist, and they who received it not 'rejected the counsel of God' concerning their salvation (Luke 7:10), and so perished in their sins. This is the sum of the blessed invitation given by Wisdom (Prov. 9:1–5). And here men stumble, fall, and perish (Prov. 1:29–30).

You that have found grace and favour to accept of these terms, and thereby to obtain peace with God, learn to live in a holy admiration of his condescension and love therein. That he would provide such terms; that he would reveal them to you; that he would enable you to receive them; unspeakable love and grace lies in it all. Many have not these terms revealed to them; few find favour to accept of them. And of whom is it that you have obtained this peculiar mercy?

Do you aright consider the nature of this matter? The Scripture proposes it as an object of eternal admiration: 'so God loved the world;' 'Herein is love, not that we loved God, but that he loved us first.' Live in this admiration, and do your utmost, in your several capacities, to prevail with your friends, relations, acquaintance, to hearken after this great treaty of peace with God, whose terms we shall nextly consider, as before in general they were expressed.

Secondly, the terms provided for you, and proposed to you, are equal, holy, righteous, yea, pleasant and easy (Hos. 2:18–19). They are not such as a cursed, guilty sinner might justly expect, but such as are meet for an infinitely good and gracious God to propose; not suited to the wisdom of man, but full of the 'wisdom of God' (1 Cor. 2:6–7). The poor, convinced wretch thinking of dealing with God (Mic. 6:6–7), rolls in his mind what terms he is like to meet withal; and fixes on the most dreadful, difficult, and impossible that can be imagined. 'If,' says he, 'any thing be done with this great and most high God, it must be by "rivers," "thousands," and "ten thousands," children, "first-born;" whatever is dreadful and terrible to nature, whatever is impossible for me to perform, that is it which he looks for.' But the matter is quite otherwise. The terms are wholly of another nature: it is a way of mere mercy, a way of free forgiveness. The apostle lays it down (Rom. 3:21–6). It is a way of propitiation, of pardon, of forgiveness in the blood of Christ; the terms are, the acceptance of the forgiveness that we have described. Who would not think, now, that the whole world would run in to be made partakers of these terms, willingly accepting of them? But it proves for the most part quite otherwise. Men like not this way, of all others. 'It had been something,' says Naaman, 'if the prophet had come and done so and so; but this, "Go wash, and be clean." I do not like it; I am but deluded.' Men think within themselves, that had it been some great thing that was required of them that they might be saved, they would with all speed address themselves thereunto; but to come to God by Christ, to be freely forgiven, without more ado, they like it not. Some rigid, austere penances, some compensatory obedience, some satisfactory mortification or purgatory, had been a more likely way. This of mere pardon in and by the cross, it is but folly (1 Cor. 1:18, 20). 'I had rather,' says the

Jew, 'have it "as it were by the works of the law," (Rom. 9:32, 10:3). This way of grace and forgiveness I like not.' So say others also; so practise others every day. Either this way is wholly rejected, or it is mended by some additions; which with God is all one with the rejection of it.

Here multitudes of souls deceive themselves and perish. I know not whether it be more difficult to persuade an unconvinced person to think of any terms, or a convinced person to accept of these. Let men say what they will, and pretend what they please, yet practically they like not this way of forgiveness. I shall therefore offer some subservient considerations, tending to the furtherance of your souls in the acceptance of the terms proposed.

## God Chose the Terms

This is the way, these are the terms of God's own choosing; he found out this way, he established it himself. He did it when all was lost and undone. He did it, not upon our desire, request, or proposal, but merely of his own accord; and why should we contend with him about it? If God will have us saved in a way of mere mercy and forgiveness, if his wisdom and sovereignty be in it, shall we oppose him, and say we like it not? Yet this is the language of unbelief (Rom. 10:3). Many poor creatures have disputed it with God, until at length, being overpowered as it were by the Spirit, [they] have said, 'If it must be so, and God will save us by mercy and grace, let it be so; we yield ourselves to his will;' and yet throughout their disputes dreamed of nothing but that their own unworthiness only kept them from closing with the promise of the gospel.

Of this nature was that way of Satan whereby he deceived our first parents of their interest in the covenant of works. 'The terms of it,' says he, 'as apprehended by you, are unequal. "Yea, has God said, You shall eat of every tree of the garden, but of the tree of knowledge of good and evil you shall not eat, lest you die?" Come; "you shall not die: for God knows that in the day you eat thereof then your eyes shall be opened." There is no proportion between the disobedience and the threatening; the issue cannot be such as is feared.' And by these means he ruined them. Thus, also, he proceeds to deprive souls of their interest in the covenant of grace, whereunto they are invited: 'The terms of it are unequal, how can any man believe them? There is no proportion between the obedience and the promise. To have pardon, forgiveness, life, and a blessed eternity, on believing! Who can rest in it?' And here lies a conspiracy between Satan and unbelief, against the wisdom, goodness, love, grace, and sovereignty of God. The poison of this deceit lies in this, that neither the righteousness nor the mercy of God is of that infiniteness as indeed they are. The apostle, to remove this fond imagination, calls us to the pleasure of God: 'It pleased God by the foolishness of preaching' (1 Cor. 1:21) — that is, by the gospel preached, which they esteemed foolishness — 'to save them that believe.' He suffered men, indeed, to make trial of other ways; and when their insufficiency for the ends men proposed to themselves was sufficiently manifested, it pleased him to reveal his way. And what are we, that we should contend about it with him? This rejection of the way of personal righteousness, and choosing the way of grace and forgiveness, God asserts: 'Behold, the days come, says the LORD, that I will make a new covenant with the house of Israel, and with the house of Judah: not according to the covenant that I made with their fathers' (in which administration of the covenant, as far as it had respect to typical mercies, much depended on their personal obedience): 'but this shall be the covenant that I will make with the house of Israel; After those days, says the LORD, I will put my law…' 'for I will forgive their iniquity, and I will remember their sin no more' (Jer. 31:31–5). Let, then, this way stand, and the way of man's wisdom and self-righteousness perish for ever.

## To the Glory of God

This is the way that above all others tends directly and immediately to the glory of God. God has managed and ordered all things in this way of forgiveness, so as 'no flesh should glory in his presence,' but that 'he that glories should glory in the Lord' (1 Cor. 1:29, 31). 'Where is boasting then? It is excluded. By what law? By the law of works? Nay; but by the law of faith' (Rom. 3:27). It might be easily manifested that God has so laid the design of saving sinners by forgiveness according to the law of faith, that it is utterly impossible that any soul should, on any account whatever, have the least ground of glorying or boasting in itself, either absolutely or in comparison with them that perish. 'If Abraham,' says the same apostle, 'were justified by works, he had whereof to glory; but not before God' (Rom. 4:2). The obedience of works would have been so infinitely disproportionate to the reward, which was God himself, that there had been no glorying before God, but therein his goodness and grace must he acknowledged; yet in comparison with others who yielded not the obedience required, he would have had wherein to glory: but now this also is cut off by the way of forgiveness, and no pretence is left for any to claim the least share in the glory of it but God alone. And herein lies the excellency of faith, that it 'gives glory to God' (Rom. 4:20); the denial whereof, under various pretences, is the issue of proud unbelief. And this is that which God will bring all to, or they shall perish—namely, that shame be ours, and the whole glory of our salvation be his alone. So he expresses his design (Isa. 45:22–5). He proposes himself as the only relief for sinners: 'Look to me,' says he, 'and be saved, all the ends of the earth' (v. 22) But what if men take some other course, and look well to themselves, and so decline this way of mere mercy and grace? Why, says he, 'I have sworn by myself, the word is gone out of my mouth in righteousness, and shall not return, That to me every knee shall bow, every tongue shall swear' (v. 23). Look you to that, 'But I have sworn that you shall either do so, or answer your disobedience at the day of judgment;' whereunto Paul applies those words (Rom. 14:11). What do the saints hereupon? 'Surely, shall one say, in the LORD have I righteousness and strength. In the LORD shall all the seed of Israel be justified, and shall glory' (Isa. 45:24–5). They bring their hearts to accept of all righteousness from him, and to give all glory to him.

God at first placed man in a blessed state and condition—in

such a dependence on himself as that he might have wrought out his eternal happiness with a great reputation of glory to himself. 'Man being in this honour,' says the psalmist, 'abode not.' God now fixes on another way, as I said, wherein all the glory shall be his own, as the apostle at large sets it forth (Rom. 3:21–6). Now, neither the way from which Adam fell, nor that wherein some of the angels continued, which for the substance were the same, is to be compared with this of forgiveness, as to the bringing glory to God. I hate curiosities and conjectures in the things of God, yet, upon the account of the interposition of the blood of Christ, I think I may boldly say there comes more glory to God by saving one sinner in this way of forgiveness, than in giving the reward of blessedness to all the angels in heaven: so seems it to appear from that solemn representation we have of the ascription of glory to God by the whole creation (Rev. 5:9–14). All centres in the bringing forth forgiveness by the blood of the Lamb.

I insist the more on this, because it lies so directly against that cursed principle of unbelief which reigns in the hearts of the most, and often disquiets the best. That a poor ungodly sinner, going to God with the guilt of all his sins upon him, to receive forgiveness at his hand, brings more glory to him than the obedience of an angel, men are not over ready to think, nor can be prepared for it but by itself. And the formal nature of that unbelief which works in convinced sinners lies in a refusal to give to God the whole glory of salvation. There are many hurtful controversies in religion that are managed in the world with great noise and clamour, but this is the greatest and most pernicious of them all; and it is for the most part silently transacted in the souls of men, although under various forms and pretences. It has also broken forth in writings and disputations; that is, whether God or man shall have the glory of salvation; or whether it shall wholly be ascribed to God, or that man also, on one account or other, may come in for a share. Now, if this be the state and condition with any of you, that you will rather perish than God should have his glory, what shall we say but, 'Go, you cursed souls, perish for ever, without the least compassion from God, or any that love him, angels or men.'

If you shall say, for your parts you are contented with this course—let God have the glory, so you may be forgiven and saved; there is yet just cause to suspect lest this be a selfish contempt of God. It is a great thing to give glory to God by believing in a due manner. Such slight returns seem not to have the least relation to it. Take heed that, instead of believing, you be not found mockers, and so your bands be made strong.

But a poor convinced sinner may here find encouragement.

You would willingly come to acquaintance with God, and so attain salvation?

'Oh, my soul longs for it!'

Would you willingly take that course for the obtaining those ends which will bring most glory to God?

'Surely it is meet and most equal that I should do so.'

What, now, if one should come and tell you from the Lord of a way whereby you, poor, sinful, self-condemned creature, might bring as much glory to God as any angel in heaven is able to do?

'Oh, if I might bring the least glory to God, I should rejoice in it!'

Behold, then, the way which himself has fixed on for the exaltation of his glory, even that you should come to him merely upon the account of grace in the blood of Christ for pardon and forgiveness; and the Lord strengthen you to give yourself up thereunto!

### No Other Terms

Consider that if this way of salvation be refused, there is no other way for you. We do not propose this way of forgiveness as the best and most pleasant, but as the only way. There is no other name given but that of Christ; no other way but this of forgiveness. Here lies your choice; take this path, or perish for ever. It is a shame, indeed, to our cursed nature that there should be any need to use this argument—that we will neither submit to God's sovereignty nor delight in his glory; but seeing it must be used, let it be so. I intend neither to flatter men nor to frighten them, but to tell them the truth as it is. If you continue in your present state and condition; if you rest on what you do or what you hope to do; if you support yourselves with general hopes of mercy, mixed with your own endeavours and obedience; if you come not up to a thorough gospel-closure with this way of God; if you make it not your all, giving glory to God therein—perish you will, you must, and that to eternity. There remains no sacrifice for your sins, nor way of escape for your souls. You have not, then, only the excellency of this way to invite you, but the absolute, indispensable necessity of this way to enforce you. And now, let me add that I am glad this word is spoken, is written to you. You and I must one day be accountable for this discourse. That word that has already been spoken, if neglected, will prove a sore testimony against you. It will not fare with you as with other men who have not heard the joyful sound. All those words that shall be found consonant to the gospel, if they are not turned to grace in your hearts here, will turn into torment to your souls hereafter. Choose not any other way; it will be in vain for you; it will not profit you. And take heed lest you suppose you embrace this way when indeed you do not; about which I have given caution before.

### Free and Open to Sinners

This way is free and open for and to sinners. He that fled to the city of refuge might well have many perplexed thoughts, whether he should find the gates of it opened to him or no, and whether the avenger of blood might not overtake and slay him whilst he was calling for entrance. Or if the gates were always open, yet some crimes excluded men thence (Num. 35:16). It is not so here (Acts 13:38–9).

This is the voice of God, even the Father: 'Come,' says he, 'to the marriage, for all things are prepared'—no fear of want of entertainment (Matt. 22:4); whence the preachers of the gospel are said in his stead to beseech men to be reconciled (2 Cor. 5:20).

And it is the voice of the Son: 'Whosoever,' says he, 'comes to God by me, "I will in no wise cast out."' (John 6:37). Whoever he be that comes shall assuredly find entertainment. The same is his call and invitation in other places (as Matt. 11:28; John 7:37).

And this is the voice of the Spirit, and of the church, and of all believers: 'The Spirit and the bride say, Come. And let him that hears say, Come. And let him that is athirst come. And whosoever will, let him take the water of life freely' (Rev. 22:17). All centre in this, that sinners may come freely to the grace of the gospel.

And it is the known voice of the gospel itself (as Isa. 40:1–3; Prov. 9:1–5).

And it is the voice of all the saints in heaven and earth, who have been made partakers of forgiveness; they all testify that they received it freely.

Some, indeed, endeavour to abuse this concurrent testimony of God and man. What is spoken of the freedom of the grace of God, they would wrest to the power of the will of man; but the riches and freedom of God's mercy do not in the least interfere with the efficacy of his grace. Though he proclaim pardon in the blood of Christ indefinitely, according to the fullness and excellency of it, yet he gives out his quickening grace to enable men to receive it as he pleases; for he has mercy on whom he will have mercy. But this lies in the thing itself; the way is opened and prepared, and it is not because men cannot enter, but because they will not, that they do not enter. As our Saviour Christ tells the Pharisees, 'You therefore hear not God's word, because you are not of God' (John 8:47, 6:44); so he does, 'You will not come to me that you might have life' (John 5:40). In the neglect and inadvertency of the most excusable, there is a positive act of their will put forth in the refusing of Christ and grace by him; and this is done by men under the preaching of the gospel every day. There is nothing that at the last day will tend more immediately to the advancement of the glory of God, in the inexcusableness of them who obey not the gospel, than this, that terms of peace, in the blessed way of forgiveness, were freely tendered to them. Some that hear or read this word may perhaps have lived long under the dispensation of the word of grace, and yet it may be have never once seriously pondered on this way of coming to God by forgiveness through the blood of Christ, but think that going to heaven is a thing of course, that men need not much trouble themselves about. Do they know what they have done? Hitherto, all their days, they have positively refused the salvation that has been freely tendered to them in Jesus Christ. Not they, they will say; they never had such a thought, nor would for all this world. But be it known to you, inasmuch as you have not effectually received him, you have refused him; and whether your day and season be past or no, the Lord only knows.

### A Safe Way

This way is safe. No soul ever miscarried in it. There is none in heaven but will say it is a safe way; there is none in hell can say otherwise. It is safe to all that venture on it so as to enter into it. In the old way we were to preserve ourselves and the way; this preserves itself and us. This will be made evident by the ensuing considerations.

THE OLD COVENANT WAS NOT A SAFE WAY. This is the way which, in the wisdom, care, and love of God in Christ, was provided in the room of another, removed and taken out of the way for this cause and reason, because it was not safe nor could bring us to God: 'For if the first covenant had been faultless, then should no place have been sought for the second. But finding fault with them, he says' (Heb. 8:7–8).

And he tells us that the first covenant was not faultless; for if it had, there would have been no need of a second. The 'commandment,' indeed, which was the matter of that covenant, the same apostle informs us to be 'holy, and just, and good' (Rom. 7:12). But this was faulty as to all ends of a covenant, considering our state and condition as sinners; it could not bring us to God. So he acquaints us, 'It was weak through the flesh' (Rom. 8:3)—that is, by the entrance of sin—and so became unuseful as to the saving of souls. Be it so, then: through our sin and default this good and holy law, this covenant, was made unprofitable to us; but what was that to

God? Was he bound to desert his own institution and appointment, because through our own default it ceased to be profitable to us? Not at all. He might righteously have tied us all to the terms of that covenant, to stand or fall by them to eternity; but he would not do so.

But, in his love and grace he 'finds fault with it' (Heb. 8:8); not in itself and absolutely, but only so far as that he would provide another way, which should supply all its defects and wants in reference to the end aimed at. What way that is the apostle declares in the following verses to the end of that chapter. The sum is, 'I will be merciful to their unrighteousness, and their sins and their iniquities will I remember no more' (v. 12). It is the way of pardon and forgiveness. This is substituted in the room of that insufficient way that was removed.

Let us consider, then, whether the infinitely wise and holy God, pursuing his purpose of bringing souls to himself—laying aside one way of his own appointment as useless and infirm, because of the coming in of sin, against which there was no relief found in it, and substituting another way in the room of it—would not provide such a one as should be absolutely free from the faults and inconveniences which he charged upon that which he did remove. That which alone rendered the former way faulty was sin; it could do any thing but save a sinner. This, then, was to be, and is, principally provided against in this way of forgiveness. And we see here how clearly God has severed, yea, and in this matter opposed, these two things—namely, the way of personal righteousness and the way of forgiveness. He finds fault with the first. What then does he do? What course does he take? Does he mend it, take from it what seems to be redundant, mitigate its severity, and supply it where it was wanting by forgiveness, and so set it up anew? This, indeed, is the way that many proceed in their notions, and the most in their practice; but this is not the way of God. He takes the one utterly away, and establishes the other in its place. And men's endeavours to mix them will be found of little use to them at the last. I can have no great expectation from that which God pronounced faulty.

UNCHANGEABLE FOUNDATIONS MAKE IT SAFE. The unchangeable principles and foundations that this way is built upon render it secure and safe for sinners.

For, it is founded on the purpose of God: 'The Scripture foreseeing that God would justify the heathen through faith' (Gal. 3:8). God would do so; he had purposed and determined to proceed this way; and all the purposes of God are attended with immutability.

And, his promise also is engaged in it, and that given out in the way of a covenant, as has been already declared.

This promise is confirmed by an oath; and it may be observed, that God does not in any thing interpose with an oath, but what relates to this way of coming to himself by forgiveness; for the oath of God, wherever it is used, respects either Christ typically or personally, or the covenant established in him.

For, this way is confirmed and ratified in his blood; from whence the apostle at large evinces its absolute security and safety (Heb. 9): Whatever soul, on the invitation under consideration, shall give up himself to come to God by the way proposed, he shall assuredly find absolute peace and security in it. Neither our own weakness or folly from within, nor the opposition of any or all our enemies from without, shall be able to turn us out of this way (see Isa. 35:4–10).

WE STAND ON THE ACCOUNT OF A COMMON MEDIATOR. In the other way, every individual person stands upon his own bottom, and must do so to the last and utmost of his continuance in this world. You are desirous to go to God, to obtain his favour, and come to an enjoyment of him. What will you do, what course will you fix upon, for the obtaining of these ends? If you were so holy, so perfect, so righteous, so free from sin as you could desire, you should have some boldness in going to God. Why, if this be the way you fix upon, take this along with you: You stand upon your own personal account all your days: and if you fail in the least, you are gone for ever; 'for whosoever shall keep the whole law, and yet offend in one point, he is guilty of all' (James 2:10). And what peace can you possibly obtain, were you as holy as ever you aimed or desired to be, whilst this is your condition? But in this way of forgiveness we all shall stand upon the account of one common Mediator, in whom we are 'complete' (Col. 2:10). And a want of a due improvement of this truth is a great principle of disconsolation to many souls. Suppose a man look upon himself as loosed from the covenant of works, wherein exact and perfect righteousness is rigidly required, and to be called to gospel, evangelical obedience, to be performed in the room thereof in sincerity and integrity; yet if he be not cleared in this also, that he stands not in this way purely on his own account, he will never be able to make his comforts hold out to the end of his journey. There will be found in the best of men so many particular failings, as will seem in difficult seasons to impeach their integrity; and so many questionings will after arise, through the darkness of their minds and power of their temptations, as will give but little rest to their souls. Here lies the great security of this way—we abide in it on the account of the faithfulness and ability of our common Mediator, Jesus Christ.

And this is another consideration, strengthening our invitation to a closure with the way of coming to God under proposal. There is nothing wanting that is needful to give infallible security to any soul that shall venture himself into it and upon it. There are terms of peace proposed, as you have heard. These terms are excellent, and holy, and chosen of God, tending to the interest of his glory—free, safe, and secure to sinners. What has any soul in the world to object against them? Or wherein do men repose their trust and confidence in the neglect of this so great salvation? Is it in their lusts and sins, that they will yield them as much satisfaction and contentment as they shall need to desire? Alas! They will ruin them, and bring forth nothing but death. Is it in the world? It will deceive them; the figure of it passes away. Is it in their duties and righteousness? They will not relieve them; for, did they follow the law of righteousness, they could not obtain the righteousness of the law. Is it in the continuance of their lives? Alas! It is but a shadow, 'a vapour that appears for a little while.' Is it in a future amendment and repentance? Hell is full of souls perishing under such resolutions. Only this way of pardon remains; and yet of all others is most despised! But yet I have one consideration more to add before I farther enforce the exhortation.

### The Only Way to Obey

Consider that this is the only way and means to enable you to obedience, and to render what you do therein acceptable to God. It may be that some of you are under the power of convictions, and have made engagements to God to live to him, to keep yourselves from sin, and to follow after holiness. It may be you have done so in afflictions, dangers, sicknesses, or upon receipt of mercies, but yet you find that you cannot come to stability or constancy in your course—you break with God and your own souls; which fills you with new disquietments, or else hardens you and makes you secure and negligent, so that you return to your purposes no oftener than your convictions or afflictions befall you anew. This condition is ruinous and pernicious, which nothing can deliver you from but this closing with forgiveness.

APART FROM THIS GOD ACCEPTS NOTHING. For all that you do without this, however it may please your minds or ease your consciences, is not at all accepted with God. Unless this foundation be laid, all that you do is lost; all your prayers, all your duties, all your amendments, are an abomination to the Lord. Until peace is made with him, they are but the acts of enemies, which he despises and abhors. You run, it may be earnestly, but you run out of the way; you strive, but not lawfully, and shall never receive the crown. True gospel obedience is the fruit of the faith of forgiveness. Whatever you do without it is but a building without a foundation, a castle in the air. You may see the order of gospel obedience (Eph. 2:7–10). The foundation must be laid in grace, riches of grace by Christ—in the free pardon and forgiveness of sin. From hence must the works of obedience proceed, if you would have them to be of God's appointment, or find acceptance with him. Without this God will say of all your services, worship, obedience, as he did to the Israelites of old, 'I despise all, reject it all' (Amos 5:21–3). It is not to him nor to his glory. Now, if you are under convictions of any sort, there is nothing you more value, nothing you more place your confidence in, than your duties, your repentance, your amendment, what you do, and what in good time you will be. Is it nothing to you to lose all your hopes and all your expectations which you have from hence; to have no other reception with God than if all this while you had been wallowing in your sins and lusts? Yet thus it is with you. If you have not begun with God on his own terms, if you have not received the atonement in the blood of his Son, if you are not made partakers of forgiveness, if your persons are not pardoned, all your duties are accursed.

MOTIVES AND ENCOURAGEMENTS. This alone will give you such motives and encouragements to obedience as will give you life, alacrity, and delight in it. You perform duties, abstain from sins, but with heaviness, fear, and in bondage. Could you do as well without them as with them, would conscience be quiet, and hope of eternity hold out, you would omit them for ever. This makes all your obedience burdensome, and you cry out in your thoughts with him in the prophet, 'Behold, what a weariness is it!' The service of God is the only drudgery of your lives, which you dare not omit, and delight not to perform. From this wretched and cursed frame there is nothing can deliver you but this closing with forgiveness. This will give you such motives, such encouragements, as will greatly influence your hearts and souls. It will give you freedom, liberty, delight, and cheerfulness, in all duties of gospel obedience. You will find a constraining power in the love of Christ therein—a freedom from bondage, when the Son truly has made you free. Faith and love will work genuinely and naturally in your spirits; and that which was your greatest burden will become your chief joy (2 Cor. 7:1). Thoughts of the love of God, of the blood of Christ, or of the covenant of grace, and sense of pardon in them, will enlarge your hearts and sweeten all your duties. You will find a new life, a new pleasure, a new satisfaction, in all that you do. Have you yet ever understood that of the wise man (Prov. 3:17), 'Wisdom's ways are ways of pleasantness, and all her paths are peace?' Have the ways of holiness, of obedience, of duties, been so to you? Whatever you pretend, they are not, they cannot be so, whilst you are strangers to that which alone can render them so to you. I speak to them that are under the law. Would you be free from that bondage, that galling yoke in duties of obedience? Would you have all that you do towards God a delight and pleasantness to you? This, and this alone, will effect it for you.

NOT LABOURING TO PAY A MOUNTAIN OF DEBT. This will place all your obedience upon a sure foot of account in your own souls and consciences, even the same that is fixed on in the gospel. For the present, all that you do is indeed but to compound with God for your sin. You hope, by what you do for him and to him, to buy off what you have done against him, that you may not fall into the hands of his wrath and vengeance. This makes all you do to be irksome. As a man that labours all his days to pay an old debt, and brings in nothing to lay up for himself, how tedious and wearisome is his work and labour to him! It is odds but that, at one time or other, he will give over and run away from his creditor. So it is in this case: men who have secret reserves of recompensing God by their obedience, every day find their debt growing upon them, and have every day less hopes of making a satisfactory payment. This makes them weary, and for the most part they faint under their discouragements, and at length they fly wholly from God. This way alone will state things otherwise in your consciences: it will give you to see that all your debts are paid by Christ, and freely forgiven to you by God; so that what you do is of gratitude or thankfulness, has an influence into eternity, leads to the glory of God, the honour of Christ in the gospel, and your own comfortable account at the last day. This encourages the soul to labour, to trade, to endeavour; all things now looking forward, and to his advantage.

A SPIRIT OF LIFE AND POWER. Find you not in yourselves an impotency, a disability to the duties of obedience, as to their performance to God in an acceptable manner? It may be you are not so sensible hereof as you ought to be; for, respecting only or principally the outward part and performance of duties, you have not experience of your own weakness. How to enliven and fill up duties with faith, love, and delight, you know not; and are therefore unacquainted with your own insufficiency in this matter. Yet if you have any light, any convictions (and to such I speak at present), you cannot but perceive and understand that you are not able in your obedience to answer what you aim at; you have not strength or power for it. Now it is this faith of forgiveness alone that will furnish you with the ability whereof you stand in need. Pardon comes not to the soul alone, or rather, Christ comes not to the soul with pardon only; it is that which he opens the door and enters by, but he comes with a Spirit of life and power. And as 'without him we can do nothing,' so through his enabling us we may 'do all things.' Receiving of gospel forgiveness engages all the grace of the gospel to our assistance.

This is the sum of what has been spoken—the obedience that you perform under your convictions is burdensome and unpleasant to you; it is altogether unacceptable to God. You lose all you do, and all that you hope to do hereafter, if the foundation be not laid in the receiving of pardon in the blood of Christ. It is high time to cast down all that vain and imaginary fabric which you have been erecting, and to go about the laying of a new foundation, which you may safely and cheerfully build upon—a building that will abide for ever.

### Neglect It at a Terrible Cost

Again: it is such a way, so excellent, so precious, so near the heart of God, so relating to the blood of Christ, that the neglect of it will assuredly be sorely revenged of the Lord. Let not men think that they shall despise the wisdom and love of the Father, the blood of the Son, and the promises of the gospel, at an easy rate. Let us in a very few words take a view of what the Holy Ghost speaks to this purpose. There are three ways whereby the vengeance due to the neglect of closing with forgiveness or gospel grace is expressed:

That is done positively: 'He that believes not shall be damned' (Mark 16:16). That is a hard word; many men cannot endure to hear of it. They would not have it named by their good wills, and are ready to fly in the face of him from whose mouth it proceeds. But let not men deceive themselves; this is the softest word that mercy and love itself, that Christ, that the gospel speaks to despisers of forgiveness. It is Christ who is this legal terrifying preacher; it is he that cries out, 'If you believe not, you shall be damned;' and he will come himself 'in flaming fire, to take vengeance on them that obey not the gospel' (2 Thess. 2:8). This is the end of the disobedient, if God, if Christ, if the gospel may be believed.

Comparatively, in reference to the vengeance due to the breach of the law. We are in the preaching of forgiveness by Christ, to them that perish, 'a savour of death to death' (2 Cor. 2:16), a deep death, a sore condemnation. So Hebrews 10:29: 'Of how much sorer punishment suppose you shall he be thought worthy?' Sorer than ever was threatened by the law, or inflicted for the breach of it—not as to the kind of punishment but as to the degrees of it; hence arises the addition of 'Many stripes.'

By way of admiration at the inexpressibleness and unavoidableness of the punishment due to such sinners: 'How shall we escape, if we neglect so great salvation!' (Heb. 2:3)—'Surely there is no way for men to escape, they shall unavoidably perish, who neglect so great salvation.' So the Holy Ghost says, 'What shall the end be of them that obey not the gospel?' (1 Pet. 4:17)—'What understanding can reach to an apprehension of their miserable and woeful condition?' 'None can,' says the Holy Ghost, 'nor can it be spoken to their capacity.' Ah! What shall their end be? There remains nothing but 'a certain fearful looking for of judgment and fiery indignation, which shall devour the adversaries' (Heb. 10:27)—a certain fearful expectation of astonishable things, that cannot be comprehended.

### WHERE DOES YOUR HOPE REST?

And these are the enforcements of the exhortation in hand which I shall insist upon. On these foundations, on the consideration of these principles, let us now a little confer together, with the words of truth and sobriety. I speak to such poor souls as, having deceived themselves, or neglected utterly their eternal condition, are not as yet really and in truth made partakers of this forgiveness. Your present state is sad and deplorable. There is nothing but the woeful uncertainty of a dying life between you and eternal ruin. That persuasion you have of forgiveness is good for nothing but to harden you and destroy you. It is not the forgiveness that is with God, nor have you taken it up on gospel grounds or evidences. You have stolen painted beads, and take yourselves to be lawful possessors of pearls and jewels. As you are, then, any way concerned in your own eternal condition, which you are entering into (and how soon you shall be engaged in it you know not), prevail with yourselves to attend a little to the exhortation that lies before you; it is your own business that you are entreated to have regard to.

Consider seriously what it is you bottom your hopes and expectation upon as to eternity. Great men, and in other things wise, are here very apt to deceive themselves. They suppose they think and believe much otherwise than indeed they think and believe, as their cry at the last day will manifest. Put your souls a little to it. Do you at all seriously think of these things? Or are you so under the power of your lusts, ignorance, and darkness, that you neglect and despise them? Or do you rise up and lie down, and perform some duties, or neglect them, with a great coldness, remissness, and indifferency of spirit, like Gallio, not much caring for these things? Or do you relieve yourselves with hopes of future amendment, purposing that if you live you will be other persons than you are, when such and such things are brought about and accomplished? Or do you not hope well in general upon the account of what you have done and will do? If any of these express your condition, it is unspeakably miserable. You lie down and rise up under the wrath of the great God, who will prevail at last upon you, and there shall be none to deliver.

If you shall say, 'Nay, this is not our state; we rely on mercy and forgiveness,' then let me, in the fear of the great God, entreat a few things yet farther of you.

That you would seriously consider whether the forgiveness you rest on and hope in be that gospel forgiveness which we have before described; or is it only a general apprehension of impunity, though you are sinners—that God is merciful, and you hope in him that you shall escape the vengeance of hell-fire? If it be thus with you, forgiveness itself will not relieve you. This is that of the presumptuous man (Deut. 29:19). Gospel pardon is a thing of another nature; it has its spring in the gracious heart of the Father, is made out by a sovereign act of his will, rendered consistent with the glory of his justice and holiness by the blood of Christ, by which it is purchased in a covenant of grace; as has been showed.

### Examine Your Hearts

If you shall say, 'Yea, this is the forgiveness we rely upon, it is that which you have described,' then I desire farther that you would examine your own hearts, how you came to have an interest in this forgiveness, to close with it, and to have a right to it. a man may deceive himself as effectually by supposing that true riches are his, when they are not, as by supposing his false and counterfeit ware to be good and current. How, then, came you to be interested in this gospel forgiveness? If it has befallen you you know not how—if a lifeless, barren, inoperative persuasion of it has crept upon your minds—be not mistaken, God will come and require his forgiveness at your hands, and it shall appear that you have had no part nor portion in it.

### How Have You Used Forgiveness?

If you shall say, 'Nay, but we were convinced of sin, and rendered exceeding unquiet in our consciences, and on that account looked out after forgiveness, which has given us rest,' then I desire that you would diligently consider to what ends and purposes you have received, and do make use of, this gospel forgiveness. Has it been to make up what was wanting, and to piece up a peace in your own consciences? That whereas you could not answer your convictions with your duties, you would seek for relief from forgiveness? This and innumerable other ways there are whereby men may lose their souls when they think all is well with them, even on the account of pardon and mercy. Whence is that caution of the apostle, 'Looking diligently lest any one should seem to fall,' or come short, 'of the grace of God' (Heb. 12:15). Men miss it and come short of it when they pretend themselves to be in the pursuit of it, yea, to have overtaken and possessed it.

### Flee from the Wrath to Come

Now, if any of these should prove to be your condition, I desire that you would consider seriously whether it be not high time for you to look out for a way of deliverance and escape, that you may save yourselves from this evil world, and flee from the wrath to come. The Judge stands at the door. Before he deal with you as a judge, he knocks with a tender of mercy. Who knows but that this may be the last time of his dealing thus with you. Be you old or young, you have but your season, but your day. It may, perhaps, be night with you when it is day with the rest of the world. Your sun may go down at noon; and God may swear that you shall not enter into his rest. If you are, then, resolved to continue in your present condition, I have no more to say to you. I am pure from your blood, in that I have declared to you the counsel of God in this thing; and so I must leave you to a naked trial between the great God and your souls at the last day. Poor creatures! I even tremble to think how he will tear you in pieces when there shall be none to deliver. Methinks I see your poor, destitute, forlorn souls, forsaken of lusts, sins, world, friends, angels, men, trembling before the throne of God, full of horror and fearful expectation of the dreadful sentence. Oh, that I could mourn over you, whilst you are joined to all the living, whilst there is but hope! Oh, that in this your day you knew the things of your peace!

### When God Will not Forgive

But now if you shall say, 'Nay, but we will "seek the LORD whilst he may be found," we will draw nigh to him before he cause darkness,' then consider, I pray, what Joshua told the children of Israel, when they put themselves upon such a resolution, and cried out, 'We will serve the LORD, for he is our God' (Josh. 24:19), 'You cannot serve the LORD: for he is an holy God, a jealous God; he will not forgive your transgressions nor your sins.' Go to him upon your own account, and in your own strength, with your own best endeavours and duties, you will find him too great and too holy for you to deal withal. You will obtain neither acceptance of your persons nor pardon of your sins. But you will say, 'This is heavy tidings, "If you sit still you perish, and if you rise to be doing, it will not be better." Is there no hope left for our souls? Must we pine away under our sins and the wrath of God for ever?' God forbid. There are yet other directions remaining to guide you out of these entanglements.

### *What Do You Think of This Way?*

Wherefore, ponder seriously on what has been spoken of this way of approaching to God. Consider it in its own nature, as to all the ends and purposes for which it is proposed of God; consider whether you approve of it or no. Do you judge it a way suited and fitted to bring glory to God? Does it answer all the wants and distresses of your souls? Do you think it excellent, safe, and glorious to them who are entered into it? Or have you any thing to object against it? Return your answer to him in whose name and by whose appointment these words are spoken to you.

### *Abhor Yourselves*

If you shall say, 'We are convinced that this way of forgiveness is the only way for the relief and deliverance of souls,' then abhor yourselves for all your blindness and obstinacy, whereby you have hitherto despised the love of God, the blood of Christ, and the tenders of pardon in the gospel. Be abased and humbled to the dust in a sense of your vileness, pollutions, and abominations; which things are every day spoken to, and need not here be repeated.

### *Labour to Think of Abundant Grace*

And, labour to exercise your hearts greatly with thoughts of that abundant grace that is manifested in this way of sinners coming to God, as also of the excellency of the gospel wherein it is unfolded. Consider the eternal love of the Father, which is the fountain and spring of this whole dispensation—the inexpressible love of the Son in establishing and confirming it, in removing all hinderances and obstructions by his own blood, bringing forth to beauty and glory this redemption or forgiveness of sin at the price of it. And let the glory of the gospel, which alone makes this discovery of forgiveness in God, dwell in your hearts. Let your minds be exercised about these things. You will find effects from them above all that has as yet been brought forth in your souls. What, for the most part, have you hitherto been conversant about? When you have risen above the turmoiling of lusts and corruptions in your hearts, the entanglements of your callings, business, and affairs, what have you been able to raise your hearts to? Perplexing fears about your condition, general hopes, without savour or relish, yielding you no refreshment, legal commands, bondage duties, distracted consciences, broken purposes and promises, which you have been tossed up and down withal, without any certain rest. And what effects have these thoughts produced? Have they made you more holy and more humble? Have they given you delight in God, and strength to new obedience? Not at all. Where you were, there you still are, without the least progress. But now bring your souls to these springs, and try the Lord if from that day you be not blessed with spiritual stores.

### *Stir Yourselves Up*

If the Lord be pleased to carry on your souls thus far, then stir up yourselves to choose and close with the way of forgiveness that has been revealed. Choose it only, choose it in comparison with and opposition to all others. Say you will be for Christ, and not for another; and be so accordingly. Here venture, here repose, here rest your souls. It is a way of peace, safety, holiness, beauty, strength, power, liberty, and glory. You have the nature, the name, the love, the purposes, the promises, the covenant, the oath of God; the love, life, death or blood, the mediation, or oblation and intercession of Jesus Christ; the power and efficacy of the Spirit, and gospel grace by him administered—to give you assurance of the excellency, the oneness, the safety of the way whereunto you are engaging.

If now the Lord shall be pleased to persuade your hearts and souls to enter upon the path marked out before you, and shall carry you on through the various exercises of it to this closure of faith, God will have the glory, the gospel will be exalted, and your own souls shall reap the eternal benefit of this exhortation.

### Anathema Maranatha

But now if, notwithstanding all that has been spoken, all the invitations you have had, and encouragements that have been held out to you, you shall continue to despise this so great salvation, you will live and die in the state and condition wherein you are. Why, then, as the prophet said to the wife of Jeroboam, 'Come near, for I am sent to you with heavy tidings.' I say, then if you resolve to continue in the neglect of this salvation, and shall do so accordingly, then cursed be you of the Lord, with all the curses that are written in the law, and all the curses that are denounced against despisers of the gospel. Yea, be *Anathema Maranatha*—cursed in this world always, until the coming of the Lord; and when the Lord comes, be cursed from his presence into everlasting destruction. Yea, curse them, all you holy angels of God, as the obstinate enemies of your king and head, the Lord Jesus Christ. Curse them, all you churches of Christ, as despisers of that love and mercy which is your portion, your life, your inheritance. Let all the saints of God, all that love the Lord, curse them, and rejoice to see the Lord coming forth mightily and prevailing against them, to their everlasting ruin. Why should any one have a thought of compassion towards them who despise the compassion of God, or of mercy towards them who trample on the blood of Christ? Whilst there is yet hope, we desire to have continual sorrow for you, and to travail in soul for your conversion to God; but if you be hardened in your way, shall we join with you against him? Shall we prefer you above his glory? Shall we desire your salvation with the despoiling God of his honour? Nay, God forbid. We hope to rejoice in seeing all that vengeance and indignation that is in the right hand of God poured out to eternity upon your souls (Prov. 1:24–33).

# 6

## RULES FOR FINDING GOSPEL PEACE

---

That which remains to be farther carried on, upon the principles laid down, is to persuade with souls more or less entangled in the depths of sin to close with this forgiveness by believing, to their peace and consolation. And because such persons are full of pleas and objections against themselves, I shall chiefly, in what I have to say, endeavour to obviate these objections, so to encourage them to believing and bring them to settlement. And herein whatever I have to offer flows naturally from the doctrine at large laid down and asserted. Yet I shall not in all particulars apply myself thereunto, but in general fix on those things that may tend to the establishment and consolation of both distressed and doubting souls. And I shall do what I purpose these two ways.

First, I shall lay down such general rules as are necessary to be observed by all those who intend to come to gospel peace and comfort. And then, secondly, shall consider some such objections as seem to be most comprehensive of those special reasonings wherewith distressed persons do usually entangle themselves.

I shall begin with general rules, which, through the grace of Christ and supplies of his Spirit, may be of use to believers in the condition under consideration.

I

## LET CHRIST BE YOUR JUDGE

Be not judges of your own condition, but let Christ judge. You are invited to take the comfort of this gospel truth, that 'there is forgiveness with God.' You say, not for you. So said Jacob, 'My way is hid from the LORD' (Isa. 40:27); and Zion said so too, 'The LORD has forsaken me, and my Lord has forgotten me' (Isa. 49:14). But did they make a right judgment of themselves? We find in those places that God was otherwise minded. This false judgment, made by souls in their entanglements, of their own condition, is ofttimes a most unconquerable hinderance to the bettering of it. They fill themselves with thoughts of their own about it, and on them they dwell, instead of looking out after a remedy. Misgiving thoughts of their distempers are commonly a great part of some men's sickness. Many diseases are apt to cloud the thoughts, and to cause misapprehensions concerning their own nature and danger. And these delusions are a real part of the person's sickness. Nature is no less impaired and weakened by them, the efficacy of remedies no less obstructed, than by any other real distemper. In such cases we persuade men to acquiesce in the judgment of their skilful physician; not always to be wasting themselves in and by their own tainted imaginations, and so despond upon their own mistakes, but to rest in what is informed them by him who is acquainted with the causes and tendency of their indisposition better than themselves. It is ofttimes one part of the soul's depths to have false apprehensions of its condition. Sin is a madness (Eccles. 9:3); so far as any one is under the power of it, he is under the power of madness. Madness does not sooner nor more effectually discover itself in any way or thing than in possessing them in whom it is with strange conceits and apprehensions of themselves. So does this madness of sin, according to its degrees and prevalency. Hence some cry, 'Peace, peace,' when 'sudden destruction is at hand' (1 Thess. 5:3). It is that madness, under whose power they are, which gives them such groundless imaginations of themselves and their own condition. And some say they are lost for ever, when God is with them.

Do you, then, your duty, and let Christ judge of your state. Your concern is too great to make it a reasonable demand to commit the judgment of your condition to any other. When eternal welfare or woe are at the stake, for a man to renounce his own thoughts, to give up himself implicitly to the judgment of men fallible and liars like himself, is stupidity. But there is no danger of being deceived by the sentence of Christ. The truth is, whether we will or no, he will judge; and according as he determines, so shall things be found at the last day: 'The Father judges no man' (that is, immediately and in his own person), 'but has committed all judgment to the Son' (John 5:22). All judgment that respects eternity, whether it be to be passed in this world or in that to come, is committed to him. Accordingly in that place he judges both of things and persons. Things he determines upon, 'He that hears my word, and believes on him that sent me, has everlasting life, and shall not come into condemnation; but is passed from death to life' (v. 24). Let men say what they please, this sentence shall stand; faith and eternal life are inseparably conjoined. And so of persons, 'You have not' (says he to the Pharisees, who were much otherwise minded) 'the word of God abiding in you' (v. 38).

## His Judgments often Contradict Men's Judgments

Take not, then, the office and prerogative of Christ out of his hand, by making a judgment, upon your own reasonings and conclusions and deductions, of your estate and condition. You will find that he oftentimes, both on the one hand and on the other, determines quite contrary to what men judge of themselves, as also to what others judge of them. Some he judges to be in an evil condition, who are very confident that it is well with them, and who please themselves in the thoughts of many to the same purpose. And he judges the state of some to be good, who are diffident in themselves, and, it may be, despised by others. We may single out an example or two in each kind.

### 'I Need Nothing'

Laodicea's judgment of herself and her spiritual state we have: 'I am rich, and increased with goods, and have need of nothing' (Rev. 3:17). a fair state it seems, a blessed condition. She wants nothing that may contribute to her rest, peace, and reputation: she is orthodox, and numerous, and flourishing; makes a fair profession, and all is well within! So she believes, so she reports of herself; wherein there is a secret reflection also upon others whom she despises: 'Let them shift as they list, I am thus as I say.' But was it so with her indeed? Was that her true condition, whereof she was so persuaded as to profess it to all? Let Jesus Christ be heard to speak in this cause, let him come and judge. 'I will do so,' says he: 'Thus says the Amen, the faithful and true Witness' (v. 14). Coming to give sentence in a case of this importance, he gives himself this title, that we may know his word is to be acquiesced in. 'Every man,' says he, 'is a liar; their testimony is of no value, let them pronounce what they win of themselves or of one another, "I am the Amen," and I will see whose word shall stand, mine or theirs.' What, then, says he of Laodicea? 'You are wretched, and miserable, and poor, and blind, and naked.' Oh, woeful and sad disappointment! Oh, dreadful surprisal! Ah! How many Laodicean churches have we in the world! How many professors are members of these churches! Not to mention the generality of men that live under the means of grace; all which have good hopes of their eternal condition, whilst they are despised and abhorred by the only Judge. Among professors themselves, it is dreadful to think how many will be found light when they come to be weighed in this balance.

### 'But You Are Rich'

Again, he judges some to be in a good condition, be they themselves never so diffident. Says he to the church of Smyrna, 'I know your poverty' (Rev. 2:9). Smyrna was complaining that she was a poor, contemptible congregation, not fit for him to take any notice of. 'Well,' says he, 'fear not. "I know your poverty," whereof you complain; "but you are rich." That is my judgment, testimony, and sentence, concerning you and your condition.' Such will be his judgment at the last day, when both those on the one hand and on the other shall be surprised with his sentence—the one with joy at the riches of his grace, the other with terror at the severity of his justice (Matt. 25:37–40, 44–5). This case is directly stated in both the places mentioned in the entrance of this discourse; as in that, for instance, 'Zion said, The LORD has forsaken me' (Isa. 49:14). That is Zion's judgment of herself, and her state and condition; a sad report and conclusion. But does Christ agree with Zion in this sentence? The next verse gives us his resolution of this matter: 'Can,' says he, 'a woman forget her sucking child, that she should not have compassion on the son of her womb? Yea, they may forget, yet will I not forget you.' The state of things, in truth, is as much otherwise as can possibly be thought or imagined.

To what purpose is it for men to be passing a judgment upon themselves, when there is no manner of certainty in their determinations, and when their proceeding thereon will probably lead them to farther entanglements, if not to eternal ruin? The judging of souls, as to their spiritual state and condition, is the work of Jesus Christ, especially as to the end now under inquiry. Men may, men do, take many ways to make a judgment of themselves. Some do it on slight and trivial conjectures; some on bold and wicked presumptions; some on desperate atheistic notions (as Deut. 29:19); some, with more sobriety and sense of eternity, lay down principles that may be good and true in themselves, from them they draw conclusions, arguing from one thing to another, and in the end ofttimes either deceive themselves, or sit down no less in the dark than they were at the entrance of their self-debate and examination. a man's judgment upon his own reasonings is seldom true, more seldom permanent. I speak not of self-examination, with a due discussion of graces and actions, but of the final sentence as to state and condition, wherein the soul is to acquiesce. This belongs to Christ.

### HOW CHRIST PRONOUNCES HIS SENTENCE

Now, there are two ways whereby the Lord Jesus Christ gives forth his decretory sentence in this matter.

#### By His Word

He determines, in the word of the gospel, of the state and condition of all men indefinitely. Each individual coming to that word receives his own sentence and doom. He told the Jews that Moses accused them (John 5:45). His law accused and condemned the transgressors of it. And so he acquits every one that is discharged by the word of the gospel. And our self-judging is but our receiving by faith his sentence in the word. His process herein we have recorded: 'His soul' (that is, of the sinner) 'draws near to the grave, and his life to the destroyers' (Job 33:22–3). This seems to be his state; it is so indeed: he is at the very brink of the grave and hell. What then? Why, if there be with him or stand over him מַלְאָךְ מֵלִיץ, the angel interpreting, or the angel of the covenant, who alone אֶחָד מִנִּי־אָלֶף, the 'one of a thousand,' what shall he do? 'He shall shew to him his uprightness.' He shall give to him a right determination of his interest in God, and of the state and frame of his heart towards God; whereupon God shall speak peace to his soul, and deliver him from his entanglements (v. 24). Jesus Christ has, in the word of the gospel, stated the condition of every man. He tells us that sinners, of what sort soever they are, that believe, are accepted with him, and shall receive forgiveness from God—that none shall be refused or cast off that come to God by him. The soul of whom we are treating is now upon the work of coming to God for forgiveness by Jesus Christ. Many and weighty objections it has in and against itself why it should not come, why it shall not be accepted. Our Lord Jesus, the wisdom of God, foresaw all these objections, he foreknew what could be said in the case, and yet he has determined the matter as has been declared. In general, men's arguings against themselves arise from sin and the law. Christ knows what is in them both. He tried them to the uttermost, as to their penalties, and yet he has so determined as we have showed. Their particular objections are from particular considerations of sin, their greatness, their number, their aggravations. Christ knows all these also, and yet stands to his former determination. Upon the whole matter, then, it is meet his word should stand. I know, when a soul brings itself to be judged by the word of the gospel, it does not always in a like manner receive and rest in the sentence given. But when Christ is pleased to speak the word with power to men, they shall 'hear the voice of the Son of God,' and be concluded by it. Let the soul, then, that is rising out of depths and pressing towards a sense of forgiveness, lay itself down before the word of Christ in the gospel. Let him attend to what he speaks; and if for a while it has not power upon him to quiet his heart, let him wait a season, and light shall arise to him out of darkness. Christ will give in his sentence into his conscience with that power and efficacy as he shall find rest and peace in it.

## By His Spirit

Christ also judges by his Spirit, not only in making this sentence of the gospel to be received effectually in the soul, but in and by peculiar actings of his upon the heart and soul of a believer: 'We have received the Spirit which is of God, that we might know the things that are freely given to us of God' (1 Cor. 2:12). The Spirit of Christ acquaints the soul that this and that grace is from him, that this or that duty was performed in his strength. He brings to mind what at such and such times was wrought in men by himself, to give them support and relief in the times of depths and darkness. And when it has been clearly discovered to the soul at any time by the Holy Ghost, that any thing wrought in it or done by it has been truly saving, the comfort of it will abide in the midst of many shakings and temptations.

He also by his Spirit bears witness with our spirits as to our state and condition. Of this I have spoken largely elsewhere, and therefore shall now pass it by.

This, then, is our first general rule and direction. Self-determinations concerning men's spiritual state and condition, because their minds are usually influenced by their distempers, are seldom right and according to rule; mistakes in such determinations are exceedingly prejudicial to a soul seeking out after relief and sense of forgiveness: let Christ, then, be the judge in this case by his word and Spirit, as has been directed.

## II

### EXPECT TO CARRY HELL IN ONE HAND AND HEAVEN IN THE OTHER

Self-condemnation and abhorrency do very well consist with gospel justification and peace. Some men have no peace, because they have that without which it is impossible they should have peace. Because they cannot but condemn themselves, they cannot entertain a sense that God acquits them. But this is the mystery of the gospel, which unbelief is a stranger to; nothing but faith can give a real subsistence to these things in the same soul, at the same time. It is easy to learn the notion of it, but it is not easy to experience the power of it. For a man to have a sight of that within him which would condemn him, for which he is troubled, and at the same time to have a discovery of that without him which will justify him, and to rejoice therein, is that which he is not led to but by faith in the mystery of the gospel. We are now under a law for justification which excludes all boasting (Rom. 3:27); so that though we have joy enough in another, yet we may have, we always have, sufficient cause of humiliation in ourselves. The gospel will teach a man to feel sin and believe righteousness at the same time. Faith will carry heaven in one hand and hell in the other; showing the one deserved, the other purchased. a man may see enough of his own sin and folly to bring *'gehennam e coelo'*—a hell of wrath out of heaven; and yet see Christ bring '*coelum ex inferno*'—a heaven of blessedness out of a hell of punishment. And these must needs produce very divers, yea, contrary effects and operations in the soul; and he who knows not how to assign them their proper duties and seasons must needs be perplexed. The work of self-condemnation, then, which men in these depths cannot but abound with, is, in the disposition of the covenant of grace, no way inconsistent with nor unsuited to justification and the enjoyment of peace in the sense of it. There may be a deep sense of sin on other considerations besides hell. David was never more humbled for sin than when Nathan told him it was forgiven. And there may be a view of hell as deserved, which yet the soul may know itself freed from as to the issue.

To evidence our intendment in this discourse, I shall briefly consider what we intend by gospel assurance of forgiveness, that the soul may not be solicitous and perplexed about the utter want of that which, perhaps, it is already in some enjoyment of.

Some men seem to place gospel assurance in a high, unassaulted confidence of acceptance with God. They think it is in none but such as, if a man should go to them and ask them, 'Are you certain you shall be saved?' have boldness, and confidence, and ostentation to answer presently, 'Yea, they are certain they shall be saved.' But as the blessed truth of assurance has been reproached in the world under such a notion of it, so such expressions become not them who know what it is to have to do with the holy God, who is 'a consuming fire.' Hence some conclude that there are very few believers who have any assurance, because they have not this confidence, or are more free to mention the opposition they meet with than the support they enjoy. And thus it is rendered a matter not greatly to be desired, because it is so rarely to be obtained, most of the saints serving God and going to heaven well enough without it. But the matter is otherwise. The importance of it, not only as it is our life of comfort and joy, but also as it is the principal means of the flourishing of our life of holiness, has been declared before, and might be farther manifested, were that our present business; yea, and in times of trial, which are the proper seasons for the effectual working and manifestation of assurance, it will and does appear that many, yea, that most of the saints of God are made partakers of this grace and privilege.

I shall, then, in the pursuit of the rule laid down, do these two things: 1. Show what things they are which are not only consistent with assurance, but are even necessary concommitants of it; which yet, if not duly weighed and considered, may seem so far to impeach a man's comfortable persuasion of his condition before God as to leave him beneath the assurance sought after. And, 2. I shall speak somewhat of its nature, especially as manifesting itself by its effects.

### A Deep Sense of the Evil of Sin

A deep sense of the evil of sin, of the guilt of man's own sin, is no way inconsistent with gospel assurance of acceptance with God through Christ, and of forgiveness in him. By a sense of the guilt of sin I understand two things – First, a clear conviction of sin, by the Holy Ghost saying to the soul, 'You are the man;' and, Secondly, a sense of the displeasure of God, or the wrath due to sin, according to the sentence of the law. Both these David expresses in that complaint, 'My life is spent with grief, and my years with sighing: my strength fails because of mine iniquity, and my bones are consumed' (Ps. 31:10). His iniquity was before him, and a sense of it pressed him sore. But yet, notwithstanding all this, he had a comfortable persuasion that God was his God in covenant: 'I trusted in you, O LORD: I said, you are my God' (v. 14). And the tenor of the covenant, wherein alone God is the God of any person, is, that he will be merciful to their sin and iniquity. To whom he is a God, he is so according to the tenor of that covenant; so that here these two are conjoined. Says he, 'Lord, I am pressed with the sense of the guilt of mine iniquities; and you are my God, who forgivest them.' And the ground hereof is, that God by the gospel has divided the work of the law, and taken part of it out of its hand. Its whole work and duty is, to condemn the sin and the sinner. The sinner is freed by the gospel, but its right lies against the sin still; that it condemns, and that justly. Now, though the sinner himself be freed, yet finding his sin laid hold of and condemned, it fills him with a deep sense of its guilt and of the displeasure of God against it; which yet hinders not but that, at the same time, he may have such an insight as faith gives into his personal interest in a gospel acquitment. a man, then, may have a deep sense of sin all his days, walk under the sense of it continually, abhor himself for his ingratitude, unbelief, and rebellion against God, without any impeachment of his assurance.

### A Deep Sorrow for Sin

Deep sorrow for sin, is consistent with assurance of forgiveness; yea, it is a great means of preservation of it. Godly sorrow, mourning, humiliation, contriteness of spirit, are no less gospel graces and fruits of the Holy Ghost than faith itself, and so are consistent with the highest flourishings of faith whatever. It is the work of heaven itself, and not of the assurance of it, to wipe all tears from our eyes. Yea, these graces have the most eminent promises annexed to them (as Isa. 57:15, 66:2), with blessedness itself (Matt. 5:4); yea, they are themselves the matter of many gracious gospel promises (Zech. 12:10): so that they are assuredly consistent with any other grace or privilege that we may be made partakers of, or [any that] are promised to us. Some, finding the weight and burden of their sins, and being called to mourning and humiliation on that account, are so taken up with it as to lose the sense of forgiveness, which, rightly improved, would promote their sorrow, as their sorrow seems directly to sweeten their sense of forgiveness. Sorrow, absolutely exclusive of the faith of forgiveness, is legal, and tends to death; assurance, absolutely exclusive of godly sorrow, is presumption, and not a persuasion from Him that calls us: but gospel sorrow and gospel assurance may well dwell in the same breast at the same time. Indeed, as in all worldly joys there is a secret wound, so in all godly sorrow and mourning, considered in itself, there is a secret joy and refreshment; hence it does not wither and dry up, but rather enlarge, open, and *...they mourn most who have most assurance.* sweeten the heart. I am persuaded that, generally, they mourn most who have most assurance. And all true gospel mourners will be found to have the root of assurance so grafted in them, that in its proper season—a time of trouble—it will undoubtedly flourish.

### A Deep Sense of the Indwelling Power of Sin

A deep sense of the indwelling power of sin is consistent with gospel assurance. Sense of indwelling sin will cause manifold perplexities in the soul. Trouble, disquietments, sorrow and anguish of heart, expressing themselves in sighs, mourning, groaning for deliverance, always attend it. To what purpose do you speak to a soul highly sensible of the restless power of indwelling sin concerning assurance?

'Alas,' says he, 'I am ready to perish every moment. My lusts are strong, active, restless, yea, outrageous; they give me no rest, no liberty, and but little success do I obtain. Assurance is for conquerors, for them that live at rest and peace. I lie grovelling on the ground all my days, and must needs be uncertain what will be the issue.'

But when such a one has done all he can, he will not be able to make more woeful complaints of this matter than Paul has done before him (Rom. 7); and yet he closes the discourse of it with as high an expression of assurance as any person needs to seek after (v. 25, and Rom. 8:1). It is not assurance but enjoyment that excludes this sense and trouble. But if men will think they can have no assurance because they have that without which it is impossible they should have any, it is hard to give them relief. a little cruse of salt of the gospel cast into these bitter waters will make them sweet and wholesome. Sense of the guilt of sin may consist with faith of its pardon and forgiveness in the blood of Christ. Godly sorrow may dwell in the same heart, at the same time, with joy in the Holy

Ghost, and groaning after deliverance from the power of sin with a gracious persuasion that 'sin shall not have dominion over us, because we are not under the law, but under grace.'

## *Doubts, Fears, and Temptations*

Doubtings, fears, temptations, if not ordinarily prevailing, are consistent with gospel assurance. Though the devil's power be limited in reference to the saints, yet his hands are not tied; though he cannot prevail against them, yet he can assault them. And although there be not 'an evil heart of unbelief' in believers, yet there will still be unbelief in their hearts. Such an evidence, conviction, and persuasion of acceptance with God as are exclusive of all contrary reasonings, that suffer the soul to hear nothing of objections, that free and quiet it from all assaults, are neither mentioned in the Scripture, nor consistent with that state wherein we walk before God, nor possible on the account of Satan's will and ability to tempt, or of our own remaining unbelief. Assurance encourages us in our combat; it delivers us not from it. We may have peace with God when we have none from the assaults of Satan.

Now, unless a man do duly consider the tenor of the covenant wherein we walk with God, and the nature of that gospel obedience which he requires at our hands, with the state and condition which is our lot and portion whilst we live in this world, the daily sense of these things, with the trouble that must be undergone on their account, may keep him in the dark to himself, and hinder him from that establishment in believing which otherwise he might attain to. On this account, some as holy persons as any in this world, being wholly taken up with the consideration of these home-bred perplexities, and not clearly acquainted with the way and tenor of assuring their souls before God according to the rule of the covenant of grace, have passed away their days in a bondage-frame of spirit, and unacquaintance with that strong consolation which God is abundantly willing that all the heirs of promise should receive.

## THE EFFECTS OF EVANGELICAL ASSURANCE

Evangelical assurance is not a thing that consists in any point, and so incapable of variation. It may be higher or lower, greater or less, obscure or attended with more evidence. It is not quite lost when it is not quite at its highest. God sometimes marvellously raises the souls of his saints with some close and near approaches to them—gives them a sense of his eternal love, a taste of the embraces of his Son and the inhabitation of the Spirit, without the least intervening disturbance; then this is their assurance. But this life is not a season to be always taking wages in; our work is not yet done; we are not always to abide in this mount; we must down again into the battle—fight again, cry again, complain again. Shall the soul be thought now to have lost its assurance? Not at all. It had before assurance with joy, triumph, and exultation; it has it now, or may have, with wrestling, cries, tears, and supplications. And a man's assurance may be as good, as true, when he lies on the earth with a sense of sin, as when he is carried up to the third heaven with a sense of love and foretaste of glory. In brief, this assurance of salvation is such a gracious, evangelical persuasion of acceptance with God in Christ, and of an interest in the premises of preservation to the end, wrought in believers by the Holy Ghost, in and through the exercise of faith, as for the most part produces these effects following.

### Delight in Obedience

It gives delight in obedience, and draws out love in the duties that to God we do perform. So much assurance of a comfortable issue of their obedience, of a blessed end of their labours and duties, of their purifying their hearts, and pressing after universal renovation of mind and life, as may make them cheerful in them, as may give love and delight in the pursuit of what they are engaged in, is needful for the saints, and they do not often go without it; and where this is, there is gospel assurance. To run as men uncertain, to fight as those that beat the air, to travel as not any way persuaded of a comfortable entertainment or refreshment at the journey's end, is a state and condition that God does not frequently leave his people to; and when he does, it is a season wherein he receives very little of glory from them, and they very little increase of grace in themselves. Many things, as has been showed, do interpose—many doubts arise and entangling perplexities; but still there is a comfortable persuasion kept alive that there is a rest provided, which makes them willing to, and cheerful in, their most difficult duties. This prevails in them, that their labour in the Lord, their watchings, praying, suffering, alms, mortification, fighting against temptation, crucifying the flesh with the lusts thereof, shall not be in vain. This gives them such a delight in their most difficult duties as men have in a hard journey towards a desirable home or a place of rest.

### Fear Cast Out

It casts out fear, tormenting fear, such as fills the soul with perplexing uncertainties, hard thoughts of God, and dreadful apprehensions of wrath to come. There are three things spoken concerning that fear which is inconsistent with the assurance of forgiveness.

First, with respect to its principle, it is from a 'spirit of bondage' (Rom. 8:15), 'We have not received the spirit of bondage again to fear.' It is not such a fear as makes an occasional incursion upon the mind or soul, such as is excited and occasioned by incident darkness and temptation, such as the best, and persons of the highest assurance, are liable and obnoxious to; but it is such as has a complete abiding principle in the soul, even a 'spirit of bondage'—a prevailing frame constantly inclining it to fear, or dreadful apprehensions of God and its own condition.

Secondly, that it tends to bondage. It brings the soul into bondage: he died 'to deliver them who through fear of death were all their lifetime subject to bondage' (Heb. 2:14–15). Fear of death as penal, as it lies in the curse, which is that fear that proceeds from a 'spirit of bondage,' brings the persons in whom it is into bondage; that is, it adds weariness, trouble, and anxiety of mind to fear, and puts them upon all ways and means imaginable, unduly and disorderly, to seek for a remedy or relief.

Thirdly, it has torment: 'Fear has torment' (1 John 4:18). It gives no rest, no quietness, to the mind. Now, this is so cast out by gospel assurance of forgiveness, that, though it may assault the soul, it shall not possess it; though it make incursions upon it, it shall not dwell, abide, and prevail in it.

### Hope of Glory

It gives the soul a hope and expectation of 'the glory that shall be revealed,' and secretly stirs it up and enlivens it to a support in sufferings, trials, and temptations. This is the 'hope which makes not ashamed' (Rom. 5:5), and that because it will never expose the soul to disappointment. Wherever there is the root of assurance, there will be this fruit of hope. The proper object of it is things absent, invisible, eternal—the promised reward, in all the notions, respects, and concerns of it. This, hope goes out to, in distresses, temptations, failings, and under a sense of the guilt and power of sin. Hence arises a spring of secret relief in the soul, something that calms the heart and quiets the spirit in the midst of many a storm. Now, as, wherever assurance is, there will be this hope; so wherever this secret relieving hope is, it grows on no other root but a living persuasion of a personal interest in the things hoped for.

### Willingness to Die for Christ

As it will do many other things, so, that I may give one comprehensive instance, it will carry them out, in whom it is, to die for Christ. Death, to men who saw not one step beyond it, was esteemed of all things most terrible. The way and means of its approach add to its terror. But this is nothing in comparison of what it is to them who look through it as a passage into ensuing eternity. For a man, then, to choose death rather than life, in the most terrible manner of its approach, expecting an eternity to ensue, it argues a comfortable persuasion of a good state and condition after death. Now, I am persuaded that there are hundreds who, upon gospel, saving accounts, would embrace a stake for the testimony of Jesus, who yet know not at all that they have the assurance we speak of; and yet nothing else would enable them thereunto. But these things being beside the main of my intendment, I shall pursue them no farther; only, the rule is of use. Let the soul be sure to be well acquainted with the nature of that which it seeks after, and confesses a sense of the want of.

## III

### WAIT

Whatever your condition be, and your apprehension of it, yet continue waiting for a better issue, and give not over through weariness or impatience. This rule contains the sum of the great example given us in this psalm. Forgiveness in God being discovered, though no sense of a particular interest therein as yet obtained, that which the soul applies itself to is diligent, careful, constant, persevering waiting; which is variously expressed in the fifth and sixth verses. The Holy Ghost tells us that 'light is sown for the righteous, and gladness for the upright in heart' (Ps. 97:11). Light and gladness are the things now inquired after. Deliverance from darkness, misapprehensions of God, hard and misgiving thoughts of his own condition, is that which a soul in its depths reaches towards. Now, says the Holy Ghost, 'These things are sown for the righteous.' Does the husbandman, after he casts his seed into the earth, immediately the next day, the next week, expect that it will be harvest? Does he think to reap so soon as he has sown? Or does he immediately say, 'I have laboured in vain, here is no return; I will pull up the hedge of this field and lay it waste?' Or, 'I see a little grass in the blade, but no corn; I will give it to the beasts to devour it?' No; 'his God,' as the prophet speaks, 'instructs him to discretion, and teaches him,' namely, what he must do, and how he must look for things in their season. And shall not we be instructed by him? 'Behold, the husbandman,' says James, 'waits for the precious fruit of the earth, and has long patience for it, until he receive the early and latter rain' (James 5:7). And is light sown for them that are in darkness, and shall they stifle the seed under the clods, or spoil the tender blade that is springing up, or refuse to wait for the watering of the Spirit, that may bring it forth to perfection? Waiting is the only way to establishment and assurance; we cannot speed by our haste; yea, nothing puts the end so far away as making too much haste and speed in our journey. The ground hereof is, that a sense of a special interest in forgiveness and acceptance is given in to the soul by a mere act of sovereignty. It is not, it will not be, obtained by or upon any rational conclusions or deductions that we can make. All that we can do is but to apply ourselves to the removal of hinderances, for the peace and rest sought for come from mere prerogative: 'When he gives quietness, who then can make trouble? And when he hides his face, who then can behold him?' (Job 34:29). Now, what is the way to receive that which comes from mere sovereignty and prerogative? Does not the nature of the thing require humble waiting? If, then, either impatience cast the soul into frowardness, or weariness make it slothful (which are the two ways whereby waiting is ruined), let not such a one expect any comfortable issue of his contending for deliverance out of his depths. And let not any think to make out their difficulties any other way: their own reasonings will not bring them to any establishing conclusion; for they may lay down propositions, and have no considerable objections to lie against either of them, and yet be far enough from that sweet consolation, joy, and assurance which is the product of the conclusion, when God is not pleased to give it in. Yea, a man may sometimes gather up consolation to himself upon such terms, but it will not abide. So did David (Ps. 30:6–7). He thus argues with himself: 'He whose mountain is made strong, to whom God is a defence, he shall never be moved nor be shaken; but I am thus settled of God: therefore I shall not be moved.' And therein he rejoices. It is an expression of exultation that he uses; but what is the issue of it? In the midst of these pleasing thoughts of his, 'God hides his face,' and 'he is troubled;' he cannot any longer draw out the sweetness of the conclusion mentioned. It was in him before from the shinings of God's countenance, and not from any arguings of his own.

No disappointment, then, no tediousness or weariness, should make the soul leave waiting on God, if it intend to attain consolation and establishment. So deals the church (Lam. 3:21), 'This I recall to mind, therefore have I hope.' What is that she calls to mind? This, that 'it is of the LORD's mercy that we are not consumed, because his compassions fail not' (v. 22)—'I will yet hope, I will yet continue in my expectation upon the account of never-failing compassion, of endless mercies in him, whatever my present condition be.' And thence she makes a blessed conclusion, 'It is good that a man should both hope and quietly wait for the salvation of the LORD' (v. 26). And this is our third rule: It is good to hope and wait, whatever our present condition be, and not to give over, if we would not be sure to fall; whereunto I speak no more, because the close of this psalm insists wholly on this duty, which must be farther spoken to.

## IV

### Search Out Sin

Seeing, in the course of our believing and obedience, that which is chiefly incumbent on us, for our coming up to establishment and consolation, is spiritual diligence in the removal of the hinderances thereof, let the soul that would attain thereunto make thorough work in the search of sin, even to the sins of youth, that all scores on that account may clearly be wiped out. If there be much rubbish left in the foundation of the building, no wonder if it always shake and totter. Men's leaving of any sin unsearched to the bottom will poison all their consolation. David knew this when, in dealing with God in his distresses, he prays that he would not 'remember the sins and transgressions of his youth' (Ps. 25:7). Youth is oftentimes a time of great vanity and unmindfulness of God; many stains and spots are therein usually brought upon the consciences of men. 'Childhood and youth are vanity' (Eccles. 11:10); not because they soon pass away, but because they are usually spent in vanity, as the following advice of chapter 12:1, to remember God in those days, manifests. The way of many is to wear such things out of mind, and not to walk in a sense of their folly and madness—never to make thorough work with God about them. I speak of the saints themselves; for with others that live under the means of grace, whom God intends any way to make useful and industrious in their generation, this is the usual course—by convictions, restraining grace, afflictions, love of employment and repute, God gives them another heart than they had for a season; another heart, but not a new heart. Hence, another course of life, another profession, other actions than formerly, do flow. With this change they do content themselves; they look on what is past perhaps with delight, or as things fit enough for those days, but not for those they have attained to. Here they rest; and therefore never come to rest,

But I speak of the saints themselves, who make not such thorough, full, close work in this kind as they ought. An after-reckoning may come in on this hand to their own disturbance, and an unconquerable hinderance of their peace and settlement be brought in, on this account. So was it with Job, 'He makes me to possess the iniquities of my youth' (Job 13:26). God filled his heart, his thoughts, his mind, with these sins—made them abide with him, so that he possessed them; they were always present with him. He made the sins of his youth the sufferings of his age. And it is a sad thing, as one speaks, when young sins and old bones meet together; as Zophar, 'His bones are full of the sins of his youth' (Job 20:11). The joyous frame of some men's youth makes way for sad work in their age. Take heed, young ones! You are doing that which will abide with you to age, if not to eternity. This possessing of the sins of youth, Job calls the 'writing of bitter things against him;' as, indeed, it is impossible but that sin should be bitter one time or other. God calls it 'a root that bears gall and wormwood' (Deut. 29:18); 'a root of bitterness springing up into defilement,' (Heb. 12:15). This, then, is to be searched out to the bottom. Israel will not have success nor peace whilst there is an Achan in the camp. Neither success in temptation nor consolation in believing is to be expected, whilst any Achan, any sin unreckoned for, lies on the conscience.

Now, for them who would seriously accomplish a diligent search in this matter, which is of such importance to them, let them take these two directions.

## Consider What Areas of Sin Disturb Your Peace

Let them go over the consideration of those sins, and others of the like nature, which may be reduced to the same general heads with them, which we laid down before as the sins which generally cast men into depths and entanglements. And if they find they have contracted the guilt of any of them, let them not think it strange that they are yet bewildered in their condition, and do come short of a refreshing sense of peace with God or an interest in forgiveness. Rather let them admire the riches of patience, grace, and forbearance, that they are not cast utterly out of all hopes of a recovery. This will speed an end to their trouble, according to the direction given.

## Consider Sin at Various Stages of Life

Let them cast the course of their times under such heads and seasons as may give them the more clear and distinct view and apprehension of the passages in them between God and their souls which may have been provoking to him.

### *Before Conversion*

As, first, for the state of their inward man, let them consider the unregenerate part of their lives, that which was confessedly so, before they had any real work of God upon their hearts; and therein inquire after two things. First, if there were then any great and signal eruptions of sins against God; for of such God requires that a deep sense be kept on our souls all our days. How often do we find Paul calling over the sins of his life and ways before his conversion! 'I was,' says he, 'injurious, and a blasphemer.' Such reflections ought persons to have on any great provoking occasions of sin, that may keep them humble, and necessitate them constantly to look for a fresh sense of pardon through the blood of Christ. If such sins lie neglected, and not considered according to their importance, they will weaken the soul in its comforts whilst it lives in this world. Secondly, if there were any signal intimations made of the good-will and love of God to the soul, which it broke off from through the power of its corruption and temptation, they require a due humbling consideration all our days. But this has been before spoken to.

### As Believers

In that part of our lives which, upon the call of God, we have given up to him, there are two sorts of sins that do effectually impeach our future peace and comfort; which ought therefore to be frequently reviewed and issued in the blood of Christ. First, such as, by reason of any aggravating circumstances, have been accompanied with some especial unkindness towards God. Such are sins after warnings, communications of a sense of love, after particular engagements against them, relapses, omissions of great opportunities and advantages for the furtherance of the glory of God in the world. These kinds of sins have much unkindness attending them, and will be searched out if we cover them. Secondly, sins attended with scandal towards fewer or more, or any one single person who is or may be concerned in us. The aggravations of these kinds of sins are commonly known.

### In Prosperity and Affliction

The various outward states and conditions which we have passed through, as of prosperity and afflictions, should in like manner fall under this search and consideration. It is but seldom that we fill up our duty or answer the mind of God in any dispensation of providence, and if our neglect herein be not managed aright, they will undoubtedly hinder and interrupt our peace.

## V

## Distinguish Between Unbelief and Jealousy

Learn to distinguish between unbelief and jealousy.

There is a twofold unbelief: 1. That which is universal and privative, such as is in all unregenerate persons; they have no faith at all—that is, they are dead men, and have no principles of spiritual life. This I speak not of; it is easily distinguished from any grace, being the utter enemy and privation as it were of them all. 2. There is an unbelief partial and negative, consisting in a staggering at or questioning of the promises. This is displeasing to God, a sin which is attended with unknown aggravations, though men usually indulge it in themselves. It is well expressed (Ps. 78:19–20). God had promised his presence to the people in the wilderness to feed, sustain, and preserve them. How did they entertain these promises of God? 'Can he,' say they, 'give bread? Can he provide flesh for his people?' (v. 20). What great sin, crime, or offence is in this inquiry? Why, this is called speaking against God: 'They spoke against God; they said, "Can he furnish a table in the wilderness?"' (v. 19). Unbelief in question of the promises is a 'speaking against God;' a 'limiting of the Holy One of Israel,' as it is called (v. 41); an assigning of bounds to his goodness, power, kindness, and grace, according to what we find in ourselves, which he abhors. By this unbelief we make God like ourselves; that is, our limiting of him, expecting no more from him than either we can do, or see how it may be done. This, you will say, was a great sin in the Israelites, because they had no reason to doubt or question the promises of God. It is well we think so now; but when they were so many thousand families, that had not one bit of bread nor drop of water aforehand for themselves and their little ones, there is no doubt but they thought themselves to have as good reason to question the promises as any one of you can think that you have. We are ready to suppose that we have all the reasons in the world: every one supposes he has those that are more cogent than any other has to question the promises of grace, pardon, and forgiveness; and therefore the questioning of them is not their sin, but their duty. But pretend what we will, this is speaking against God, limiting of him; and that which is our keeping off from steadfastness and comfort.

But now there may be a jealousy in a gracious heart concerning the love of Christ, which is acceptable to him, at least which he is tender towards, that may be mistaken for this questioning of the promises by unbelief, and so help to keep the soul in darkness and disconsolation. This the spouse expresses in herself: 'Love is strong as death; jealousy is hard as the grave: the coals thereof are coals of fire, which has a most vehement flame' (S. of S. 8:6). Love is the foundation, the root; but yet it bears that fruit which is bitter, although it be wholesome—that which fills the soul with great perplexities, and makes it cry out for a nearer and more secure admission into the presence of Christ. 'Set me,' says the spouse, 'as a seal upon your heart, as a seal upon your arm: for jealousy is cruel as the grave'—'I cannot bear this distance from you, these fears of my being disregarded by you. "Set me as a seal upon your heart."'

Now, this spiritual jealousy is the solicitousness of the mind of a believer, who has a sincere love for Christ, about the heart, affection, and good-will of Christ towards it, arising from a consciousness of its own unworthiness to be beloved by him or accepted with him. All causeless jealousy arises from a secret sense and conviction of unworthiness in the person in whom it is, and a high esteem of him that is the object of it, or concerning whose love and affection any one is jealous. So it is with this spiritual jealousy. The root of it is love, sincere love, that cannot be 'quenched by waters' nor 'drowned by floods' (v. 7)—which nothing can utterly prevail against or overcome. This gives the soul high thoughts of the glorious excellencies of Christ, fills it with admiration of him; these are mixed with a due sense of its own baseness, vileness, and unworthiness to be owned by him or accepted with him. Now, if these thoughts, on the one hand and on the other, be not directed, guided, and managed aright by faith—which alone can show the soul how the glory of Christ consists principally in this, that he, being so excellent and glorious, is pleased to love us with love inexpressible who are vile and sinful—questionings about the love of Christ, and those attended with much anxiety and trouble of mind, will arise. Now, this frame may sometimes be taken for a questioning of the promises of God, and that to be a defect in faith which is an excess of love, or at most such an irregular acting of it as the Lord Christ will be very tender towards, and which is consistent with peace and a due sense of the forgiveness of sins. Mistake not, then, these one for another, lest much causeless unquietness ensue in the judgment which you are to make of yourselves.

But you will say, 'How shall we distinguish between these two, so as not causelessly to be disquieted and perplexed?' I answer briefly.

### UNBELIEF WEAKENS

Unbelief, working in and by the questioning of the promises of God, is a weakening, disheartening, dispiriting thing. It takes off the edge of the soul from spiritual duties, and weakens it both as to delight and strength. The more any one questions the promises of God, the less life, power, joy, and delight in obedience he has; for faith is the spring and root of all other graces, and according as that thrives or goes backwards so do they all. Men think sometimes that their uncertainty of the love of God, and of acceptance with him by the forgiveness of sin, does put them upon the performance of many duties; and they can have no rest or peace in the omission of them. It may be it is so; yea, this is the state and condition with many. But what are these duties? And how are they performed? And what is their acceptance with God? The duties themselves are legal; which denomination arises not from the nature, substance, or matter of them, for they may be the same that are required and enjoined in the gospel, but from the principle from whence they proceed and the end to which they are used. Now these in this case are both legal; their principle is legal fear, and their end is legal righteousness—the whole attendance to them a 'seeking of righteousness as it were by the works of the law.' And how are they performed? Plainly, with a bondage-frame of spirit, without love, joy, liberty, or delight. To quiet conscience, to pacify God, are the things in them aimed at, all in opposition to the blood and righteousness of Christ. And are they accepted with God? Let them be multiplied never so much, he everywhere testifies that they are abhorred by him. This, then, unbelief mixed with convictions will do. It is the proper way of venting and exercising itself where the soul is brought under the power of conviction. But as to gospel obedience, in all the duties of it, to he carried on in communion with God by Christ and delight in him, all questioning of the promises weakens and discourages the soul, and makes them all wearisome and burdensome to it.

But the jealousy that is exercised about the person and love of Christ to the soul is quite of another nature, and produces other effects. It cheers, enlivens, and enlarges the soul, stirs up to activity, earnestness, and industry in its inquiries and desires after Christ. 'Jealousy,' says the spouse, '"is hard as the grave;" therefore, "set me as a seal upon your heart, as a seal upon your arm."' It makes the soul restlessly pant after nearer, more sensible, and more assured communion with Christ; it stirs up vigorous and active spirits in all duties. Every doubt and fear that it ingenerates concerning the love of Christ stirs up the soul to more earnestness after him, delight in him, and sedulous watching against every thing that may keep it at a distance from him, or occasion him to hide, withdraw, or absent himself from it.

## UNBELIEF IS SELFISH

Unbelief, that works by questioning of the promises, is universally selfish; it begins and ends in self. Self-love, in desires after freedom from guilt, danger, and punishment, is the life and soul of it. May this end be attained, it has no delight in God; nor does it care what way it be attained, so it may be attained. May such persons have any persuasions that they shall be freed from death and hell, be it by the works of the law or by the observance of any inventions of their own, whether any glory arises to God from his grace and faithfulness or no, they are not solicitous.

The jealousy we speak of has the person of Christ and his excellency for its constant object. These it fills the mind with in many and various thoughts, still representing him more and more amiable and more desirable to the soul: so does the spouse upon the like occasion, as you may see at large (S. of S. 5:9–16). Being at some loss for his presence, for he had withdrawn himself, not finding her wonted communion and intercourse with him, fearing that, upon her provocation, she might forfeit her interest in his love, she falls upon the consideration of all his excellencies; and thereby the more inflames herself into desires after his company and enjoyment. All these diverse things may be thus distinguished and discerned.

## VI

### DISTINGUISH BETWEEN FAITH AND FEELING

Learn to distinguish between faith and spiritual sense.

This rule the apostle gives us, 'We walk by faith, and not by sight' (2 Cor. 5:7). It is the sight of glory that is especially here intended. But faith and sense in any kind are clearly distinguished. That may be believed which is not felt; yea, it is the will and command of God that faith should stand and do its work where all sense fails (Isa. 50:10). And it is with spiritual sense in this matter as it is with natural. Thomas would not believe unless he saw the object of his faith with his eyes, or felt it with his hand. But says our Saviour, 'Blessed are they that have not seen, and yet believe'—who believe upon the testimony of God, without the help of their own sense or reason. And if we will believe no more of God, of his love, of his grace, of our acceptance with him, than we have a spiritual affecting sense of, we shall be many times at a loss. Sensible impressions from God's love are great springs of joy; but they are not absolutely necessary to peace, nor to an evidence that we do believe.

We will deal thus with the vilest person living—we will believe

347

him whilst we have the certainty of our sense to secure us. And if we deal so with God, what's there in our so doing praiseworthy? The prophet tells us what it is to believe in respect of providence (Hab. 3:17). When there is nothing left outward and visible to support us, then to rest quietly on God, that is to believe (Ps. 73:26). And the apostle, in the example of Abraham, shows us what it is to believe with respect to a special promise: 'Against hope, he believed in hope' (Rom. 4:18). When he saw not any outward ordinary means for the accomplishment of the promise, when innumerable objections arose against any such hope as might have respect to such means, yet he resolved all his thoughts into the faithfulness of God in the promise, and therein raised a new hope in its accomplishment; so in hope believing against hope.

To clear this matter, you must observe what I intend by this spiritual sense, which you must learn to distinguish faith from, and to know that true faith interesting the soul in forgiveness may be without it; that so you may not conclude to a real want of pardon from the want of the refreshing sense of it.

Grace in general may be referred to two heads. 1. Our acceptation with God through Christ, the same upon the matter with the forgiveness of sin that we are treating of. 2. Grace of sanctification from God in Christ. Of each of these there is a spiritual sense or experience to be obtained, in both distinguished from faith that gives us a real interest in forgiveness.

### PEACE AND JOY ARE NOT ESSENTIAL TO FAITH

Of the first, or the spiritual sense that we have of acceptance with God, there are sundry parts or degrees; as, first, hereunto belongs peace with God: 'Being justified by faith, we have peace with God' (Rom. 5:1). This peace is the rest and composure of the soul emerging out of troubles, upon the account of the reconciliation and friendship made for it by the blood of Christ. And it has, as all peace has, two parts—first, a freedom from war, trouble, and distress; and, secondly, rest, satisfaction, and contentment in the condition attained; and this, at least the second part of it, belongs to the spiritual sense that we inquire after. Again: there is in it 'joy in the Holy Ghost,' called 'joy unspeakable, and full of glory' (1 Pet. 1:8); as also 'glorying in the Lord' upon the account of his grace (Isa. 45:25); with many the like effects, proceeding from a 'shedding abroad of the love of God in our hearts' (Rom. 5:5).

Yea, you say, these are the things you aim at; these are the things you would attain, and be filled withal. It is this peace, this joy, this glorying in the Lord, that you would always be in the possession of. I say, you do well to desire them, to seek and labour after them—they are purchased by Christ for believers; but you will do well to consider under what notion you do desire them. If you look on these things as belonging to the essence of faith, without which you can have no real interest in forgiveness or acceptance with God, you greatly deceive your own souls, and put yourselves out of the way of obtaining of them. These things are not believing, nor adequate effects of it, so as immediately to be produced wherever faith is; but they are such consequents of it as may or may not ensue upon it, according to the will of God. Faith is a seed that contains them virtually, and out of which they may be in due time educed by the working of the word and Spirit; and the way for any soul to be made partaker of them is to wait on the sovereignty of God's grace, who creates peace in the exercise of faith upon the promises. He, then, that would place believing in these things, and will not be persuaded that he does believe until he is possessed of them, he does both lose the benefit, advantage, and comfort of what he has, and, neglecting the due acting of faith, puts himself out of the way of attaining what he aims at.

These things, therefore, are not needful to give you a real saving interest in forgiveness, as it is tendered in the promise of the gospel by the blood of Christ. And it may be it is not the will of God that ever you should be intrusted with them. It may be it would not be for your good and advantage so to be. Some servants that are ill husbands must have their wages kept for them to the year's end, or it will do them no good. It may be, some would be such spendthrifts of satisfying peace and joy, and be so diverted by them from attending to some necessary duties—as of humiliation, mortification, and self-abasement, without which their souls cannot live—that it would not be much to their advantage to be intrusted with them. It is from the same care and love that peace and joy are detained from some believers, and granted to others.

You are therefore to receive forgiveness by a pure act of believing, in the way and manner before at large described. And do not think that it is not in you unless you have constantly a spiritual sense of it in your hearts. See, in the meantime, that your faith brings forth obedience, and God in due time will cause it to bring forth peace.

### Grace May Work Unrecognised

The like may be said concerning the other head of grace, though it be not so direct to our purpose, yet tending also to the relief of the soul in its depths. This is the grace that we have from God in Christ for our sanctification. When the soul cannot find this in himself; when he has not a spiritual sense and experience of its inbeing and power; when it cannot evidently distinguish it from that which is not fight or genuine—it is filled with fears and perplexities, and thinks it is yet in its sin. He is so, indeed, who has no grace in him; but not he always who can find none in him. But these are different things. a man may have grace, and yet not have it at sometimes much acting; he may have grace for life, when he has it not for fruitfulness and comfort, though it be his duty so to have it (Rev. 3:2; 2 Tim. 1:6). And a man may have grace acting in him, and yet not know, not be sensible, that he has acting grace. We see persons frequently under great temptations of apprehension that they have no grace at all, and yet at the same time, to the clearest conviction of all who are able to discern spiritual things, sweetly and genuinely to act faith, love, submission to God, and that in a high and eminent manner. Heman complains that he was 'free among the dead,' 'a man of no strength' (Ps. 88:4–5)—as one that had no spiritual life, no grace. This afflicted his mind, and almost distracted him (v. 15); and yet there can be no greater expressions of faith and love to God than are mixed with his complaints.

These things, I say then, are not to be judged of by spiritual sense, but we are to live by faith about them. And no soul ought to conclude, that because it has not the one it has not the other—that because it has not joy and peace, it has no interest in pardon and forgiveness.

## VII

## Do Not Mix Foundation and Building Work

Mix not too much foundation and building work together. Our foundation in dealing with God is Christ alone, mere grace and pardon in him.

Our building is in and by holiness and obedience, as the fruits of that faith by which we have received the atonement. And great mistakes there are in this matter, which bring great entanglements on the souls of men. Some are all their days laying of the foundation, and are never able to build upon it to any comfort to themselves or usefulness to others; and the reason is, because they will be mixing with the foundation stones that are fit only for the following building. They will be bringing their obedience, duties, mortification of sin, and the like, to the foundation. These are precious stones to build with, but unmeet to be first laid, to bear upon them the whole weight of the building. The foundation is to be laid, as was said, in mere grace, mercy, pardon in the blood of Christ. This the soul is to accept of and to rest in merely as it is grace, without the consideration of any thing in itself, but that it is sinful and obnoxious to ruin. This it finds a difficulty in, and would gladly have something of its own to mix with it. It cannot tell how to fix these foundation-stones without some cement of its own endeavours and duty; and because these things will not mix, they spend a fruitless labour about it all their days. But if the foundation be of grace, it is not at all of works; for 'otherwise grace is no more grace.' If any thing of our own be mixed with grace in this matter, it utterly destroys the nature of grace; which if it be not alone, it is not at all. But does this not tend to licentiousness? Does not this render obedience, holiness, duties, mortification of sin, and good works needless? God forbid; yea, this is the only way to order them aright to the glory of God. Have we nothing to do but to lay the foundation? Yes; all our days we are to build upon it, when it is surely and firmly laid. And these are the means and ways of our edification. This, then, is the soul to do who would come to peace and settlement. Let it let go all former endeavours, if it have been engaged to any of that kind, and let it alone receive, admit of, and adhere to, mere grace, mercy, and pardon, with a full sense that in itself it has nothing for which it should have an interest in them, but that all is of mere grace through Jesus Christ: 'Other foundation can no man lay.' Depart not hence until this work be well over. Surcease not an earnest endeavour with your own hearts to acquiesce in this righteousness of God, and to bring your souls to a comfortable persuasion that 'God for Christ's sake has freely forgiven you all your sins.' Stir not hence until this be effected. If you have been engaged in another way—that is, to seek for an interest in the pardon of sin by some endeavours of your own—it is not unlikely but that you are filled with the fruit of your own doings; that is, that you go on with all kinds of uncertainties, and without any kind of constant peace. Return, then, again hither; bring this foundation-work to a blessed issue in the blood of Christ; and when that is done, up and be doing.

You know how fatal and ruinous it is for souls to abuse the grace of God and the apprehension of the pardon of sins in the course of their obedience—to countenance themselves in sin or the negligence of any duty; this is to turn the grace of God into wantonness, as we have elsewhere at large declared. And it is no less pernicious to bring the duties of our obedience, any reserves for them, any hopes about them, into the matter of pardon and forgiveness, as we are to receive them from God. But these things, as they are distinct in themselves, so they must be distinctly managed in the soul; and the confounding of them is that which disturbs the peace and weakens the obedience of many. In a confused manner they labour to keep up a life of grace and duty; which will be in their places conjoined, but not mixed or compounded.

First, to take up mercy, pardon, and forgiveness absolutely on the account of Christ, and then to yield all obedience in the strength of Christ and for the love of Christ, is the life of a believer (Eph. 2:8–10).

## VIII

### 'Get Up!'

Take heed of spending time in complaints when vigorous actings of grace are your duty.

Fruitless and heartless complaints, bemoanings of themselves and their condition, is the substance of the profession that some make. If they can object against themselves, and form complaints out of their conditions, they suppose they have done their duty. I have known some who have spent a good part of their time in going up and down from one to another with their objections and complaints. These things are contrary to the life of faith. It is good, indeed, in our spiritual distresses, to apply ourselves to them who are furnished with the tongue of the learned, to know how to speak a word in season to him that is weary; but for persons to fill their minds and imaginations with their own objections and complaints, not endeavouring to mix the words that are spoken for their relief and direction with faith, but going on still in their own way, this is of no use or advantage. And yet some, I fear, may please themselves in such course, as if it had somewhat of eminency in religion in it.

Others, it may be, drive the same trade in their thoughts, although they make not outwardly such complaints. They are conversant, for the most part, with heartless despondings. And in some they are multiplied by their natural constitutions or distempers. Examples of this kind occur to us every day. Now, what is the advantage of these things? What did Zion get when she cried, 'The Lord has forsaken me, and my Lord has forgotten me?' Or Jacob, when he said, 'My way is hid from the Lord, and my judgment is passed over from my God?' Doubtless they did prejudice themselves. How does David rouse up himself when he found his mind inclinable to such a frame? For having said, 'Why do you cast me off? Why go I mourning because of the oppression of the enemy?' He quickly rebukes and recollects himself, saying, 'Why are you cast down, O my soul? And why are you disquieted within me? Hope in God' (Ps. 43:2–5).

We must say, then, to such heartless complainers, as God did to Joshua, 'Get up; why lie you thus upon your faces?' Do you think to mend your condition by wishing it better, or complaining it is so bad? Are your complaints of want of an interest in forgiveness a sanctified means to obtain it? Not at all; you will not deal so with yourselves in things natural or civil. In such things you will take an industrious course for a remedy or for relief. In things of the smallest importance in this world and to this life, you will not content yourselves with wishing and complaining; as though industry in the use of natural means, for the attaining of natural ends, were the ordinance of God, and diligence in the use of spiritual means, for the obtaining of spiritual ends, were not.

Do not consult your own hearts only. What is it that the Scripture calls for in your condition? Is it not industry and activity of spirit? And what does the nature of the thing require? Distress that is yet hoped to be conquered evidently calls for industry and diligence in the use of means for deliverance. If you are past hope, it avails not to complain; if you are not, why do you give up yourselves to despondencies? Our Saviour tells us that 'the kingdom of heaven suffers violence, and the violent take it by force' (Matt. 11:12). It is not of the outward violence of its enemies seeking to destroy it that our Saviour speaks, but of that spiritual fervency and ardency of mind that is in those who intend to be partakers of it; for βιάζεται, 'is taken by force' (Luke 16:16), is no more but εὐαγγελίζεται, 'is preached'—'The kingdom of God is preached, and every man presses into it.' Pressing into it, and taking it by force, are the same thing. There is, then, a violence, a restless activity and vigour of spirit, to be used and exercised for an interest in this kingdom. Apply this to your condition. Are you in depths and doubts, staggering and uncertain, not knowing what is your condition, nor whether you have any interest in the forgiveness that is with God. Are you tossed up and down between hopes and fears? [Do you] want peace, consolation, and establishment? Why lie you upon your faces? Get up, watch, pray, fast, meditate, offer violence to your lusts and corruptions; fear not, startle not at their crying or importunities to be spared; press to the throne of grace by prayers, supplications, importunities, restless requests. This is the way to take the kingdom of heaven. These things are not peace, they are not assurance; but they are part of the means that God has appointed for the attainment of them.

What, then, is the peculiar instruction that is proper for souls in this condition? That, plainly, of the apostle, 'Give diligence to make your calling and election sure' (2 Pet. 1:10). 'Alas!' says the soul, 'I am at no certainty, but rather am afflicted and tossed, and not comforted. My heart will come to no stability. I have no assurance, know not whether I am chosen or called; yea, fear that my latter end will be darkness and sorrow. There is, I confess, forgiveness with God, but [I] justly fear I shall never be made partaker of it.' What is the usual course that is taken in such complaints by them to whom they are made? Mostly, they have a good opinion of them that come with these complaints; they judge them to be godly and holy, though much in the dark. If they knew them not before, yet upon these complaints they begin to be well persuaded of them. Hereupon, they are moved with pity and compassion, and troubled to see them in their perplexities, and set themselves to tender relief to them: they mind them of the gracious promises of the gospel; it may be, fix upon some one or more of them in particular, which they explain to them; thence they mind them of the abundant grace and tender love of the Father, of the merciful care of our High Priest, his readiness and ability to save, his communications of such favours to them as they perceive not. By such ways and means, by such applications, do they seek to relieve them in the state and condition wherein they are. But what is the issue? Does not this relief prove, for the most part, like the morning cloud, and as the early dew? a little refreshment it may be it yields for a season, but is quickly again dried up, and the soul left in its heartless, withering condition.

You will say, then, 'Do you condemn this manner of proceeding with the souls of men in their doubts, fears, and distresses? Or would you have them pine away under the sense of their condition, or abide in this uncertainty all their days?' I answer, No; I condemn not the way; I would not have any left comfortless in their depths. But yet I would give these two cautions.

### Spiritual Wisdom Is Essential

That spiritual wisdom and prudence is greatly required in this matter, in the administration of consolation to distressed souls. If in any thing, the tongue of the spiritually learned is required herein—namely, in speaking a word in season to them that are weary. a promiscuous drawing out of gospel consolations, without a previous right judgment concerning the true state and condition of the souls applied to, is seldom useful, ofttimes pernicious. And let men take care how they commit their souls and consciences to such who have good words in readiness for all comers.

### Beware Unbalanced Spiritual Counsel

If counsel and consolation of this kind be given, special and distinct from the advice we are upon of watchfulness, diligence, spiritual violence in a way of duty, it is exceeding dangerous, and will assuredly prove useless; for let us see what counsel the Holy Ghost gives in this condition to them who would make their 'calling and election sure,' who would be freed from their present fears and uncertainties, who complain of their darkness and dangers. Why, says he, 'Giving all diligence, add to your faith virtue' (2 Pet. 1:5–7) and so on; 'for,' says he, 'if you do these things you shall never fall: for so an entrance shall be ministered to you abundantly into the everlasting kingdom of our Lord and Saviour Jesus Christ' (v. 11). You who are now in the skirts of it, who know not whether you belong to it or no, you shall have an entrance into the kingdom of Christ, and all the joy, comforts, consolations, and glory of it shall be richly administered to you. This is the advice that the Holy Ghost gives in this case; and this is the blessed promise annexed to the following of this advice; and this the former compassionate course of administering consolation is not to be separated from.

But you will, it may be, here say, 'We are so dead and dull, so chained under the power of corruptions and temptations, that we are not able thus to put forth the fruit of a spiritual life in adding one grace to another.' But do you use diligence, study, endeavours, all diligence, diligence at all times, in all ways by God appointed, all manner of diligence within and without, in private and public, to this end and purpose? Do you study, meditate, pray, watch, fast, neglect no opportunity, keep your hearts, search, try, examine yourselves, flee temptations and occasions of cooling, deadening, and stifling grace? Do these things abound in you? Alas! You cannot do thus, you are so weak, so indisposed. But, alas! You will not, you will not part with your ease, you will not crucify your lusts, you will not use all diligence; but must come to it, or be contented to spend all your days in darkness, and to lie down in sorrow.

Thus do men frequently miscarry. Is it any news, for persons to bewail the folly of their nature and ways in the morning and evening, and yet scarce stand upon their watch any part of the day, or in any occasion of the day? Is this 'giving all diligence?' Is this 'working out our salvation with fear and trembling?' And may we not see professors even indulging themselves in ways of vanity, folly, wrath, envy, sloth, and the like, and yet complain at what a loss they are, how unquiet, how uncertain? God forbid it should be otherwise with you, or that we should endeavour to speak peace to you in any such a frame. To hear of a person that he walks slothfully, carelessly, or indulges his corruptions, and to find him complaining that he is at a loss whether he have any interest in pardon or no; to give or tender comfort to such mourners, without a due admonition of their duty to use diligence in the use of means, for to help on their delivery out of the condition wherein they are, is to tender poison to them.

To this, then, the soul must come that is in depths, if it intend to be delivered. Heartless complaints, with excuses to keep it from vigorous, spiritual diligence, must be laid aside; if not, ordinarily, peace, rest, and stability will not be obtained. a great example hereof we have in the spouse (S. of S. 5:2–8). She is drowsy and indisposed to communion with Christ, whereunto she is invited (v. 2); this puts her upon making excuses, from the unfitness of the time, and her present indisposition and unpreparedness as to the duty whereunto she was called (v. 3). Hereupon Christ withdraws his presence from her, and leaves her at a loss as to her former comforts (v. 6). What course does she now take? Does she now lie down again in her former slumber? Does she make use of her former excuses and pretences why she should not engage into the duties she was called to? No such thing; but now, with all earnestness, diligence, sedulity, and importunity, she engages in all manner of duties, whereby she may recover her former comforts, as you may see in the text. And this must be the course of others who would obtain the same success. Spiritual peace and sloth will never dwell together in the same soul and conscience.

## IX

### GUARD YOUR THOUGHTS OF GOD

Take heed, in doubts, distresses, and perplexities, of hard thoughts of God, hasty unweighed expressions concerning him or his ways, or of secret resolves that it were as good give over waiting as continue in the state wherein you are, seeing your condition is remediless.

On three occasions are such thoughts and resolves apt to befall the minds of men; which sometimes break forth into unwarrantable expressions concerning God himself and his ways:

1. In deep perplexities of mind, by reason of some pressing terror from the Lord.
2. On the long wearisome continuance of some tempting distress; and hereof we have many examples, some whereof shall be mentioned.
3. In spiritual disappointments, through the strength of lust

or temptation. When a person has, it may be, recovered himself, through grace, from a perplexing sense of the guilt of some sin, or it may be from a course, shorter or longer, lesser or greater, of backsliding and negligent walking with God, and therein goes on cheerfully for a season in the course of his obedience; if this person, through the power of temptation, subtilty of lusts, neglect of watchfulness, by one means or other, is surprised in the sins or ways that he had relinquished, or is turned aside from the vigour of that course wherein he was engaged, he may be exposed not only to great despondencies, but also be overtaken with secret resolves to give over contending, seeing it is to no more purpose, nay, to no purpose, and that God regards him not at all.

Take an instance or two in each kind:

The first we have in Job, in the extremity of his trials and terrors from the Lord (see, among other places, Job 10:3). 'Is it,' says he to God, 'good to you that you should oppress, that you should despise the work of your hands?' Ah! Poor worms, with whom have we to do? 'Who shall say to a king, you are wicked? And to princes, You are ungodly? And will you speak to Him who respects not the person of princes, nor regards them more than the poorest in the earth?' And see what conclusions from such thoughts as these he infers: 'You number my steps: do you not watch over my sin? My transgression is sealed up in a bag, and you sew up my iniquity' (Job 14:16–17). He charges God to be his enemy, one that watched for all opportunities and advantages against him, that seemed to be glad at his halting, and take care that none of his sins should be missing when he intended to deal with him. Had this indeed been the case with him, he had perished to eternity, as elsewhere he acknowledged.

Of the other we have an instance in the church: 'I said, "My strength and my hope is perished from the Lord"' (Lam. 3:18). Present grace in spiritual strength and future expectation of mercy are all gone. And what is got by this? Secret hard thoughts of God himself are hereby ingenerated, 'When I cry and shout, he shuts out my prayer' (v. 8), 'You have covered yourself with a cloud, that our prayer should not pass through' (v. 44). These things are grievous to God to bear, and no way useful to the soul in its condition; yea, they more and more unfit it for every duty that may lie in a tendency to its relief and deliverance.

So was it with Jonah: 'I said, I am cast out of your sight' (ch. 2:4). 'All is lost and gone with me; as good give over as contend; I do but labour in vain. Perish I must, as one cast out of the sight of God.' The like complaints fell also from Heman in his distress (Ps. 88).

The general who heard one of his soldiers cry out, upon a fresh onset of the enemy, 'Now we are undone, now we are ruined,' called him a traitor, and told him it was not so whilst he could wield his sword. It is not for every private soldier on every danger to make judgment of the battle; that is the work of the general. Jesus Christ is 'the captain of our salvation;' he has undertaken the leading and conduct of our souls through all our difficulties. Our duty is to fight and contend; his work is to take care of the event, and to him it is to be committed.

That, then, you make a due use of this rule, keep always in your minds these two considerations:

1. That it is not for you to take the judgment of Christ out of his hand, and to be passing sentence upon your own souls. Judgment as to the state and condition of men is committed to Christ, and to him it is to be left. This we were directed to in our first rule, and it is of special use in the case under consideration. Self-judging in reference to sin and the demerit of it is our duty. The judging of our state and condition in relation to the remedy provided is the office and work of Jesus Christ, with whom it is to be left.

2. Consider that hard thoughts of what God will do with you, and harsh desponding sentences pronounced against yourselves, will insensibly alienate your hearts from God. It may be when men's perplexities are at the height, and the most sad expressions are as it were wrested from them, they yet think they must justify God, and that they do so accordingly.

But yet such thoughts as those mentioned are very apt to infect the mind with other inclinations: for after a while they will prevail with the soul to look on God as an enemy, as one that has no delight in it; and what will be the consequence thereof is easily discernible. None will continue to love long where they expect no returns. Suffer not, then, your minds to be tainted with such thoughts; and let not God be dishonoured by any such expressions as reflect on that infinite grace and compassion which he is exercising towards you.

## X

### Lay Hold of Every Appearance of Grace

If you would come to stability, and a comforting persuasion of an interest in forgiveness by the blood of Christ, improve the least appearances of him to your souls, and the least intimations of his love in pardon, that are made to you in the way of God. The spouse takes notice of her Husband, and rejoices in him, when he stands behind the wall, when he does but look forth at the window and show himself at the lattice—when she could have no clear sight of him (S. of S. 2:9). She lays hold on the least appearance of him to support her heart withal, and to stir up her affections towards him. Men in dangers do not sit still to wait until something presents itself to them that will give assured deliverance; but they close with that which first presents itself to them, that is of the same kind and nature with what they look after. And thus God in many places expresses such supports as give the soul little more than a possibility of attaining the end aimed at: 'It may be you shall be hid in the day of the LORD's anger' (Zeph. 2:3). And Joel 2:14, 'Who knows but he will return and leave a blessing?'—'It maybe we shall be hid; it may be we shall have a blessing.' And this was the best ground that Jonathan had for the great undertaking against the enemies of God: 'It may be that the LORD will work for us' (1 Sam. 14:6). And to what end does God at any time make these seemingly dubious intimations of grace and mercy? Is it that we should, by the difficulty included in them, be discouraged and kept from him? Not at all; he speaks nothing to deter sinners, especially distressed sinners, from trusting in him. But his end is, that we should close with, and lay hold upon and improve, the least appearances of grace, which this kind of expressions gives to us. When men are in a voyage at sea, and meet with a storm or a tempest which abides upon them, and they fear will at last prevail against them, if they make so far a discovery of land as that they can say, 'It may be there is land, it may be it is such a place where there is a safe harbour,' none can positively say it is not; there lies no demonstration against it. In this condition, especially if there be no other way of escape, delivery, or safety proposed to them, this is enough to make them to follow on that discovery, and with all diligence to steer their course that way, until they have made a trial of it to the utmost. The soul of which we speak is afflicted and tossed, and not comforted. There is in the intimation of grace and pardon intended a remote discovery made of some relief. This may be Christ; it may be forgiveness. This it is convinced of; it cannot deny but at such or such a time, under such ordinances, or in such duties, it was persuaded that yet there might be mercy and pardon for it. This is enough to carry it to steer its course constantly that way—to press forward to that harbour which will give it rest. How little was it that David had to bring his soul to a composure in his great distress! 'If,' says he, 'I shall find favour in the eyes of the LORD, he will bring me again, and shew me the ark, and his habitation: but if he thus say, I have no delight in you; behold, here am I, let him do to me as seems good to him' (2 Sam. 15:25-6). He has nothing but sovereign grace to rest upon, and that he gives himself up to.

Faith is indeed the soul's venture for eternity. Something it is to venture on as to its eternal condition. It must either adhere to itself or its own vain hopes of a righteousness of its own; or it must give over all expectation and lie down in darkness; or it must shut out all dreadful apprehensions of eternity, by the power and activity of its lusts and carnal affections; or it must, whatever its discouragements be, cast itself upon pardon in the blood of Jesus Christ. Now, if all the former ways be detestable and pernicious, if the best of them be a direct opposition to the gospel, what has the soul that inquires after these things to do but to adhere to the last, and to improve every encouragement, even the least, to that purpose?

XI

## Pinpoint the Cause of Your Restlessness

As a close to these general rules, I shall only add this last direction: consider in particular where the stress and hinderance lies that keeps you off from peace, through an established persuasion of an interest in evangelical pardon. Do not always fluctuate up and down in generals and uncertainties; but drive things to a particular issue, that it may be tried whether it be of sufficient efficacy to keep you in your present entanglements and despondencies. Search out your wound, that it may be tried whether it be curable or no.

Now, in this case, we cannot expect that persons should suggest their own particular concerns, that so they might be considered and be brought to the rule; but we must ourselves reduce such distresses as may or do in this matter befall the minds of men to some general heads, and give a judgment concerning them according to the word of truth. Indeed, particular cases, as varied by circumstances, are endless, nor can they be spoken to in this way of instruction and direction; but they must be left to occasional considerations of them, as they are represented to them who are intrusted to dispense the mysteries of God. Besides, many have laboured already in this matter, and their endeavours are in and of general use; although it must be said, as was before observed, that special cases are so varied By their circumstances, that it is very rare that any resolutions of them are every way adequate and suited to the apprehensions of them that are exercised with them. I shall therefore call things to some general heads, whereunto most of the objections that distressed sinners make against their own peace may be reduced, and leave the light of them to be applied in particular to the relief of the souls of men, as God shall be pleased to make them effectual.

7

## CAUSES OF SPIRITUAL DISQUIET

That which now lies before us is the second part of the second general use educed from the truth insisted on. Our aim is, to lead on souls towards peace with God, through a gracious persuasion of their interest in that forgiveness which is with him; and it consists, as was declared, in a consideration of some of those disquietments which befall the minds of men, and keep them off from establishment in this matter.

### AFFLICTIONS

And, first, such disquietments and objections against the peace of the soul and its acceptance with God will arise from afflictions; they have done so of old, they do so in many at this day. Afflictions, I say, greatened to the mind from their nature or by their concomitants, do ofttimes variously affect it, and sometimes prevail to darken it so far as to ingenerate thoughts that they are all messengers of wrath, all tokens of displeasure, and so, consequently, evidences that we are not pardoned or accepted with God.

### WHAT AGGRAVATES AFFLICTIONS

Now, this is a time of great afflictions to many, and those, some of them, such as have innumerable aggravating circumstances accompanying of them. Some have come with a dreadful surprisal in things not looked for, such as falls not out in the providence of God in many generations. Such is the condition of them who are reduced to the utmost extremity by the late consuming fire; some have had their whole families, all their posterity, taken from them. In a few days they have been suddenly bereaved, as in the plague. Some in their own persons, or in their relations, have had sore, long, and grievous trials from oppressions and persecutions. And these things have various effects on the minds of men. Some we find crying, with that wicked king, 'This evil is of the LORD; why should we wait any longer for him?' and give up themselves to seek relief from their own lusts; some bear up under their troubles with a natural stoutness of spirit; some have received a sanctified use and improvement of their trials with joy in the Lord: but many we find to go heavily under their burdens, having their minds darkened with many misapprehensions of the love of God and of their own personal interest in his grace. It is not, therefore, unseasonable to speak a little to this head of trouble in our entrance. Outward troubles, I say, are oftentimes occasions, if not the causes, of great inward distresses. You know how the saints of old expressed their sense of them and conflicts with them. The complaints of David are familiar to all who attend to any communion with God in these things; so are those of Job, Heman, Jonah, Jeremiah, and others: neither do they complain only of their troubles, but of the sense which they had of God's displeasure in and under them, and of his hiding of his face from them whilst they were so exercised.

It is not otherwise at present, as is known to such as converse with many who are either surprised with unexpected troubles, or worn out with trials and disappointments of an expected end. They consider themselves both absolutely and with respect to others, and upon both accounts are filled with dark thoughts and despondencies. Says one, 'I am rolled from one trial to another.

The clouds with me return still after the rain. All the billows and water-spouts of God go over me. In my person, it may be, pressed with sickness, pains, troubles; in my relations, with their sins, miscarriages, or death; in my outward state, in want, losses, disreputation. I am even as a withered branch. Surely if God had any especial regard to my soul, it would not be thus with me, or some timely end would have been put to these dispensations.' On the other hand, they take a view of some other professors; they see that their tables are spread day by day, that the candle of the Lord shines continually on their tabernacle, and that in all things they have their hearts' desire, setting aside the common attendancies of human nature, and nothing befalls them grievous in the world. 'Thus it is with them. And surely, had I an interest in his grace, in pardon, the God of Israel would not thus pursue a flea in the mountains, nor set himself in battle army against a leaf driven to and fro with the wind; he would spare me a little, and let me alone for a moment. But as things are with me, I fear "my way is hidden from the LORD, and my judgment is passed over from my God."' This kind of thoughts do perplex the minds of men, and keep them off from partaking of that strong consolation which God is abundantly willing they should receive, by a comfortable persuasion of a blessed interest in that forgiveness that is with him.

And this was the very case of David; or at least these outward troubles were a special part of those depths out of which he cried for relief, by a sense of pardon, grace, and redemption with God.

I answer to these complaints, first, that there are so many excellent things spoken concerning afflictions, their necessity, their usefulness, and the like—such blessed ends are assigned to them, and in many have been compassed and fulfilled by them—that a man, unacquainted with the exercise wherewith they are attended, would think it impossible that any one should be shaken in mind as to the love and favour of God on their account. But as the apostle tells us that no afflictions are joyous at present, but grievous, so he who made, in the close of his trials, that solemn profession, that 'it was good for him that he had been afflicted,' yet we know, as has been declared, how he was distressed under them. There are, therefore, sundry accidental things which accompany great afflictions, that seem to exempt them from the common rule and the promise of love and grace.

### Remembering Past Sins

The remembrance of past and buried miscarriages and sins lies in the bosom of many afflictions. It was so with Job: 'You make me,' says he, 'possess the iniquities of my youth.' See his plea to that purpose (Job 13:23–7). In the midst of his troubles and distresses, God revived upon his spirit a sense of former sins, even the sins of his youth, and made him to possess them; he filled his soul and mind with thoughts of them and anxiety about them. This made him fear lest God was his enemy, and would continue to deal with him in all severity. So was it with Joseph's brethren in their distresses: 'They said one to another, We are verily guilty concerning our brother, in that we saw the anguish of his soul, when he besought us, and we would not hear; therefore is this distress come upon us' (Gen. 42:21); and verse 22, 'Behold, his blood is required.' Their distress revives a deep, perplexing sense of the guilt of sin many years past before, and that under all its aggravating circumstances; which spoiled them of all their reliefs and comforts, filling them with confusion and trouble, though absolutely innocent as to what was come on them. And the like appeared in the widow of Zarephath, with whom Elijah sojourned during the famine. Upon the death of her son, which, it seems, was somewhat extraordinary, she cried out to the prophet, 'What have I to do with you, O you man of God? Are you come to call my sin to remembrance, and to slay my son?' (1 Kgs 17:18). It seems some great sin she had formerly contracted the guilt of, and now, upon her sore affliction in the death of her only child, the remembrance of it was recalled and revived upon her soul. Thus 'deep calls to deep at the noise of God's water-spouts,' and then 'all his waves and billows go over' a person (Ps. 42:7). The deep of afflictions calls up the deep of the guilt of sin, and both in conjunction become as billows and waves passing over the soul. We see only the outside of men's afflictions; they usually complain only of what appears: and an easy thing it is supposed to be to apply relief and comfort to those that are distressed. The rule in this matter is so clear, so often repeated and inculcated, the promises annexed to this condition so many and precious, that every one has in readiness what to apply to them who are so exercised. But oftentimes we know nothing of the gall and wormwood that is in men's affliction; they keep that to themselves, and their souls feed upon them in secret (Lam. 3:19). God has stirred up the remembrance of some great sin or sins, and they look upon their afflictions as that wherein he is come or beginning to enter into judgment with them. And is it any wonder if they be in darkness, and filled with disconsolation?

### Sharp Edges

There is in many afflictions something that seems new and peculiar, wherewith the soul is surprised, and cannot readily reduce its condition to what is taught about afflictions in general. This perplexes and entangles it. It is not affliction it is troubled withal, but some one thing or other in it that appears with an especial dread to the soul, so that he questions whether ever it were so with any other or no, and is thereby deprived of the support which from former examples it might receive. And, indeed, when God intends that which shall be a deep affliction, he will put an edge upon it, in matter, or manner, or circumstances, that shall make the soul feel its sharpness. He will not take up with our bounds and measures, and with which we think we could be contented; but he will put the impress of his own greatness and terror upon it, that he may be acknowledged and submitted to. Such was the state with Naomi, when, from a full and plentiful condition, she went into a strange country with a husband and two sons, where they all died, leaving her destitute and poor. Hence, in her account of God's dealing with her, she says, 'Call me not Naomi' (that is, pleasant), 'call me Mara' (that is, bitter): 'for the Almighty has dealt very bitterly with me. I went out full, and the LORD has brought me home again empty: why then do you call me Naomi, seeing the LORD has testified against me, and the Almighty has afflicted me?' (Ruth 1:20–21). So was it with Job, with the widow of Zarephath, and with her at Nain who was burying her only child. And still in many afflictions God is pleased to put in an entangling speciality, which perplexes the soul, and darkens it in all its reasonings about the love of God towards it and its interest in pardon and grace.

### One's Natural Disposition

In some, affections are very strong and importunate as fixed on lawful things, whereby their nature is made sensible and tender, and apt to receive very deep impressions from urgent afflictions. Now, although this in itself be a good natural frame, and helps to preserve the soul from that stout-heartedness which God abhors, yet if it be not watched over, it is apt to perplex the soul with many entangling temptations. The apostle intimates a double evil that we are obnoxious to under trials and afflictions, 'My son, despise not the chastening of the Lord, nor faint when you are rebuked of him' (Heb. 12:5). Men may either, through a natural stoutness, despise and contemn their sufferings, and be obstinate under them, or faint and despond; and so come short of the end which God aims at for them, to be attained in a way of duty. Now, though the frame spoken of be not obnoxious to the first extreme, yet it is greatly to the latter; which, if not watched against, is no less pernicious than the former. Affections in such persons being greatly moved, they cloud and darken the mind, and fill it with strange apprehensions concerning God and themselves. Every thing is presented to them through a glass composed of fear, dread, terror, sorrow, and all sorts of disconsolations. This makes them faint and despond, to very sad apprehensions of themselves and their conditions.

### Unmortified Corruptions

Afflictions find some entangled with very strong corruptions—as love of the world, or the pleasure of it, of name or reputation, of great contrivances for posterity, and the like; or it may be in things carnal or sensual. Now, when these unexpectedly meet together—great afflictions and strong corruptions—it is not conceivable what a combustion they will make in the soul. As a strong medicine or potion meeting with a strong or tough distemper in the body—there is a violent contention in nature between them and about them, so that oftentimes the very life of the patient is endangered; so it is where a great trial, a smart stroke of the hand of God, falls upon a person in the midst of his pursuit of the effects of some corruptions—the soul is amazed even to distraction, and can scarce have any thought but that God is come to cut the person off in the midst of his sin. Every unmortified corruption fills the very fear and expectation of affliction with horror. And there is good reason that so it should do; for although God should be merciful to men's iniquities, yet if he should come to take vengeance of their inventions, their condition would be dark and sorrowful.

## Satan's Opportunism

Satan is never wanting in such occasions to attempt the compassing of his ends upon persons that are exercised under the hand of God. In the time of suffering it was that he fell upon the Head of the church, turning it into the very hour of the power of darkness. And he will not omit any appearing opportunities of advantage against his members. And this is that which he principally, in such seasons, attacks them withal—namely, that God regards them not, that they are fallen under his judgment and severity, as those who have no share in mercy, pardon, or forgiveness.

### How to Avoid Spiritual Trouble Under Affliction

From these and the like reasons, I say, it is, that whereas afflictions in general are so testified to, to be such pledges and tokens of God's love and care, to be designed to blessed ends as conformity to Christ, and a participation of the holiness of God; yet, by reason of these circumstances, they often prove means of casting the soul into depths, and of hindering it from a refreshing interest in the forgiveness that is with God. That this may prove no real or abiding ground of inward spiritual trouble to the soul, the following rules and directions may be observed:

### Most Affliction—Most Grace

Not only afflictions in general, but great and manifold afflictions, and those attended with all sorts of aggravating circumstances, are always consistent with the pardon of sin, after signal tokens and pledges of it, and of the love of God therein: 'What is man, that you should magnify him? And that you should set your heart upon him? And that you should visit him every morning, and try him every moment?' (Job 7:17–18). What were the considerations that cast him into this admiration of the care and love of God is expressed (v. 12–16). There are no words of a more dismal import in the whole book than those here expressed: yet, when he recollected himself from his overwhelming distress, he acknowledges that all this proceeded from the love and care of God; yea, his fixing his heart upon a man to magnify him, to set him up and do him good. For this end he chastens a man every morning, and tries him every moment; and that with such afflictions as are for the present so far from being joyous as that they give no rest, but even weary the soul of life, as he expresses their effects on himself (v. 15–16). And hence it is observed of this Job, that when none in the earth was like to him in trouble, God gave him three testimonies from heaven that there was none in the earth like to him in grace. And although it may not be laid down as a general rule, yet for the most part in the providence of God, from the foundation of the world, those who have had most of afflictions have had most of grace and the most eminent testimonies of acceptance with God.

Christ Jesus, the Son of God, the head of the church, had all afflictions gathered into a head in him, and yet the Father always loved him, and was always well pleased with him.

When God solemnly renewed his covenant with Abraham, and he had prepared the sacrifice whereby it was to be ratified and confirmed, God made a smoking furnace to pass between the pieces of the sacrifice (Gen. 15:17). It was to let him know that there was a furnace of affliction attending the covenant of grace and peace. And so he tells Zion that he 'chose her in the furnace of affliction' (Isa. 48:10)—that is, in Egyptian affliction; burning, flaming afflictions; 'fiery trials,' as Peter calls them (1 Pet. 4:12). There can, then, no argument be drawn from affliction, from any kind of it, from any aggravating circumstance wherewith it may be attended, that should any way discourage the soul in the comforting, supporting persuasion of an interest in the love of God and forgiveness thereby.

### Long Afflictions no Cause for Spiritual Disconsolation

No length or continuance of afflictions ought to be any impeachment of our spiritual consolation. Take for the confirmation hereof the great example of the Son of God. How long did his afflictions continue? What end or issue was put to them? No longer did they abide than until 'he cried with a loud voice, and gave up the ghost.' To the moment of his death, from his manger to his cross, his afflictions still increased, and he ended his days in the midst of them. Now, he was the head of the church, and the great representative of it, to a conformity with whom we are predestinated. And if God will have it so with us even in this particular, so as that we shall have no rest, no peace from our trials, until we lie down in the grave, that whatever condition we pass through they shall be shut out of none, but only from immortality and glory, what have we herein to complain of?

### Deal with Past Sins in Isolation

Where the remembrance and perplexing sense of past sins is revived by present afflictions, separate them in your minds and deal distinctly about them. So long as you carry on the consideration of them jointly, you will be rolled from one to another, and never obtain rest to your souls. They will mutually aggravate each other. The sharpness of affliction will add to the bitterness of the sense of sin; and the sense of sin will give an edge to affliction, and cause it to pierce deeply into the soul, as we showed in the former instances. Deal, therefore, distinctly about them, and in their proper order. So does the psalmist here. He had at present both upon him; and together they brought him into these depths, concerning which he so cries out for deliverance from them (see Ps. 32:3–5). And what course does he take? He applies himself in the first place to his sin and the guilt of it, and that distinctly and separately. And when he has got a discharge of sin, which he waited so earnestly for, his faith quickly arose above his outward trials, as appears in his blessed close of all: "'He shall redeem Israel out of all his trouble;" the whole Israel of God, and myself amongst them.' This do, then—single out the sin or sins that are revived in the sense of their guilt upon the conscience; use all diligence to come to an issue about them in the blood of Christ. This God by your affliction calls you to. This is the disease, whereof your trouble is but the symptom. This, therefore, in the cure you seek after, is first and principally to be attended to; when that is once removed, the other, as to any prejudice to your soul, will depart of itself. The root being once digged up, you shall not long feed on the bitter fruit that it has brought forth; or if you do, the wormwood shall be taken out of it, and it shall be very pleasant to you, as well as wholesome. How this is to be done, by an application to God for forgiveness, has been at large declared. But if men will deal with confused thoughts about their sins and their troubles, their wound will be incurable and their sorrow endless.

### Afflictions Bring Temptations

Remember that a time of affliction is a time of temptation. Satan, as we have showed, will not be wanting to any appearing opportunity or advantage of setting upon the soul. When Pharaoh heard that the people were entangled in the wilderness, he pursued them; and when Satan sees a soul entangled with its distresses and troubles, he thinks it his time and hour to assault it. He seeks to winnow, and comes when the corn is under the flail. Reckon, therefore, that when trouble comes, the prince of the world comes also, that you may be provided for him. Now is the time to take the shield of faith, that we may be able to quench his fiery darts. If they be neglected, they will inflame the soul. Watch, therefore, and pray, that you enter not into temptation, that Satan do not represent God falsely to you. He that durst represent Job falsely to the all-seeing God will with much boldness represent God falsely to us, who see and know so little. Be not, then, ignorant of his devices, but every way set yourselves against his interposing between God and your souls in a matter which he has nothing to do withal. Let not this make-bate by any means inflame the difference.

## Distinguish Natural Depression from Spiritual Distress

Learn to distinguish the effect of natural distempers from spiritual distresses. Some have sad, dark, and tenacious thoughts fixed on their minds from their natural distempers. These will not be cured by reasonings, nor utterly quelled by faith. Our design must be, to abate their efficacy and consequents by considering their occasions. And if men cannot do this in themselves, it is highly incumbent on those who make application of relief to them to be careful to discern what is from such principles, whereof they are not to expect a speedy cure.

## Be Vigilant in Good Times

Take heed in times of peace and ease that you lay not up, by your negligence or careless walking, sad provision for a day of darkness, a time of afflictions. It is sin that imbitters troubles; the sins of peace are revived in time of distress. Fear of future affliction, of impendent troubles, should make us careful not to bring that into them which will make them bitter and sorrowful.

## *Labour to Benefit from Afflictions*

Labour to grow better under all your afflictions, lest your afflictions grow worse, lest God mingle them with more darkness, bitterness, and terror. As Joab said to David, if he ceased not his scandalous lamentation on the death of Absalom, all the people would leave him, and he then should find himself in a far worse condition than that which he bemoaned, or any thing that befell him from his youth; the same may be said to persons under their afflictions. If they are not managed and improved in a due manner, that which is worse may, nay, in all probability will, befall them. Wherever God takes this way, and engages in afflicting, he does commonly pursue his work until he has prevailed, and his design towards the afflicted party be accomplished. He will not cease to thresh and break the bread-corn until it be meet for his use. Lay down, then, the weapons of your warfare against him; give up yourselves to his will; let go every thing about which he contends with you; follow after that which he calls you to; and you will find light arising to you in the midst of darkness. Has he a cup of affliction in one hand? Lift up your eyes, and you will see a cup of consolation in another. And if all stars withdraw their light whilst you are in the way of God, assure yourselves that the sun is ready to rise.

## *Chastisement Is Compatible with Assurance*

According to the tenor of the covenant of grace, a man may be sensible of the respect of affliction to sin, yea, to this or that sin in particular, and yet have a comfortable persuasion of the forgiveness of sin. Thus it was in general in God's dealing with his people. He 'forgave them,' but he 'took vengeance of their inventions' (Ps. 89:8). Whatever they suffered under the vengeance that fell upon their inventions (and that is as hard a word as is applied anywhere to God's dealing with his people), yet, at the same time, he assured them of the pardon of their sin. So, you know, was the case of David. His greatest trial and affliction, and that which befell him on the account of a particular sin, and wherein God took vengeance on his invention, was ushered in with a word of grace—that God had done away or pardoned his sin, and that he should not die. This is expressed in the tenor of the covenant with the seed of Christ (Ps. 89:31–4).

## INNER TURMOIL ABOUT THE STATE OF THE SOUL

Another head of objections and despondencies arises from things internal—things that are required in the soul, that it may have an interest in the forgiveness that is with God, some whereof we shall speak to. And these respect, first, the state of the soul; and, secondly, some actings in the soul.

### UNCERTAINTY ABOUT REGENERATION

First, as to the state. Say some, 'Unless a man be regenerate and born again, he is not, he cannot be made partaker of mercy and pardon. Now, all things here are in the dark to us; for, first, we know not well what this regeneration is, and it is variously disputed amongst men. Some would place it only in the outward signs of our initiation into Christ, and some otherwise express it. Again, it is uncertain whether those that are regenerate do or may know that they are so, or whether this may be in any measure known to others with whom they may treat about it. And if it may not be known, we must be uncertain in this also. And then, it may be, for their parts, they neither know the time when, nor the manner how, any such work was wrought in them; and yet, without this, seeing it is wrought by means, and springs from certain causes, they can have no establishment in a not-failing persuasion of their acceptance with God by the pardon of their sins in the blood of Christ.'

This is the head and sum of most of the objections which perplexed souls do manage against themselves as to their state and condition. Hence, indeed, they draw forth reasonings with great variety, according as they are suggested by their particular occasions and temptations. And many proofs, taken from their sins, miscarriages, and fears, do they enforce their objections withal. My purpose is, to lay down some general rules and principles, which may be applied to particular occasions and emergencies; and this shall be done in answer to the several parts of the general objection mentioned before. I say, then:

## Two Conditions Divide Mankind

It is most certain that there are two estates and conditions that divide all mankind, and every one that lives in the world does completely and absolutely belong to one of them. These are, the state of nature and the state of grace—of sin and of righteousness by Christ. Every man in the world belongs to one of these states or conditions. This the Scripture so abounds in that it seems to be the first principal thing that we are taught in it. It is as clear that there are two different states in this world as that there are so in that to come. Yea, all our faith and obedience depend on this truth; and not only so, but the covenant of God, the mediation of Christ, and all the promises and threats of the law and gospel, are built on this supposition. And this lays naked to a spiritual eye that abounding atheism that is in the world. Men are not only, like Nicodemus, ignorant of these things, and wonder how they can be, but they scorn them, despise them, scoff at them. To make mention of being regenerate is exposed to reproach in the world. But whether men will or no, to one of these conditions they must belong.

## Distinct Characteristics

As these two estates differ morally in themselves, and physically in the causes constitutive of that difference, so there is a specifical difference between the things that place men in the one condition and in the other. Whatever there is of goodness, virtue, duty, grace, in an unregenerate person, there is in him that is regenerate somewhat of another kind that is not in the other at all. For the difference of these states themselves, it is plain in Scripture—the one is a state of death, the other of life; the one of darkness, the other of light; the one of enmity against God, the other of reconciliation with him. And that the one state is constituted by that of grace, which is of a peculiar kind, and which is not in the other, I shall briefly declare.

FRUITS OF ELECTING LOVE. The grace of regeneration proceeds from an especial spring and fountain, which empties much of its living waters into it, no one drop whereof falls on them that are not regenerate. This is electing love; it is given out in the pursuit of the decree of election: 'God has chosen us that we should be holy' (Eph. 1:4). Our holiness, whose only spring is our regeneration, is an effect of our election—that which God works in our souls, in the pursuit of his eternal purpose of love and good-will towards us. So again says the apostle, 'God has from the beginning chosen you to salvation, through sanctification of the Spirit' (2 Thess. 2:13). God having designed us to salvation as the end, has also appointed the sanctification of the Spirit to be the means to bring us orderly to the attainment of that end. But the best of common grace or gifts that may be in men unregenerate are but products of the providence of God, ordering all things in general to his own glory and the good of them that shall be heirs of salvation. They are not fruits of electing eternal love, nor designed means for the infallible attaining of eternal salvation.

GRACES OF THE REGENERATE INSEPARABLE FROM CHRIST. The graces of those that are regenerate have a manifold respect or relation to the Lord Christ, that the common graces of others have not. I shall name one or two of these respects:

First, they have an especial moral relation to the mediatory acts of Christ in his oblation and intercession. Especial grace is an especial part of the purchase of Christ by his death and blood-shedding. He made a double purchase of his elect—of their persons, to be his; of especial grace, to be theirs: 'He gave himself for the church, that he might sanctify and cleanse it with the washing of water by the word, that he might present it to himself a glorious church, not having spot or wrinkle, or any such thing; but that it should be holy and without blemish' (Eph. 5:25–7). The design of Christ in giving himself for his church was, to procure for it that especial grace whereby, through the use of means, it might be regenerate, sanctified, and purified: so, 'He gave himself for us, that he might redeem us from all iniquity, and purify to himself a peculiar people, zealous of good works' (Tit. 2:14). Real purification in grace and holiness has this especial relation to the death of Christ, that he designed therein to procure it for them for whom he died; and in the pursuit of his purchase or acquisition of it, his purpose was really to bestow it upon them, or effectually to work it in them. Moreover, it has an especial relation to his intercession, and that in a distinguishing manner from any other gifts or common graces that other men may receive. Giving us the rule and pattern of his intercession (John 17), he tells us that he so prays not for the world, but for his elect, those which the Father had given him; because they were his (v. 9). And what is it that he prays for them, in distinction from all other men whatever? Amongst others this is one principal thing that he insists on (v. 17), 'Sanctify them through your truth.' Their sanctification and holiness is granted upon that prayer and intercession of Christ; which is peculiar to them, with an exclusion of all others: 'I pray for them; I pray not for the world.' Now, the common grace of unregenerate persons, whereby they are distinguished from other men, whatever it be, it has not this especial relation to the oblation and intercession of Christ. Common grace is not the procurement of especial intercession.

Secondly, they have a real relation to Christ, as he is the living, quickening head of the church; for he is so, even the living spiritual fountain of the spiritual life of it, and of all vital acts whatever: 'Christ is our life; and our life is hid with him in God' (Col. 3:2–3). That eternal life which consists in the knowledge of the Father and the Son (John 17:3), is in him as the cause, head, spring, and fountain of it. In him it is in its fullness, and from thence it is derived to all that believe, who receive from his fullness 'grace for grace' (John 1:16). All true, saving, sanctifying grace, all spiritual life, and every thing that belongs thereunto, is derived directly from Christ, as the living head of his church and fountain of all spiritual life to them. This the apostle expresses, 'speaking the truth in love, grow up into him in all things, which is the head, even Christ: from whom the whole body fitly joined together and compacted by that which every joint supplies, according to the effectual working in the measure of every part, makes increase of the body to the edifying of itself in love' (Eph. 4:15–16). To the same purpose he again expresses the same matter (Col. 2:19). All grace in the whole body comes from the head, Christ Jesus; and there is no growth or furtherance of it but by his effectual working in every part, to bring it to the measure designed to it. Nothing, then, no, not the least of this grace, can be obtained but by virtue of our union to Christ as our head; because it consists in a vital, effectual influence from him and his fullness. And this kind of relation to Christ, all grace that is or may be in unregenerate men is incapable of.

GRACE IS ADMINSTERED ACCORDING TO THE COVENANT. The grace of regeneration and the fruits of it are administered in and by the covenant. This is the promise of the covenant, that God will write his law in our hearts, and put his fear in our inward parts, that we shall not depart from him (Jer. 31). This is that grace whereof we speak, whatever it be, or of what kind soever. It is bestowed on none but those who are taken into covenant with God; for to them alone it is promised, and by virtue thereof is it wrought in and upon their souls. Now, all unregenerate men are strangers from the covenant, and are not made partakers of that grace which is peculiarly and only promised thereby and exhibited therein.

A NEVER-FAILING SPRING. The least spark of saving, regenerating grace is wrought in the soul by the Holy Ghost, as given to men to dwell in them and to abide with them. He is the water given by Jesus Christ to believers, which is in them 'a well of water springing up into everlasting life' (John 4:14). First they receive the water, the spring itself, that is, the Holy Spirit—and from thence living waters do arise up in them; they are wrought, effected, produced by the Spirit, which is given to them. Now, although the common gifts and graces of men unregenerate are effects of the power of the Holy Ghost wrought in them and bestowed on them, as are all other works of God's providence, yet it does not work in them, as received by them, to dwell in them and abide with them, as a never-failing spring of spiritual life; for our Saviour says expressly that the world, or unbelievers, do not know the Spirit, nor can receive him, or have him abiding in them—all which, in a contradistinction to all unregenerate persons, are affirmed of all them that do believe.

THAT WHICH IS BORN OF THE SPIRIT IS SPIRIT. The least of saving grace, such as is peculiar to them that are regenerate, is spirit: 'That which is born of the Spirit is spirit' (John 3:6). Whatever it is that is so born, it is spirit; it has a spiritual being, and it is not educible by any means out of the principles of nature. So it is said to be a 'new creature' (2 Cor. 5:17). Be it never so little or so great, however it may differ in degrees in one and in another, yet the nature of it is the same in all—it is a 'new creature.' As the least worm of the earth, in the order of the old creation, is no less a creature than the sun, yea, or the most glorious angel in heaven; so, in the order of the new creation, the least spark or dram of true grace that is from the sanctifying Spirit is a new creature, no less than the highest faith or love that ever was in the chiefest of the apostles. Now, that which is spirit, and that which is not spirit—that which has a new spiritual being, and that which has none—whatever appearance of agreement there may be among them, do yet differ specifically from one another. And thus it is with the saving grace that is in a regenerate, and those common graces that are in others which are not so. So that as these are divers states, so they are eminently different and distinct the one from the other. And this answers the second thing laid down in the objections taken from the uncertainty of these states and of regeneration itself, and the real difference of it from the contrary state, which is exclusive of an interest in forgiveness.

## *Regeneration Is Discernible*

This is laid down in the inquiry, 'Whether this state may be known to him who is really partaker of it or translated into it, or to others that may be concerned therein?' To which I say, The difference that is between these two states, and the constitutive causes of them, as it is real, so it is discernible. It may be known by themselves who are in those states, and others. It may be known who are born of God, and who are yet children of the devil—who are quickened by Christ, and who are yet 'dead in trespasses and sins.'

NOT ALWAYS TO THOSE CONCERNED. But here also observe that I do not say this is always known to the persons themselves concerned in this distribution. Many cry, 'Peace, peace,' when sudden destruction is at hand. These either think themselves regenerate when they are not, or else wilfully despise the consideration of what is required in them that they may have peace, and so delude their own souls to their ruin. And many that are truly born of God yet know it not; they may for a season walk in darkness, and have no light.

NOT ALWAYS TO OTHERS. Nor, that this is always known to others. It is not known to unregenerate men in respect of them that are so; for they know not really and substantially what it is to be so. Natural men perceive not the things of God; that is, spiritually, in their own light and nature (1 Cor. 2). And as they cannot aright discern the things which put men into that condition (for they are foolishness to them), so they cannot judge aright of their persons in whom they are. And if they do at any time judge aright notionally concerning any things or persons, yet they do not judge so upon right grounds, nor with any evidence in or to themselves of what they do judge. Wherefore generally they judge amiss of such persons; and because they make profession of somewhat which they find not in themselves, they judge them hypocrites, and false pretenders to what is not: for those things which evince their union with Christ, and which evidence their being born of God, they savour them not, nor can receive them. Nor is this always known to or discerned by them that are regenerate. They may sometimes, with Peter, think Simon Magus to be a true believer, or, with Eli, an Hannah to be a daughter of Belial. Many hypocrites are set forth with gifts, common graces, light, and profession, so that they pass amongst all believers for such as are born of God; and many poor saints may be so disguised, under darkness, temptation, sin, as to be looked on as strangers from that family whereunto indeed they do belong. The judgment of man may fail, but the judgment of God is according to righteousness.

BY THE DILIGENT USE OF MEANS. Wherefore, this is that we say, It may be known, in the sedulous use of means appointed for that end, to a man's self and others, which of the conditions mentioned he belongs to, that is, whether he be regenerate or no—so far as his or their concern lies therein. This, I say, may be known, and that infallibly and assuredly, with reference to any duty wherein from hence we are concerned. The discharge of some duties in ourselves and towards others depends on this knowledge; and therefore we may attain it so far as it is necessary for the discharge of such duties to the glory of God.

## A DIGRESSION ON JUDGING OTHERS

Now because it is not directly in our way, yet having been mentioned, I shall briefly, in our passage, touch upon the latter, or what duties do depend upon our judging of others to be regenerate, and the way or principles whereby such a judgment may be made.

### MANY CHRISTIAN DUTIES REQUIRE US TO JUDGE OTHERS

There are many duties incumbent on us to be performed with and towards professors, which, without admitting a judgment to be made of their state and condition, cannot be performed in faith. And in reference to these duties alone it is that we are called to judge the state of others; for we are not giving countenance to a rash, uncharitable censuring of men's spiritual conditions, nor to any judging of any men, any other than what our own duty towards them indispensably requires. Thus, if we are to 'lay down our lives for the brethren,' it is very meet we should so far know them so to be as that we may hazard our lives in faith when we are called thereunto. We are also to join with them in those ordinances wherein we make a solemn profession that we are members of the same body with them, that we have the same Head, the same Spirit, faith, and love. We must love them because they are begotten of God, children of our heavenly Father; and therefore must on some good ground believe them so to be. In a word, the due performance of all principal mutual gospel duties, to the glory of God and our own edification, depends on this supposition, that we may have such a satisfying persuasion concerning the spiritual condition of others as that from thence we may take our aim in what we do.

## ONE SPIRIT—ONE BODY

For the grounds hereof I shall mention one only, which all others do lean upon. This is pressed, 'As the body is one, and has many members, and all the members of that one body, being many, are one body: so also is Christ. For by one Spirit we are all baptized into one body, whether we be Jews or Gentiles, whether we be bond or free; and have been all made to drink into one Spirit' (1 Cor. 12:12–13). They are all united to and hold of one head; for as are the members of the body natural, under one head, so is Christ mystical, that is, all believers, under Christ their head. And this union they have by the inhabitation of the same quickening Spirit which is in Christ their head; and by him they are brought all into the same spiritual state and frame—they are made to drink into one and the same Spirit: for this same Spirit produces the same effects in them all—the same in kind, though differing in degrees—as the apostle fully declares (Eph. 4:3–6). And this Spirit is in them, and not in the world (John 16). And as this gives them a naturalness in their duties one towards another, or in mutual caring for, rejoicing or sorrowing with, one another, as members one of another (1 Cor. 12:25–6);

so it reveals and discovers them to each other so far as is necessary for the performance of the duties mentioned, in such a manner as becomes members of the same body. There is on this account a spiritually natural answering of one to another, as face answers face in the water. They can see and discern that in others whereof they have experience in themselves—they can taste and relish that in others which they feed upon in themselves, and wherein the lives of their souls consist; the same Spirit of life being in them, they have the same spiritual taste and savour. And unless their palates are distempered by temptations, or false opinions, or prejudices, they can in their communion taste of that Spirit in each other which they are all made to drink into. This gives them the same likeness and image in the inward man, the same heavenly light in their minds, the same affections; and being thus prepared and enabled to judge and discern of the state of each other, in reference to their mutual duties, they have, moreover, the true rule of the word to judge of all spirits and spiritual effects by. And this is the ground of all that love without dissimulation and real communion that is among the saints of God in this world. But here two cautions must be allowed:

### Do Not Judge Beyond What Is Essential

That we would not judge the state and condition of any men in the world—no farther than we are called thereunto in a way of duty; and we are so called only with reference to the duties that we are to perform towards them. What have we to do to judge them that are without—that is, any one that we have not a call to consider in reference to our own duty? Herein that great rule takes place, 'Judge not, that you be not judged.' Let us leave all men, the worst of men, unless where evident duty requires other actings, to the judgment-seat of God. They are the servants of another, and they stand or fall to their own master. There have been great miscarriages amongst us in this matter; some have been ready to condemn all that go not along with them in every principle, yea, opinion or practice. And every day slight occasions and provocations are made the grounds and reasons of severe censures; but nothing is more contrary to the conduct of the meek and holy spirit of Christ. This is our rule: Are we called to act towards any as saints, as living members of the body of Christ, and that in such duties as we cannot perform in faith unless we are persuaded that so they are? Then are we, on the grounds and by the ways before mentioned, to satisfy ourselves in one another.

### Fulfill the Purpose of Judgment—to Love Fellow Believers

Do we endeavour mutually to discern the condition of one another in reference to such ends? Let us be sure to look to and pursue those ends when we have attained our satisfaction. What these ends are has been showed. It is, that we may love them without dissimulation, as members of the same mystical body with us; that we may naturally take care of them, and for them; that we may delight sincerely in them; that we may minister to their wants, temporal and spiritual; that we may watch over them with pity and compassion. These and the like are the only ends for which we are at any time called to the consideration of the spiritual condition of one another; if these be neglected, the other is useless. And here lies a great aggravation of that neglect, in that such a way is made for the avoidance of it. Here lies the life or death of all church society. All church society and relation is built on this supposition, that the members of it are all regenerate. Some lay this foundation in baptism only, professing that all that are baptized are regenerate; others require a farther satisfaction, in the real work itself; but all build on the same foundation, that all church members are to be regenerate. And to what end is this? Namely, that they may all mutually perform those duties one towards another which are incumbent mutually on regenerate persons. If these are omitted, there is an end of all profitable use of church society. Churches without this are but mere husks and shells of churches, carcasses without souls; for as there is no real union to Christ without faith, so there is no real union among the members of any church without love, and that acting itself in all the duties mentioned. Let not this ordinance be in vain.

But we must return from this digression to that which lies before us, which is concerning what a man may discern concerning his own being regenerate or born again.

## SOME DUTIES REQUIRE CERTAINTY OF REGENERATION

Secondly, men may come to an assured, satisfactory persuasion that themselves are regenerate, and that such as is so far infallible as that it will not deceive them when it is brought to the trial. For there are many duties whose performance in faith, to the glory of God and the edification of our own souls, depends on this persuasion and conviction.

### *Childlike Dependence on God*

A due sense of our relation to God, and an answerable comportment of our spirits and hearts towards him. He that is born again is born of God; he is begotten of God by the immortal seed of the word. Without a persuasion hereof, how can a man on grounds of faith carry himself towards God as his Father? And how great a part of our obedience towards him and communion with him depends hereon, we all know. If men fluctuate all their days in this matter, if they come to no settlement in it, no comfortable persuasion of it, they scarce ever act any genuine childlike acts of love or delight towards God, which exceedingly impeaches their whole obedience.

### *Thankfulness for Grace*

Thankfulness for grace received is one of the principal duties that is incumbent on believers in this world. Now, how can a man in faith bless God for that which he is utterly uncertain whether he have received it from him or no? I know some men run on in a rote in this matter. They will bless God in a formal way for regeneration, sanctification, justification, and the like; but if you ask them whether themselves are regenerate or no, they will be ready to scoff at it, or at least to profess that they know no such thing.

What is this but to mock God, and in a presumptuous manner to take his name in vain? But if we will praise God as we ought for his grace, as we are guided and directed in the Scripture, as the nature of the matter requires, with such a frame of heart as may influence our whole obedience, surely it cannot but be our duty to know the grace that we have received.

### The Pursuit of Godliness

Again: the main of our spiritual watch and diligence consists in the cherishing, improving, and increasing of the grace that we have received, the strengthening of the new creature that is wrought in us. Herein consists principally the life of faith, and the exercise of that spiritual wisdom which faith furnishes the soul withal. Now, how can any man apply himself hereunto whilst he is altogether uncertain whether he has received any principle of living, saving grace, or no? Whereas, therefore, God requires our utmost diligence, watchfulness, and care in this matter it is certain that he requires also of us, and grants to us, that which is the foundation of all these duties, which lies in an acquaintance with that state and condition whereunto we do belong. In brief, there is nothing we have to do, in reference to eternity, but one way or other it has a respect to our light and convictions, as to our state and condition in this world; and those who are negligent in the trial and examination thereof do leave all things between God and their souls at absolute uncertainties and dubious hazards, which is not to lead the life of faith.

#### RULES FOR DEALING WITH DOUBTS OF REGENERATION

We shall now, upon these premises, return to that part of the objection which is under consideration. Say some, 'We know not whether we are regenerate or no, and are therefore altogether uncertain whether we have an interest in that forgiveness that is with God; nor dare we, on that account, admit of the consolation that is tendered on the truth insisted on.'

Supposing what has been spoken in general, I shall lay down the grounds of resolving this perplexing doubt in the ensuing rules.

## I. Do not Seek Extraordinary Assurance

See that the persuasion and assurance hereof which you look after and desire be regular, and not such as is suited merely to your own imaginations. Our second and third general rules about the nature of all spiritual assurance, and what is consistent therewithal, are here to be taken into consideration. If you look to have such an evidence, light into, and absolute conviction of, this matter, as shall admit of no doubts, fears, questionings, just occasions and causes of new trials, teachings, and self-examinations, you will be greatly deceived. Regeneration induces a new principle into the soul, but it does not utterly expel the old; some would have security, not assurance. The principle of sin and unbelief will still abide in us, and still work in us. Their abiding and their acting must needs put the soul upon a severe inquiry, whether they are not prevalent in it beyond what the condition of regeneration will admit. The constant conflicts we must have with sin will not suffer us to have always so clear an evidence of our condition as we would desire. Such a persuasion as is prevalent against strong objections to the contrary, keeping up the heart to a due performance of those duties in faith which belong to the state of regeneration, is the substance of what in this kind you are to look after.

## II. Do not Seek Immediate Assurance from the Spirit

If you are doubtful concerning your state and condition, do not expect an extraordinary determination of it by an immediate testimony of the Spirit of God. I do grant that God does sometimes, by this means, bring in peace and satisfaction to the soul. He gives his own Spirit immediately 'to bear witness with ours that we are the children of God,' both upon the account of regeneration and adoption. He does so; but, as far as we can observe, in a way of sovereignty, when and to whom he pleases. Besides, that men may content and satisfy themselves with his ordinary teachings, consolations, and communications of his grace, he has left the nature of that peculiar testimony of the Spirit very dark and difficult to be found out, few agreeing wherein it consists or what is the nature of it. No one man's experience is a rule to others, and an undue apprehension of it is a matter of great danger. Yet it is certain that humble souls in extraordinary cases may have recourse to it with benefit and relief thereby. This, then, you may desire, you may pray for, but not with such a frame of spirit as to refuse that other satisfaction which in the ways of truth and peace you may find. This is the putting of the hand into the side of Christ; but 'blessed are they that have not seen, and yet have believed.'

### III. Remember Past Pledges from God

If you have at any time formerly received any especial or immediate pledge or testimony of God, given to your souls as to their sincerity, and consequently their regeneration, labour to recover it, and to revive a sense of it upon your spirits now in your darkness and trouble. I am persuaded there are but few believers, but that God does, at one time or other, in one duty or other, entering into or coming out of one temptation or another, give some singular testimony to their own souls and consciences concerning their sincerity and his acceptance of them. Sometimes he does this in a duty, wherein he has enabled the soul to make so near an approach to him as that it has been warmed, enlivened, sweetened, satisfied with the presence, the gracious presence, of God, and which God has made to him as a token of his uprightness; sometimes, when a man is entering into any great temptation, trial, difficult or dangerous duty, that death itself is feared in it, God comes in, by one means or other, by a secret intimation of his love, which he gives him to take along with him for his furniture and provision in his way, and thereby testifies to him his sincerity; and this serves, like the food of Elijah, for forty days in a wilderness condition; sometimes he is pleased to shine immediately into the soul in the midst of its darkness and sorrow; wherewith it is surprised, as not looking for any such expression of kindness, and is thereby relieved against its own pressing self-condemnation; – and sometimes the Lord is pleased to give these tokens of love to the soul as its refreshment, when it is coming off from the storm of temptations wherewith it has been tossed. And many other times and seasons there are wherein God is pleased to give to believers some especial testimony in their consciences to their own integrity. But now these are all wrought by a transient operation of the Spirit, exciting and enabling the heart to a spiritual, sensible apprehension and receiving of God's expressing kindness towards it. These things abide not in their sense and in their power which they have upon our affections, but immediately pass away. They are, therefore, to be treasured up in the mind and judgment, to be improved and made use of by faith, as occasion shall require. But we are apt to lose them. Most know no other use of them but whilst they feel them; yea, through ignorance in our duty to improve them, they prove like a sudden light brought into a dark place and again removed, which seems to increase, and really aggravates, our sense of the darkness. The true use of them is, to lay them up and ponder them in our hearts, that they may be supports and testimonies to us in a time of need. Have you, then, who are now in the dark as to your state or condition, whether you are regenerate or no, ever received any such refreshing and cheering testimony from God given to your integrity, and your acceptance with him thereupon? Call it over again, and make use of it against those discouragements which arise from your present darkness in this matter, and which keep you off from sharing in the consolation tendered to you in this word of grace.

### IV. Consider the Causes and Effects of Regeneration

A due spiritual consideration of the causes and effects of regeneration is the ordinary way and means whereby the souls of believers come to be satisfied concerning that work of God in them and upon them. The principle or causes of this work are, the Spirit and the word. He that is born again, 'is born of the Spirit' (John 3:6);

and of the word, 'Of his own will begat he us with the word of truth' (James 1:18); 'We are born again by the word of God, which lives and abides for ever' (1 Pet. 1:23). Wherever, then, a man is regenerate, there has been an effectual work of the Spirit and of the word upon the soul. This is to be inquired into and after. Ordinarily it will discover itself. Such impressions will be made in it upon the soul, such a change will be wrought and produced in it, as will not escape a spiritual diligent search and inquiry. And this is much of the duty of such as are in the dark, and uncertain concerning the accomplishment of this work in themselves. Let them call to mind what have been the actings of the Spirit by the word upon their souls; what light thereby has been communicated to their minds; what discoveries of the Lord Christ and way of salvation have been made to them; what sense and detestation of sin have been wrought in them; what satisfaction has been given to the soul, to choose, accept, and acquiesce in the righteousness of Christ; what resignation of the heart to God, according to the tenor of the covenant of grace, it has been wrought to. Call to mind what transactions there have been between God and your souls about these things; how far they have been carried on; whether you have broken off the treaty with God, and refused his terms, or if not, where the stay is between you; and what is the reason, since God has graciously begun to deal thus with you, that you are not yet come to a thorough close with him in the work and design of his grace? The defect must of necessity lie on your parts God does nothing in vain. Had he not been willing to receive you, he would not have dealt with you so far as he has done. There is nothing, then, remains to firm your condition but a resolved act of your own wills in answering the mind and will of God. And by this search may the soul come to satisfaction in this matter, or at least find out and discover where the stick is whence their uncertainty arises, and what is wanting to complete their desire.

Again: this work may be discovered by its effects. There is something that is produced by it in the soul, which may also be considered either with respect to its being and existence, or to its actings and operations. In the first regard it is spirit: 'That which is born of the Spirit' (John 3:6) which is produced by the effectual operation of the Spirit of God, it 'is spirit'—'a new creature' (2 Cor. 5:17). He that is in Christ Jesus, who is born again, is a new creature, a new life, a spiritual life (Gal. 2:20; Eph. 2:1). In brief, it is an habitual furnishment of all the faculties of the soul with new spiritual, vital principles, enabling a person in all instances of obedience to lead a spiritual life to God. This principle is by this work produced in the soul. And in respect of its actings, it consists in all the gracious operations of the mind, will, heart, or affections, in the duties of obedience which God has required of us. This is that which gives life to our duties (without which the best of our works are but dead works), and renders them acceptable to the living God. It is not my business at large to pursue and declare these things; I only mention them, that persons who are kept back from a participation of the consolation tendered from the forgiveness that is with God, because they cannot comfortably conclude that they are born again, as knowing that it is such persons alone to whom these consolations do truly and really belong, may know how to make a right judgment of themselves. Let such persons, then, not fluctuate up and down in generals and uncertainties, with heartless complaints, which is the ruin of the peace of their souls; but let them really put things to the trial, by the examination of the causes and effects of the work they inquire after. It is by the use of such means whereby God will be pleased to give them all the assurance and establishment concerning their state and condition which is needful for them, and which may give them encouragement in their course of obedience.

But supposing all that has been spoken, what if a man, by the utmost search and inquiry that he is able to make, cannot attain any satisfactory persuasion that indeed this great work of God's grace has passed upon his soul; is this a sufficient ground to keep him off from accepting of support and consolation from this truth, that there is forgiveness with God? which is the design of the objection laid down before.

## Regeneration Does not Occur Before Forgiveness

I say therefore farther, that, regeneration does not in order of time precede the soul's interest in the forgiveness that is with God, or its being made partaker of the pardon of sin. I say no more but that it does not precede it in order of time, not determining which has precedency in order of nature. That, I confess, which the method of the gospel leads to is, that absolution, acquitment, or the pardon of sin, is the foundation of the communication of all saving grace to the soul, and so precedes all grace in the sinner whatever. But because this absolution or pardon of sin is to be received by faith, whereby the soul is really made partaker of it and all the benefits belonging thereunto, and that faith is the radical grace which we receive in our regeneration—for it is by faith that our hearts are purified, as an instrument in the hand of the great purifier, the Spirit of God—I place these two together, and shall not dispute as to their priority in nature; but in time the one does not precede the other.

## Assurance of Regeneration Is not a Prerequesite to Believing

It is hence evident, that an assurance of being regenerate is no way previously necessary to the believing of an interest in forgiveness; so that although a man have not the former, it is, or may be, his duty to endeavour the latter. When convinced persons cried out, 'What shall we do to be saved?' the answer was, 'Believe, and you shall be so.' 'Believe in Christ, and in the remission of sin by his blood,' is the first thing that convinced sinners are called to. They are not directed first to secure their souls that they are born again, and then afterward to believe; but they are first to believe that the remission of sin is tendered to them in the blood of Christ, and that 'by him they may be justified from all things from which they could not be justified by the law.' Nor upon this proposition is it the duty of men to question whether they have faith or no, but actually to believe. And faith in its operation will evidence itself (see Acts 13:38–9). Suppose, then, that you do not know that you are regenerate, that you are born of God—that you have no prevailing, refreshing, constant evidence or persuasion thereof—should this hinder you? Should this discourage you from believing forgiveness, from closing with the promises, and thereby obtaining in yourselves an interest in that forgiveness that is with God? Not at all; nay, this ought exceedingly to excite and stir you up to your duty herein:

1. Suppose that it is otherwise—that, indeed, you are yet in the state of sin, and are only brought under the power of light and conviction—this is the way for a translation into an estate of spiritual life and grace. If you will forbear the acting of faith upon and for forgiveness until you are regenerate, you may, and probably you will, come short both of forgiveness and regeneration also. Here lay your foundation, and then your building will go on. This will open the door to you, and give you an entrance into the kingdom of God. Christ is the door; do not think to climb up over the wall; enter by him, or you will be kept out.

2. Suppose that you are born again, but yet know it not—as is the condition of many—this is a way whereby you may receive an evidence thereof. It is good, the embracing of all signs, tokens, and pledges of our spiritual condition, and it is so to improve them; but the best course is, to follow the genuine natural actings of faith, which will lead us into the most settled apprehensions concerning our relation to God and acceptance with him. Believe first the forgiveness of sin as the effect of mere grace and mercy in Christ. Let the faith hereof be nourished and strengthened in your souls. This will insensibly influence your hearts into a comforting gospel persuasion of your state and condition towards God; which will be accompanied with assured rest and peace.

To wind up this discourse. Remember that that which has been spoken with reference to the state of regeneration in general may be applied to every particular objection or cause of fear and discouragement that may be reduced to that head. Such are all objections that arise from particular sins, from aggravations of sins by their greatness or circumstances, or relapses into them. The way that the consideration of these things prevails upon the mind to fear, is by begetting an apprehension in men that they are not regenerate; for if they were, they suppose they could not be so overtaken or entangled. The rules thereof laid down are suited to the straits of the souls of sinners in all such particular cases.

### 'I Have no Conversion Story'

Lastly, there was somewhat in particular added in the close of the objection, which, although it be not directly in our way nor of any great importance in itself, yet having been mentioned, it is not unmeet to remove it out of the way, that it may not leave entanglement upon the minds of any. Now this is, that some know not nor can give an account of the time of their conversion to God, and therefore cannot be satisfied that the saving work of his grace has passed upon them. This is usually and ordinarily spoken to; and I shall therefore briefly give an account concerning it

CONSIDER ALL THE EVIDENCE. It has been showed that, in this matter, there are many things whereon we may regularly found a judgment concerning ourselves, and it is great folly to waive them all, and put the issue of the matter upon one circumstance. If a man have a trial at law, wherein he has many evidences speaking for him, only one circumstance is dubious and in question, he will not cast the weight of his cause on that disputed circumstance, but will plead those evidences that are more clear and testify more fully in his behalf. I will not deny but that this matter of the time of conversion is ofttimes an important circumstance—in the affirmative, when it is known, it is of great use, tending to stability and consolation; but yet it is still but a circumstance, such as that the being of the thing itself does not depend upon. He that is alive may know that he was born, though he know neither the place where nor the time when he was so; and so may he that is spiritually alive, and has ground of evidence that he is so, that he was born again, though he know neither when, nor where, nor how. And this case is usual in persons of quiet natural tempers, who have had the advantage of education under means of light and grace. God ofttimes, in such persons, begins and carries on the work of his grace insensibly, so that they come to good growth and maturity before they know that they are alive. Such persons come at length to be satisfied in saying, with the blind man in the gospel, 'How our eyes were opened we know not; only one thing we know, whereas we were blind by nature, now we see.'

LIVE BY FAITH. Even in this matter also, we must, it may be, be content to live by faith, and to believe as well what God has done in us, if it be the matter and subject of his promises, as what he has done for us; the ground whereof also is the promise, and nothing else.

### INNER TURMOIL OVER A SENSE OF SPIRITUAL POVERTY

Thirdly, there is another head of objections against the soul's receiving consolation from an interest in forgiveness, arising from the consideration of its present state and condition as to actual holiness, duties, and sins. Souls complain, when in darkness and under temptations, that they cannot find that holiness, nor those fruits of it in themselves, which they suppose an interest in pardoning mercy will produce. Their hearts they find are weak, and all their duties worthless. If they were weighed in the balance, they would be all found too light. In the best of them there is such a mixture of self, hypocrisy, unbelief, vain-glory, that they are even ashamed and confounded with the remembrance of them. These things fill them with discouragements, so that they refuse to be comforted or to entertain any refreshing persuasion from the truth insisted on, but rather conclude that they are utter strangers from that forgiveness that is with God, and so continue helpless in their depths.

According to the method proposed, and hitherto pursued, I shall only lay down some such general rules as may support a soul under the despondencies that are apt in such a condition to befall it, that none of these things may weaken it in its endeavour to lay hold of forgiveness.

## ADD ONE GRACE TO ANOTHER

And this is the proper place to put in execution our eighth rule, to take heed of heartless complaints when vigorous actings of grace are expected at our hands. If it be thus, indeed, why lie you on your faces? Why do you not rise and put out yourselves to the utmost, giving all diligence to add one grace to another, until you find yourselves in a better frame? Supposing, then, the putting of that rule into practice, I add:

### Know Holiness Tends to Self-righteousness

That known holiness is apt to degenerate into self-righteousness. What God gives us on the account of sanctification we are ready enough to reckon on the score of justification. It is a hard thing to feel grace, and to believe as if there were none. We have so much of the Pharisee in us by nature, that it is sometimes well that our good is hid from us. We are ready to take our corn and wine and bestow them on other lovers. Were there not in our hearts a spiritually sensible principle of corruption, and in our duties a discernible mixture of self, it would be impossible we should walk so humbly as is required of them who hold communion with God in a covenant of grace and pardoning mercy. It is a good life which is attended with a faith of righteousness and a sense of corruption. Whilst I know Christ's righteousness, I shall the less care to know my own holiness. To be holy is necessary; to know it, sometimes a temptation.

### God Abhors Duties Turned into Self-righteousness

Even duties of God's appointment, when turned into self-righteousness, are God's great abhorrency (Isa. 66:2–3). What has a good original may be vitiated by a bad end.

## *Holiness Is Known by Its Opposition*

Oftentimes holiness in the heart is more known by the opposition that is made there to it, than by its own prevalent working. The Spirit's operation is known by the flesh's opposition. We find a man's strength by the burdens he carries, and not the pace that he goes. 'O wretched man that I am! Who shall deliver me from the body of this death?' is a better evidence of grace and holiness than 'God, I thank you I am not as other men.' a heart pressed, grieved, burdened, not by the guilt of sin only, which reflects with trouble on an awakened conscience, but by the close, adhering power of indwelling sin, tempting, seducing, soliciting, hindering, captivating, conceiving, restlessly disquieting, may from thence have as clear an evidence of holiness as from a delightful fruit-bearing. What is it that is troubled and grieved in you? What is it that seems to be almost killed and destroyed; that cries out, complains, longs for deliverance? Is it not the new creature? Is it not the principle of spiritual life, whereof you are partaker? I speak not of troubles and disquietments for sin committed; nor of fears and perturbations of mind lest sin should break forth to loss, shame, ruin, dishonour; nor of the contending of a convinced conscience lest damnation should ensue; but of the striving of the Spirit against sin, out of a hatred and a loathing of it, upon all the mixed considerations of love, grace, mercy, fear, the beauty of holiness, excellency of communion with God, that are proposed in the gospel. If you seem to yourself to be only passive in these things, to do nothing but to endure the assaults of sin; yet if you are sensible, and stand under the stroke of it as under the stroke of an enemy, there is the root of the matter. And as it is thus as to the substance and being of holiness, so it is also as to the degrees of it. Degrees of holiness are to be measured more by opposition than self-operation. He may have more grace than another who brings not forth so much fruit as the other, because he has more opposition, more temptation (Isa. 41:17). And sense of the want of all is a great sign of somewhat in the soul.

## MORE SPIRITUAL MEN SEE THEIR UNSPIRITUALNESS MORE

As to what was alleged as to the nothingness, the selfishness of duty, I say, it is certain, whilst we are in the flesh, our duties will taste of the vessel whence they proceed. Weakness, defilements, treachery, hypocrisy, will attend them. To this purpose, whatever some pretend to the contrary, is the complaint of the church (Isa. 64:6). The chaff oftentimes is so mixed with the wheat that corn can scarce be discerned. And this know, that the more spiritual any man is, the more he sees of his unspiritualness in his spiritual duties. An outside performance will satisfy an outside Christian. Job abhorred himself most when he knew himself best. The clearer discoveries we have had of God, the viler will every thing of self appear. Nay, farther, duties and performances are oftentimes very ill measured by us; and those seem to be first which indeed are last, and those to be last which indeed are first. I do not doubt but a man, when he has had distractions to wrestle withal, no outward advantage to farther him, no extraordinary provocation of hope, fear, or sorrow, on a natural account in his duty, may rise from his knees with thoughts that he has done nothing in his duty but provoked God; when there has been more workings of grace, in contending with the deadness cast on the soul by the condition that it is in, than when, by a concurrence of moved natural affections and outward provocations, a frame has been raised that has, to the party himself, seemed to reach to heaven: so that it may be this perplexity about duties is nothing but what is common to the people of God, and which ought to be no obstruction to peace and settlement.

### HYPOCRISY

As to the pretence of hypocrisy, you know what is usually answered. It is one thing to do a thing in hypocrisy, another not to do it without a mixture of hypocrisy. Hypocrisy, in its long extent, is every thing that, for matter or manner, comes short of sincerity. Now, our sincerity is no more perfect than our other graces; so that in its measure it abides with us and adheres to all we do. In like manner, it is one thing to do a thing for vain-glory and to be seen of men, another not to be able wholly to keep off the subtle insinuations of self and vain-glory. He that does a thing in hypocrisy and for vain-glory is satisfied with some corrupt end obtained, though he be sensible that he sought such an end. He that does a thing with a mixture of hypocrisy—that is, with some breaches upon the degrees of his sincerity, with some insensible advancements in performance on outward considerations—is not satisfied with a self-end obtained, and is dissatisfied with the defect of his sincerity. In a word, would you yet be sincere, and endeavour so to be in private duties, and in public performances—in praying, hearing, giving alms, zealous actings for God's glory and the love of the saints; though these duties are not, it may be, sometimes done without sensible hypocrisy—I mean, as traced to its most subtle insinuations of self and vain-glory—yet are they not done in hypocrisy, nor do they denominate the persons by whom they are performed hypocrites. Yet I say of this, as of all that is spoken before, it is of use to relieve us under a troubled condition—of none to support us or encourage us to an abode in it.

## God Does not Despise Small Things

Know that God despises not small things. He takes notice of the least breathings of our hearts after him, when we ourselves can see nor perceive no such thing. He knows the mind of the Spirit in those workings which are never formed to that height that we can reflect upon them with our observation. Every thing that is of him is noted in his book, though not in ours. He took notice that, when Sarah was acting unbelief towards him, yet that she showed respect and regard to her husband, calling him 'lord' (Gen. 18:12; 1 Pet. 3:6). And even whilst his people are sinning, he can find something in their hearts, words, or ways, that pleases him; much more in their duties. He is a skilful refiner, that can find much gold in that ore where we see nothing but lead or clay. He remembers the duties which we forget, and forgets the sins which we remember. He justifies our persons, though ungodly; and will also our duties, though not perfectly godly.

### CHRIST MAKES OUR LITTLE A GREAT DEAL

To give a little farther support in reference to our wretched, miserable duties, and to them that are in perplexities on that account, know that Jesus Christ takes whatever is evil and unsavoury out of them, and makes them acceptable. When an unskilful servant gathers many herbs, flowers, and weeds in a garden, you gather them out that are useful, and cast the rest out of sight. Christ deals so with our performances. All the ingredients of self that are in them on any account he takes away, and adds incense to what remains, and presents it to God (Exod. 30:36). This is the cause that the saints at the last day, when they meet their own duties and performances, they know them not, they are so changed from what they were when they went out of their hand. 'Lord, when saw we you naked or hungry?' So that God accepts a little, and Christ makes our little a great deal.

### BELIEVE NOW TO OBEY NOW

Is this an argument to keep you from believing? The reason why you are no more holy is because you have no more faith. If you have no holiness, it is because you have no faith. Holiness is the purifying of the heart by faith, or our obedience to the truth. And the reason why you are no more in duty is, because you are no more in believing. The reason why your duties are weak and imperfect is, because your faith is weak and imperfect. Have you no holiness? Believe, that you may have. Have you but a little, or that which is imperceptible? Be steadfast in believing, that you may abound in obedience. Do not resolve not to eat your meat until you are strong, when you have no means of being strong but by eating your bread, which strengthens the heart of man.

## THE POWER OF INDWELLING SIN

The powerful tumultuating of indwelling sin or corruption is another cause of the same kind of trouble and despondency. "'They that are Christ's have crucified the flesh with the lusts thereof.' But we find,' say some, 'several corruptions working effectually in our hearts, carrying us captive to the law of sin. They disquiet with their power as well as with their guilt. Had we been made partakers of the law of the Spirit of life, we had, ere this, been more set free from the law of sin and death. Had sin been pardoned fully, it would have been subdued more effectually.'

There are three considerations which make the actings of indwelling sin to be so perplexing to the soul.

### UNEXPECTED

Because they are unexpected. The soul looks not for them upon the first great conquest made of sin, and universal engagement of the heart to God. When it first says, 'I have sworn, and am steadfastly purposed to keep your righteous judgments,' commonly there is peace, at least for a season, from the disturbing vigorous actings of sin. There are many reasons why so it should be. 'Old things are then passed away, all things are become new;' and the soul, under the power of that universal change, is utterly turned away from those things that should foment, stir up, provoke, or cherish, any lust or temptation. Now, when some of these advantages are past, and sin begins to stir and act again, the soul is surprised, and thinks the work that he has passed through was not true and effectual, but temporary only; yea, he thinks, perhaps, that sin has more strength than it had before, because he is more sensible than he was before. As one that has a dead arm or limb, whilst it is mortified, endures deep cuts and lancings, and feels them not; so when spirits and sense are brought into the place again, he feels the least cut, and may think the instruments sharper than they were before, when all the difference is, that he has got a quickness of sense, which before he had not. It may be so with a person in this case: he may think lust more powerful than it was before, because he is more sensible than he was before. Yea, sin in the heart is like a snake or serpent: you may pull out the sting of it, and cut it into many pieces; though it can sting mortally no more, nor move its whole body at once, yet it will move in all its parts, and make an appearance of a greater motion than formerly. So it is with lust: when it has received its death's wound, and is cut to pieces, yet it moves in so many parts as it were in the soul, that it amazes him that has to do with it; and thus coming unexpectedly, fills the spirit oftentimes with disconsolation.

## UNIVERSAL

It has also in its actings a universality. This also surprises. There is a universality in the actings of sin, even in believers. There is no evil that it will not move to; there is no good that it will not attempt to hinder; no duty that it will not defile. And the reason of this is, because we are sanctified but in part; not in any part wholly, though savingly and truly in every part. There is sin remaining in every faculty, in all the affections, and so may be acting in and towards any sin that the nature of man is liable to. Degrees of sin there are that all regenerate persons are exempted from; but to solicitations to all kinds of sin they are exposed: and this helps on the temptation.

## ENDLESS

It is endless and restless, never quiet, conquering nor conquered; it gives not over, but rebels being overcome, or assaults afresh having preveiled. Ofttimes after a victory obtained and an opposition subdued, the soul is in expectation of rest and peace from its enemies: but this holds not; it works and rebels again and again, and will do so whilst we live in this world, so that no issue will be put to our conflict but by death. This is at large handled elsewhere, in a treatise lately published on this peculiar subject.

These and the like considerations attending the actings of indwelling sin, oftentimes entangle the soul in making a judgment of itself, and leave it in the dark as to its state and condition.

## NOT INCONSISTENT WITH GRACE

A few things shall be offered to this objection also. The sensible powerful actings of indwelling sin are not inconsistent with a state of grace (Gal. 5:17). There are in the same person contrary principles—'the flesh and the Spirit' these are contrary. And there are contrary actings from these principles—'the flesh lusts against the Spirit, and the Spirit against the flesh;' and these actings are described to be greatly vigorous in other places. Lust wars against our souls (James 4:1; 1 Pet. 2:11). Now, to war is not to make faint or gentle opposition, to be slighted and contemned; but it is to go out with great strength, to use craft, subtlety, and force, so as to put the whole issue to a hazard. So these lusts war; such are their actings in and against the soul. And therefore, says the apostle, 'You cannot do the things that you would' (see Rom. 7:14–17). In this conflict, indeed, the understanding is left unconquered—it condemns and disapproves of the evil led to; and the will is not subdued—it would not do the evil that is pressed upon it; and there is a hatred or aversion remaining in the affections to sin: but yet, notwithstanding, sin rebels, fights, tumultuates, and leads captive. This objection, then, may receive this speedy answer—Powerful actings and workings, universal, endless strugglings of indwelling sin, seducing to all that is evil, putting itself forth to the disturbance and dissettlement of all that is good, are not sufficient ground to conclude a state of alienation from God. See for this the other treatise before mentioned at large.

## YOUR OPPOSITION TO SIN IS THE MEASURE

Your state is not at all to be measured by the opposition that sin makes to you, but by the opposition you make to it. Be that never so great, if this be good—be that never so restless and powerful, if this be sincere—you may be disquieted, you can have no reason to despond.

I have mentioned these things only to give a specimen of the objections which men usually raise up against an actual closing with the truth insisted on to their consolation. And we have also given in upon them some rules of truth for their relief; not intending in them absolute satisfaction as to the whole of the cases mentioned, but only to remove the darkness raised by them so out of the way, as that it might not hinder any from mixing the word with faith that has been dispensed from this blessed testimony, that 'there is forgiveness with God, that he may be feared.'

# 8

## MY SOUL WAITS

---

5 I wait for the LORD,
my soul waits,
and in his word do I hope.
6 My soul waits for the Lord
more than they that watch for the morning:
I say, more than they
that watch for the morning.

Proceed we now to the second part of this psalm, which contains the deportment of a sin-perplexed soul, when by faith it has discovered where its rest lies, and from whom its relief is to be expected; even from the forgiveness which is with God, whereof we have spoken.

There are two things in general, as was before mentioned, that the soul in that condition applies itself to; whereof the first respects itself, and the other the whole Israel of God.

That which respects itself is the description of that frame of heart and spirit that he was brought into upon faith's discovery of forgiveness in God, with the duties that he applied himself to, the grounds of it, and the manner of its performance: 'I wait for the

LORD, my soul waits, and in his word do I hope. My soul waits for the Lord more than they that watch for the morning: I say, more than they that watch for the morning' (Ps. 130:5–6)

Herein, I say, he describes both his frame of spirit and the duty he applied himself to, both as to matter and manner.

I shall, as in the method hitherto observed, first consider the reading of the words, then their sense and importance, with the suitableness of the things mentioned in them to the condition of the soul under consideration; all which yield us a foundation of the observations that are to be drawn from them.

The words rendered strictly, or word for word, lie thus: 'I have earnestly expected Jehovah; my soul has expected, and in his word have I tarried,' or waited. 'My soul to the Lord more than' (or before) 'the watchmen in the morning; the watchmen in the morning,' or 'unto the morning.'

'I have waited' or 'expected:' קִוִּיתִי from קָוָה, 'to expect,' 'to hope,' 'to wait.' *Verbum hoc est, magno animi desiderio in allquem intenturn esse, et respicere ad eum, ex eo pendere*—'The word denotes to be intent on any one with great desire; to behold or regard him, and to depend upon him;' and it also expresses the earnest inclination and intention of the will and mind.

Paul seems to have expressed this word to the full by ἀποκαραδοκία (Rom. 8:19), an intent or earnest expectation, expressing itself by putting forth the head, and looking round about with earnestness and diligence. And this is also signified expressly by this word, וָאֲקַוֶּה לָנוּד—'And I looked for some to take pity' (Ps. 69:21). *'Huc illuc anxie circumspexi, siquis forte me commiseraturus esset'*—'I looked round about, this way and that way, diligently and solicitously, to see if any would pity me or lament with me.'

Thus, 'I have waited,' is as much as, 'I have diligently, with intension of soul, mind, will, and affections, looked to God, in earnest expectation of that from him that I stand in need of, and which must come forth from the forgiveness that is with him.'

'I have,' says he, 'waited for, or expected Jehovah.' He uses the same name of God in his expectation that he first fixed on in his application to him.

And it is not this or that means, not this or that assistance, but it is Jehovah himself that he expects and waits for. It is Jehovah himself that must satisfy the soul—his favour and loving-kindness, and what flows from them; if he come not himself, if he give not himself, nothing else will relieve.

'My soul waits,' or expects—'It is no outward duty that I am at, no lip-labour, no bodily work, no formal, cold, careless performance of a duty. No; "my soul waits." It is soul-work, heart-work I am at. I wait, I wait with my whole soul.'

'In His words do I hope,' or 'Wait.' There is not any thing of difficulty in these words. The word used, הוֹחָלְתִּי, is from יָחַל, 'sunt qui, quod affine sit verbo' חָלַל, 'velint anxietatem et nisum includere, ut significet anxie, seu enixe expectare, sustinere, et sperare.' It signifies to hope, expect, endure, and sustain with care, solicitousness, and endeavours. Hence the LXX have rendered the word by ὑπέμεινεν, and the Vulgar Latin 'sustinui'—' I have sustained and waited with patience.'

And this on the word; or, he sustained his soul with the word of promise that it should not utterly faint, seeing he had made a discovery of grace and forgiveness, though yet at a great distance; he had a sight of land, though he was yet in a storm at sea; and therefore encourages himself, or his soul, that it does not despond.

But yet all this that we have spoken reaches not the intenseness of the soul of the psalmist, in this his expectation of Jehovah. The earnest engagement of his soul in this duty rises up above what he can express. Therefore he proceeds, verse 6: 'My soul,' says he, 'waits for the Lord' (that is, expects him, looks for him, waits for him, waits for his coming to me in love and with forgiveness), 'more than the watchers for the morning, the watchers for the morning.'

These latter words are variously rendered, and variously expounded. The LXX and Vulgar Latin render them, 'From the morning watch until night;' others, 'From those that keep the morning watch, to those that keep the evening watch;' 'More than the watchers in the morning, more than the watchers in the morning.' The words also are variously expounded. Augstine would have it to signify the placing of our hopes on the morning of Christ's resurrection, and continuing in them until the night of our own death.

Jerome, who renders the words, 'From the morning watch to the morning watch,' expounds them of continuing our hopes and expectations from the morning that we are called into the Lord's vineyard to the morning when we shall receive our reward; as much to the sense of the place as the former. And so Chrysostom interprets it of our whole life.

It cannot be denied but that they were led into these mistakes by the translation of the LXX and that of the Vulgar Latin, who both of them have divided these words quite contrary to their proper dependence, and read them thus, 'My soul expected the Lord. From the morning watch to the night watch, let Israel trust in the Lord;' so making the words to belong to the following exhortation to others, which are plainly a part of the expression of his own duty.

The words, then, are a comparison, and an allusion to watchmen, and may be taken in one of these two senses:

1. In things civil, as those who keep the watch of the night do look, and long for, and expect the morning, when, being dismissed from their guard, they may take that sleep that they need and desire; which expresses a very earnest expectation, inquiry, and desire.
2. Or, in things sacred, with the Chaldee paraphrast, which renders the words, 'More than they that look for the morning watch,' which they carefully observe, that they may offer the morning sacrifice. In this sense, 'As,' says he, 'the warders and watchers in the temple do look diligently after the appearance of the morning, that they may with joy offer the morning sacrifice in the appointed season; so, and with more diligence, does my soul wait for Jehovah.'

You see the reading of the words, and how far the sense of them opens itself to us by that consideration.

Let us, then, next see briefly the several parts of them, as they stand in relation one to another. We have, then:

1. The expression of the duty wherein he was exercised; and that is, earnest waiting for Jehovah.
2. The bottom and foundation of that his waiting and expectation; that is, the word of God, the word of promise—he diligently hoped in the word.
3. The frame of his spirit in, and the manner of his performance of, this duty; expressed: (1.) In the words themselves that he uses, according as we opened them before. (2.) In the emphatical reduplication, yea, triplecation of his expression of it: 'I wait for the LORD;' 'My soul waits for God;' 'My soul waits for the Lord.' (3.) In the comparison instituted between his discharge of his duty and others' performances of a corporal watch—with the greatest care and diligence: 'More than they that watch for the morning.'

So that we have:

1. The duty he performed—earnest waiting and expectation.
2. The object of his waiting—Jehovah himself.
3. His support in that duty—the word of promise.
4. The manner of his performance of it: (1.) With earnestness and diligence. (2.) With perseverance.

Let us, then, now consider the words as they contain the frame and working of a sin-entangled soul.

Having been raised out of his depths by the discovery of forgiveness in God, as was before declared, yet not being immediately made partaker of that forgiveness, as to a comforting sense of it, he gathers up his soul from wandering from God, and supports it from sinking under his present condition.

'It is,' says he, 'Jehovah alone, with whom is forgiveness, that can relieve and do me good. His favour, his loving-kindness, his communication of mercy and grace from thence, is that which I stand in need of. On him, therefore, do I with all heedfulness attend; on him do I wait. My soul is filled with expectation from him. Surely he will come to me, he will come and refresh me.

Though he seem as yet to be afar off, and to leave me in these depths, yet I have his word of promise to support and stay my soul; on which I will lean until I obtain the enjoyment of him, and his kindness which is better than life.'

And this is the frame of a sin-entangled soul who has really by faith discovered forgiveness in God, but is not yet made partaker of a comforting, refreshing sense of it. And we may represent it in the ensuing observations:

1. The first proper fruit of faith's discovery of forgiveness in God, to a sin-distressed soul, is waiting in patience and expectation.
2. The proper object of a sin-distressed soul's waiting and expecting is God himself, as reconciled in Christ: 'I have waited for Jehovah.'
3. The word of promise is the soul's great support in waiting for God: 'In your word do I hope.'
4. Sin-distressed souls wait for God with earnest intension of mind, diligence, and expectation—from the redoubling of the expression.
5. Continuance in waiting until God appears to the soul is necessary and prevailing—necessary, as that without which we cannot attain assistance; and prevailing, as that wherein we shall never fail.
6. Establishment in waiting, when there is no present sense of forgiveness, yet gives the soul much secret rest and comfort. This observation arises from the influence that these verses have to those that follow. The psalmist, having attained thus far, can now look about him and begin to deal with others, and exhort them to an expectation of grace and mercy.

And thus, though the soul be not absolutely in the haven of consolation where it would be, yet it has cast out an anchor that gives it establishment and security. Though it be yet tossed, yet it is secured from shipwreck, and is rather sick than in danger. a waiting condition is a condition of safety.

Hence it is that he now turns himself to others; and upon the experience of the discovery that he had made of forgiveness in God, and the establishment and consolation he found in waiting on him, he calls upon and encourages others to the same duty (v. 7–8).

The propositions laid down I shall briefly pass through, still with respect to the state and condition of the soul represented in the psalm. Many things that might justly be insisted on in the improvement of these truths have been anticipated in our former general rules. To them we must therefore sometimes have recourse, because they must not be again repeated. On this account, I say, we shall pass through them with all briefness possible; yet so as not wholly to omit any directions that are here tendered to us as to the guidance of the soul, whose condition, and the working of whose faith, is here described. This, therefore, in the first place is proposed.

## 'I WAIT...'

The first proper fruit of faith's discovery of forgiveness in God, to a sin-distressed soul, is waiting in patience and expectation.

This the psalmist openly and directly applies himself to, and expresses to have been as his duty, so his practice. And he does it so emphatically, as was manifested in the opening of the words, that I know not that any duty is anywhere in the Scripture so recommended and lively represented to us.

You must, therefore, for the right understanding of it, call to mind what has been spoken concerning the state of the soul inquired into—its depths, entanglements, and sense of sin, with its application to God about those things; as also remember what has been delivered about the nature of forgiveness, with the revelation that is made of it to the faith of believers, and that this may be done where the soul has no refreshing sense of its own interest therein. It knows not that its own sins are forgiven, although it believes that there is forgiveness with God. Now, the principal duty that is incumbent on such a soul is that laid down in the proposition—namely, patient waiting and expectation.

Two things must be done in reference hereunto. First, the nature of the duty itself is to be declared; and, secondly, the necessity and usefulness of its practice is to be evinced and demonstrated.

### HOW WE WAIT

For the nature of it, something has been intimated giving light into it, in the opening of the words here used by the psalmist to express it by. But we may observe, that these duties, as required of us, do not consist in any particular acting of the soul, but in the whole spiritual frame and deportment of it, in reference to the end aimed at in and by them. And this waiting, as here and elsewhere commended to us, and which is comprehensive of the especial duties of the soul, in the case insisted on and described, comprehends these three things:

1. Quietness, in opposition to haste and tumultuating of spirit.
2. Diligence, in opposition to spiritual sloth, despondency, and neglect of means.
3. Expectation, in opposition to despair, distrust, and other proper immediate actings of unbelief.

### *Quietly*

Quietness. Hence this waiting itself is sometimes expressed by silence. To wait is to be silent (Lam. 3:26): 'It is good both to hope, וְדוּמָם, and to be silent for the salvation of the LORD;' that is, to 'wait quietly,' as we have rendered the word. And the same word we render sometimes 'to rest' (as Ps. 37:7), 'Rest on the LORD, דּוֹם לַיהוָה, be silent to him,' where it is joined with hoping or waiting, as that which belongs to the nature of it; and so in sundry other places. And this God, in an especial manner, calls souls to in straits and distresses. 'In quietness and confidence,' says he, 'shall be your strength' (Isa. 30:15). And the effect of the righteousness of God by Christ is said to be 'quietness and assurance for ever'

(Isa. 32:17)—first quietness, and then assurance. Now, this silence and quietness which accompanies waiting, yea, which is an essential part of it, is opposed, first, to haste; and haste is the soul's undue lifting up itself, proceeding from a weariness of its condition, to press after an end of its troubles not according to the conduct of the Spirit of God. Thus, when God calls his people to waiting, he expresses the contrary acting to this duty by the lifting up of the soul: 'Though the vision tarry, wait for it. Behold, his soul which is lifted up is not upright in him: but the just shall live by his faith' (Hab. 2:3–4). God has given to the soul a vision of peace, through the discovery of that forgiveness which is with him; but he will have us wait for an actual participation of it to rest and comfort. He that will not do so, but lifts up his soul—that is, in making haste beyond the rule and method of the Spirit of God in this matter—his heart is not upright in him, nor will he know what it is to live by faith. This ruins and disappoints many a soul in its attempts for forgiveness. The prophet, speaking of this matter, tells us that 'he that believes shall not,' nor will not, 'make haste' (Isa. 28:16), which words the apostle twice making use of (Rom. 9:33, 10:11), in both places renders them, 'Whosoever believes on him shall not be ashamed,' or confounded; and that because this haste turns men off from believing, and so disappoints their hopes, and leaves them to shame and confusion. Men with a sense of the guilt of sin, having some discovery made to them of the rest, ease, and peace which they may obtain to their souls by forgiveness, are ready to catch greedily at it, and to make false, unsound, undue applications of it to themselves. They cannot bear the yoke that the Lord has put upon them, but grow impatient under it, and cry with Rachel, 'Give me children, or else I die.' Any way they would obtain it.

Now, as the first duty of such a soul is to apply itself to waiting, so the first entrance into waiting consists in this silence and quietness of heart and spirit. This is the soul's endeavour to keep itself humble, satisfied with the sovereign pleasure of God in its condition, and refusing all ways and means of rest and peace but what it is guided and directed to by the word and Spirit.

Secondly, as it is opposed to haste, so it is to tumultuating thoughts and vexatious disquietments. The soul is silent. 'I was dumb, I opened not my mouth; because you did it' (Ps. 39:9). He redoubles the expression, whereby he sets out his endeavour to quiet and still his soul in the will of God. In the condition discoursed of, the soul is apt to have many tumultuating thoughts, or a multitude of perplexing thoughts, of no use or advantage to it. How they are to be watched against and rejected was before declared in our general rules. This quietness in waiting will prevent them. And this is the first thing in the duty prescribed.

### Diligently

Diligence, in opposition to spiritual sloth, is included in it also. Diligence is the activity of the mind, in the regular use of means, for the pursuit of any end proposed. The end aimed at by the soul is a comforting, refreshing interest in that forgiveness that is with God. For the attaining thereof, there are sundry means instituted and blessed of God. a neglect of them, through regardlessness or sloth, will certainly disappoint the soul from attaining that end.

It is confessedly so in things natural. He that sows not must not think to reap; he that clothes not himself will not be warm; nor he enjoy health who neglects the means of it. Men understand this as to their outward concerns; and although they have a due respect to the blessing of God, yet they expect not to be rich without industry in their ways. It is so also in things spiritual. God has appointed one thing to be the means of obtaining another; in the use of them does he bless us, and from the use of them does his glory arise, because they are his own appointments. And this diligence wholly respects practice, or the regular use of means. a man is said to be diligent in business, to have a diligent hand; though it be an affection of the mind, yet it simply respects practice and operation. This diligence in his waiting David expresses (Ps. 40:1): קַוֹּה קִוִּיתִי. We render it, 'I have waited patiently,' that is, 'Waiting I have waited;' that is, diligently, earnestly, in the use of means. So he describes this duty by an elegant similitude, 'Behold, as the eyes of servants look to the hand of their masters, and as the eyes of a maiden to the hand of her mistress; so our eyes wait upon the LORD our God, until he have mercy upon us' (Ps. 123:2). Servants that wait on their masters and look to their hands, it is to expect an intimation of their minds as to what they would have them do, that they may address themselves to it. 'So,' says he, 'do we wait for mercy'—not in a slothful neglect of duties, but in a constant readiness to observe the will of God in all his commands. An instance hereof we have in the spouse when she was in the condition here described (S. of S. 3:1–2). She wanted the presence of her Beloved; which amounts to the same state which we have under consideration; for where the presence of Christ is not, there can be no sense of forgiveness. At first she seeks him upon her bed: 'By night upon my bed I sought him whom my soul loves: I sought him, but I found him not.' She seems herein to have gone no farther than desires, for she was in her bed, where she could do no more; and the issue is, she found him not. But does she so satisfy herself, and lie still, waiting until he should come there to her? No; she says, 'I will rise now, and go about the city in the streets, and in the broad ways I will seek him whom my soul loves.' She resolves to put herself into the use of all means whereby one may be sought that is wanting. In the city, streets, and fields, she would inquire after him. And the blessed success she had herein is reported (v. 4); she 'found him, she held him, she would not let him go.' This, then, belongs to the waiting of the soul: diligence in the use of means, whereby God is pleased ordinarily to communicate a sense of pardon and forgiveness, is a principal part of it. What these means are is known. Prayer, meditation, reading, hearing of the word, dispensation of the sacraments, they are all appointed to this purpose; they are all means of communicating love and grace to the soul. Be not, then, heartless or slothful: up and be doing; attend with diligence to the word of grace; be fervent in prayer, assiduous in the use of all ordinances of the church; in one or other of them, at one time or other, you will meet with Him whom your soul loves, and God through Him will speak peace to you.

## *Expectantly*

There is expectation in it; which lies in a direct opposition to all the actings of unbelief in this matter, and is the very life and soul of the duty under consideration. So the psalmist declares it, 'My soul, wait you only upon God; for my expectation is only from him' (Ps. 62:5) The soul will not, cannot, in a due manner wait upon God, unless it has expectations from him—unless, as James speaks, he looks to receive somewhat from him (ch. 1:7). The soul in this condition regards forgiveness not only as by itself it is desired, but principally as it is by God promised. Thence they expect it. This is expressed in the fourth proposition before laid down—namely, that sin-distressed souls wait for God with earnestness, intension of mind, and expectation. As this arises from the redoubling of the expression, so principally from the nature of the comparison that he makes on himself in his waiting with them that watch for the morning. Those that watch for the morning do not only desire it and prepare for it, but they expect it, and know assuredly that it will come. Though darkness may for a time be troublesome, and continue longer than they would desire, yet they know that the morning has its appointed time of return, beyond which it will not tarry; and, therefore, they look out for its appearance on all occasions. So it is with the soul in this matter. So says David, 'I will direct my prayer to you, וַאֲצַפֶּה, and look up' (Ps. 5:3). So we: the words before are defective: בֹּקֶר אֶעֱרָךְ־לְךָ, 'In the morning,' or rather every morning, 'I will order to you.' We restrain this to prayer: 'I will direct my prayer to you.' But this was expressed directly in the words foregoing: 'In the morning you shall hear my voice;' that is, 'the voice of my prayer and supplications,' as it is often supplied. And although the psalmist does sometimes repeat the same thing in different expressions, yet here he seems not so to do, but rather proceeds to declare the general frame of his spirit in walking with God. 'I will,' says he, 'order all things towards God, so as that I may wait upon him in the ways of his appointment, וַאֲצַפֶּה, and will look up.' It seems in our translation to express his posture in his prayer; but the word is of another importance. It is diligently to look out after that which is coming towards us, and looking out after the accomplishment of our expectation. This is a part of our waiting for God; yea, as was said, the life of it, that which is principally intended in it. The prophet calls it his 'standing upon his watch tower, and watching to see what God would speak to him' (Hab. 2:1)—namely, in answer to that prayer which he put up in his trouble. He is now waiting in expectation of an answer from God. And this is that which poor, weak, trembling sinners are so encouraged to (Isa. 35:3–4): 'Strengthen the weak hands, and confirm the feeble knees. Say to them that are of a fearful heart, Be strong, fear not: behold, your God will come.' Weakness and discouragements are the effects of unbelief. These he would have removed, with an expectation of the coming of God to the soul, according to the promise. And this, I say, belongs to the waiting of the soul in the condition described. Such a one expects and hopes that God will in his season manifest himself and his love to him, and give him an experimental sense of a blessed interest in forgiveness. And the accomplishment of this purpose and promise of God, it looks out after continually. It will not despond and be heartless, but stir up and strengthen itself to a full expectation to have the desires of his soul satisfied in due time: as we find David doing in places almost innumerable.

This is the duty that, in the first place, is recommended to the soul who is persuaded that there is forgiveness with God, but sees not his own interest therein. Wait on, or for, the Lord. And it has two properties when it is performed in a due manner—namely, patience and perseverance. By the one men are kept to the length of God's time; by the other they are preserved in a due length of their own duty.

## Why We Wait

And this is that which was laid down in the first proposition drawn from the words—namely, that continuance in watching, until God appears to the soul, is necessary, as that without which we cannot attain what we look after; and prevailing, as that wherein we shall never fail.

### Our Times Are in His Hand

God is not to be limited, nor his times prescribed to him. We know our way and the end of our journey; but our stations of especial rest we must wait for at his mouth, as the people did in the wilderness. When David comes to deal with God in his great distress, he says to him, 'O LORD, you are my God; my times are in your hand' (Ps. 31:14–15). His times of trouble and of peace, of darkness and of light, he acknowledged to be in the hand and at the disposal of God, so that it was his duty to wait his time and season for his share and portion in them.

### We Shall Reap if We Faint Not

During this state the soul meets with many oppositions, difficulties, and perplexities, especially if its darkness be of long continuance; as with some it abides many years, with some all the days of their lives. Their hope being hereby deferred makes their heart sick, and their spirit oftentimes to faint; and this fainting is a defect in waiting, for want of perseverance and continuance, which frustrates the end of it. So David, 'I had fainted, unless I had believed to see the goodness of the LORD' (Ps. 27:13) – 'Had I not received support by faith, I had fainted.' And wherein does that consist? What was the fainting which he had been overtaken withal, without the support mentioned? It was a relinquishment of waiting on God, as he manifests by the exhortation which he gives to himself and others, 'Wait on the LORD; be of good courage, and he shall strengthen your heart: wait, I say, on the LORD' (v. 14) – 'Wait with courage and resolution, that you faint not.' And the apostle puts the blessed event of faith and obedience upon the avoidance of this evil: 'We shall reap, if we faint not' (Gal. 6:9). Hence we have both encouragements given against it, and promises that in the way of God we shall not be overtaken with it. 'Consider the Lord Christ,' says the apostle, 'the captain of your salvation, "lest you be wearied and faint in your minds"' (Heb. 12:1). Nothing else can cause you to come short of the mark aimed at. 'They,' says the prophet, 'that wait upon the LORD'—that is, in the use of the means by him appointed—'shall not faint' (Isa. 40:31).

This continuance, then, in waiting is to accompany this duty, upon the account of both the things mentioned in the proposition— that it is indispensably necessary on our own account, and it is assuredly prevailing in the end; it will not fail.

It is necessary. They that watch for the morning, to whose frame and actings the waiting of the soul for God is compared, give not over until the light appears; or if they do, if they are wearied and faint, and so cease watching, all their former pains will be lost, and they will lie down in disappointments. So will it be with the soul that deserts its watch, and faints in its waking. If upon the eruption of new lusts or corruptions—if upon the return of old temptations, or the assaults of new ones—if upon a revived perplexing sense of guilt, or on the tediousness of working and labouring so much and so long in the dark—the soul begins to say in itself, 'I have looked for light and behold darkness, for peace and yet trouble comes; the summer is past, the harvest is ended, and I am not relieved; such and such blessed means have been enjoyed, and yet I have not attained rest;' and so give over its waiting in the way and course before prescribed—it will at length utterly fail, and come short of the grace aimed at. 'You have laboured, and have not fainted,' brings in the reward (Rev. 2:3).

Perseverance in waiting is assuredly prevalent; and this renders it a necessary part of the duty itself. If we continue to wait for the vision of peace it will come, it will not tarry, but answer our expectation of it. Never soul miscarried that abode in this duty to the end. The joys of heaven may sometimes prevent consolations in this life; God sometimes gives in the full harvest without sending of the first-fruits aforehand; but spiritual or eternal peace and rest is the infallible end of permanent waiting for God.

This is the duty that the psalmist declares himself to be engaged in, upon the encouraging discovery which was made to him of forgiveness in God: 'There is forgiveness with you, that you may be feared. I wait for the LORD, my soul waits, and in his word do I hope.' And this is that which, in the like condition, is required of us. This is the great direction which was given us, in the example and practice of the psalmist, as to our duty and deportment in the condition described. This was the way whereby he rose out of his depths and escaped out of his entanglements. Is this, then, the state of any of us? Let such take directions from hence.

ENCOURAGE YOUR SOULS TO WAITING ON GOD. Do new fears arise, do old disconsolations continue? Say to your souls, 'Yet wait on God. "Why are you cast down, O our souls? And why are you disquieted within us? Hope in God; for we shall yet praise him, who is the health of our countenance, and our God;"' as the psalmist does in the like case (Ps. 43:5). So he speaks elsewhere, 'Wait on God, and be of good courage'—'Shake off sloth, rouse up yourselves from under despondencies; let not fears prevail.' This is the only way for success, and it will assuredly be prevalent. Oppose this resolution to every discouragement, and it will give new life to faith and hope. Say, 'My flesh and my heart fails; but God is the rock of my heart, and my portion for ever' (Ps. 73:26). Though your perplexed thoughts have even wearied and worn out the outward man, as in many they do, so that flesh fails—and though you have no refreshing evidence from within, from yourself, or your own experience, so that your heart fails—yet resolve to look to God; there is strength in him, and satisfaction in him, for the whole man; he is a rock, and a portion. This will strengthen things which otherwise will be ready to die. This will keep life in your course, and stir you up to plead it with God in an acceptable season, when he will be found. Job carried up his condition to a supposition that God might slay him—that is, add one stroke, one rebuke to another, until he was consumed, and so take him out of the world in darkness and in sorrow—yet he resolved to trust, to hope, to wait on him, as knowing that he should not utterly miscarry so doing. This frame the church expresses so admirably that nothing can be added thereunto (Lam. 3:17–26):

> You have removed my soul far off from peace: I forgot prosperity. And I said, My strength and my hope is perished from

the LORD: remembering mine affliction and my misery, the wormwood and the gall. My soul has them still in remembrance, and is humbled in me. This I recall to my mind, therefore have I hope. It is of the LORD's mercies that we are not consumed, because his compassions fail not. They are new every morning: great is your faithfulness. The LORD is my portion, says my soul; therefore will I hope in him. The LORD is good to them that wait for him, to the soul that seeks him. It is good that a man should both hope and quietly wait for the salvation of the LORD.

We have here both the condition and the duty insisted on, with the method of the soul's actings in reference to the one and the other fully expressed. The condition is sad and bitter; the soul is in depths, far from peace and rest (v. 17). In this state it is ready utterly to faint, and to give up all for lost and gone, both strength for the present and hopes for the future (v. 18). This makes its condition full of sorrow and bitterness, and its own thoughts become to it like 'wormwood and gall' (v. 19–20). But does he lie down under the burden of all this trouble? Does he despond and give over? No; says he, 'I call to mind that "there is forgiveness with God;" grace, mercy, goodness for the relief of distressed souls, such as are in my condition' (v. 21–3). Thence the conclusion is, that as all help is to be looked for, all relief expected from him alone, so 'it is good that a man should quietly wait and hope for the salvation of God' (v. 24–6). This he stirs up himself to as the best, as the most blessed course for his deliverance.

MAKE DILIGENT USE OF MEANS. Remember that diligent use of the means for the end aimed at is a necessary concomitant of, and ingredient to, waiting on God. Take in the consideration of this direction also. Do not think to be freed from your entanglements by restless, heartless desiring that it were otherwise with you. Means are to be used that relief may be obtained. What those means are is known to all. Mortification of sin, prayer, meditation, due attendance upon all gospel ordinances; conferring in general about spiritual things, advising in particular about our own state and condition, with such who, having received the tongue of the learned, are able to speak a word in season to them that are weary— are required to this purpose. And in all these are diligence and perseverance to be exercised, or in vain shall men desire a delivery from their entanglements.

### '...FOR THE LORD'

We have seen what the duty is intended in the proposition. We are next to consider the reason also of it, why this is the great, first, and principal duty of souls who in their depths have it discovered to them that there is forgiveness with God; and the reason hereof is that which is expressed in our second observation before mentioned, namely, that the proper object of a sin-distressed soul's waiting and expectation is God himself as revealed in Christ. 'I have,' says the psalmist, 'waited for Jehovah'—'It is not this or that mercy or grace, this or that help or relief, but it is Jehovah himself that I wait for.'

Here, then, we must do two things—first, show in what sense God himself is the object of the waiting of the soul; secondly, how it appears from hence that waiting is so necessary a duty.

### HIMSELF

First, it is the Lord himself, Jehovah himself, that the soul waits for. It is not grace, mercy, or relief absolutely considered, but the God of all grace and help, that is the full adequate object of the soul's waiting and expectation; only, herein he is not considered absolutely in his own nature, but as there is forgiveness with him. What is required hereunto has been at large before declared. It is as he is revealed in and by Jesus Christ; as in him he has found a ransom, and accepted the atonement for sinners in his blood; as he is a God in covenant, so he is himself the object of our waiting.

And that, first, because all troubles, depths, entanglements arise from: 1. The absence of God from the soul; and, 2. From his displeasure.

### His Absence Is Our Distress

The absence of God from the soul, by his departure, withdrawing, or hiding himself from it, is that which principally casts the soul into its depths. 'Woe to them,' says the Lord, 'when I depart from them!' (Hos. 9:12). And this woe, this sorrow, does not attend only a universal, a total departure of God from any; but that also which is gradual or partial, in some things, in some seasons. When God withdraws his enlightening, his refreshing, his comforting presence, as to any ways or means whereby he has formerly communicated himself to the souls of any, then—'woe to them!'—sorrows will befall them, and they will fall into depths and entanglements. Now, this condition calls for waiting. If God be withdrawn, if he hide himself, what has the soul to do but to wait for his return? So says the prophet Isaiah, 'I will wait upon the LORD, that hides his face from the house of Jacob, and I will look for him' (Isa. 8:17). If God hide himself, this is the natural and proper duty of the soul, to wait and to look for him. Other course of relief it cannot apply itself to. What that waiting is, and wherein it consists, has been declared. Patient seeking of God in the ways of his appointment is comprised in it. This the prophet expresses in that word, 'I will look for him;' indeed, the same in the original with that in the psalm, וְקִוִּיתִי־לוֹ—'And I will earnestly look out after him, with expectation of his return to me.'

### A Sense of His Displeasure Is Our Trouble

A sense of God's displeasure is another cause of these depths and troubles, and of the continuance of the soul in them, notwithstanding it has made a blessed discovery by faith that there is with him forgiveness. This has been so fully manifested through the whole preceding discourse, that it need not again be insisted on. All has respect to sin; and the reason of the trouble that arises from sin is because of the displeasure of God against it. What, then, is the natural posture and frame of the soul towards God as displeased? Shall he contend with him? Shall he harden himself against him?

Shall he despise his wrath and anger, and contemn his threatenings? Or shall he hide himself from him, and so avoid the effects of his wrath? Who knows not how ruinous and pernicious to the soul such courses would be? And how many are ruined by them every day? Patient waiting is the soul's only reserve on this account also.

## A Great and Sovereign Ruler

Secondly, this duty in the occasion mentioned is necessary upon the account of the greatness and sovereignty of him with whom we have to do: 'My soul waits for Jehovah.' Indeed, waiting is a duty that depends on the distance that is between the persons concerned in it—namely, he that waits, and he that is waited on; so the psalmist informs us (Ps. 123:2). It is an action like that of servants and handmaids towards their masters or rulers. And the greater this distance is, the more cogent are the reasons of this duty on all occasions. And because we are practically averse from the due performance of this duty, or at least quickly grow weary of it, notwithstanding our full conviction of its necessity, I shall a little insist on some such considerations of God and ourselves, as may not only evince the necessity of this duty, but also satisfy us of its reasonableness; that by the first we may be engaged into it, and by the latter preserved in it.

Two things we may to this purpose consider in God, in Jehovah, whom we are to wait for—First, his being, and the absolute and essential properties of his nature; secondly, those attributes of his nature which respect his dealing with us; both which are suited to beget in us affections and a frame of spirit compliant with the duty proposed.

### His Infinite & Glorious Being

First, let us consider the infinite glorious being of Jehovah, with his absolute, incommunicable, essential excellencies; and then try whether it does not become us in every condition to wait for him, and especially in that under consideration. This course God himself took with Job to recover him from his discontents and complaints, to reduce him to quietness and waiting. He sets before him his own glorious greatness, as manifested in the works of his power, that thereby, being convinced of his own ignorance, weakness, and infinite distance in all things from him, he might humble his soul into the most submissive dependence on him and waiting for him. And this he does accordingly: 'I abhor myself,' says he, 'and repent in dust and ashes' (Job 42:6). His soul now comes to be willing to be at God's disposal; and therein he found present rest and a speedy healing of his condition. It is 'the high and lofty One that inhabits eternity, whose name is Holy' (Isa. 57:15), with whom we have now to do (Isa. 50:22, 15, 17):

> He sits upon the circle of the earth, and the inhabitants of it are as grasshoppers before him; yea, the nations are as a drop of a bucket, and are counted as the small dust of the balance; he takes up the isles as a very little thing. All nations before him are as nothing; and they are counted to him less than nothing, and vanity.

To what end does the Lord set forth and declare his glorious greatness and power? It is that all might be brought to trust in him and to wait for him, as at large is declared in the close of the chapter; for shall 'grasshoppers,' a 'drop of the bucket,' 'dust of the balance,' things 'less than nothing,' repine against, or wax weary of, the will of the immense, glorious, and lofty One? He that 'takes up the isles as a very little thing,' may surely, if he please, destroy, cast, and forsake one isle, one city in an isle, one person in a city; and we are before him but single persons. Serious thoughts of this infinite, all-glorious Being will either quiet our souls or overwhelm them. All our weariness of his dispensations towards us arises from secret imaginations that he is such a one as ourselves—one that is to do nothing but what seems good in our eyes. But if we cannot comprehend his being, we cannot make rules to judge of his ways and proceedings. And how small a portion is it that we know of God! The nearest approaches of our reasons and imaginations leave us still at an infinite distance from him. And, indeed, what we speak of his greatness, we know not well what it signifies; we only declare our respect to that which we believe, admire, and adore, but are not able to comprehend. All our thoughts come as short of his excellent greatness as our natures do of his—that is, infinitely. Behold the universe, the glorious fabric of heaven and earth; how little is it that we know of its beauty, order, and disposal!—yet was it all the product of the word of his mouth; and with the same facility can he, when he pleases, reduce it to its primitive nothing. And what are we, poor worms of the earth, an inconsiderable, unknown part of the lower series and order of the works of his hands, few in number, fading in condition, unregarded to the residue of our fellow-creatures, that we should subduct ourselves from under any kind of his dealings with us, or be weary of waiting for his pleasure? This he presses on us, 'Be still, and know that I am God' (Ps. 46:10)—'Let there be no more repinings, no more disputings; continue waiting in silence and patience. Consider who I am. "Be still, and know that I am God."'

Farther to help us in this consideration, let us a little also fix our minds towards some of the glorious, essential, incommunicable properties of his nature distinctly.

HIS ETERNITY. This Moses proposes, to bring the souls of believers to submission, trust, and waiting: 'From everlasting to everlasting you are God' (Ps. 90:1)—'One that has his being and subsistence not in a duration of time, but in eternity itself.' So does Habakkuk also, 'Are you not from everlasting, O LORD my God, mine Holy One?' (Hab. 1:12), and hence he draws his conclusion against making haste in any condition, and for tarrying and waiting for God. The like consideration is managed by David also (Ps. 102:27). How inconceivable is this glorious divine property to the thoughts and minds of men! How weak are the ways and terms whereby they go about to express it! One says, it is a *'nunc stans;'* another, that it is a 'perpetual duration.' He that says most, only signifies what he knows of what it is not. We are of yesterday, change every moment, and are leaving our station tomorrow. God is still the same, was so before the world was—from eternity. And now I cannot think what I have said, but only have intimated what I adore. The whole duration of the world, from the beginning to the end, takes up no space in this eternity of God: for how long soever it has continued or may yet continue, it will all amount but to so many thousand years, so long a time; and time has no place in eternity. And for us who have in this matter to do with God, what is our continuance to that of the world? a moment, as it were, in comparison of the whole. When men's lives were of old prolonged beyond the date and continuance of empires or kingdoms now, yet this was the winding up of all—such a one lived so many years, 'and he died' (Gen. 5). And what are we, poor worms, whose lives are measured by inches, in comparison of their span? What are we before the eternal God, God always immutably subsisting in his own infinite being? a real consideration hereof will subdue the soul into a condition of dependence on him and of waiting for him.

HIS IMMENSITY. The immensity of his essence and his omnipresence is of the same consideration: 'Do not I fill heaven and earth? says the LORD' (Jer. 23:24). 'The heavens, even the heaven of heavens,' the supreme and most comprehensive created being, 'cannot contain him,' says Solomon. In his infinitely glorious being he is present with, and indistant from all places, things, times, all the works of his hands; and is no less gloriously subsisting where they are not. God is where heaven and earth are not, no less than where they are; and where they are not is himself. Where there is no place, no space, real or imaginary, God is; for place and imagination have nothing to do with immensity. And he is present everywhere in creation—where I am writing, where you are reading; he is present with you, indistant from you. The thoughts of men's hearts for the most part are, that God as to his essence is in heaven only; and it is well if some think he is there, seeing they live and act as if there were neither God nor devil but themselves. But on these apprehensions such thoughts are ready secretly to arise, and effectually to prevail, as are expressed, 'How does God know? Can he judge through the dark? Thick clouds are a covering to him, that he sees not; and he walks in the circuit of heaven' (Job 22:13-14).

Apprehensions of God's distance from men harden them in their ways. But it is utterly otherwise. God is everywhere, and a man may on all occasions say with Jacob, 'God is in this place, and I knew it not.' Let the soul, then, who is thus called to wait on God, exercise itself with thoughts about this immensity of his nature and being. Comprehend it, fully understand it, we can never; but the consideration of it will give that awe of his greatness upon our hearts, as that we shall learn to tremble before him, and to be willing to wait for him in all things.

HIS HOLINESS. Thoughts of the holiness of God, or infinite self-purity of this eternal, immense Being, are singularly useful to the same purpose. This is that which Eliphaz affirms that he received by vision to reply to the complaint and impatience of Job (ch. 4:17–21). After he has declared his vision, with the manner of it, this he affirms to be the revelation that by voice was made to him: 'Shall mortal man be more just than God? Shall a man be more pure than his Maker? Behold, he put no trust in his servants; and his angels he charged with folly. How much less in them that dwell in houses of clay, whose foundation is in the dust, who are crushed before the moth?' If the saints and angels in heaven do not answer this infinite holiness of God in their most perfect condition, is it meet for worms of the earth to suppose that any thing which proceeds from him is not absolutely holy and perfect, and so best for them? This is the fiery property of the nature of God, whence he is called a 'consuming fire' and 'everlasting burnings.' And the law, whereon he had impressed some representation of it, is called a 'fiery law,' as that which will consume and burn up whatever is perverse and evil. Hence the prophet who had a representation of the glory of God in a vision, and heard the seraphim proclaiming his holiness, cried out, 'Woe is me! for I am undone; because I am a man of unclean lips' (Isa. 6:5). He thought it impossible that he should bear that near approach of the holiness of God. And with the remembrance hereof does Joshua still the people—with the terror of the Lord (ch. 14:19). Let such souls, then, as are under troubles and perplexities on any account, endeavour to exercise their thoughts about this infinite purity and fiery holiness of God. They will quickly find it their wisdom to become as weaned children before him, and content themselves with what he shall guide them to; which is to wait for him. This fiery holiness streams from his throne (Dan. 7:10), and would quickly consume the whole creation, as now under the curse and sin, were it not for the interposing of Jesus Christ.

HIS MAJESTY. His glorious majesty as the Ruler of all the world. Majesty relates to government, and it calls us to such an awe of him as renders our waiting for him comely and necessary. God's throne is said to be in heaven, and there principally do the glorious beams of his terrible majesty shine forth; but he has also made some representation of it on the earth, that we might learn to fear before him. Such was the appearance that he gave of his glory in the giving of the law, whereby he will judge the world, and condemn the transgressors of it who obtain not an acquitment in the blood of Jesus Christ. See the description of it in Exodus 19:16–18. 'So terrible was the sight' hereof, 'that Moses' himself 'said, I exceedingly fear and quake' (Heb. 12:21). And what effect it had upon all the people is declared (Exod. 20:18–19). They were not able to bear it, although they had good assurance that it was for their benefit and advantage that he so drew nigh and manifested his glory to them. Are we not satisfied with our condition? Cannot we wait under his present dispensations? Let us think how we may approach to his presence, or stand before his glorious majesty. Will not the dread of his excellency fall upon us? Will not his terror make us afraid? Shall we not think his way best, and his time best, and that our duty is to be silent before him? And the like manifestation has he made of his glory, as the great Judge of all upon the throne, to sundry of the prophets: as to Isaiah (ch. 6:1–4); to Ezekiel (ch. 1); to Daniel (ch. 7:9–10); to John (Rev. 1). Read the places attentively, and learn to tremble before him. These are not things that are foreign to us. This God is our God. The same throne of his greatness and majesty is still established in the heavens. Let us, then, in all our hastes and heats that our spirits in any condition are prone to, present ourselves before this throne of God, and then consider what will be best for us to say or do; what frame of heart and spirit will become us, and be safest for us. All this glory encompasses us every moment, although we perceive it not. And it will be but a few days before all the veils and shades that are about us shall be taken away and depart; and then shall all this glory appear to us to endless bliss or everlasting woe. Let us therefore know, that nothing, in our dealings with him, does better become us than silently to wait for him, and what he will speak to us in our depths and straits.

AS CREATOR. It is good to consider the instances that God has given of this his infinite greatness, power, majesty, and glory. Such was his mighty work of creating all things out of nothing. We dwell on little mole-hills in the earth, and yet we know the least part of the excellency of that spot of ground which is given us for our habitation here below. But what is it to the whole habitable world and the fullness thereof? And what an amazing thing is its greatness, with the wide and large sea, with all sorts of creatures therein! The least of these has a beauty, a glory, an excellency, that the utmost of our inquiries end in admiration of. And all this is but the earth, the lower, depressed part of the world. What shall we say concerning the heavens over us, and all those creatures of light that have their habitations in them? Who can conceive the beauty, order, use, and course of them? The consideration hereof caused the psalmist to cry out, 'LORD, our Lord, how excellent and glorious you are!' (Ps. 8:1). And what is the rise, spring, and cause of these things? Are they not all the effect of the word of the power of this glorious God? And does he not in them, and by them, speak us into a reverence of his greatness? The like, also, may be said concerning his mighty and strange works of providence in the rule of the world. Is not this he who brought the flood of old upon the world of ungodly men? Is it not he who consumed Sodom and Gomorrah with fire from heaven, setting them forth as examples to them that should afterward live ungodly, suffering the vengeance of eternal fire? Is it not he who destroyed Egypt with his plagues, and drowned Pharaoh with his host in the Red Sea? Is it not he, one of whose servants slew a hundred and fourscore and five thousand in Sennacherib's army in one night? That opened the earth to swallow up Dathan and Abiram? And sent out fire from the altar to devour Nadab and Abihu? And have not all ages been filled with such instances of his greatness and power?

The end why I have insisted on these things is, to show the reasonableness of the duty which we are pressing to—namely, to wait on God quietly and patiently in every condition of distress; for what else becomes us when we have to do with this great and holy One?

And a due consideration of these things will exceedingly influence our minds thereunto.

### Him & Us

Secondly, this waiting for God respects the whole of the condition expressed in the psalm; and this contains not only spiritual depths about sin, which we have at large insisted on, but also providential depths, depths of trouble or affliction, that we may be exercised withal in the holy, wise providence of God. In reference also to these, waiting in patience and silence is our duty. And there are two considerations that will assist us in this duty, with respect to such depths—that is, of trouble or affliction. And the first of these is the consideration of those properties of God which he exercises in an especial manner in all his dealings with us, and which in all our troubles we are principally to regard. The second is the consideration of ourselves, what we are, and what we have deserved.

Let us begin with the former. And there are four things in God's dispensations towards us and dealing with us that in this matter we should consider, all suited to work in us the end aimed at.

HIS SOVEREIGNTY. The first is his sovereignty. This he declares, this we are to acknowledge and submit to, in all the great and dreadful dispensations of his providence, in all his dealings with our souls. May he not do what he will with his own? Who shall say to him, "What are you doing?" Or if they do so, what shall give them countenance in their so doing? He made all this world of nothing, and could have made another, more, or all things, quite otherwise than they are. It would not subsist one moment without his omnipotent support. Nothing would be continued in its place, course, use, without his effectual influence and countenance. If any thing can be, live, or act a moment without him, we may take free leave to dispute its disposal with him, and to haste to the accomplishment of our desires. But from the angels in heaven to the worms of the earth and the grass of the field, all depend on him and his power continually. Why was this part of the creation an angel, that a worm; this a man, that a brute beast? Is it from their own choice, designing, or contrivance, or brought about by their own wisdom? Or is it merely from the sovereign pleasure and will of God? And what a madness is it to repine against what he does, seeing all things are as he makes them and disposes them, nor can be otherwise! Even the repiner himself has his being and subsistence upon his mere pleasure. This sovereignty of God Elihu pleads in his dealings with Job (ch. 33:8–13). He apprehended that Job had reasoned against God's severe dispensations towards him, and that he did not humble himself under his mighty hand wherewith he was exercised, nor wait for him in a due manner; and, therefore, what does he propose to him to bring him to this duty? What does he reply to his reasonings and complaints? 'Behold,' says he (v. 12), 'in this you are not just: I will answer you, that God is greater than man.' 'Why do you strive against him? For he gives not account of any of his matters' (v. 13)—'Be it that in other things you are just and innocent, that you are free from the things wherewith your friends have charged you, yet in this matter you are not just; it is neither just nor equal that any man should complain of or repine against any of God's dispensations.'

'Yea, but I suppose that these dealings of God are very grievous, very dreadful, such as he has, it may be, scarce exercised towards any from the foundation of the world; to be utterly destroyed and consumed in a day, in all relations arid enjoyments, and that at a time and season when no such thing was looked for or provided against; to have a sense of sin revived on the conscience, after pardon obtained, as it is with me?'

'All is one,' says he; 'if you complain you are not just.'

And what reason does he give thereof? Why, '"God is greater than man;" infinitely so in power and sovereign glory. He is so absolutely therein that "he gives not account of any of his matters;" and what folly, what injustice is it, to complain of his proceedings! Consider his absolute dominion over the works of his hands, over yourself, and all that you have; his infinite distance from you, and greatness above you; and then see whether it be just or no to repine against what he does.'

And he pursues the same consideration: 'If when kings and princes rule in righteousness, it is a contempt of their authority to say to them they are wicked and ungodly, then will you speak against him, contend with him, "that accepts not the persons of princes, nor regards the rich more than the poor? For they are all the work of his hands"' (ch. 34:18–19). And, verse 29, 'When he gives quietness, who then can make trouble? And when he hides his face, who then can behold him? Whether it be done against a nation, or against a man only?' All is one; whatever God does, and towards whomsoever, be they many or few, a whole nation, or city, or one single person, be they high or low, rich or poor, good or bad, all are the works of his hands, and he may deal with them as seems good to him. And this man alone, as God afterward declares, made use of the right and proper mediums to take off Job from complaining, and to compose his spirit to rest and peace, and to bring him to wait patiently for God. For whereas his other friends injuriously charged him with hypocrisy, and that he had in an especial manner, above other men, deserved those judgments of God which he was exercised withal; he, who was conscious to his own integrity, was only provoked and exasperated by their arguings, and stirred up to plead his own innocency and uprightness. But this man, allowing him the plea of his integrity, calls him to the consideration of the greatness and sovereignty of God, against which there is no rising up; and this God himself afterward calls him to.

Deep and serious thoughts of God's sovereignty and absolute

dominion or authority over all the works of his hands, are an effectual means to work the soul to this duty; yea, this is that which we are to bring our souls to. Let us consider with whom we have to do. Are not we and all our concerns in his hands, as the clay in the hand of the potter? And may he not do what he will with his own? Shall we call him to an account? Is not what he does good and holy because he does it? Do any repining thoughts against the works of God arise in our hearts? Are any complaints ready to break out of our mouths? Let us lay our hands on our hearts, and our mouths in the dust, with thoughts of his greatness and absolute sovereignty, and it will work our whole souls into a better frame.

And this extends itself to the manners, times, and seasons of all things whatever. As in earthly things, if God will bring a dreadful judgment of fire upon a people, a nation; Ah! Why must it be London? If on London, why so terrible, raging, and unconquerable? Why the city, not the suburbs? Why my house, not my neighbour's? Why had such a one help, and I none? All these things are wholly to be referred to God's sovereign pleasure. There alone can the soul of man find rest and peace. It is so in spiritual dispensations also.

Thus Aaron, upon the sudden death of his two eldest sons, being minded by Moses of God's sovereignty and holiness, immediately 'held his peace,' or quietly humbled himself under his mighty hand (Lev. 10:3). And David, when things were brought into extreme confusion by the rebellion of Absalom, followed by the ungodly multitude of the whole nation, relinquishes all other arguments and pleas, and lets go complaints in a resignation of himself and all his concerns to the absolute pleasure of God (2 Sam. 15:25–6). And this, in all our extremities, must we bring our souls to before we can attain any rest or peace, or the least comfortable persuasion that we may not yet fall under greater severities, in the just indignation of God against us.

HIS WISDOM. The wisdom of God is also to be considered and submitted to: 'He is wise in heart: who has hardened himself against him, and has prospered?' (Job 9:4). This the prophet joins with his greatness and sovereignty (Isa. 40:12–14). 'There is no searching of his understanding' (v. 28). And the apostle winds up all his considerations of the works of God in a holy admiration of his knowledge and wisdom, whence his 'judgment becomes unsearchable, and his ways past finding out' (Rom. 11:33–4). He sees and knows all things, in all their causes, effects, consequences, and circumstances, in their utmost reach and tendency, in their correspondencies one to another, and suitableness to his own glory; and so alone judges aright of all things. The wisest of men, as David speaks, walk in a shade. We see little, we know little; and that but of a very few things, and in an imperfect manner; and that of their present appearances, abstracted from their issues, successes, ends, and relations to other things. And if we would be farther wise in the works of God, we shall be found to be like the wild ass's colt. What is good for us or the church of God, what is evil to it or us, we know not at all; but all things are open and naked to God. The day will come, indeed, wherein we shall have such a prospect of the works of God, see one thing so set against another, as to find goodness, beauty, and order in them all—that they were all done in number, weight, and measure—that nothing could have been otherwise without an abridgment of his glory and disadvantage of them that believe in him; but for the present, all our wisdom consists in referring all to him. He who does these things is infinitely wise; he knows what he does, and why, and what will be the end of all. We are apt, it may be, to think that at such seasons all things will go to wreck with ourselves, with the church, or with the whole world: 'How can this breach be repaired, this loss made up, this ruin recovered? Peace is gone, trade is gone, our substance is gone, the church is gone—all is gone; confusion and utter desolation lie at the door.' But if a man who is unskilled and unexperienced should be at sea, it may be, every time the vessel wherein he is seems to decline on either side, he would be apt to conceive they should be all cast away; but yet, if he be not childishly timorous, when the master shall tell him that there is no danger, bid him trust to his skill and it shall be well with him, it will yield quietness and satisfaction. We are indeed in a storm—the whole earth seems to reel and stagger like a drunken man; but yet our souls may rest in the infinite skill and wisdom of the great Pilot of the whole creation, who steers all things according to the counsel of his will. 'His works are manifold: in wisdom has he made them all' (Ps. 104:24). And in the same wisdom does he dispose of them: 'All these things come forth from the LORD of hosts, who is wonderful in counsel, and excellent in working' (Isa. 28:29). What is good, meet, useful for us, for ours, for the churches, for the city, for the land of our nativity, he knows, and of creatures not one. This infinite wisdom of God, also, are we therefore to resign and submit ourselves to. His hand in all his works is guided by infinite wisdom. In thoughts thereof, in humbling ourselves thereunto, shall we find rest and peace; and this in all our pressures will work us to a waiting for him.

HIS RIGHTEOUSNESS. The righteousness of God is also to be considered in this matter. That name in the Scripture is used to denote many excellencies of God, all which are reducible to the infinite rectitude of his nature. I intend that at present which is called *'justitia regiminis*,' his righteousness in rule or government. This is remembered by Abraham: 'Shall not the Judge of all the earth do right?' (Gen. 18:25). And by the apostle: 'Is God unjust who takes vengeance? God forbid.' This our souls are to own in all the works of God. They are all righteous—all his who 'will do no iniquity, whose throne is established in judgment.' However they may be dreadful, grievous, and seem severe, yet they are all righteous. It is true he will sometimes 'rise up and do strange works, strange acts' (Isa. 28:21), such as he will not do often nor ordinarily, such as shall fill the world with dread and amazement— he will 'answer his people in terrible things!' But yet all shall be in righteousness. And to complain of that which is righteous, to repine against it, is the highest unrighteousness that may be. Faith, then, fixing the soul on the righteousness of God, is an effectual means to humble it under his mighty hand. And to help us herein, we may consider:

That 'God judges not as man judges.' We judge by the 'seeing of the eye, and hearing of the ear'—according to outward appearances and evidences; 'but God searches the heart.' We judge upon what is between man and man; God principally upon what is between himself and man. And what do we know or understand of these things? Or what there is in the heart of man, what purposes, what contrivances, what designs, what corrupt affections, what sins; what transactions have been between God and them; what warnings he has given them; what reproofs, what engagements they have made; what convictions they have had; what use they were putting their lives, their substance, their families to? Alas! We know nothing of these things, and so are able to make no judgment of the proceedings of God upon them; but this we know, that he 'is righteous in all his ways, and holy in all his works,' yea, the most terrible of them. And when the secrets of all hearts shall be revealed, Ah! How glorious will be his drowning of the old world, firing of Sodom, swallowing up of Dathan and Abiram in the earth, the utter rejection of the Jews, with all other acts of his providence seeming to be accompanied with severity! And so will our own trials, inward or outward, appear to be.

God is judge of all the world, of all ages, times, places, persons; and disposes of all so as they may tend to the good of the whole and his own glory in the universe. Our thoughts are bounded, much more our observations and abilities, to measure things within a very small compass. Every thing stands alone to us, whereby we see little of its beauty or order, nor do know how it ought justly to be disposed of. That particular may seem deformed to us, which, when it is under His eye who sees all at once, past, present, and to come, with all those joints and bands of wisdom and order whereby things are related to one another, is beautiful and glorious: for as nothing is of itself, nor by itself, nor to itself, so nothing stands alone; but there is a line of mutual respect that runs through the creation and every particular of it, and that in all its changes and alterations from the beginning to the end, which gives it its loveliness, life, and order. He that can at once see but one part of a goodly statue or colossus might think it a very deformed piece, when he that views it altogether is assured of its due proportion, symmetry, and loveliness. Now, all things, ages, and persons, all thus at once are objected to the sight of God; and he disposes them with respect to the whole, that every one may fill up its own place, and sustain its part and share in the common tendency of all to the same end.

And hence it is that in public judgments and calamities, God oftentimes suffers the godly to be involved with the wicked, and that not on the account of their own persons, but as they are parts of that body which he will destroy. This Job expresses somewhat harshly, but there is truth in his assertion: 'This is one thing, therefore I said it, He destroys the perfect and the wicked. If the scourge slay suddenly, he will laugh at the trial of the innocent' (ch. 9:22–3). God in public desolations oftentimes takes good and bad together; a sudden scourge involves them all. And this God does for sundry reasons:

1. That he may manifest his own holiness; which is such that he can, without the least injustice or oppression, even upon the account of their own provocations, take away the houses, possessions, estates, liberties, and lives of the best of his own saints: for how should a man, any man, the best of men, be just with God, if he would contend with him? No man can answer to him 'one of a thousand' (Job 9:3). This they will also own and acknowledge; upon the account of righteousness none can open his mouth about his judgments, without the highest impiety and wickedness.

2. He does so that his own people may learn to know his terror, and to rejoice always before him with trembling. Therefore Job affirms, that 'in the time of his prosperity he was not secure,' but still trembled in himself with thoughts of the judgments of God. Doubtless much wretched carnal security would be ready to invade and possess the hearts of believers, if God should always and constantly pass them by in the dispensations of his public judgments.

3. That it may be a stone of offence and a stumbling-block to wicked men, who are to be hardened in their sins and prepared

for ruin. When they see that all things fall alike to all, and that those who have made the strictest profession of the name and fear of God fare no better than themselves, they are encouraged to despise the warnings of God and the strokes of his hand, and so to rush on to the destruction whereunto they are prepared.

4. God does it to proclaim to all the world that what he does here is no final judgment and ultimate determination concerning things and persons; for who can see the 'wise man dying as a fool,' the righteous and holy perishing in their outward concerns as the ungodly and wicked, but must conclude that the righteous God, the judge of all, has appointed another day, wherein all things must be called over again, and every one then receive his final reward, according as his works shall appear to have been? And thus are we to humble ourselves to the righteousness wherewith the hand of God is always accompanied.

5. His goodness and grace is also to be considered in all the works of his mighty hands. As there is no unrighteousness in him, so also [there is] all that is good and gracious. And whatever there is in any trouble of allay from the utmost wrath, is of mere goodness and grace. Your houses are burned, but perhaps your goods are saved—is there no grace, no goodness therein? Or perhaps your substance also is consumed, but yet your person is alive; and should a living man complain? But say what you will, this stroke is not hell, which you have deserved long ago, yea, it may be a means of preventing your going thither; so that it is accompanied with infinite goodness, patience, and mercy also. And if the considerations hereof will not quiet your heart, take heed lest a worse thing befall you.

And these things amongst others are we to consider in God, to lead our hearts into an acquiescing in his will, a submission under his mighty hand, and a patient waiting for the issue.

OUR ABJECT CONDITION. Secondly, consider our mean and abject condition, and that infinite distance wherein we stand from him with whom we have to do. When Abraham, the father of the faithful and friend of God, came to treat with him about his judgments, he does it with this acknowledgment of his condition, that he was 'mere dust and ashes' (Gen. 18:27)—a poor abject creature, that God at his pleasure had formed out of the dust of the earth, and which in a few days was to be reduced again into the ashes of it. We can forget nothing more perniciously than what we are. 'Man is a worm,' says Bildad, 'and the son of man is but a worm' (Job 25:6). 'And therefore,' says Job himself, 'I have said to corruption, you are my father: and to the worm, you are my mother and my sister' (ch. 17:14). His affinity, his relation to them, is the nearest imaginable, and he is no otherwise to be accounted of; and there is nothing that God abhors more than an elation of mind in the forgetfulness of our mean, frail condition. 'You say,' said he to the proud prince of Tyrus, 'that you are a god; but,' says he, 'will you yet say before him that slays you, I am God?' (Ezek. 28:2, 9). That severe conviction did God provide for his pride, 'You shall be a man, and no god, in the hand of him that slays you.' And when Herod prided himself in the acclamations of the vain multitude ('The voice of a god, and not of a man!') the angel of the Lord filled that god immediately with worms, which slew him and devoured him (Acts 12:23). There is, indeed, nothing more effectual to abase the pride of the thoughts of men than a due remembrance that they are so. Hence the psalmist prays, 'Put them in fear, O LORD; that the nations may know themselves to be but men' (Ps. 9:20); so, and no more: אֱנוֹשׁ הֵמָּה, 'poor, miserable, frail, mortal man,' as the word signifies. 'What is man? What is his life? What is his strength?' said one; 'The dream of a shadow; a mere nothing.' Or as David, much better, 'Every man living, in his best condition, is altogether vanity' (Ps. 39:5). And James, 'Our life,' which is our best, our all, 'is but a vapour, that appears for a little time, and then vanishes away' (ch. 4:14). But enough has been spoken by many on this subject. And we that have seen so many thousands each week, in one city, carried away to the grave, have been taught the truth of our frailty, even as with thorns and briers. But I know not how it comes to pass, there is not any thing we are more apt to forget than what we ourselves are; and this puts men on innumerable miscarriages towards God and one another. You, therefore, that are exercised under the hand of God in any severe dispensation, and are ready on all occasions to fill your mouth with complaints, sit down a little and take a right measure of yourself, and see whether this frame and posture becomes you. It is the great God against whom you repinest, and you are a man, and that is a name of a worm, a poor, frail, dying worm; and it may be whilst you are speaking, you are no more. And will you think it meet for such a one as you are to magnify yourself against the great possessor of heaven and earth? Poor clay, poor dust and ashes, poor dying worm! Know your state and condition, and fall down quietly under the mighty hand of God. Though you wrangle with men about your concerns, let God alone. 'The potsherds may contend with the potsherds of the earth, but woe to him that strives with his Maker!'

OUR GREAT SIN. Consider that in this frail condition we have all greatly sinned against God. So did Job (ch. 7:20), 'I have sinned; what shall I do to you, O you Preserver of men?' If this consideration will not satisfy your mind, yet it will assuredly stop the mouths of all the sons of men. Though all the curses of the law should be executed upon us, yet 'every mouth must be stopped;' because 'all the world is become guilty before God' (Rom. 3:19). 'Wherefore does a living man complain?' says the prophet (Lam. 3:39). Why, it may be, it is because that his trouble is great and inexpressible, and such as seldom or never befell any before him. But what then? Says he, 'shall a man complain for the punishment of his sins?' If this living man be a sinful man, as there is none that lives and sins not, whatever his state and condition be, he has no ground of murmuring or complaint. For a sinful man to complain, especially whilst he is yet a living man, is most unreasonable.

For whatever has befallen us, it is just on the account that we are sinners before God; and to repine against the judgments of God, that are rendered evidently righteous upon the account of sin, is to anticipate the condition of the damned in hell, a great part of whose misery it is that they always repine against that sentence and punishment which they know to be most righteous and holy. If this were now a place, if that were now my design, to treat of the sins of all professors, how easy were it to stop the mouths of all men about their troubles! But that is not my present business. I speak to particular persons, and that not with an especial design to convince them of their sins, but to humble their souls. Another season may be taken to press that consideration, directly and professedly also. At present let us only, when our souls are ready to be entangled with the thoughts of any severe dispensation of God, and our own particular pressures, troubles, miseries, occasioned thereby, turn into ourselves, and take a view every one of his own personal provocations; and when we have done so, see what we have to say to God, what we have to complain of. Let the man hold his tongue, and let the sinner speak. Is not God holy, righteous, wise, in what he has done? And if he be, why do we not subscribe to his ways, and submit quietly to his will?

But this is not all. We are not only such sinners as to render these dispensations of God evidently holy, these judgments of his righteous; but also to manifest that they are accompanied with unspeakable patience, mercy, and grace. To instance in one particular: Is it the burning of our houses, the spoiling of our goods, the ruin of our estates alone, that our sins have deserved? If God had made the temporary fire on earth to have been to us a way of entrance into the eternal fire of hell, we had not had whereof righteously to complain. May we not, then, see a mixture of unspeakable patience, grace, and mercy, in every dispensation? And shall we, then, repine against it? Is it not better advice, 'Go, and sin no more, lest a worse thing befall you?' For a sinner out of hell not to rest in the will of God, not to humble himself under his mighty hand, is to make himself guilty of the especial sin of hell. Other sins deserve it, but repining against God is principally, yea, only committed in it. The church comes to a blessed quieting resolution in this case, 'I will bear the indignation of the LORD, because I have sinned against him' (Micah 7:9); bear it quietly, patiently, and submit under his hand therein.

OUR POOR JUDGMENT. Consider that of ourselves we are not able to make a right judgment of what is good for us, what evil to us, or what tends most directly to our chiefest end. 'Surely man walks in a vain show' (Ps. 39:6)–בְּצֶלֶם, in an image full of false representations of things, in the midst of vain appearances, so that he knows not what to choose or do aright; and therefore spends the most of his time and strength about things that are of no use or purpose to him: 'Surely they are disquieted in vain.' And hereof he gives one especial instance: 'He heaps up riches, and knows not who shall gather;' which is but one example of the manifold frustrations that men meet withal in the whole course of their lives, as not knowing what is good for them. We all profess to aim at one chief and principal end—namely, the enjoyment of God in Christ as our eternal reward; and in order thereunto, to be carried on in the use of the means of faith and obedience, tending to that end. Now, if this be so, the suitableness or unsuitableness of all other things, being good or evil to us, is to be measured by their tendency to this end. And what know we hereof? As to the things of this life, do we know whether it will be best for us to be rich or poor, to have houses or to be harbourless, to abound or to want, to leave wealth and inheritances to our children, or to leave them naked to the providence of God? Do we know what state, what condition will most further our obedience, best obviate our temptations, or call most on us to mortify our corruptions? And if we know nothing at all of these things, as indeed we do not, were it not best for us to leave them quietly to God's disposal? I doubt not but it will appear at the last day that a world of evil in the hearts of men was stifled by the destruction of their outward concerns, more by their inward troubles; that many were delivered from temptations by it, who otherwise would have been overtaken, to their ruin, and the scandal of the gospel; that many a secret imposthume has been lanced and cured by a stroke: for God does not send judgments on his own for judgments' sake, for punishment's sake, but always to accomplish some blessed design of grace towards them. And there is no one soul in particular which shall rightly search itself, and consider its state and condition, but will be able to see wisdom, grace, and care towards itself in all the dispensations of God. And if I would here enter upon the benefits that, through the sanctifying hand of God, do redound to believers by afflictions, calamities, troubles, distresses, temptations, and the like effects of God's visitations, it would be of use to the souls of men in this case. But this subject has been so often and so well spoken to that I shall not insist upon it. I desire only that we would seriously consider how utterly ignorant we are of what is good for us or useful to us in these outward things, and so leave them quietly to God's disposal.

OUR GOOD. We may consider that all these things about which we are troubled fall directly within the compass of that good word of God's grace, that he will make 'all things work together for the good of them that love him' (Rom. 8:28). All things that we enjoy, all things that we are deprived of, all that we do, all that we suffer, our losses, troubles, miseries, distresses, in which the apostle instances in the following verses, they shall all 'work together for good'—together with one another, and all with and in subordination to the power, grace, and wisdom of God. It may be, we see not how or by what means it may be effected; but he is infinitely wise and powerful who has undertaken it, and we know little or nothing of his ways. There is nothing that we have, or enjoy, or desire, but it has turned to some to their hurt. Riches have been kept for men to their hurt. Wisdom and high places have been the ruin of many. Liberty and plenty are to most a snare. Prosperity slays the foolish. And we are not of ourselves in any measure able to secure ourselves from the hurt and poison that is in any of these things, but that they may be our ruin also, as they have already been, and every day are, to multitudes of the children of men. It is enough to fill the soul of any man with horror and amazement, to consider the ways and ends of most of them that are intrusted with this world's goods. Is it not evident that all their lives they seem industriously to take care that they may perish eternally? Luxury, riot, oppression, intemperance, and of late especially, blasphemy and atheism, they usually give up themselves to. And this is the fruit of their abundance and security. What, now, if God should deprive us of all these things? Can any one certainly say that he is worsted thereby? Might they not have turned to his everlasting perdition, as well as they do so of thousands as good by nature, and who have had advantages to be as wise as we? And shall we complain of God's dispensations about them? And what shall we say when he himself has undertaken to make all things that he guides us to to work together for our good? Anxieties of mind and perplexities of heart about our losses is not that which we are called to in our troubles. But this is that which is our duty—let us consider whether we 'love God' or no, whether 'we are called according to his purpose.' If so, all things are well in his hand, who can order them for our good and advantage. I hope many a poor soul will from hence, under all their trouble, be able to say, with him that was banished from his country, and found better entertainment elsewhere, 'My friends, I had perished, if I had not perished; had I not been undone by fire, it may be I had been ruined in eternal fire. God has made all to work for my good.'

The end of all these discourses is, to evince the reasonableness of the duty of waiting on God, which we are pressing from the psalmist. Ignorance of God and ourselves is the great principle and cause of all our disquietments; and this arises mostly, not from want of light and instruction, but for want of consideration and application. The notions insisted on concerning God are obvious and known to all; so are these concerning ourselves: but by whom almost are they employed and improved as they ought? The frame of our spirits is as though we stood upon equal terms with God, and did think, with Jonah, that we might do well to be angry with what he does. Did we rightly consider him, did we stand in awe of him as we ought, it had certainly been otherwise with us.

### 'In His Word I Hope'

Having, therefore, laid down these considerations from the second observation taken from the words—namely, that Jehovah himself is the proper object of the soul's waiting in the condition described—I shall only add one direction, how we may be enabled to perform and discharge this duty aright, which we have manifested to have been so necessary, so reasonable, so prevalent for the obtaining of relief; and this arises from another of the propositions laid down for the opening of these verses, not as yet spoken to—namely, that the word of promise is the soul's great support in waiting for God.

So says the psalmist, 'In his word do I hope;' that is, the word of promise. As the word in general is the adequate rule of all our obedience to God and communion with him, so there are especial parts of it that are suited to these especial actings of our souls towards him. Thus the word of promise, or the promise in the word, is that which our faith especially regards in our hope, trust, and waiting on God; and it is suited to answer to the immediate actings of our souls therein. From this word of promise, therefore, that is, from these promises, does the soul in its distress take encouragement to continue waiting on God; and that on these two accounts:

First, because they are declarative of God, his mind and his will; and, secondly, because they are communicative of grace and strength to the soul; of which latter we shall not here treat.

### God's Promises Reveal Him to Believers

First, the end and use of the promise is, to declare, reveal, and make known God to believers; and that, in an especial manner, in him and concerning him which may give them encouragement to wait for him.

#### *His Goodness, Grace, and Love*

The promises are a declaration of the nature of God, especially of his goodness, grace, and love. God has put an impression of all the glorious excellencies of his nature on his word, especially, as he is in Christ, on the word of the gospel. There, as in a glass, do we behold his glory in the face of Jesus Christ. As his commands express to us his holiness, his threatenings, his righteousness, and severity; so do his promises, his goodness, grace, love, and bounty. And in these things do we learn all that we truly and solidly know of God; that is, we know him in and by his word. The soul, therefore, that in this condition is waiting on or for God, considers the representation which he makes of himself and of his own nature in and by the promises, and receives support and encouragement in his duty; for if God teach us by the promises what he is, and what he will be to us, we have firm ground to expect from him all fruits of benignity, kindness, and love. Let the soul frame in itself that idea of God which is exhibited in the promises, and it will powerfully prevail with it to continue in an expectation of his gracious returns; they all expressing goodness, love, patience, forbearance, long-suffering, pardoning mercy, grace, bounty, with a full satisfactory reward. This is the beauty of the Lord mentioned with admiration by the prophet, 'How great is his goodness! How great is his beauty!' (Zech. 9:17); which is the great attractive of the soul to adhere constantly to him. Whatever difficulties arise, whatever temptations interpose, or wearisomeness grows upon us, in our straits, troubles, trials, and desertions, let us not entertain such thoughts of God as our own perplexed imaginations may be apt to suggest to us. This would quickly cast us into a thousand impatiences, misgivings, and miscarriages. But the remembrance of and meditation on God in his promises, as revealed by them, as expressed in them, is suited quite to other ends and purposes. There appear, yea, gloriously shine forth, that love, that wisdom, that goodness, tenderness, and grace, as cannot but encourage a believing soul to abide in waiting for him.

### His Will and Purpose

The word of promise does not only express God's nature as that wherein he proposes himself to the contemplation of faith, but it also declares his will and purpose of acting towards the soul suitably to his own goodness and grace: for promises are the declarations of God's purpose and will to act towards believers in Christ Jesus according to the infinite goodness of his own nature; and this is done in great variety, according to the various conditions and wants of them that do believe. They all proceed from the same spring of infinite grace, but are branched into innumerable particular streams, according as our necessities do require. To these do waiting souls repair, for stay and encouragement. Their perplexities principally arise from their misapprehensions of what God is in himself, and of what he will be to them; and whither should they repair to be undeceived but to that faithful representation that he has made of himself and his will in the word of his grace? For 'No man has seen God at any time; the only-begotten Son, who is in the bosom of the Father, he has declared him' (John 1:18). Now, the gospel is nothing but the word of promise explained, in all the springs, causes, and effects of it. Thither must we repair, to be instructed in this matter. The imaginations and reasonings of men's hearts will but deceive them in these things. The informations or instructions of other men may do so; nor have they any truth in them farther than they may be resolved into the word of promise. Here alone they may find rest and refreshment. The soul of whom we speak is under troubles, perplexities, and distresses as to its outward condition—pressed with many straits, it may be, on every hand; and as to its spiritual estate, under various apprehensions of the mind and will of God towards it; as has before at large been explained. In this condition it is brought, in some measure, to a holy submission to God, and a patient waiting for the issue of its trials. In this estate it has many temptations to, and much working of, unbelief. The whole of its opposition amounts to this, that it is neglected of God, that its way is hid, and his judgment is passed over from him, that it shall not be at present delivered, nor hereafter saved. What course can any one advise such a one to for his relief, and to preserve his soul from fainting or deserting the duty of waiting on God wherein he is engaged, but only this, to search and inquire what revelation God has made of himself and his will concerning him in his word?

And this the promise declares. Here he shall find hope, patience, faith, expectation, to be all increased, comforted, encouraged. Herein lies the duty and safety of any in this condition. Men may bear the first impression of any trouble with the strength, courage, and resolution of their natural spirits. Under some continuance of them they may support themselves with former experiences, and other usual springs and means of consolation. But if their wounds prove difficult to be cured, if they despise ordinary remedies, if their diseases are of long continuance, this is that which they must betake themselves to—they must search into the word of promise, and learn to measure things, not according to the present state and apprehensions of their mind, but according to what God has declared concerning them.

And there are sundry excellencies in the promises, when hoped in or trusted in, that tend to the establishment of the soul in this great duty of waiting; as:

GRACE FOR ALL CONDITIONS. That grace in them, that is, the good-will of God in Christ for help, relief, satisfaction, pardon, and salvation—is suited to all particular conditions and wants of the soul. As light arises from the sun, and is diffused in the beams thereof to the especial use of all creatures enabled by a visive faculty to make use of it; so comes grace forth from the eternal good-will of God in Christ, and is diffused by the promises, with a blessed contemperation to the conditions and wants of all believers. There can nothing fall out between God and any soul but there is grace suited to it, in one promise or another, as clearly and evidently as if it were given to him particularly and immediately. And this they find by experience who at any time are enabled to mix effectually a promise with faith.

GOD IS IN IT. The word of promise has a wonderful, mysterious, especial impression of God upon it. He does by it secretly and ineffably communicate himself to believers. When God appeared in a dream to Jacob, he awaked and said, 'God is in this place, and I knew it not.' He knew God was everywhere, but an intimation of his especial presence surprised him. So is a soul surprised, when God opens himself and his grace in a promise to him. It cries out, 'God is here, and I knew it not.' Such a near approach of God in his grace it finds, as is accompanied with a refreshing surprisal.

AUTHENTICITY. There is an especial engagement of the veracity and truth of God in every promise. Grace and truth are the two ingredients of an evangelical promise, the matter and form whereof they do consist. I cannot now stay to show wherein this especial engagement of truth in the promise consists; besides, it is a thing known and confessed. But it has an especial influence to support the soul, when hoped in, in its duty of waiting; for that hope can never make ashamed or leave the soul to disappointments which stays itself on divine veracity under a special engagement.

And this is that duty which the psalmist engages himself in and to the performance of, as the only way to obtain a comfortable interest in that forgiveness which is with God, and all the gracious effects thereof. And in the handling hereof, as we have declared its nature and necessity, so we have the psalmist's directions for its practice, to persons in the like condition with him, for the attaining of the end by him aimed at; so that it needs no farther application. That which remains of the psalm is the address which he makes to others, with the encouragement which he gives them to steer the same course with himself; and this he does in the two last verses, which, to complete the exposition of the whole psalm, I shall briefly explain and pass through, as having already despatched what I principally aimed at.

# HE SHALL REDEEM ISRAEL

7 Let Israel hope in the Lord:
for with the LORD there is mercy,
and with him is plenteous redemption.
8 And he shall redeem Israel
from all his iniquities.

I shall proceed, in the opening of these words, according to the method already insisted on. First, the meaning of the principal words shall be declared; then, the sense and importance of the whole; thirdly, the relation that they have to the condition of the soul expressed in the psalm must be manifested; from all which observations will arise for our instruction and direction in the like cases, wherein we are or may be concerned.

First, verse 7. 'Let Israel hope in the LORD.' יַחֵל יִשְׂרָאֵל אֶל־יְהוָה, 'Hope, Israel, in Jehovah'—'trust,' or 'expect;' the same word with that (v. 5), 'In his word do I hope;' properly, to expect, to look for, which includes hope, and adds some farther degree of the soul's acting towards God. It is an earnest looking after the thing hoped for: '*Expecta ad Dominum*'—hope in him, and look up to him.

'For with the LORD—*quia*, or *quoniam*, because seeing that with the Lord—הַחֶסֶד, 'mercy.' The verb substantive, as usual, is omitted, which we supply, 'There is mercy'—grace, bounty, goodness, good-will. This word is often joined with another, discovering its importance; and that אֱמֶת, 'truth.' חֶסֶד וֶאֱמֶת, 'goodness,' or 'mercy and truth.' These are, as it were, constituent parts of God's promises. It is of goodness, grace, bounty, to promise any undue mercy; and it is of truth or faithfulness to make good what is so promised. The LXX commonly render this word by ἔλεος—that is, 'pardoning mercy,' as it is everywhere used in the New Testament.

'And with him is plenteous redemption:' עִמּוֹ, 'with him,' as before, speaking to God, עִמְּךָ (v. 4), 'with you there is;' the meaning of which expression has been opened at large. 'Redemption:' פְּדוּת, from פָּדָה, 'to redeem;' the same with פִּדְיוֹן, λύτρωσις, ἀπολύτρωσις, 'redemption.' This word is often used for a proper redemption, such as is made by the intervention of a price, and not a mere assertion to liberty by power, which is sometimes also called redemption. Thus it is said of the money that the first-born of the children of Israel, which were above the number of the Levites, were redeemed with, that Moses took הַפִּדְיוֹם, the 'redemption;' that is, the redemption-money, the price of their redemption (Num. 3:49, Ps. 49:8). The redemption of men's souls is precious; it cost a great price. The redemption, then, that is with God relates to a price. Goodness or mercy, with respect to a price, becomes redemption; that is, actively the cause or means of it. (What that price is, see Matt. 20:28; 1 Pet. 1:18).

'Plenteous redemption,' הַרְבֵּה, '*Multa, copiosa*'—much, abundant, plenteous. It is used both for quantity and quality: much in quantity, or plenteous, abundant; and in quality—that is, precious, excellent. And it is applied in a good and bad sense. So it is said of our sins (Ezra. 9:6), 'Our sins,' רָבוּ, 'are increased' or 'multiplied,' or are 'great;' many in number, and heinous in their nature or quality. And in the other sense it is applied to the mercy of God, whereby they are removed; it is great or plenteous, it is excellent or precious.

Verse 8. 'And he,' that is, the Lord Jehovah, he with whom is plenteous redemption—פָּדָה, 'shall redeem,' or make them partakers of that redemption that is with him. 'He shall redeem Israel,' that is, those who hope and trust in him.

'From all his iniquities,' מִכֹּל עֲוֹנֹתָיו, 'His iniquities; that is, of the elect of Israel, and every individual amongst them. But the word signifies trouble as well as sin, especially that trouble or punishment that is for sin. So Cain expresses himself upon the denunciation of his sentence: גָּדוֹל עֲוֹנִי מִנְּשֹׂא, 'My sin,'—that is, the punishment you have denounced against my sin—'is too great or heavy for me to bear' (Gen. 4:13). There is a near affinity between sin and trouble: 'Noxam poena sequitur;'—'Punishment is inseparable from iniquity.' עָוֹן, then, the word here used, signifies either sin with reference to trouble due to it, or trouble with respect to sin, whence it proceeds; and both may here be well intended: 'God shall redeem Israel from all his sins, and troubles that have ensued thereon.' And this is the signification of the words; which, indeed, are plain and obvious.

And these words close up the psalm. He who began with depths—his own depths of sin and trouble—out of which and about which he cried out to God, is so encouraged by that prospect of grace and forgiveness with God, which by faith he had obtained, as to preach to others, and to support them in expectation of deliverance from all their sin and trouble also.

And such, for the most part, are all the exercises and trials of the children of God. Their entrance may be a storm, but their close is a calm; their beginning is oftentimes trouble, but their latter end is peace—peace to themselves, and advantage to the church of God: for men in all ages coming out of great trials of their own have been the most instrumental for the good of others, for God does not greatly exercise any of his but with some especial end for his own glory.

Secondly, the sense and intention of the psalmist in these words is to be considered; and that resolves itself into three general parts:

1. An exhortation or admonition: 'Israel, hope in the LORD,' or 'expect Jehovah.'
2. A ground of encouragement to the performance of the duty exhorted to: 'Because with the LORD there is much, plenteous, abundant, precious redemption.'

3. A gracious promise of a blessed issue, which shall be given to the performance of this duty: 'He shall redeem Israel from all his sins, and out of all his troubles.'

### ISRAEL, 'HOPE IN THE LORD'

In the exhortation there occur, the persons exhorted—that is, Israel: not Israel according to the flesh, for 'they are not all Israel which are of Israel' (Rom. 9:6); but it is the Israel mentioned (Ps. 73:1), the whole Israel of God, to whom he is good, 'such as are of a clean heart,' that is, all those who are interested in the covenant, and do inherit the promise of their forefather who was first called by that name, all believers.

And the psalmist treats them all in general in this matter, because there is none of them but have their trials and entanglements about sin, more or less. As there is 'none that lives and sins not,' so there is none that sins and is not entangled and troubled. Perhaps, then, they are not all of them in the same condition with him, in the depths that he was plunged into. Yet more or less, all and every one of them is so far concerned in sin as to need his direction. All the saints of God either have been, or are, or may be, in these depths. It is a good saying of Augstine on this place, *'Valde sunt in profundo qui non clamant de profundo'*—'None so in the deep as they who do not cry and call out of the deep.' They are in a deep of security who are never sensible of a deep of sin.

There is none of them, whatever their present condition be, but they may fall into the like depths with those of the psalmist. There is nothing absolutely in the covenant, nor in any promise, to secure them from it. And what befalls any one believer may befall them all. If any one believer may fall totally away, all may do so, and not leave one in the world, and so an end be put to the kingdom of Christ; which is no small evidence that they cannot so fall. But they may fall into depths of sin. That some of them have done so we have testimonies and instances beyond exception. It is good, then, that all of them should be prepared for that duty which they may all stand in need of, and for a right discharge of it. Besides, the duty mentioned is not absolutely restrained to the condition before described, but it is proper and accommodate to other seasons also. Therefore are all the Israel of God exhorted to it.

The duty itself is, hoping in Jehovah, with such a hope or trust as has an expectation of relief joined with it. And there are two things included in this duty:

1. The renunciation of any hopes, in expectation of deliverance either from sin or trouble any other way: 'Hope in Jehovah.' This is frequently expressed where the performance of this duty is mentioned (see Hos. 14:3; Jer. 3:22–3). And we have declared the nature of it in the exposition of the first and second verses.

2. Expectation from him; and this also has been insisted on, in the observations from the verses immediately preceding; wherein also the whole nature of this duty was explained, and directions were given for the due performance of it.

### 'With Him Is Plenteous Redemption'

The encouragement tendered to this duty is the next thing in the words: 'For with the Lord is plenteous redemption;' wherein we may observe:

What it is that he professes as the great encouragement to the duty mentioned; and that is redemption—the redemption that is with God: upon the matter, the same with the forgiveness before mentioned, mercy, pardon, benignity, bounty. He does not bid them hope in the Lord because they were the seed of Abraham, the peculiar people of God, made partakers of privileges above all the people in the world; much less because of their worthiness, or that good that was in themselves; but merely upon the account of mercy in God, of his grace, goodness, and bounty. The mercy of God, and the redemption that is with him, is the only ground to sinners for hope and confidence in him.

There are two great concerns of this grace—the one expressed, the other implied—in the words. The first is, that it is much, plenteous, abundant. That which principally discourages distressed souls from a comfortable waiting on God is, their fears lest they should not obtain mercy from him, and that because their sins are so great and so many, or attended with such circumstances and aggravations, as that it is impossible they should find acceptance with God. This ground of despondency and unbelief the psalmist obviates by representing the fullness, the plenty, the boundless plenty, of the mercy that is with God. It is such as will suit the condition of the greatest sinners in their greatest depths; the stores of its treasures are inexhaustible. And the force of the exhortation does not lie so much in this, that there is redemption with God, as that this redemption is plenteous or abundant. Secondly, here is an intimation in the word itself of that relation which the goodness and grace of God proposed has to the blood of Christ, whence it is called 'Redemption.' This, as was showed in the opening of the words, has respect to a price, the price whereby we are bought; that is, the blood of Christ. This is that whereby way is made for the exercise of mercy towards sinners. Redemption, which properly denotes actual deliverance, is said to be with God, or in him, as the effect in the cause. The causes of it are, his own grace and the blood of Christ. There are these prepared for the redeeming of believers from sin and trouble to his own glory. And herein lies the encouragement that the psalmist proposes to the performance of the duty exhorted to—namely, to wait on God—it is taken from God himself, as all encouragements to sinners to draw nigh to him and to wait for him must be. Nothing but himself can give us confidence to go to him; and it is suited to the state and condition of the soul under consideration. Redemption and mercy are suited to give relief from sin and misery.

### '...FROM ALL HIS INIQUITIES'

The last verse contains a promise of the issue of the performance of this duty: 'He shall redeem Israel from all his iniquities.' Two things are observable in the words.

The certainty of the issue or event of the duty mentioned: וְהוּא יִפְדֶּה, 'And he shall,' or 'he will redeem;' he will assuredly do so. Now, although this in the psalmist is given out by revelation, and is a new promise of God, yet, as it relates to the condition of the soul here expressed, and the discovery made by faith of forgiveness and redemption with God, the certainty intended in this assertion is built upon the principles before laid down. Whence, therefore, does it appear, whence may we infallibly conclude, that God will redeem his Israel from all their iniquities? I answer:

1. The conclusion is drawn from the nature of God. There is forgiveness and redemption with him, and he will act towards his people suitably to his own nature. There is redemption with him, and therefore he will redeem; forgiveness with him, and therefore he will forgive. As the conclusion is certain and infallible, that wicked men, ungodly men, shall be destroyed, because God is righteous and holy, his righteousness and holiness indispensably requiring their destruction; so is the redemption and salvation of all that believe certain on this account—namely, because there is forgiveness with him. He is good and gracious, and ready to forgive; his goodness and grace requires their salvation.
2. The conclusion is certain upon the account of God's faithfulness in his promises. He has promised that those who wait on him 'shall not be ashamed'—that their expectation shall not be disappointed; whence the conclusion is certain that in his time and way they shall be redeemed.

There is the extent of this deliverance or redemption: 'shall redeem Israel from all his iniquities.' It was showed, in the opening of the verse, that this word denotes either sin procuring trouble, or trouble procured by sin; and there is a respect to both sin and its punishment. From both, from all of both kinds, God will redeem his Israel; not this or that evil, this or that sin, but from all evil, all sin. He will take all sins from their souls, and wipe all tears from their eyes. Now, God is said to do this on many accounts:

1. On the account of the great cause of all actual deliverance

and redemption—the blood of Christ. He has laid an assured foundation of the whole work; the price of redemption is paid, and they shall in due time enjoy the effects and fruits of it.

2. Of the actual communication of the effects of that redemption to them. This is sure to all the elect of God, to his whole Israel. They shall all be made partakers of them. And this is the end of all the promises of God, and of the grace and mercy promised in them—namely, that they should be means to exhibit and give out to believers that redemption which is purchased and prepared for them. And this is done two ways: First, partially, initially, and gradually, in this life. Here God gives to them the pardon of their sins, being freely justified by his grace; and, in his sanctification of them through his Spirit, gives them delivery from the power and dominion of sin. Many troubles also he delivers them from, and from all as far as they are penal, or have any mixture of the curse in them. Secondly, completely—namely, when he shall have freed them from sin and trouble, and from all the effects and consequents of them, by bringing them to the enjoyment of himself in glory.

### 'CONSIDER HOW IT WAS WITH ME'

Thirdly, the words being thus opened, we may briefly, in the next place, consider what they express concerning the state, condition, or actings of the soul, which are represented in this psalm.

Having himself attained to the state before described, and being engaged resolvedly to the performance of that duty which would assuredly bring him into a haven of full rest and peace, the psalmist applies himself to the residue of the Israel of God, to give them encouragement to this duty with himself, from the experience that he had of a blessed success therein. As if he had said to them, 'You are now in afflictions and under troubles, and that upon the account of your sins and provocations—a condition, I confess, sad and deplorable; but yet there is hope in Israel concerning these things. For consider how it has been with me, and how the Lord has dealt with me. I was in depths inexpressible, and saw for a while no way or means of delivery; but God has been pleased graciously to reveal himself to me, as a God pardoning iniquity, transgression, and sin. And in the consolation and support which I have received thereby, I am waiting for a full participation of the fruits of his love. Let me therefore prevail with you, who are in the like condition, to steer the same course with me. Only let your expectations be fixed on mercy and sovereign grace, without any regard to any privilege or worth in yourselves. Rest in the plenteous redemption, those stores of grace which are with Jehovah; and according to his faithfulness in his promises he will deliver you out of all perplexing troubles.'

## FINAL WORDS

Having thus opened the words, I shall now only name the doctrinal observations that are tendered from them, and so put a close to these discourses:

1. The Lord Jehovah is the only hope for sin-distressed souls: 'Hope in the LORD.' This has been sufficiently discovered and confirmed on sundry passages in the psalm.
2. The ground of all hope and expectation of relief in sinners is mere grace, mercy, and redemption: 'Hope in the LORD: for with the LORD there is mercy.' All other grounds of hope are false and deceiving.
3. Inexhaustible stores of mercy and redemption are needful for the encouragement of sinners to rest and wait on God: 'With him is plenteous redemption.' Such is your misery, so pressing are your fears and disconsolations, that nothing less than boundless grace can relieve or support you; there are, therefore, such treasures and stores in God as are suited hereunto. 'With him is plenteous redemption.'
4. The ground of all the dispensation of mercy, goodness, grace, and forgiveness, which is in God to sinners, is laid in the blood of Christ; hence it is here called 'Redemption.' To this also we have spoken at large before.

5. All that wait on God on the account of mercy and grace shall have an undoubted issue of peace: 'He shall redeem Israel.' 'Let him,' says God, 'lay hold on my arm, that he may have peace, and he shall have peace' (Isa. 27:5).

6. Mercy given to them that wait on God, shall, in the close and issue, be every way full and satisfying: 'He shall redeem Israel from all his iniquities.'

And these propositions do arise from the words as absolutely considered, and in themselves. If we mind their relation to the peculiar condition of the soul represented in this psalm, they will yet afford us the ensuing observations:

1. They who out of depths have, by faith and waiting, obtained mercy, or are supported in waiting from a sense of believed mercy and forgiveness, are fitted, and only they are fitted, to preach and declare grace and mercy to others. This was the case with the psalmist. Upon his emerging out of his own depths and straits, he declares the mercy and redemption whereby he was delivered to the whole Israel of God.

2. A saving participation of grace and forgiveness leaves a deep impression of its fullness and excellency on the soul of a sinner. So was it here with the psalmist. Having himself obtained forgiveness, he knows no bounds or measure, as it were, in the extolling of it: 'There is with God, mercy, redemption, plenteous redemption, redeeming from all iniquity; I have found it so, and so will every one do that shall believe it.'

Now, these observations might all of them, especially the two last, receive a useful improvement; but whereas what I principally intended from this psalm has been at large insisted on upon the first verses of it, I shall not here farther draw forth any meditations upon them, but content myself with the exposition that has been given of the design of the psalmist and sense of his words in these last verses.